Are We Out of the Driveway Yet?

Also by Jerry Scott and Jim Borgman

Zits: Sketchbook 1
Growth Spurt: Zits Sketchbook 2
Don't Roll Your Eyes at Me, Young Man!: Zits Sketchbook 3
Are We an "Us"?: Zits Sketchbook 4
Zits Unzipped: Zits Sketchbook 5
Busted!: Zits Sketchbook 6
Road Trip: Zits Sketchbook 7
Teenage Tales: Zits Sketchbook No. 8
Thrashed: Zits Sketchbook No. 9
Pimp My Lunch: Zits Sketchbook No. 10

Treasuries
Humongous Zits
Big Honkin' Zits
Zits: Supersized
Random Zits
Crack of Noon

Are We Out of the Driveway Yet?

Zits® Sketchbook No. 11

by JERRY SCOTT and JIM BORGMAN

Andrews McMeel
Publishing, LLC
Kansas City

06 07 08 09 10 BBG 10 9 8 7 6 5 4 3 2 1

ISBN-13: 978-0-7407-6199-7
ISBN-10: 0-7407-6199-4

Library of Congress Control Number: 2006925240

Zits® may be viewed online at
www.kingfeatures.com.

www.andrewsmcmeel.com

—— **ATTENTION: SCHOOLS AND BUSINESSES** ——

Andrews McMeel books are available at quantity discounts with bulk purchase for educational, business, or sales promotional use. For information, please write to: Special Sales Department, Andrews McMeel Publishing, LLC, 4520 Main Street, Kansas City, Missouri 64111.

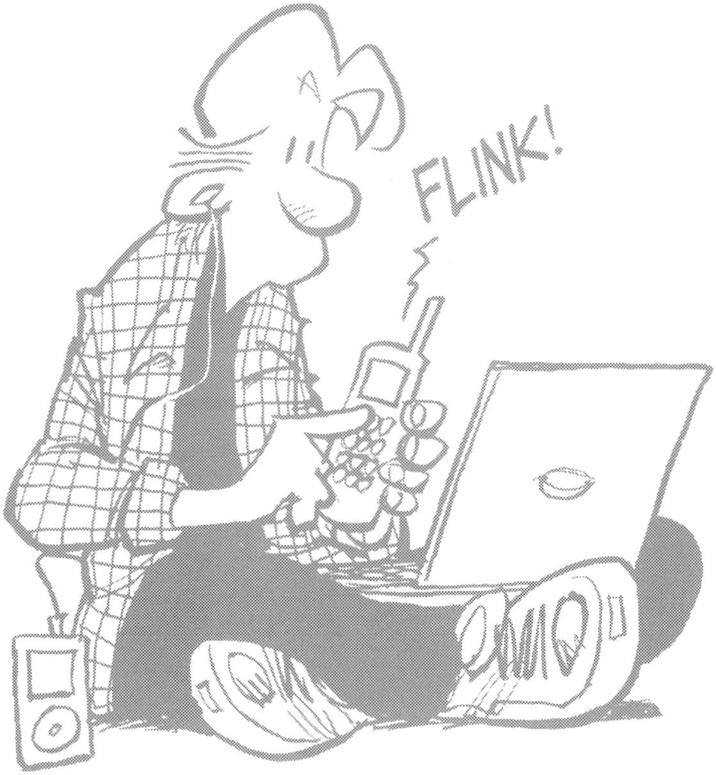
FLINK!

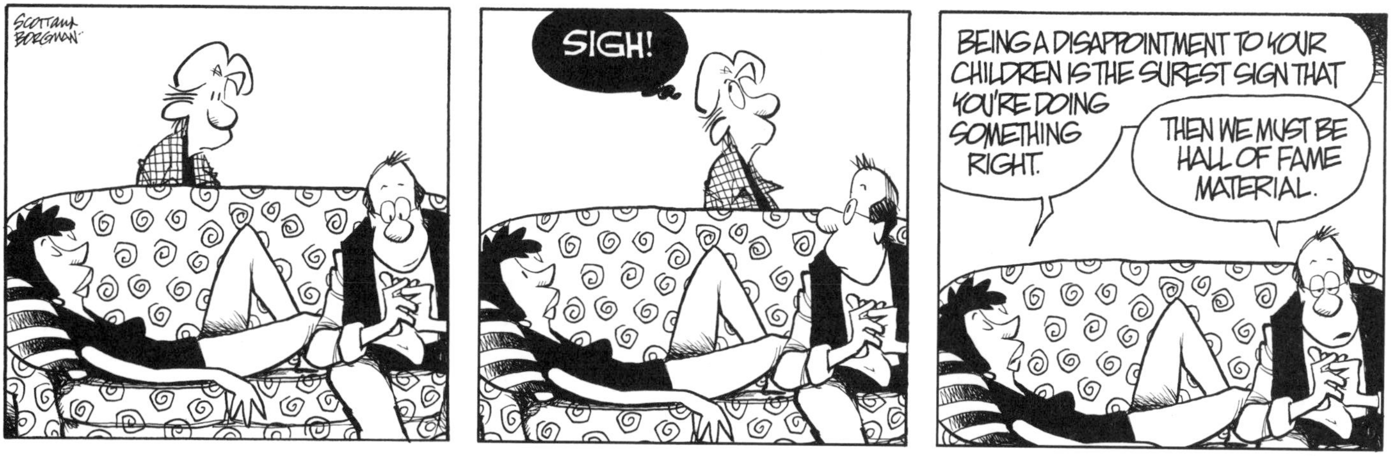
SCOTT AND BORGMAN
SIGH!
BEING A DISAPPOINTMENT TO YOUR CHILDREN IS THE SUREST SIGN THAT YOU'RE DOING SOMETHING RIGHT.
THEN WE MUST BE HALL OF FAME MATERIAL.

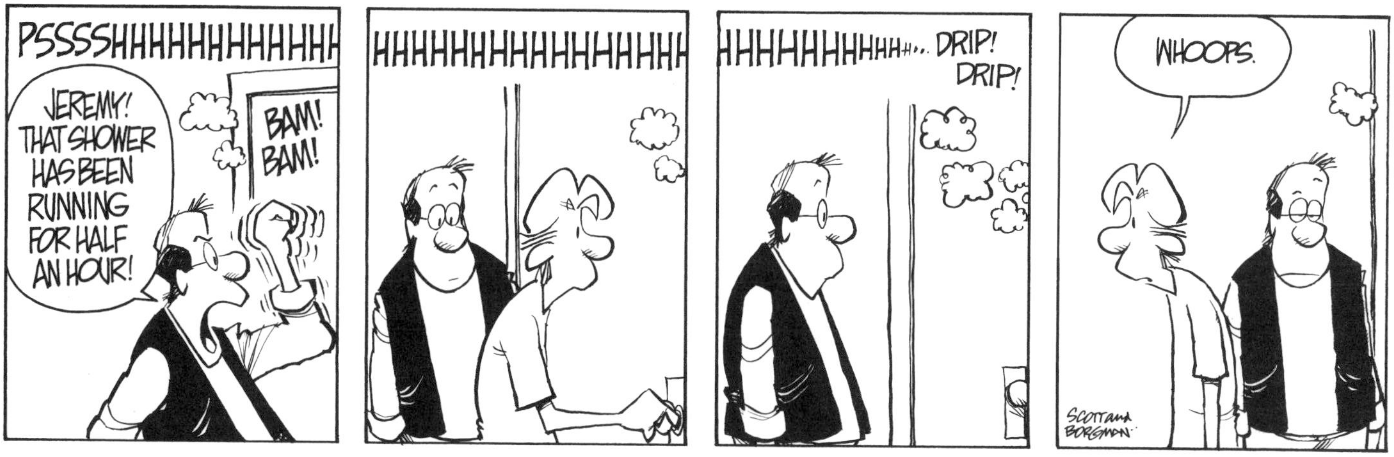
PSSSSHHHHHHHHHHHH
JEREMY! THAT SHOWER HAS BEEN RUNNING FOR HALF AN HOUR!
BAM! BAM!
HHHHHHHHHHHHHHHHH
HHHHHHHHHHHH... DRIP! DRIP!
WHOOPS.
SCOTT AND BORGMAN

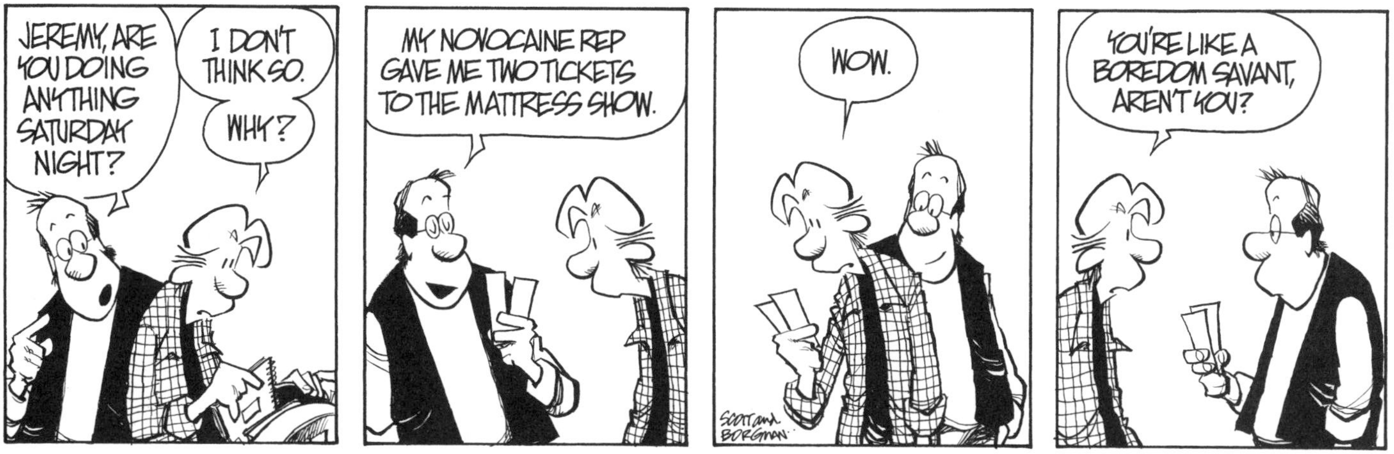
JEREMY, ARE YOU DOING ANYTHING SATURDAY NIGHT?
I DON'T THINK SO.
WHY?
MY NOVOCAINE REP GAVE ME TWO TICKETS TO THE MATTRESS SHOW.
WOW.
SCOTT AND BORGMAN
YOU'RE LIKE A BOREDOM SAVANT, AREN'T YOU?

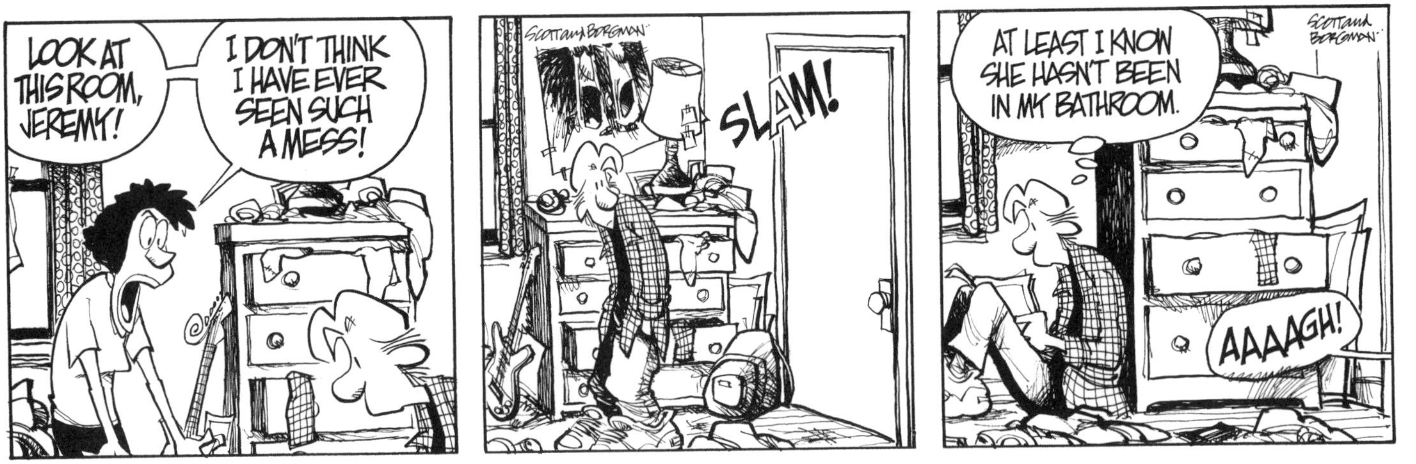
LOOK AT THIS ROOM, JEREMY!
I DON'T THINK I HAVE EVER SEEN SUCH A MESS!
SLAM!
AT LEAST I KNOW SHE HASN'T BEEN IN MY BATHROOM.
AAAAGH!

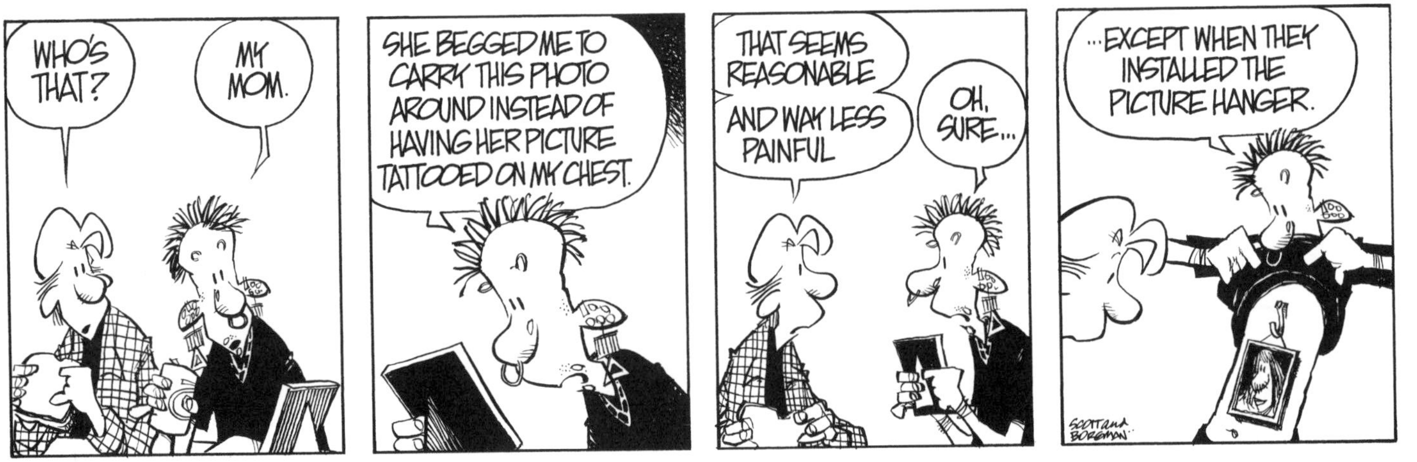
WHO'S THAT?
MY MOM.
SHE BEGGED ME TO CARRY THIS PHOTO AROUND INSTEAD OF HAVING HER PICTURE TATTOOED ON MY CHEST.
THAT SEEMS REASONABLE
AND WAY LESS PAINFUL
OH, SURE...
...EXCEPT WHEN THEY INSTALLED THE PICTURE HANGER.

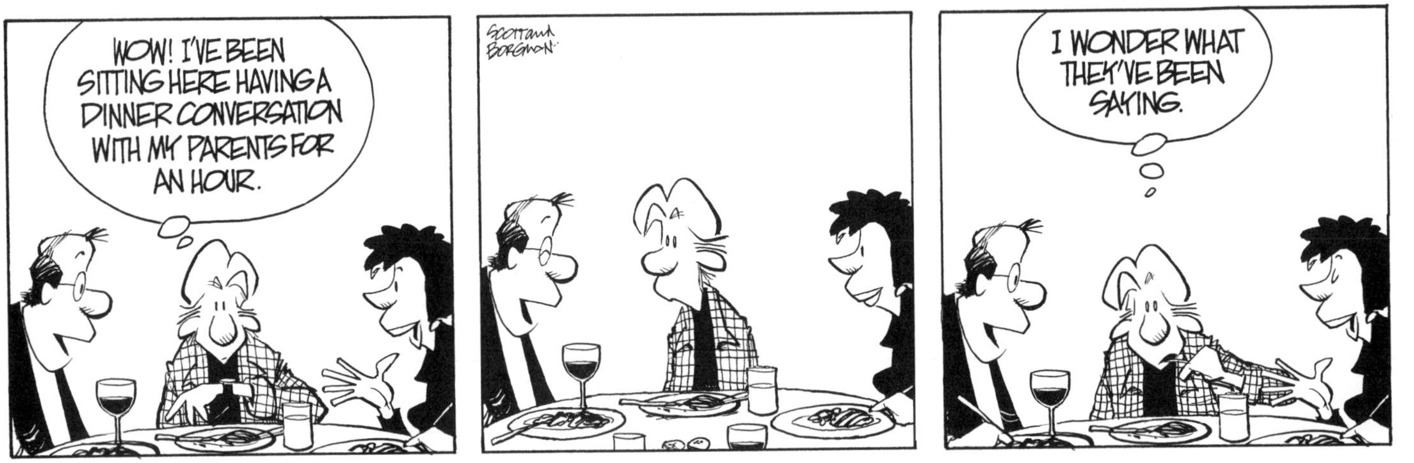
WOW! I'VE BEEN SITTING HERE HAVING A DINNER CONVERSATION WITH MY PARENTS FOR AN HOUR.
I WONDER WHAT THEY'VE BEEN SAYING.

Zits by Jerry Scott and Jim Borgman

SLAM!

HI JEREMY!

WASN'T IT A BEAUTIFUL DAY TODAY?

THE CLOUDS WERE SO PRETTY.

YOUR FATHER IS BARBECUING STEAKS...

ARE YOU HUNGRY?

HOW WAS SCHOOL?

ANYTHING INTERESTING HAPPEN TODAY?

WELL, I GUESS WE CAN TALK ABOUT IT AT DINNER.

(SIGH)

DO YOU EVER FEEL INVISIBLE AROUND TEENAGERS?

WHENEVER POSSIBLE.

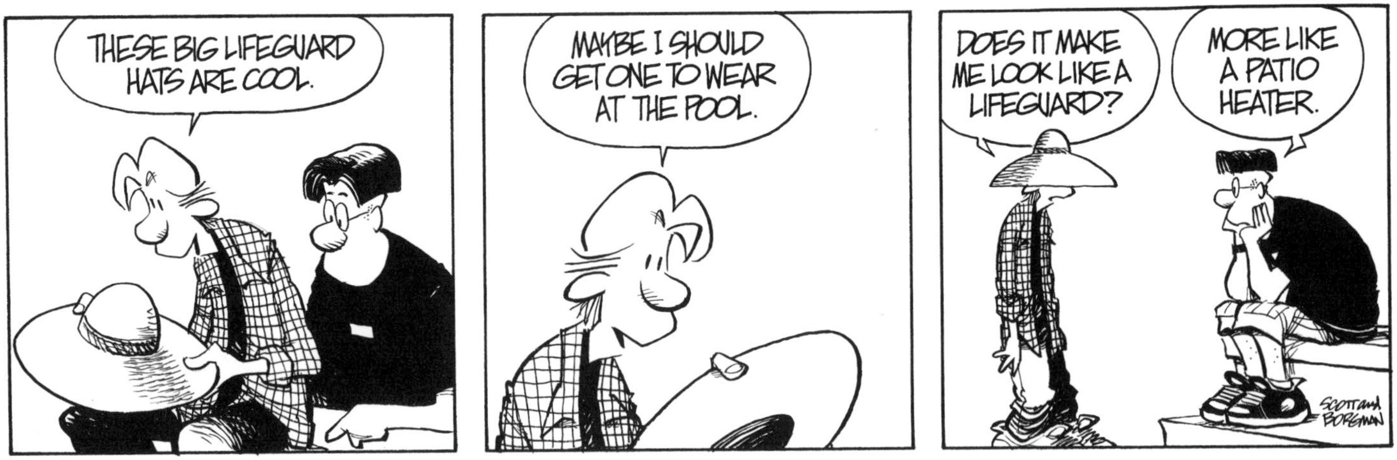
THESE BIG LIFEGUARD HATS ARE COOL.
MAYBE I SHOULD GET ONE TO WEAR AT THE POOL.
DOES IT MAKE ME LOOK LIKE A LIFEGUARD?
MORE LIKE A PATIO HEATER.
SCOTT and BORGMAN

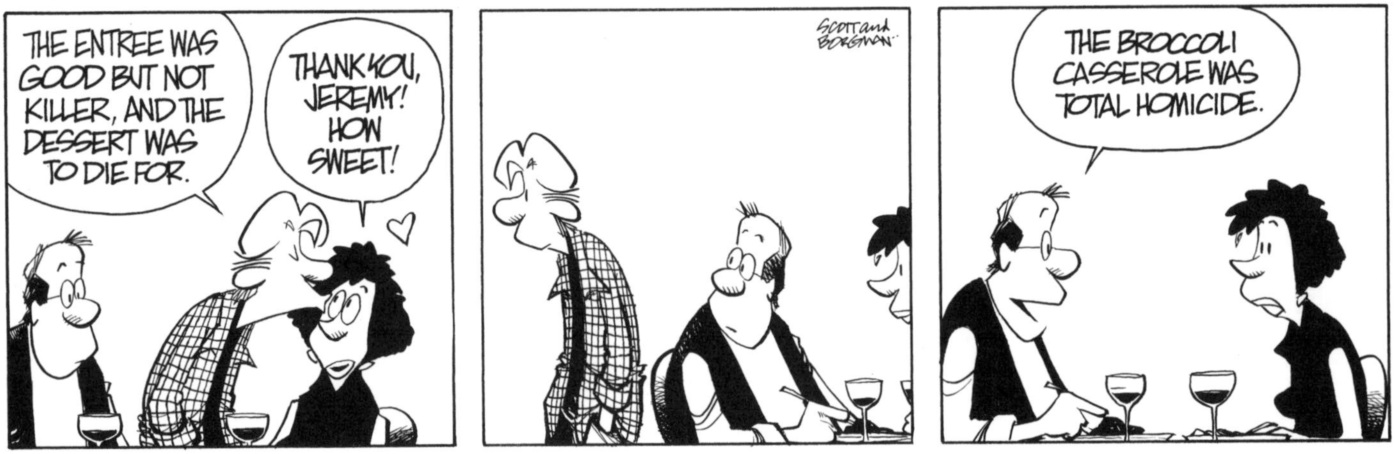
THE ENTREE WAS GOOD BUT NOT KILLER, AND THE DESSERT WAS TO DIE FOR.
THANK YOU, JEREMY! HOW SWEET!
SCOTT and BORGMAN
THE BROCCOLI CASSEROLE WAS TOTAL HOMICIDE.

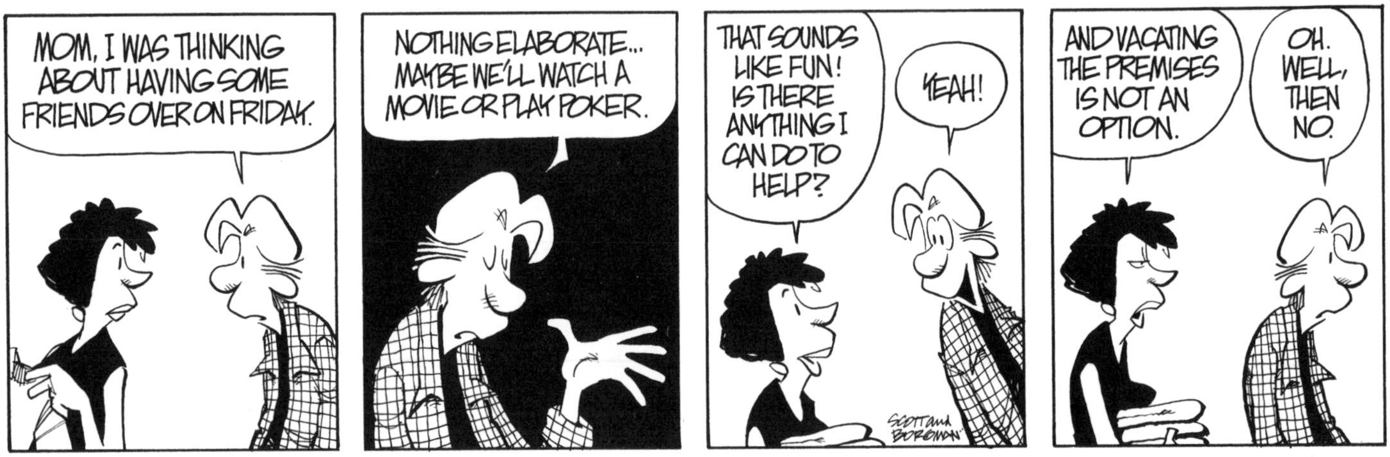
MOM, I WAS THINKING ABOUT HAVING SOME FRIENDS OVER ON FRIDAY.
NOTHING ELABORATE... MAYBE WE'LL WATCH A MOVIE OR PLAY POKER.
THAT SOUNDS LIKE FUN! IS THERE ANYTHING I CAN DO TO HELP?
YEAH!
SCOTT and BORGMAN
AND VACATING THE PREMISES IS NOT AN OPTION.
OH. WELL, THEN NO.

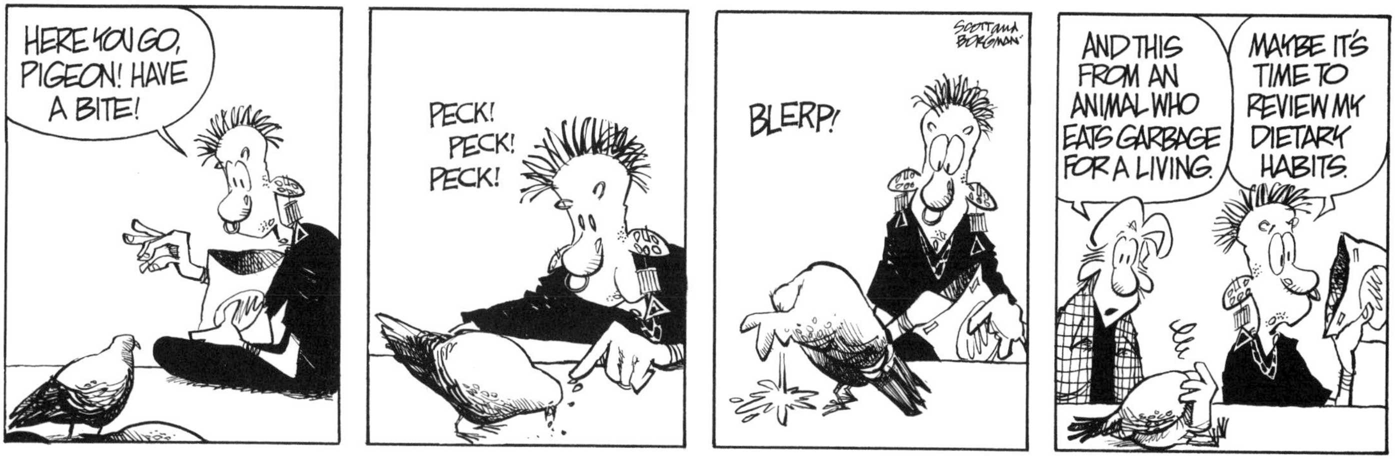
HERE YOU GO, PIGEON! HAVE A BITE!
PECK! PECK! PECK!
SCOTT and BORGMAN
BLERP!
AND THIS FROM AN ANIMAL WHO EATS GARBAGE FOR A LIVING.
MAYBE IT'S TIME TO REVIEW MY DIETARY HABITS.

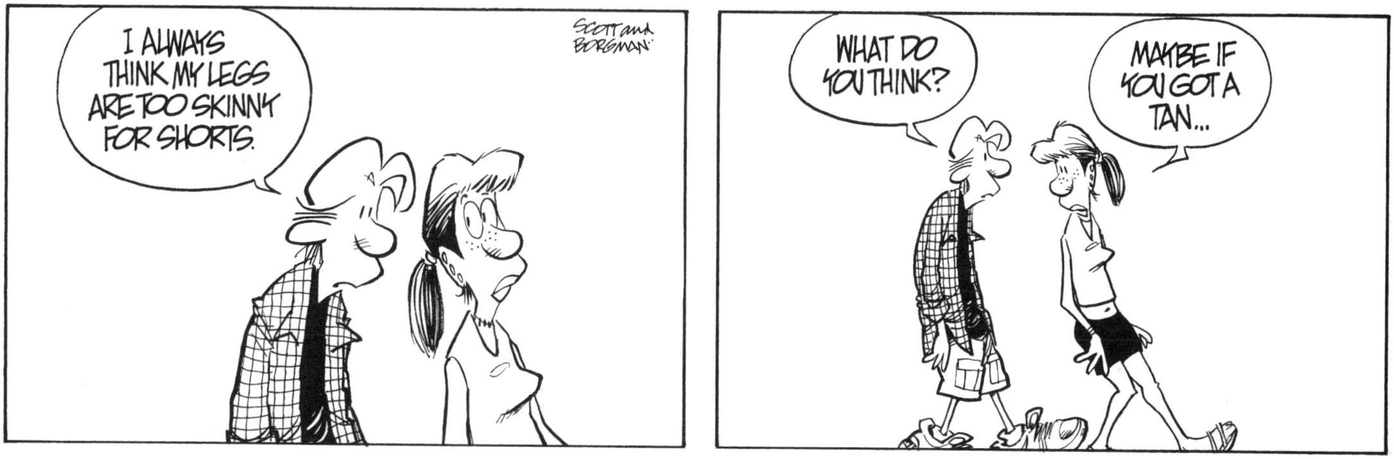
SCOTT and BORGMAN
I ALWAYS THINK MY LEGS ARE TOO SKINNY FOR SHORTS.
WHAT DO YOU THINK?
MAYBE IF YOU GOT A TAN...

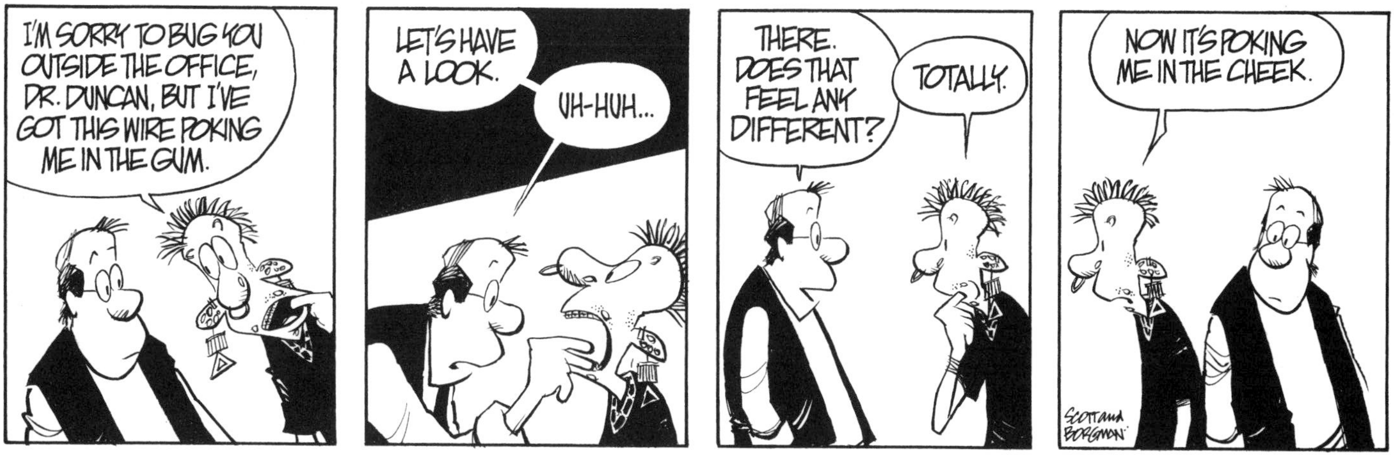
I'M SORRY TO BUG YOU OUTSIDE THE OFFICE, DR. DUNCAN, BUT I'VE GOT THIS WIRE POKING ME IN THE GUM.
LET'S HAVE A LOOK.
UH-HUH...
THERE. DOES THAT FEEL ANY DIFFERENT?
TOTALLY.
NOW IT'S POKING ME IN THE CHEEK.
SCOTT and BORGMAN

Zits
by JERRY SCOTT and JIM BORGMAN

HI DAD.
HOW MUCH?
FORTY?
TWENTY.
MIDNIGHT?
ELEVEN.
SEE YA.
THE USUAL LITANY OF CAUTIONS.
I'M SIGNING YOU TWO UP FOR A COMMUNICATION WORKSHOP.
SO WE CAN SPEND AN HOUR ACCOMPLISHING THE SAME THING?
SCOTT and BORGMAN

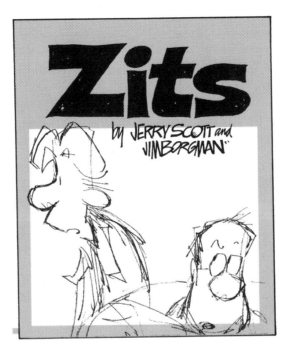

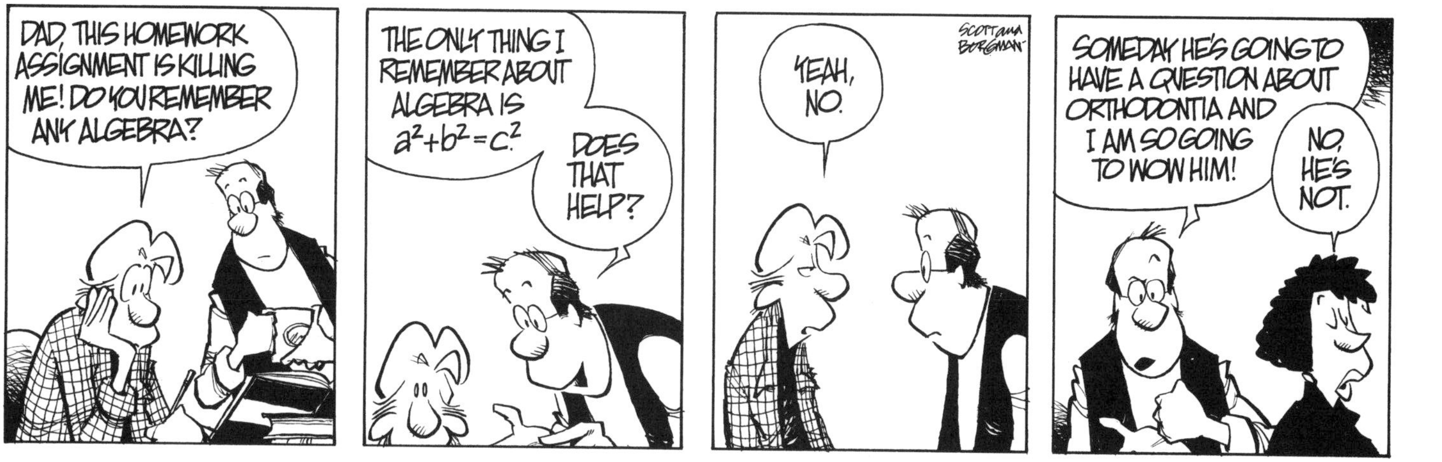
DAD, THIS HOMEWORK ASSIGNMENT IS KILLING ME! DO YOU REMEMBER ANY ALGEBRA?
THE ONLY THING I REMEMBER ABOUT ALGEBRA IS $a^2+b^2=c^2$.
DOES THAT HELP?
SCOTT and BORGMAN
YEAH, NO.
SOMEDAY HE'S GOING TO HAVE A QUESTION ABOUT ORTHODONTIA AND I AM SO GOING TO WOW HIM!
NO, HE'S NOT.

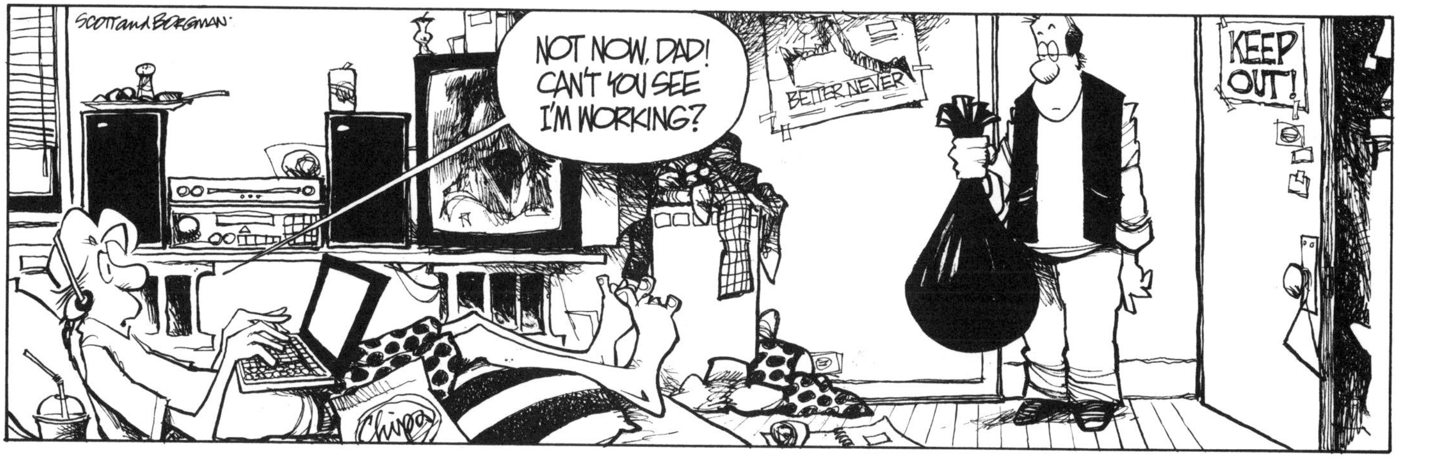
SCOTT and BORGMAN
NOT NOW, DAD! CAN'T YOU SEE I'M WORKING?
BETTER NEVER
KEEP OUT!
Chips

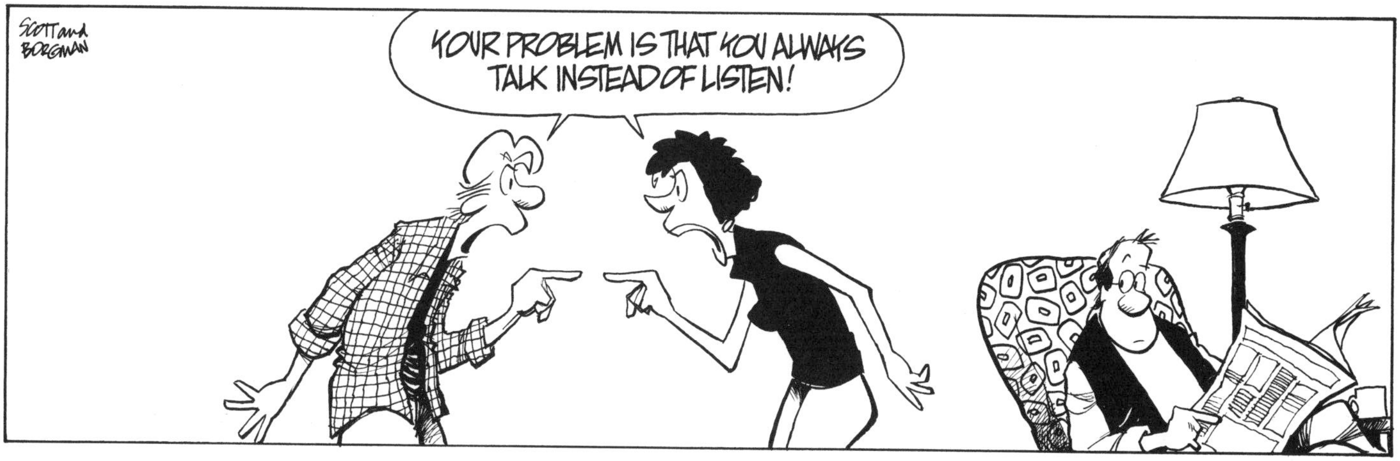
SCOTT and BORGMAN
YOUR PROBLEM IS THAT YOU ALWAYS TALK INSTEAD OF LISTEN!

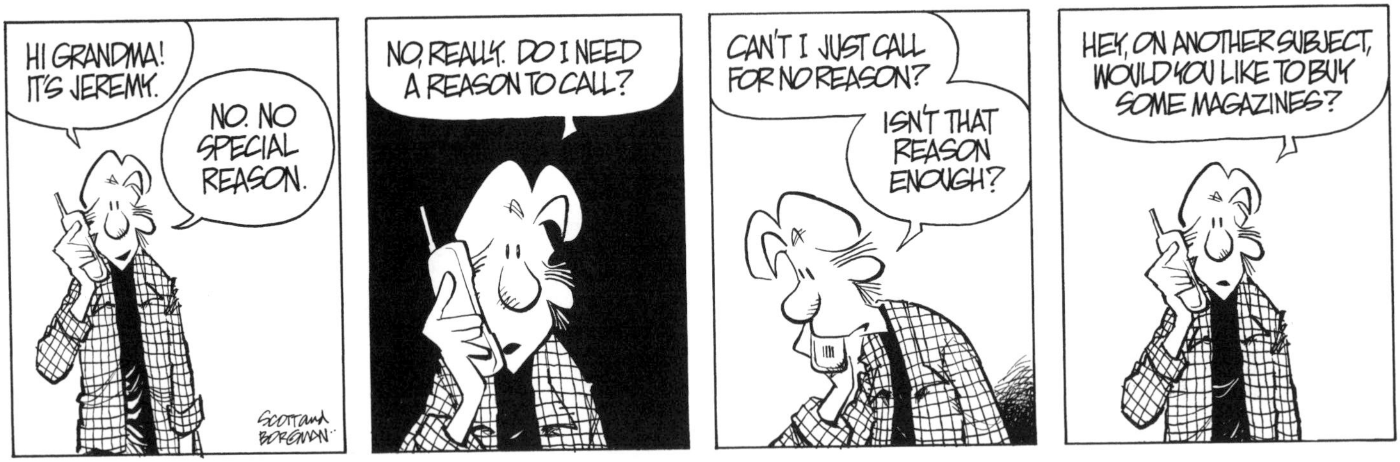
HI GRANDMA! IT'S JEREMY.
NO. NO SPECIAL REASON.
NO, REALLY. DO I NEED A REASON TO CALL?
CAN'T I JUST CALL FOR NO REASON?
ISN'T THAT REASON ENOUGH?
HEY, ON ANOTHER SUBJECT, WOULD YOU LIKE TO BUY SOME MAGAZINES?

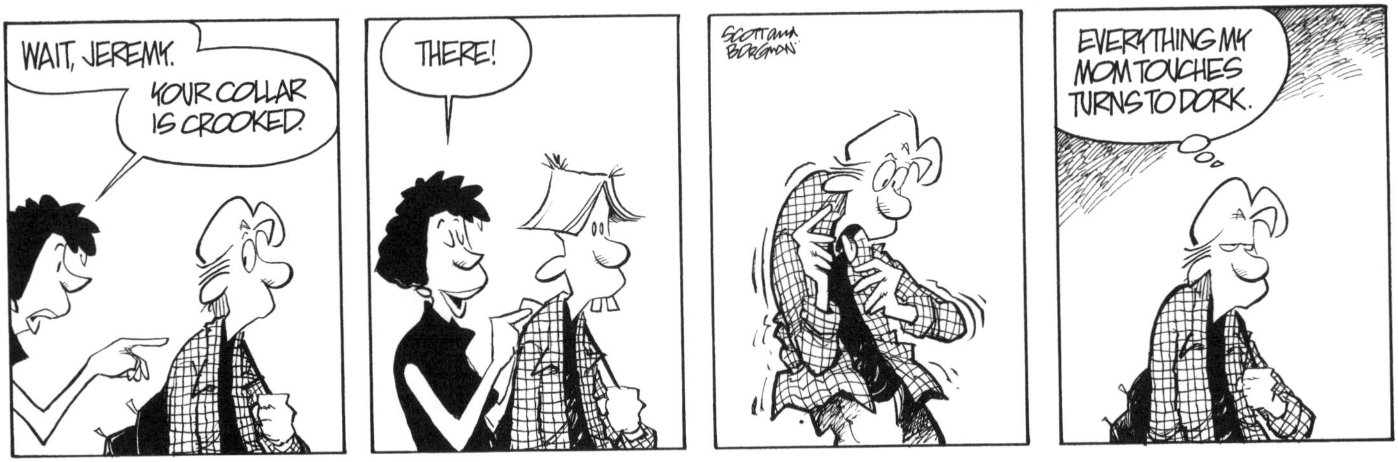
WAIT, JEREMY.
YOUR COLLAR IS CROOKED.
THERE!
EVERYTHING MY MOM TOUCHES TURNS TO DORK.

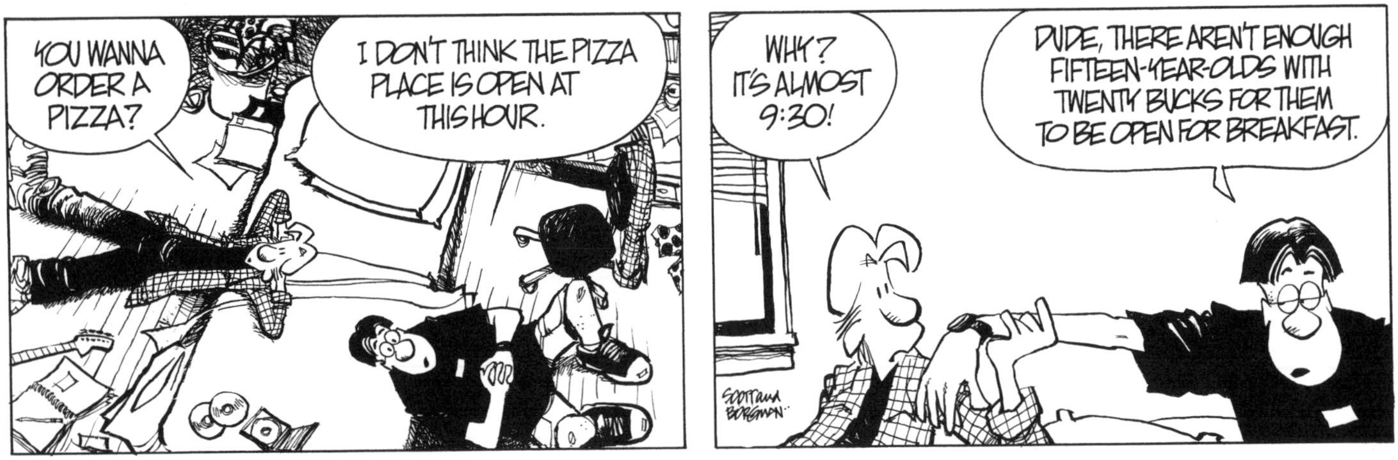
YOU WANNA ORDER A PIZZA?
I DON'T THINK THE PIZZA PLACE IS OPEN AT THIS HOUR.
WHY? IT'S ALMOST 9:30!
DUDE, THERE AREN'T ENOUGH FIFTEEN-YEAR-OLDS WITH TWENTY BUCKS FOR THEM TO BE OPEN FOR BREAKFAST.

Zits
by JERRY SCOTT and JIM BORGMAN
Z

A Day in the Life of a Desk
ACHOO!
SNIFF
Z
SCOTT and BORGMAN
COUGH!

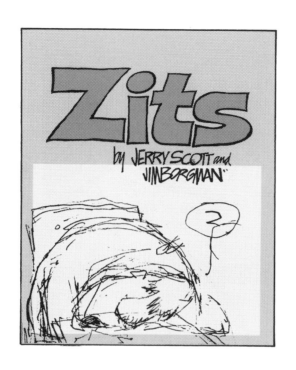

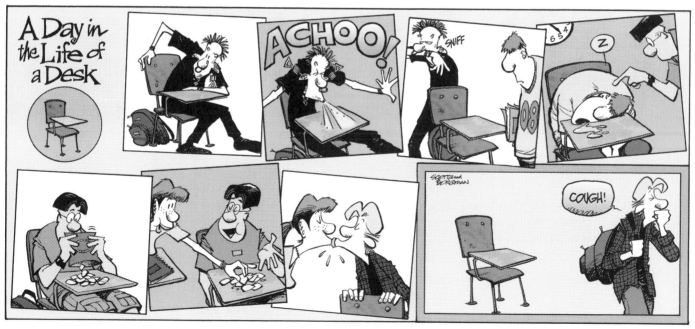

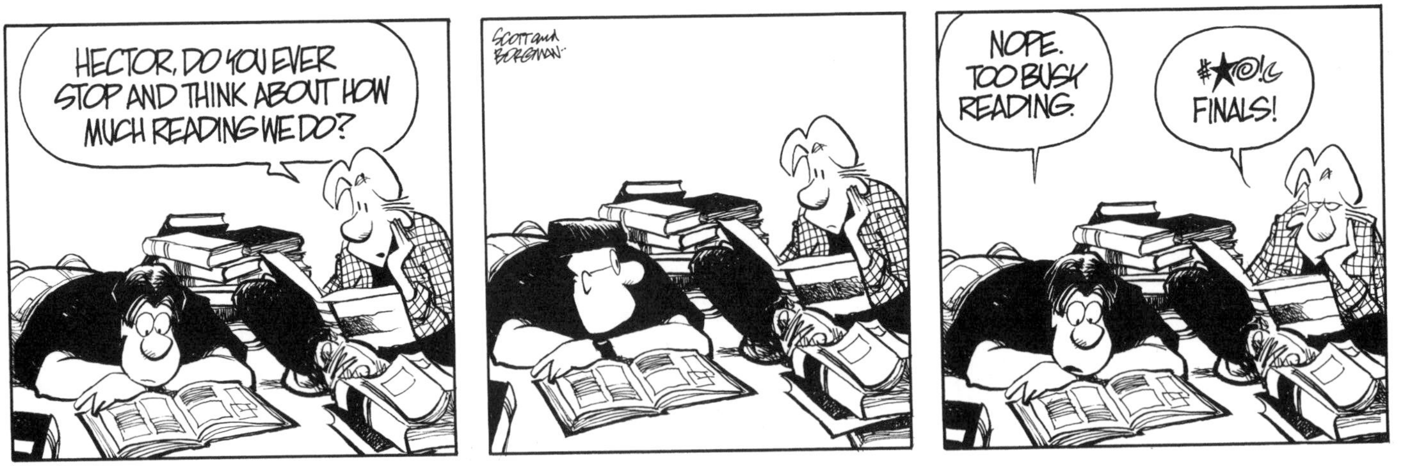
HECTOR, DO YOU EVER STOP AND THINK ABOUT HOW MUCH READING WE DO?
NOPE. TOO BUSY READING.
#★@! FINALS!

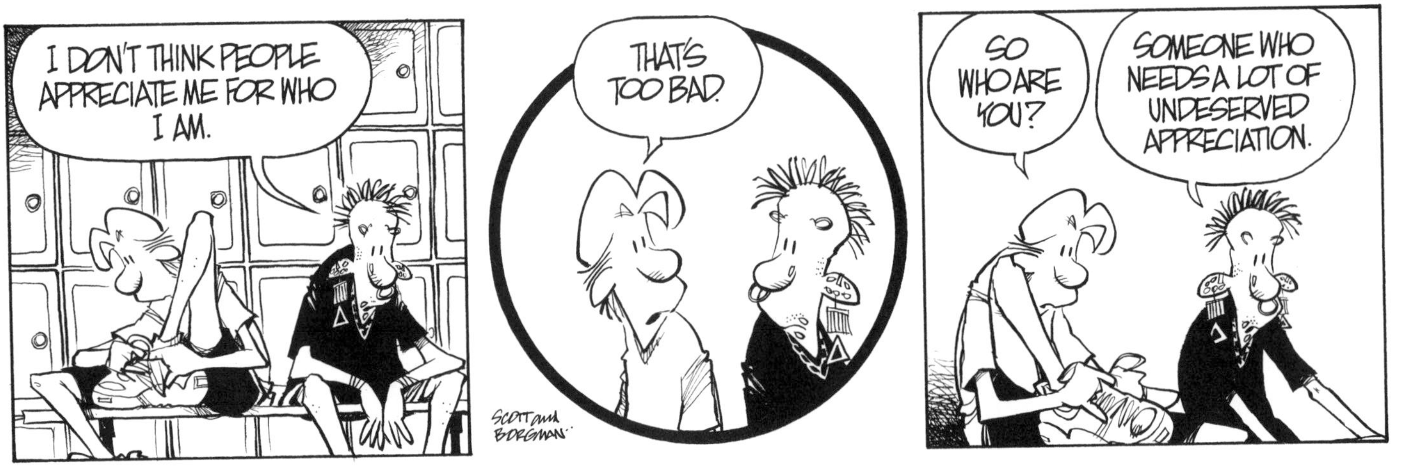
I DON'T THINK PEOPLE APPRECIATE ME FOR WHO I AM.
THAT'S TOO BAD.
SO WHO ARE YOU?
SOMEONE WHO NEEDS A LOT OF UNDESERVED APPRECIATION.

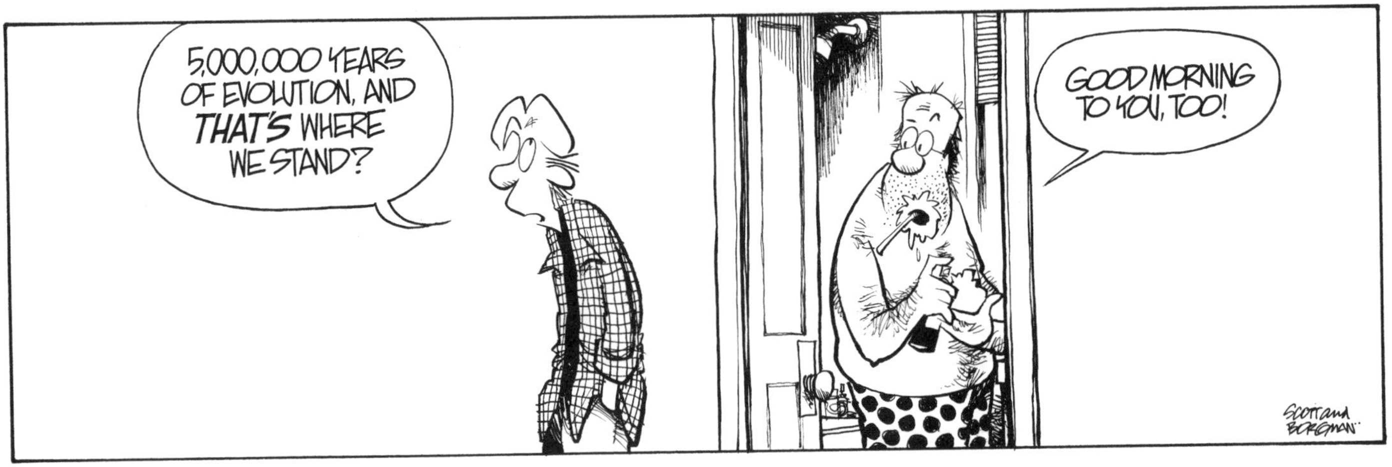
5,000,000 YEARS OF EVOLUTION, AND *THAT'S* WHERE WE STAND?
GOOD MORNING TO YOU, TOO!

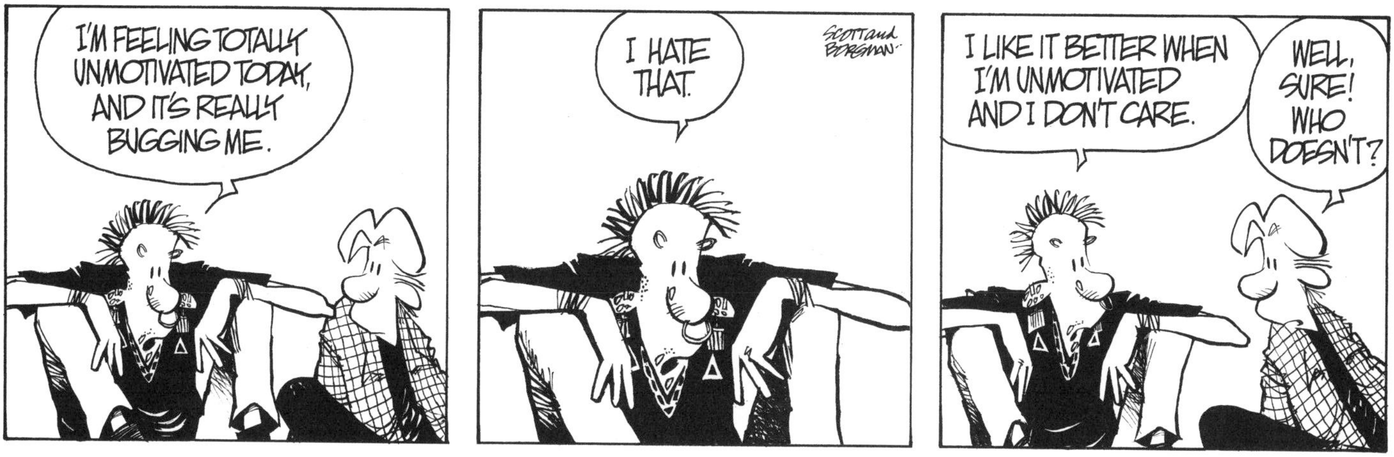
I'M FEELING TOTALLY UNMOTIVATED TODAY, AND IT'S REALLY BUGGING ME.
I HATE THAT.
I LIKE IT BETTER WHEN I'M UNMOTIVATED AND I DON'T CARE.
WELL, SURE! WHO DOESN'T?

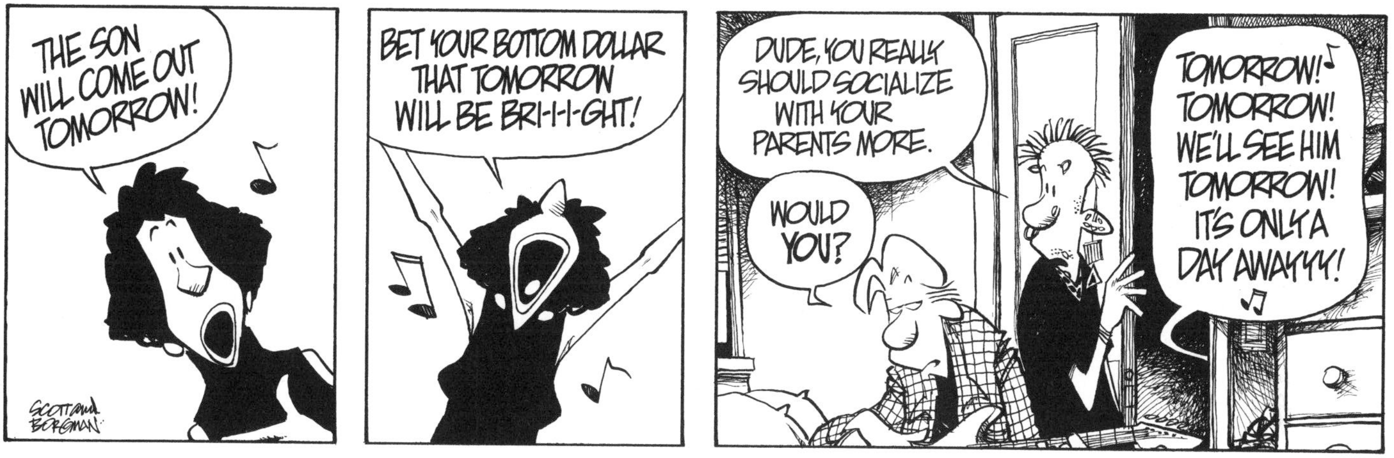
THE SON WILL COME OUT TOMORROW!
BET YOUR BOTTOM DOLLAR THAT TOMORROW WILL BE BRI-I-I-GHT!
DUDE, YOU REALLY SHOULD SOCIALIZE WITH YOUR PARENTS MORE.
WOULD YOU?
TOMORROW! TOMORROW! WE'LL SEE HIM TOMORROW! IT'S ONLY A DAY AWAYYY!

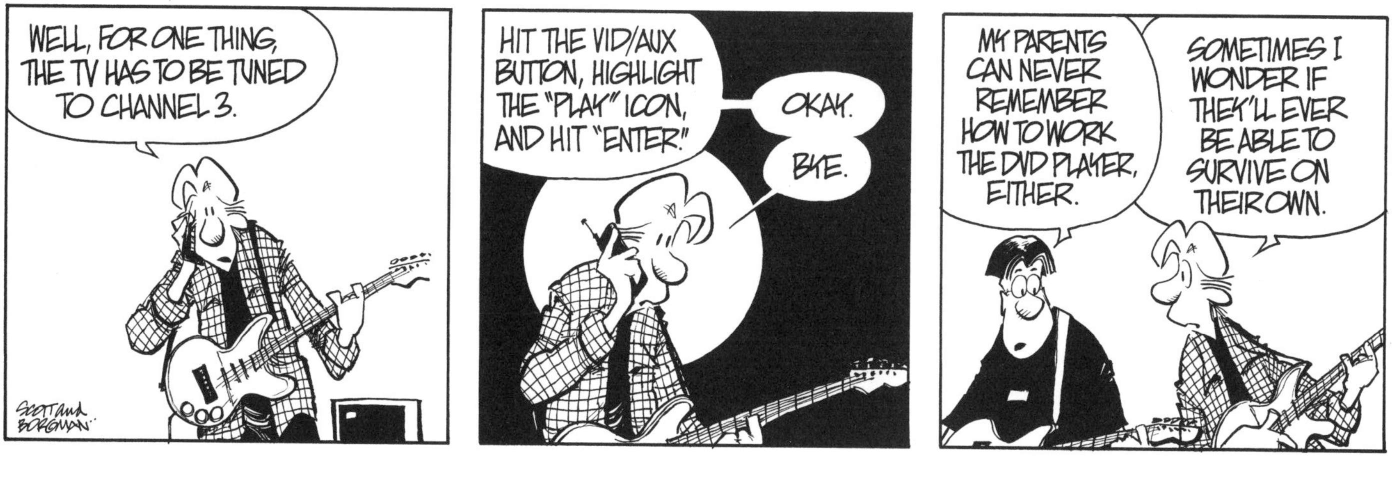
WELL, FOR ONE THING, THE TV HAS TO BE TUNED TO CHANNEL 3.
HIT THE VID/AUX BUTTON, HIGHLIGHT THE "PLAY" ICON, AND HIT "ENTER."
OKAY.
BYE.
MY PARENTS CAN NEVER REMEMBER HOW TO WORK THE DVD PLAYER, EITHER.
SOMETIMES I WONDER IF THEY'LL EVER BE ABLE TO SURVIVE ON THEIR OWN.

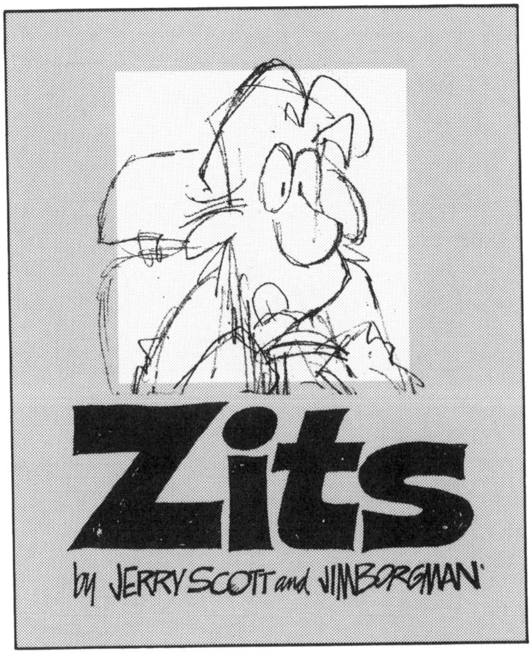
Zits
by JERRY SCOTT and JIM BORGMAN

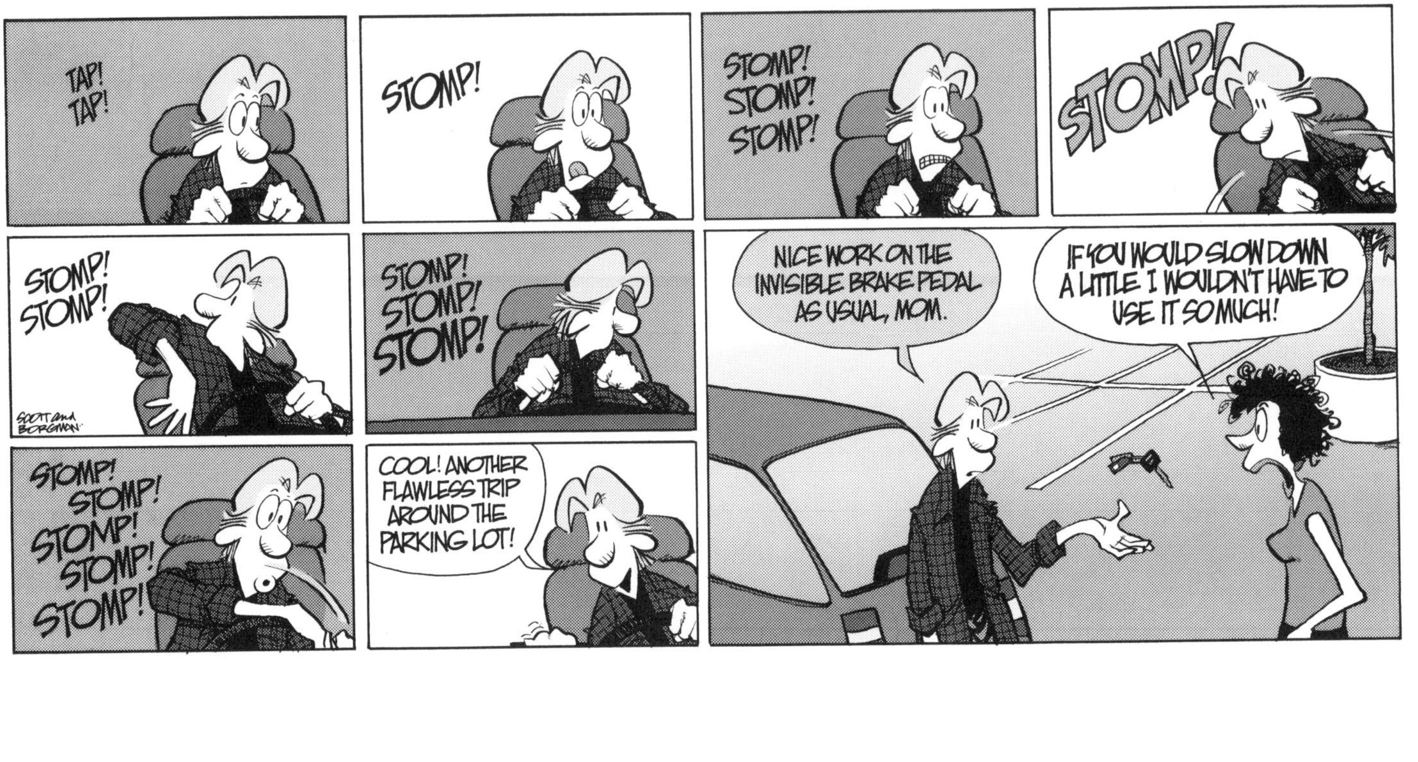
TAP! TAP!
STOMP!
STOMP! STOMP! STOMP!
STOMP!
STOMP! STOMP!
SCOTT and BORGMAN
STOMP! STOMP! STOMP!
STOMP! STOMP! STOMP! STOMP! STOMP!
COOL! ANOTHER FLAWLESS TRIP AROUND THE PARKING LOT!
NICE WORK ON THE INVISIBLE BRAKE PEDAL AS USUAL, MOM.
IF YOU WOULD SLOW DOWN A LITTLE I WOULDN'T HAVE TO USE IT SO MUCH!

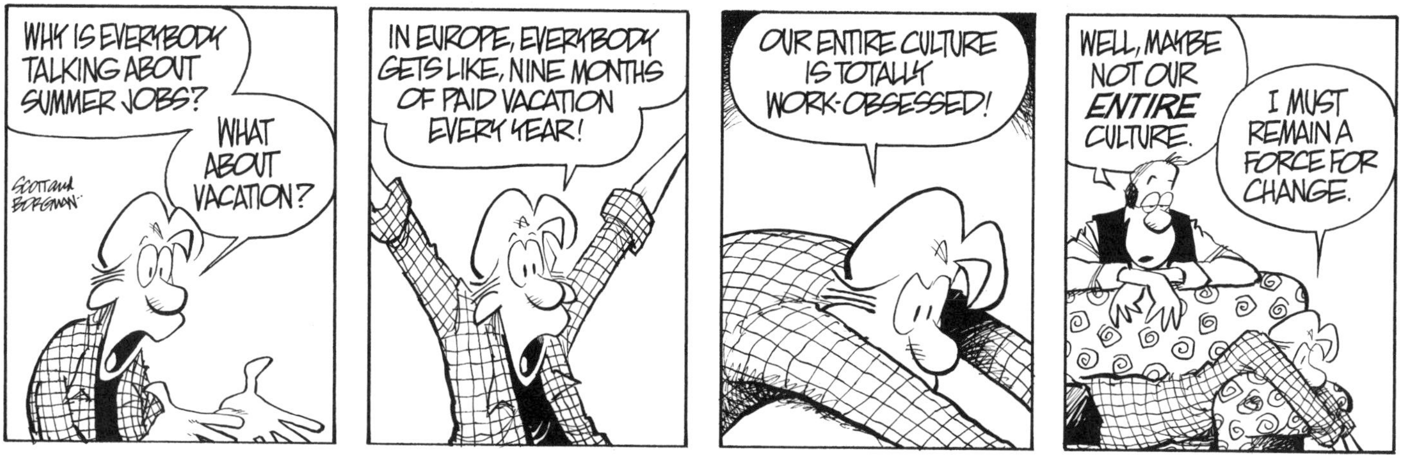
WHY IS EVERYBODY TALKING ABOUT SUMMER JOBS?
WHAT ABOUT VACATION?
IN EUROPE, EVERYBODY GETS LIKE, NINE MONTHS OF PAID VACATION EVERY YEAR!
OUR ENTIRE CULTURE IS TOTALLY WORK-OBSESSED!
WELL, MAYBE NOT OUR ENTIRE CULTURE.
I MUST REMAIN A FORCE FOR CHANGE.

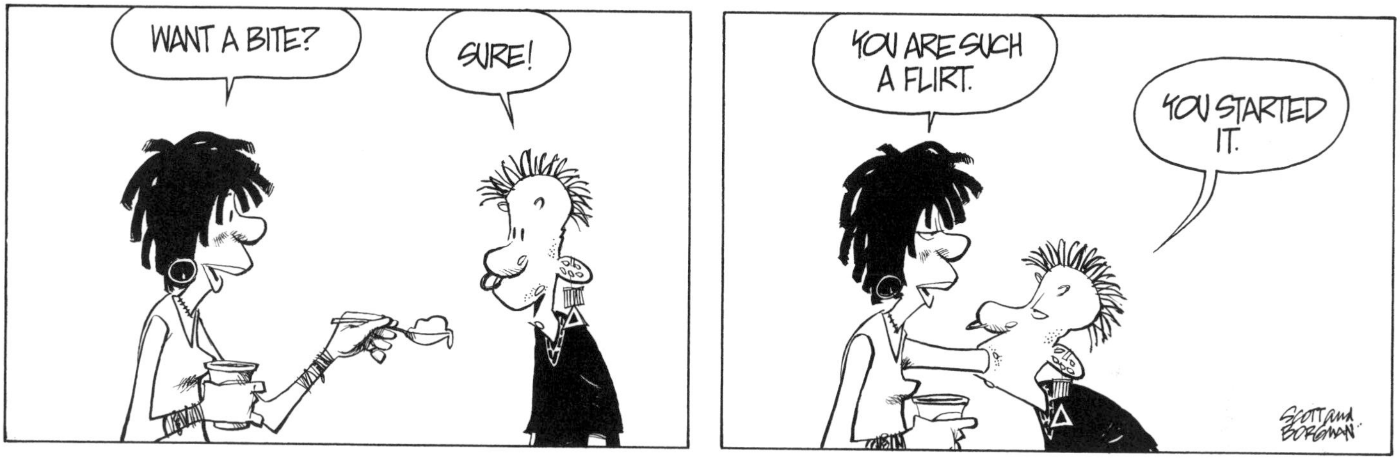
WANT A BITE?
SURE!
YOU ARE SUCH A FLIRT.
YOU STARTED IT.

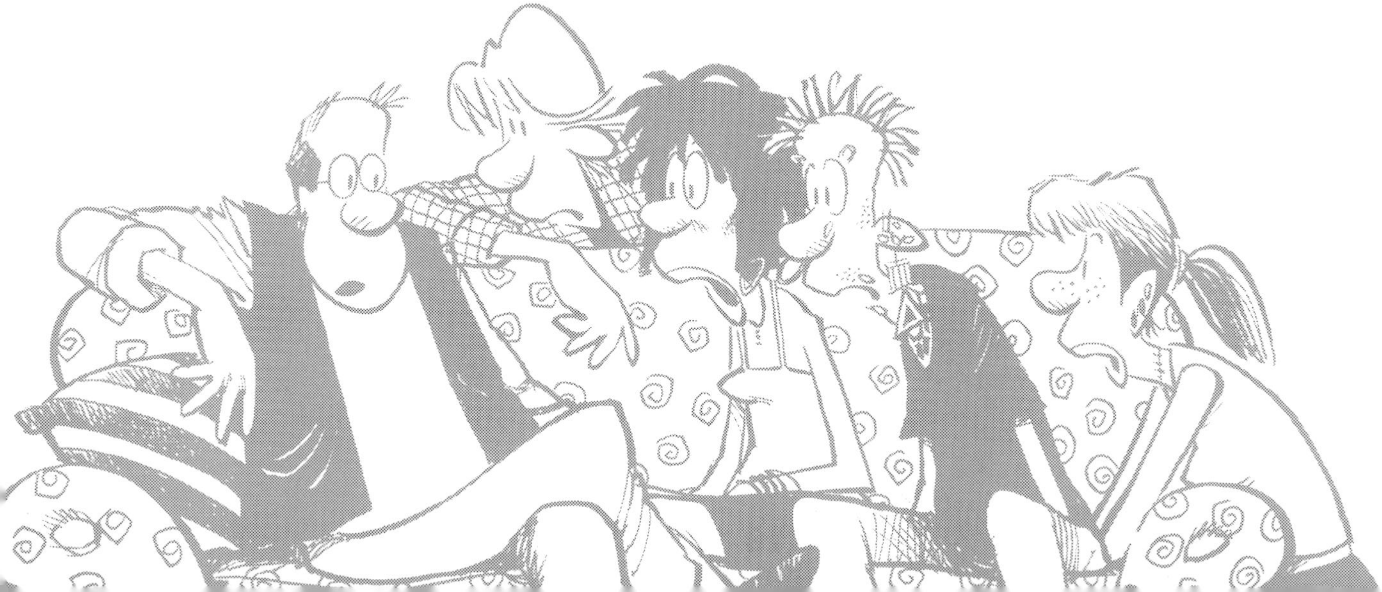

DON'T FORGET TO PUT YOUR DIRTY DISHES IN THE SINK, JEREMY.

AND TAKE YOUR SHOES UP TO YOUR ROOM, TOO.

WHEN DID LIFE BECOME SO UNBEARABLY DEMANDING?

SCOTTand BORGMAN

SO THAT'S MY PROPOSAL, BASED ON SOUND ECONOMIC PRINCIPLE.

IN THE INTEREST OF FISCAL RESPONSIBILITY, I THINK YOU HAVE TO AGREE THAT IT'S A REASONABLE REQUEST.

SCOTTand BORGMAN

I'M NOT PAYING YOUR ALLOWANCE IN EUROS.

MOM!

20

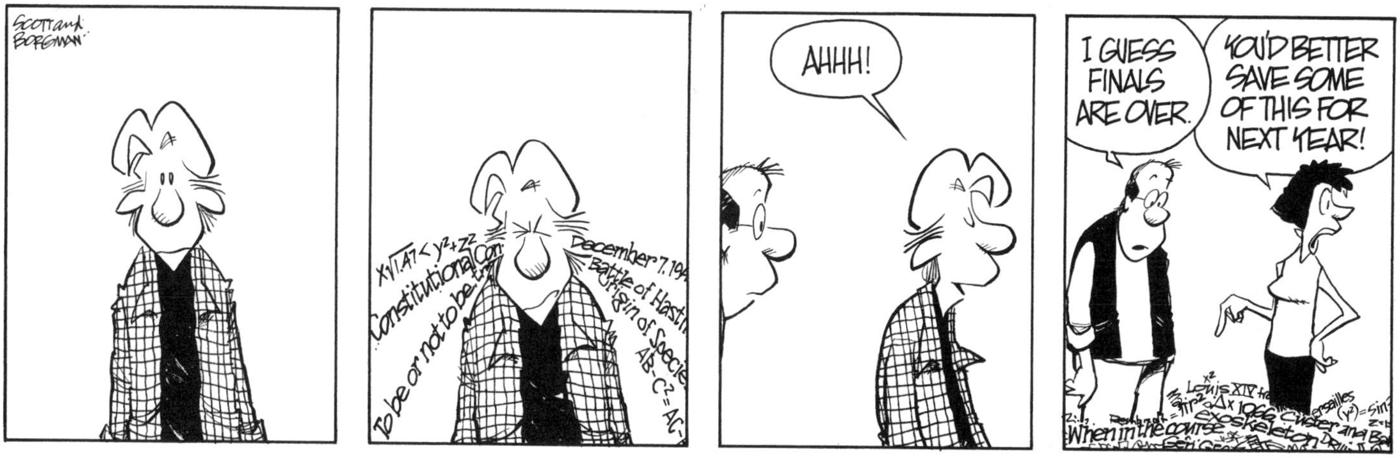
SCOTT and BORGMAN
AHHH!
I GUESS FINALS ARE OVER.
YOU'D BETTER SAVE SOME OF THIS FOR NEXT YEAR!

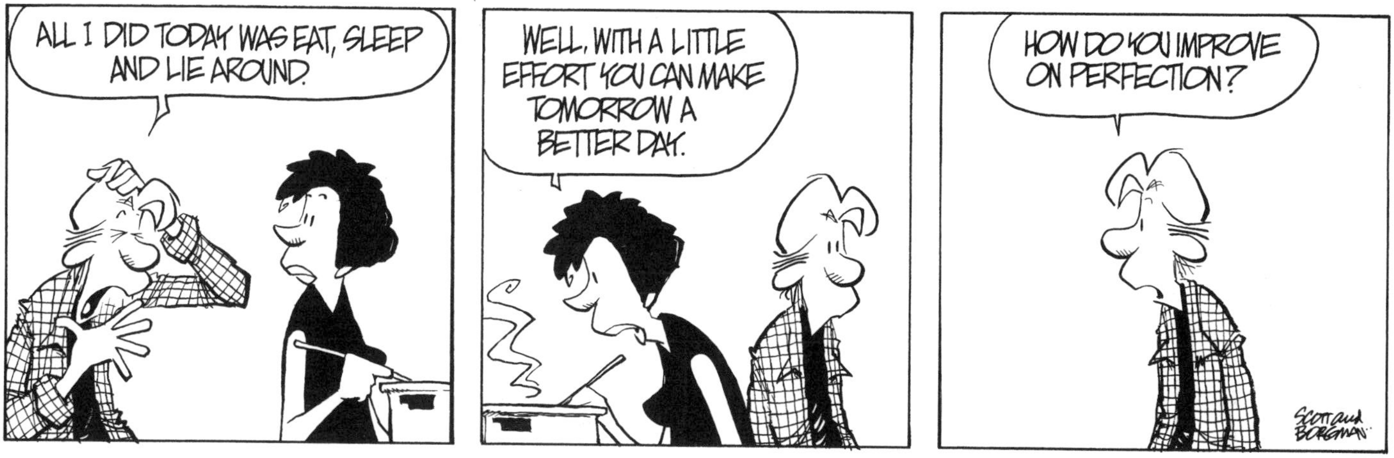
ALL I DID TODAY WAS EAT, SLEEP AND LIE AROUND.
WELL, WITH A LITTLE EFFORT YOU CAN MAKE TOMORROW A BETTER DAY.
HOW DO YOU IMPROVE ON PERFECTION?
SCOTT and BORGMAN

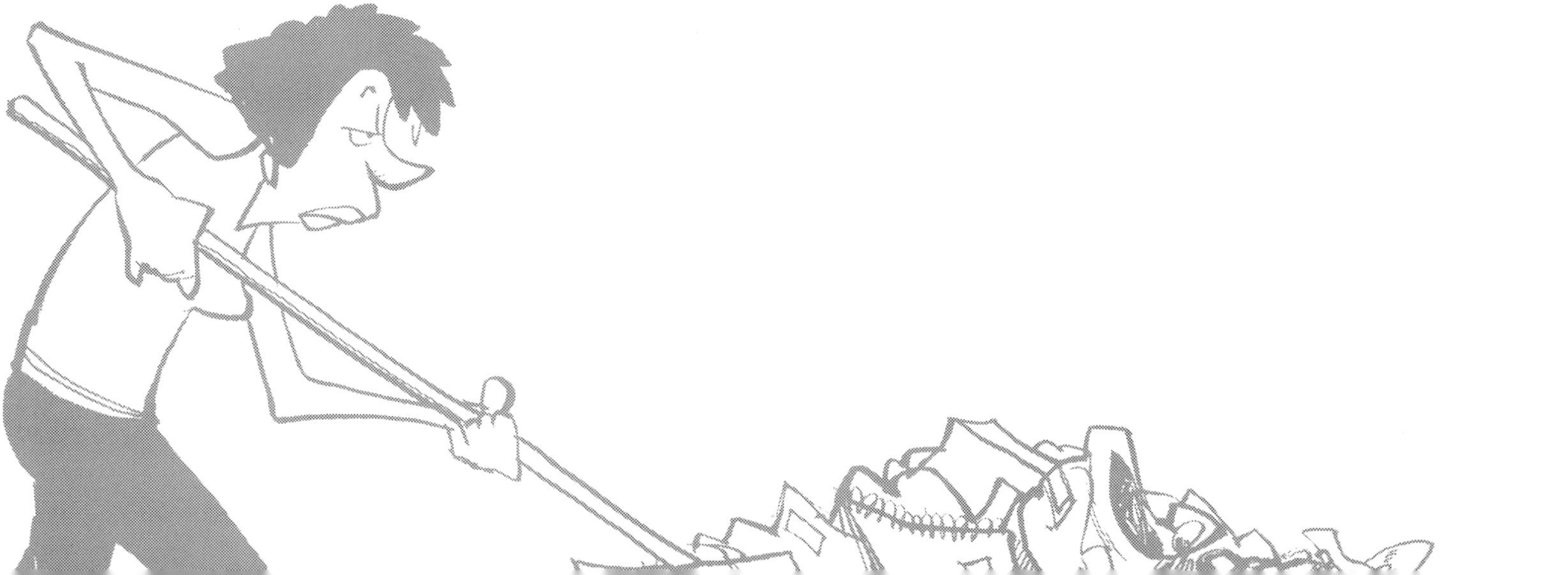

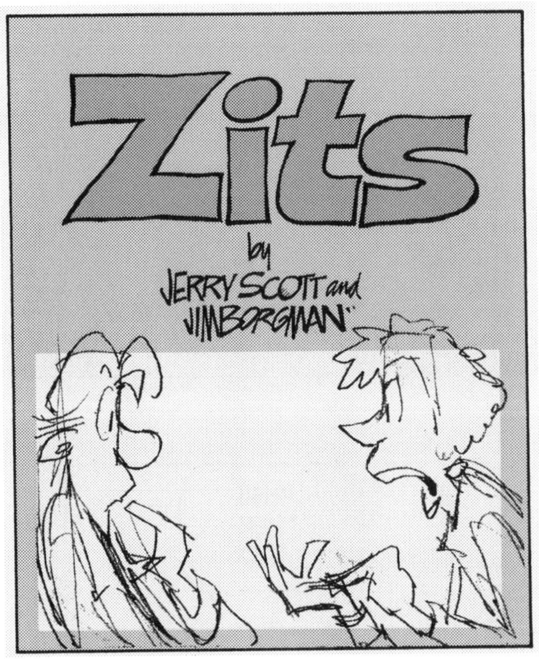
Zits
by
JERRY SCOTT and
JIM BORGMAN

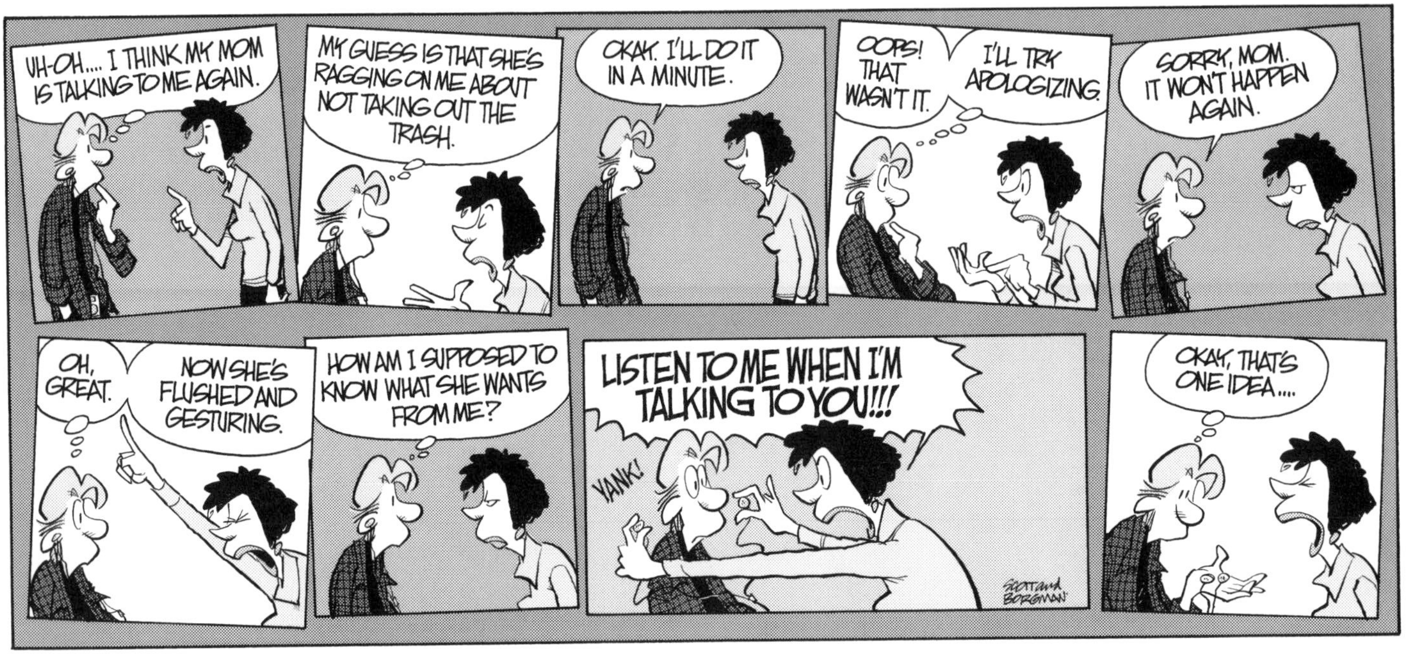
UH-OH.... I THINK MY MOM IS TALKING TO ME AGAIN.
MY GUESS IS THAT SHE'S RAGGING ON ME ABOUT NOT TAKING OUT THE TRASH.
OKAY. I'LL DO IT IN A MINUTE.
OOPS! THAT WASN'T IT.
I'LL TRY APOLOGIZING.
SORRY, MOM. IT WON'T HAPPEN AGAIN.
OH, GREAT.
NOW SHE'S FLUSHED AND GESTURING.
HOW AM I SUPPOSED TO KNOW WHAT SHE WANTS FROM ME?
LISTEN TO ME WHEN I'M TALKING TO YOU!!!
YANK!
SCOTT and BORGMAN
OKAY, THAT'S ONE IDEA....

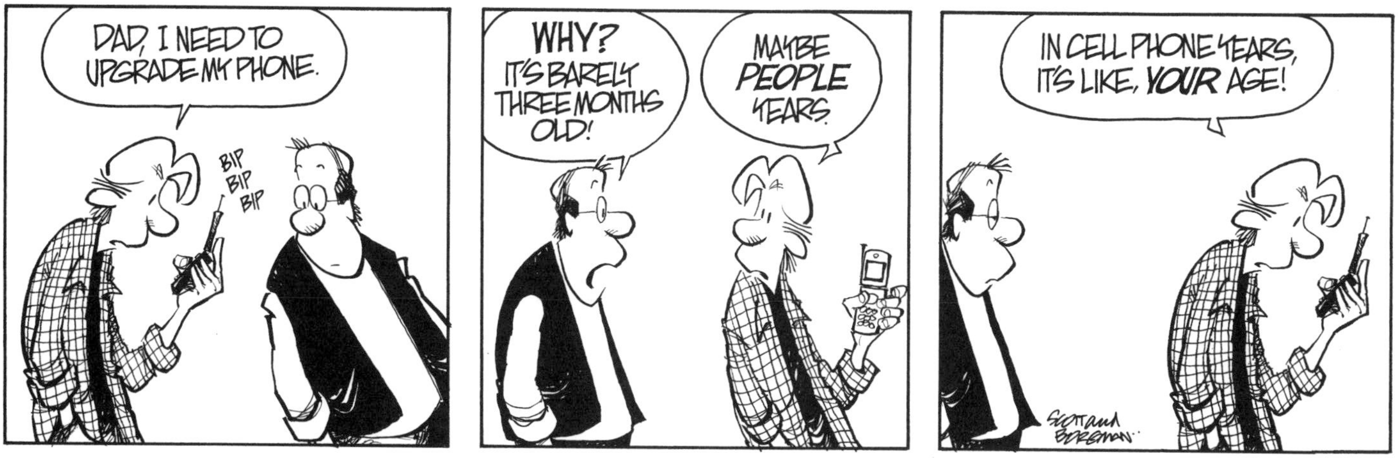
DAD, I NEED TO UPGRADE MY PHONE.
BIP BIP BIP
WHY? IT'S BARELY THREE MONTHS OLD!
MAYBE PEOPLE YEARS.
IN CELL PHONE YEARS, IT'S LIKE, YOUR AGE!

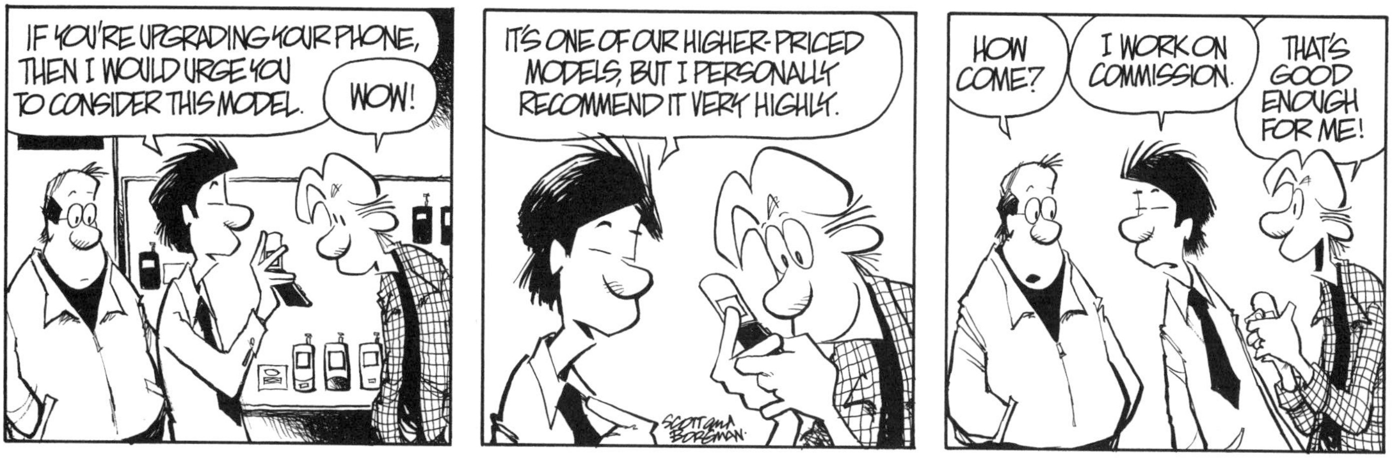
IF YOU'RE UPGRADING YOUR PHONE, THEN I WOULD URGE YOU TO CONSIDER THIS MODEL.
WOW!
IT'S ONE OF OUR HIGHER-PRICED MODELS, BUT I PERSONALLY RECOMMEND IT VERY HIGHLY.
HOW COME?
I WORK ON COMMISSION.
THAT'S GOOD ENOUGH FOR ME!

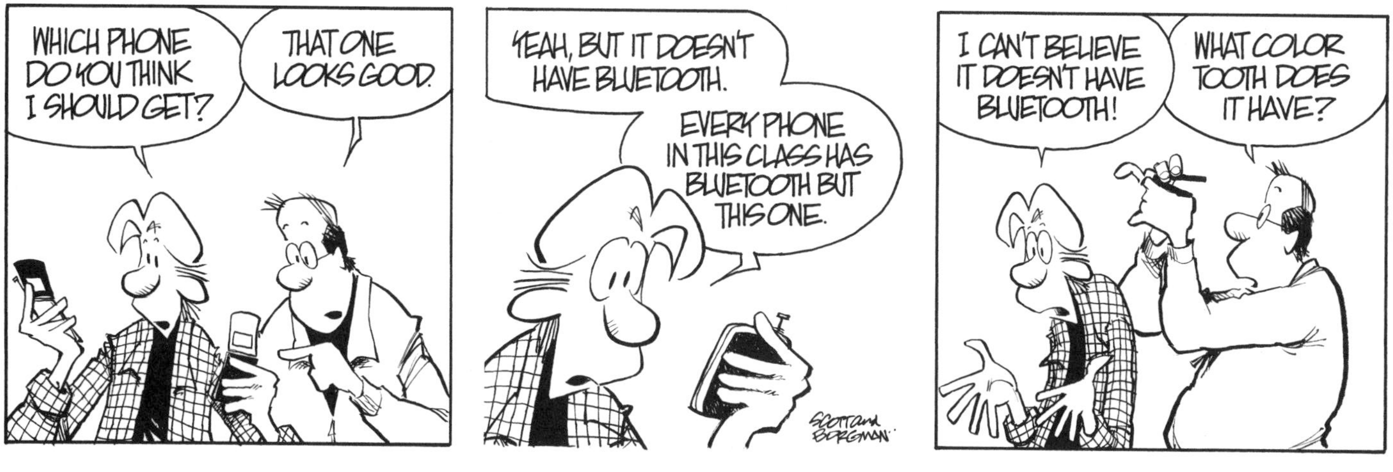
WHICH PHONE DO YOU THINK I SHOULD GET?
THAT ONE LOOKS GOOD.
YEAH, BUT IT DOESN'T HAVE BLUETOOTH.
EVERY PHONE IN THIS CLASS HAS BLUETOOTH BUT THIS ONE.
I CAN'T BELIEVE IT DOESN'T HAVE BLUETOOTH!
WHAT COLOR TOOTH DOES IT HAVE?

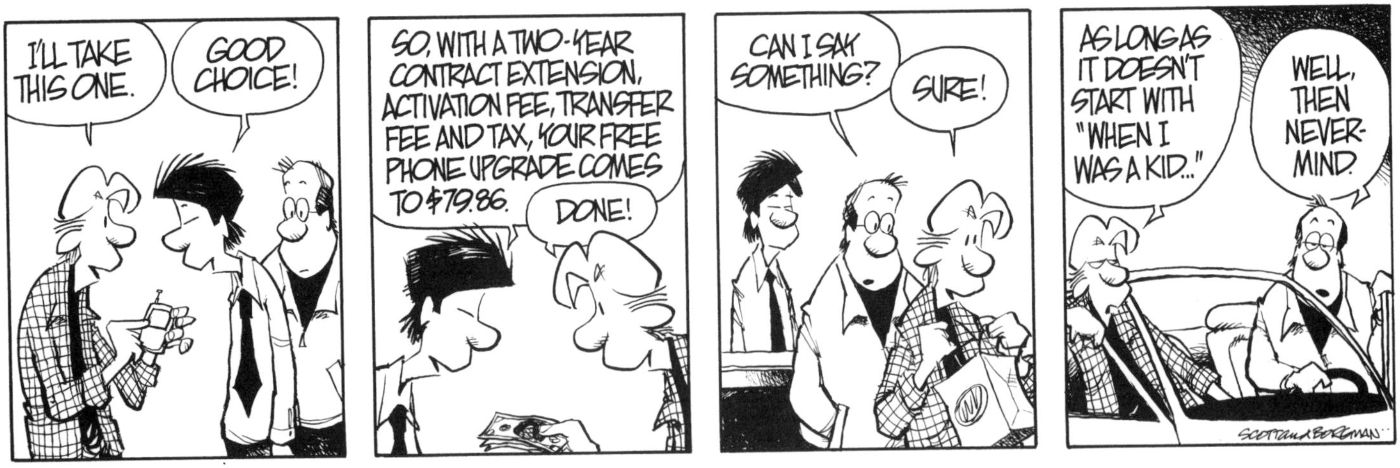
I'LL TAKE THIS ONE.
GOOD CHOICE!
SO, WITH A TWO-YEAR CONTRACT EXTENSION, ACTIVATION FEE, TRANSFER FEE AND TAX, YOUR FREE PHONE UPGRADE COMES TO $79.86.
DONE!
CAN I SAY SOMETHING?
SURE!
AS LONG AS IT DOESN'T START WITH "WHEN I WAS A KID..."
WELL, THEN NEVERMIND.
SCOTT and BORGMAN

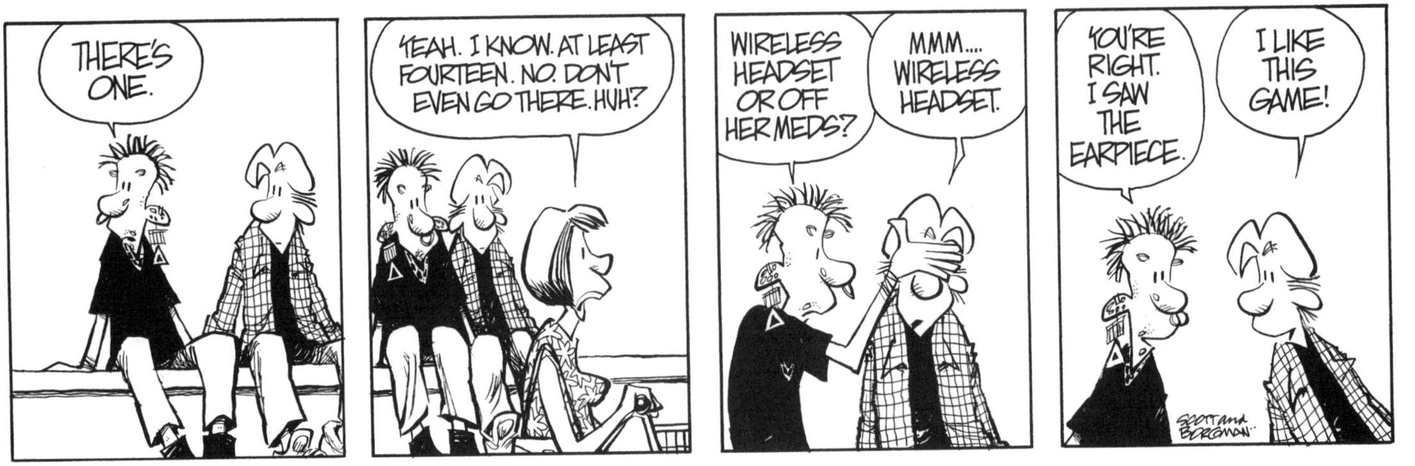
THERE'S ONE.
YEAH. I KNOW. AT LEAST FOURTEEN. NO. DON'T EVEN GO THERE. HUH?
WIRELESS HEADSET OR OFF HER MEDS?
MMM.... WIRELESS HEADSET.
YOU'RE RIGHT. I SAW THE EARPIECE.
I LIKE THIS GAME!
SCOTT and BORGMAN

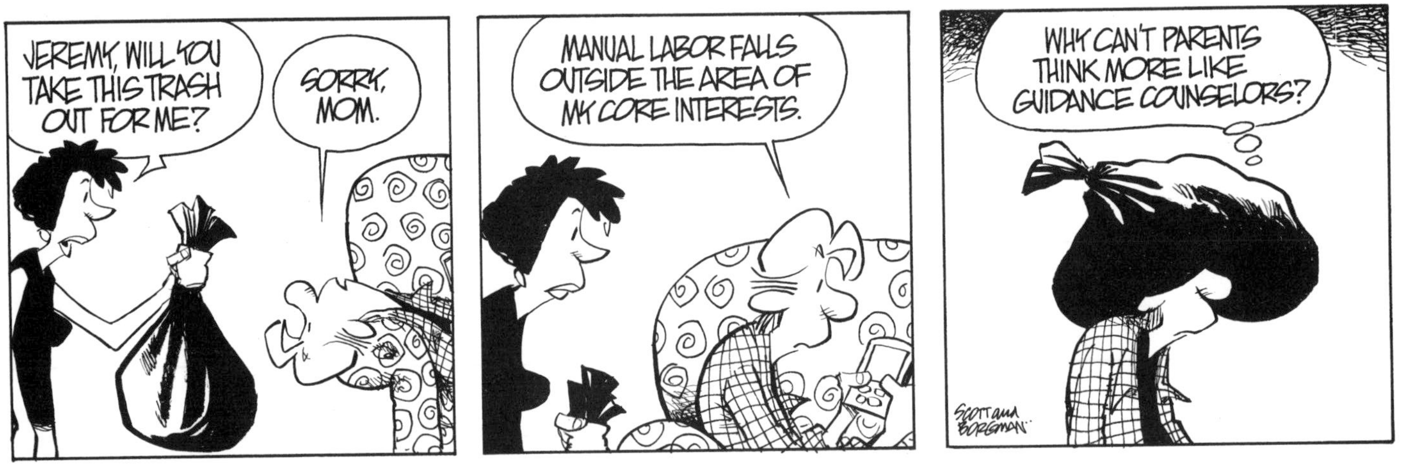
JEREMY, WILL YOU TAKE THIS TRASH OUT FOR ME?
SORRY, MOM.
MANUAL LABOR FALLS OUTSIDE THE AREA OF MY CORE INTERESTS.
WHY CAN'T PARENTS THINK MORE LIKE GUIDANCE COUNSELORS?
SCOTT and BORGMAN

Zits
by JERRY SCOTT and JIM BORGMAN

?
OH, NO.
IS THIS WHAT I THINK IT IS?
I'M AFRAID SO.
I'LL HANDLE IT.
YEEEEEEAAAGGGH!
YOUR MOTHER AND I WOULD APPRECIATE IT IF YOU WOULD WASH YOUR ATHLETIC CUP BY HAND FROM NOW ON.
WHAT? EWW! GROSS!

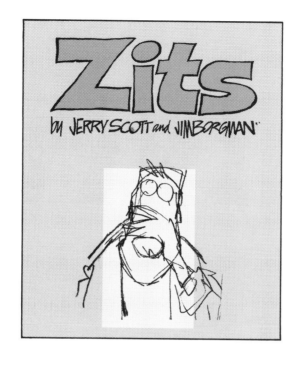

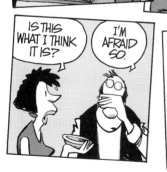

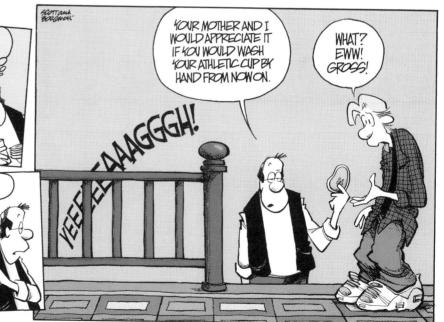

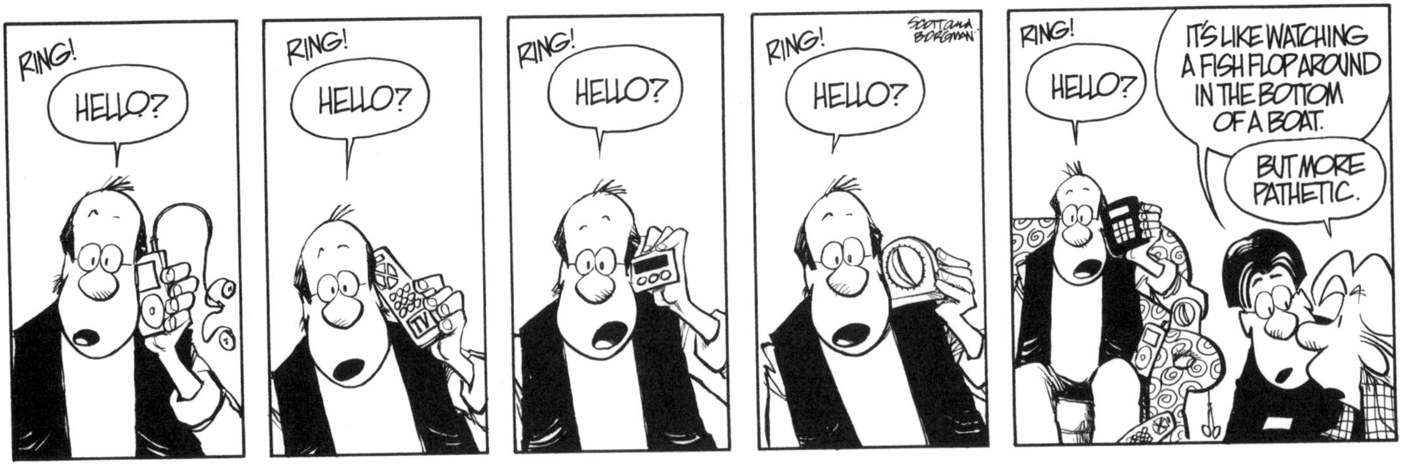
RING!
HELLO?
RING!
HELLO?
RING!
HELLO?
RING!
HELLO?
RING!
HELLO?
IT'S LIKE WATCHING A FISH FLOP AROUND IN THE BOTTOM OF A BOAT.
BUT MORE PATHETIC.

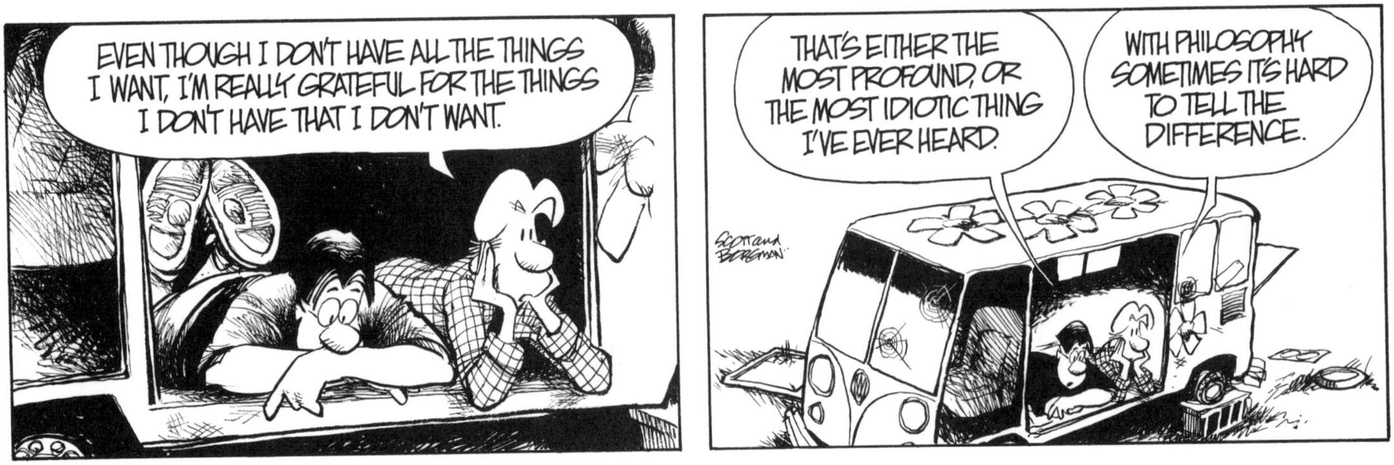
EVEN THOUGH I DON'T HAVE ALL THE THINGS I WANT, I'M REALLY GRATEFUL FOR THE THINGS I DON'T HAVE THAT I DON'T WANT.
THAT'S EITHER THE MOST PROFOUND, OR THE MOST IDIOTIC THING I'VE EVER HEARD.
WITH PHILOSOPHY SOMETIMES IT'S HARD TO TELL THE DIFFERENCE.

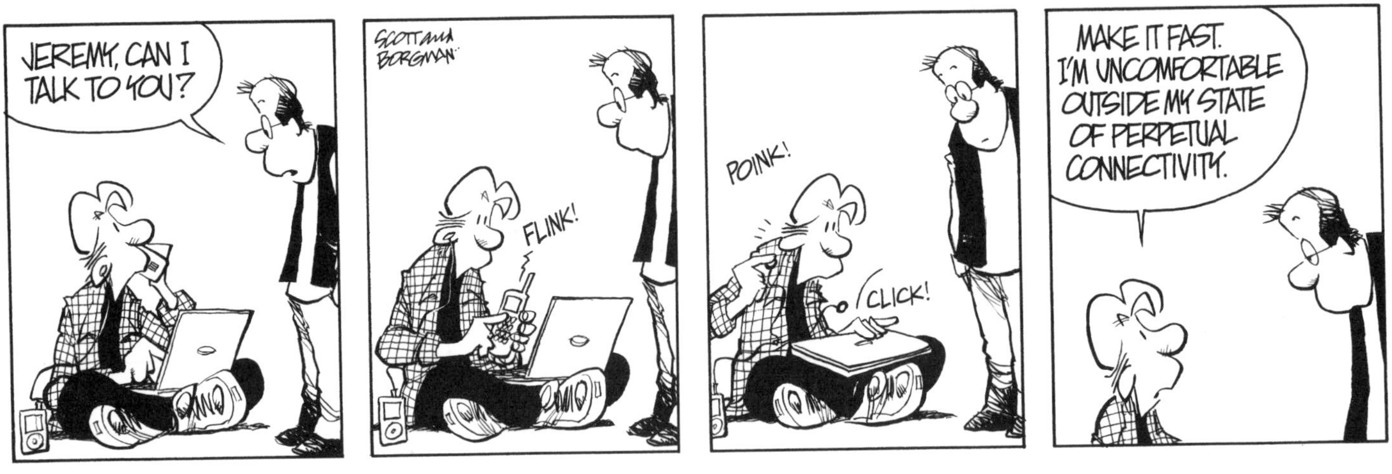
JEREMY, CAN I TALK TO YOU?
FLINK!
POINK!
CLICK!
MAKE IT FAST. I'M UNCOMFORTABLE OUTSIDE MY STATE OF PERPETUAL CONNECTIVITY.

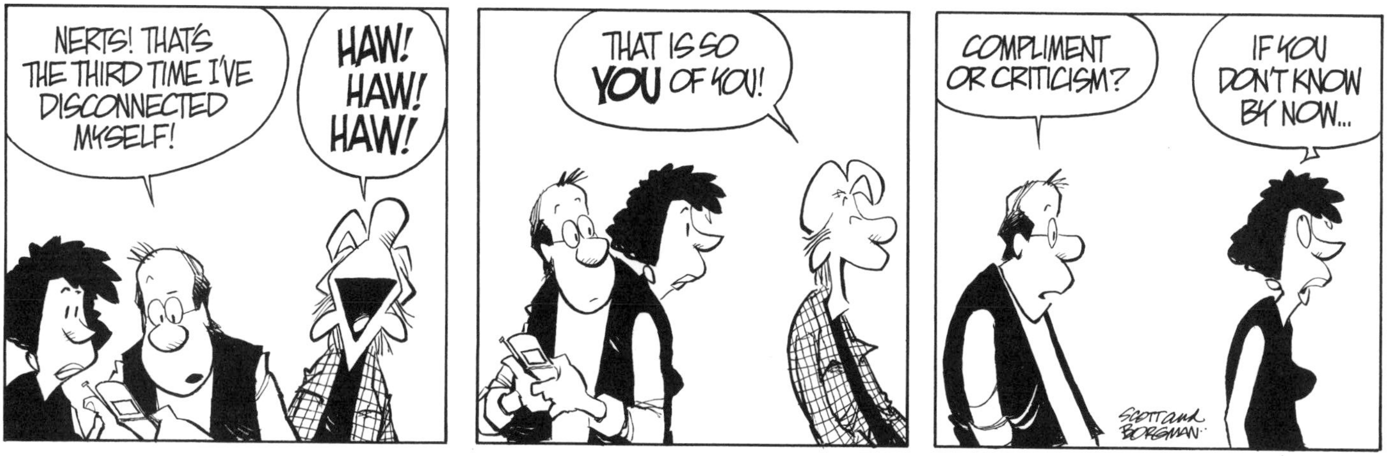
NERTS! THAT'S THE THIRD TIME I'VE DISCONNECTED MYSELF!
HAW! HAW! HAW!
THAT IS SO YOU OF YOU!
COMPLIMENT OR CRITICISM?
IF YOU DON'T KNOW BY NOW...

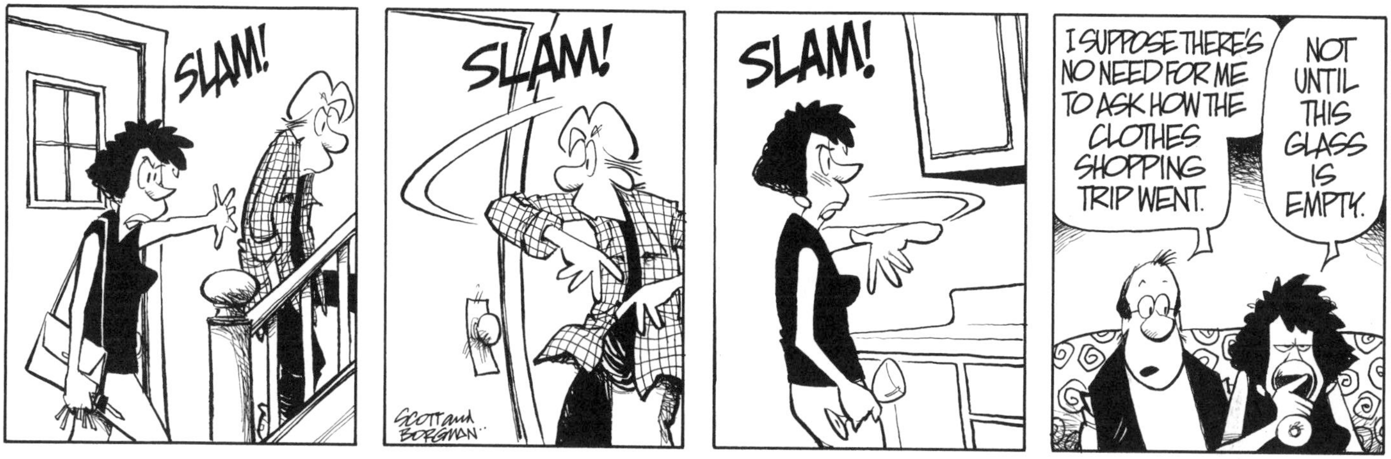
SLAM!
SLAM!
SLAM!
I SUPPOSE THERE'S NO NEED FOR ME TO ASK HOW THE CLOTHES SHOPPING TRIP WENT.
NOT UNTIL THIS GLASS IS EMPTY.

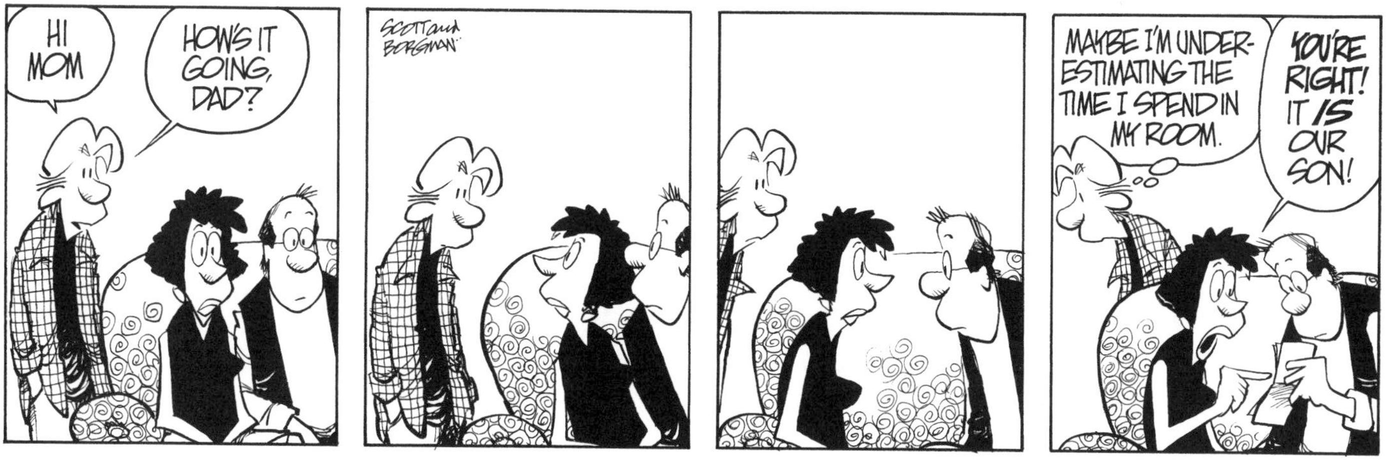
HI MOM
HOW'S IT GOING, DAD?
MAYBE I'M UNDER-ESTIMATING THE TIME I SPEND IN MY ROOM.
YOU'RE RIGHT! IT IS OUR SON!

Zits
by
JERRY SCOTT and
JIM BORGMAN
WOW!

HERE'S A ROMANCE TIP:
WHENEVER YOU WANT TO IMPRESS A GIRL, JUST SAY "CUTE SHOES."
"CUTE SHOES."
RIGHT.
WOMEN OBSESS ABOUT FOOTWEAR
IF YOU COMPLIMENT THEIR SHOES, IT'S LIKE A TOTAL VALIDATION OF THEIR WOMANHOOD.
WOW!
CUTE SHOES
CUTE SHOES
CUTE SHOES
CUTE SHOES
CUTE SHOES
CUTE SHOES
SCOTT and BORGMAN
CUTE SHOES.
YOU'RE SWEET
BUT I'M BAREFOOT.

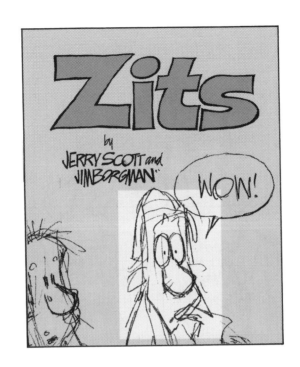

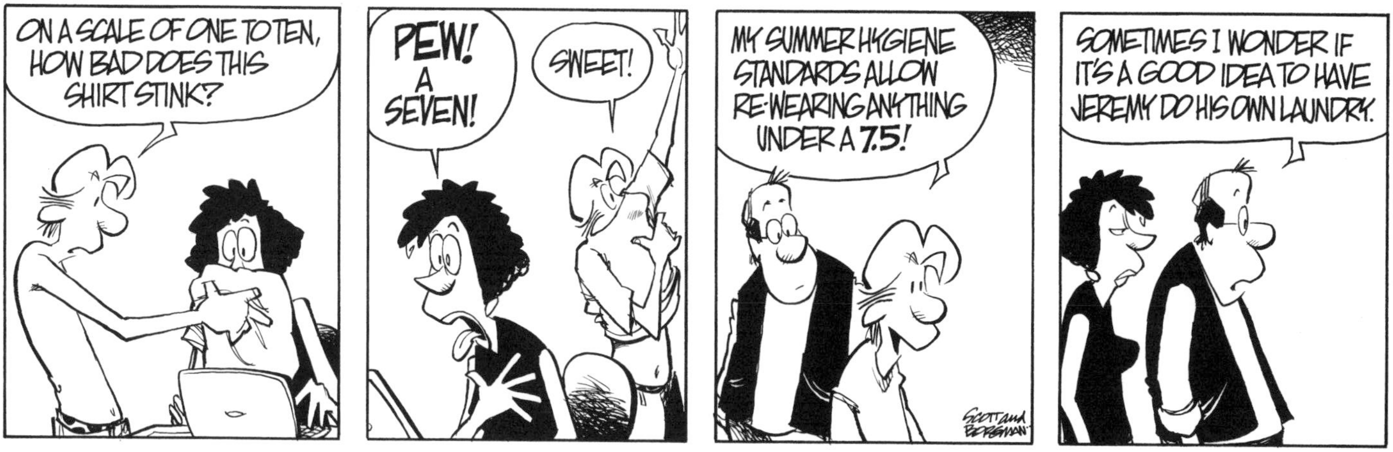
ON A SCALE OF ONE TO TEN, HOW BAD DOES THIS SHIRT STINK?
PEW! A SEVEN!
SWEET!
MY SUMMER HYGIENE STANDARDS ALLOW RE-WEARING ANYTHING UNDER A 7.5!
SOMETIMES I WONDER IF IT'S A GOOD IDEA TO HAVE JEREMY DO HIS OWN LAUNDRY.

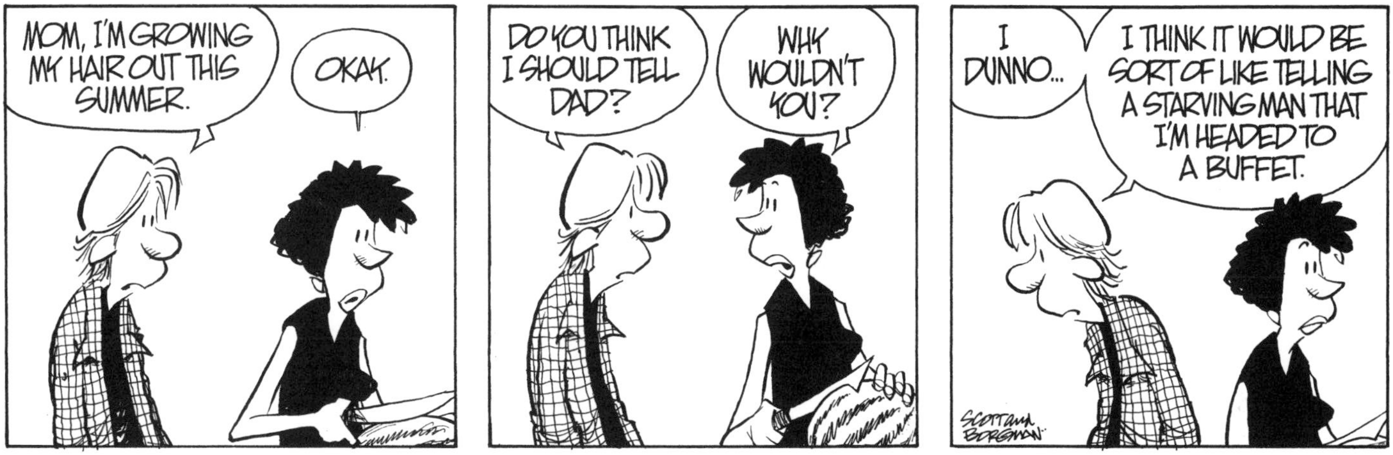
MOM, I'M GROWING MY HAIR OUT THIS SUMMER.
OKAY.
DO YOU THINK I SHOULD TELL DAD?
WHY WOULDN'T YOU?
I DUNNO...
I THINK IT WOULD BE SORT OF LIKE TELLING A STARVING MAN THAT I'M HEADED TO A BUFFET.

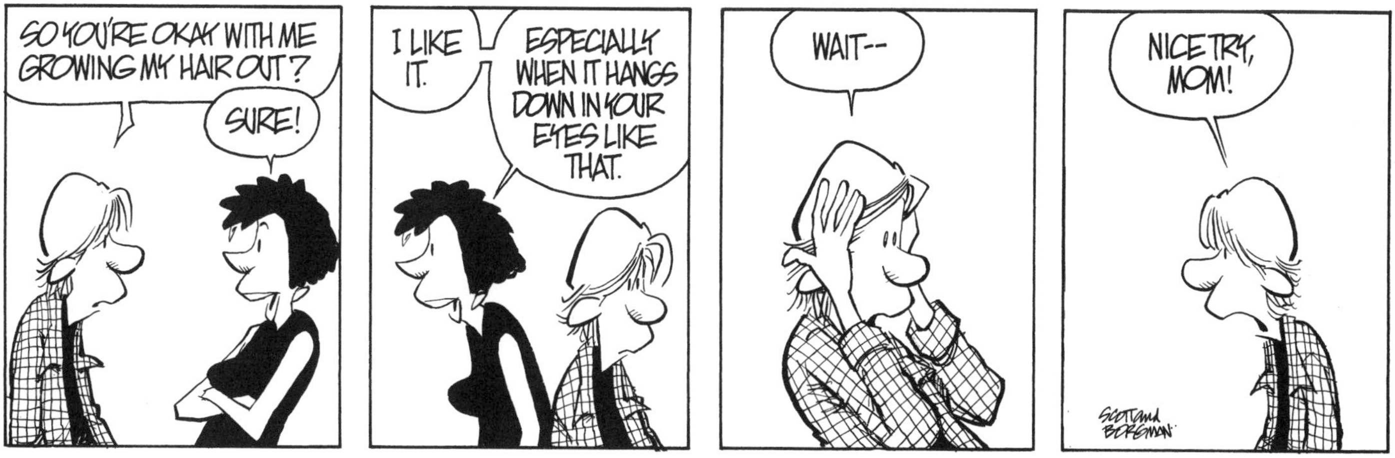
SO YOU'RE OKAY WITH ME GROWING MY HAIR OUT?
SURE!
I LIKE IT.
ESPECIALLY WHEN IT HANGS DOWN IN YOUR EYES LIKE THAT.
WAIT--
NICE TRY, MOM!

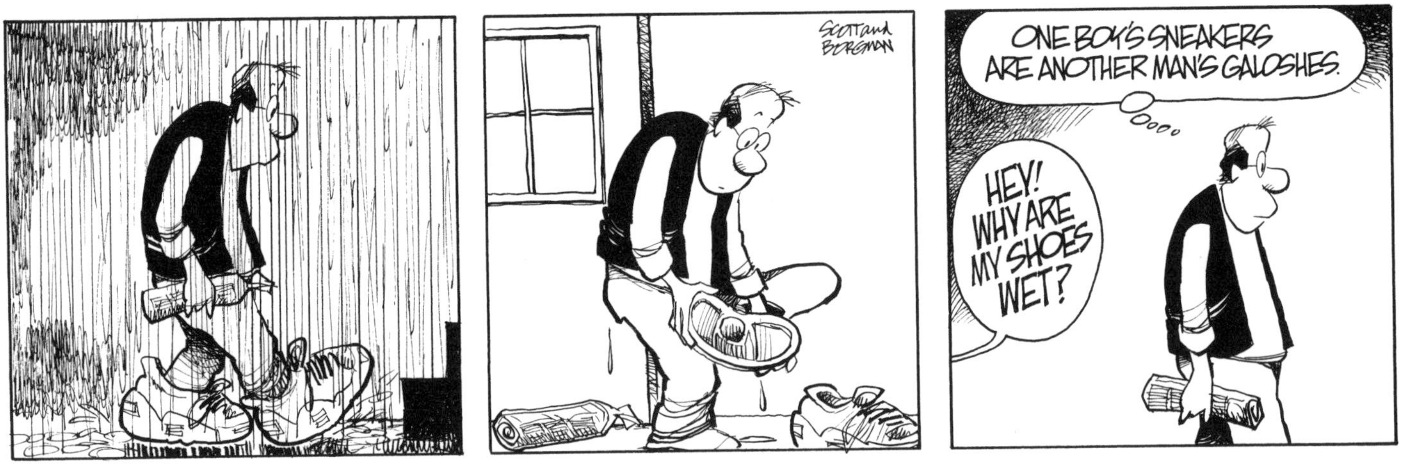
ONE BOY'S SNEAKERS ARE ANOTHER MAN'S GALOSHES.
HEY! WHY ARE MY SHOES WET?

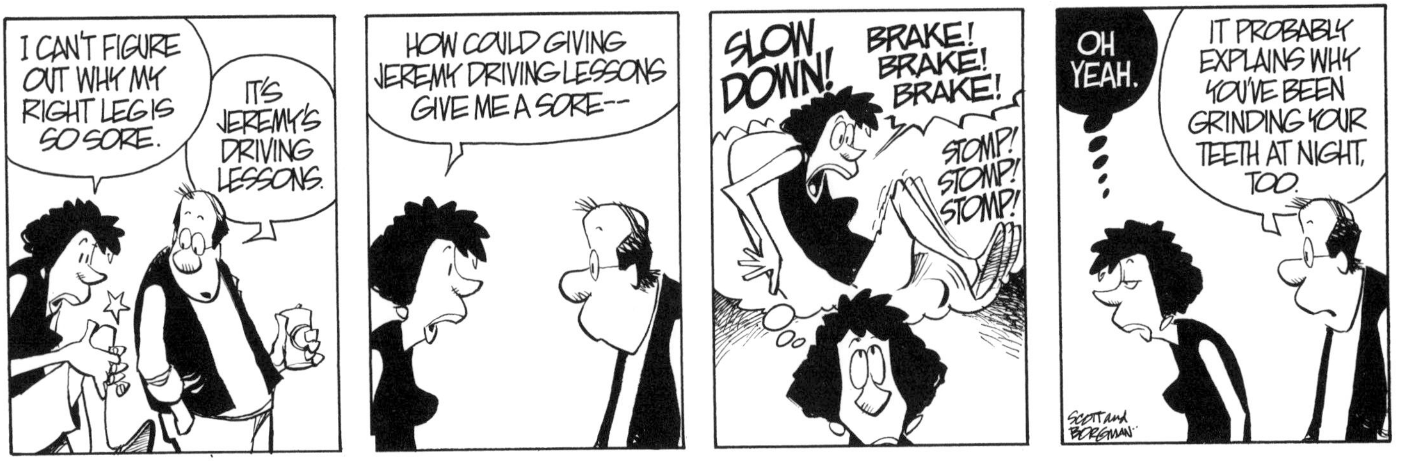
I CAN'T FIGURE OUT WHY MY RIGHT LEG IS SO SORE.
IT'S JEREMY'S DRIVING LESSONS.
HOW COULD GIVING JEREMY DRIVING LESSONS GIVE ME A SORE--
SLOW DOWN!
BRAKE! BRAKE! BRAKE!
STOMP! STOMP! STOMP!
OH YEAH.
IT PROBABLY EXPLAINS WHY YOU'VE BEEN GRINDING YOUR TEETH AT NIGHT, TOO.

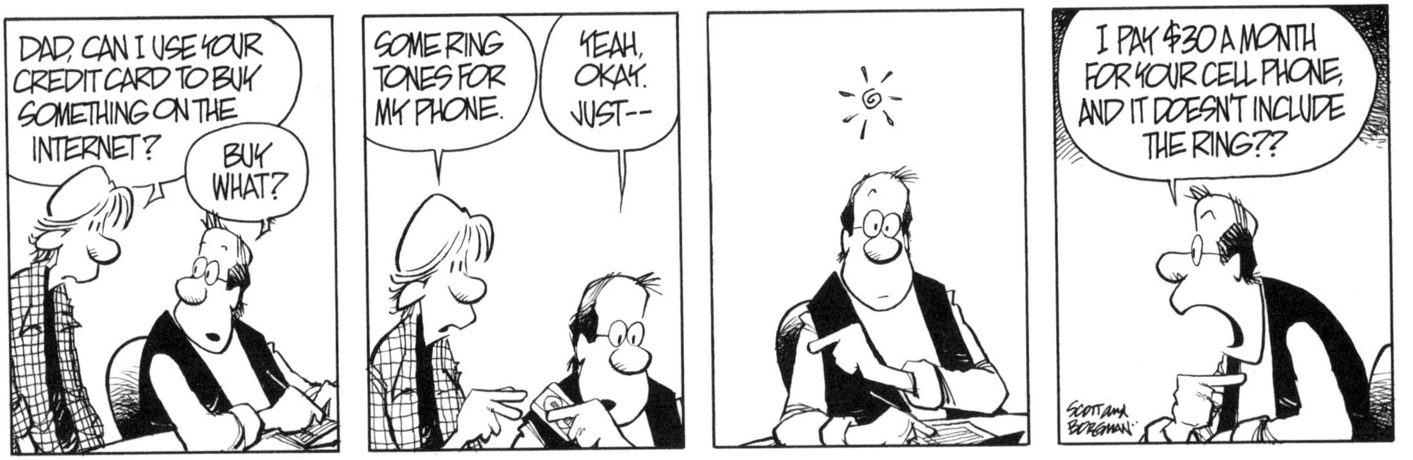
DAD, CAN I USE YOUR CREDIT CARD TO BUY SOMETHING ON THE INTERNET?
BUY WHAT?
SOME RING TONES FOR MY PHONE.
YEAH, OKAY. JUST--
I PAY $30 A MONTH FOR YOUR CELL PHONE, AND IT DOESN'T INCLUDE THE RING??

Zits

by JERRY SCOTT and JIM BORGMAN

DAD, WHO'S THIS?

THAT'S JUST ME ON MY 1946 INDIAN MOTORCYCLE.

THAT'S YOU?

I RESTORED IT WHEN I WAS IN HIGH SCHOOL, THEN RODE IT ALL THE WAY TO MONTANA.

AND THIS WAS TAKEN RIGHT AFTER MY FIRST PARACHUTE JUMP.

THAT'S YOU??

THIS IS FROM THE SUMMER IN COLLEGE WHEN I WORKED AS A FISHERMAN IN ALASKA.

THAT'S YOU??

...AND THEN I MUSHED THIS DOGSLED FROM BARROW TO DEADHORSE JUST TO WIN A BET.

THAT'S YOU?!?

SCOTT and BORGMAN 6/19

WOW.

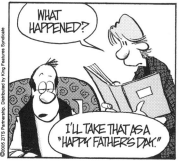

WHAT HAPPENED!?

I'LL TAKE THAT AS A "HAPPY FATHER'S DAY."

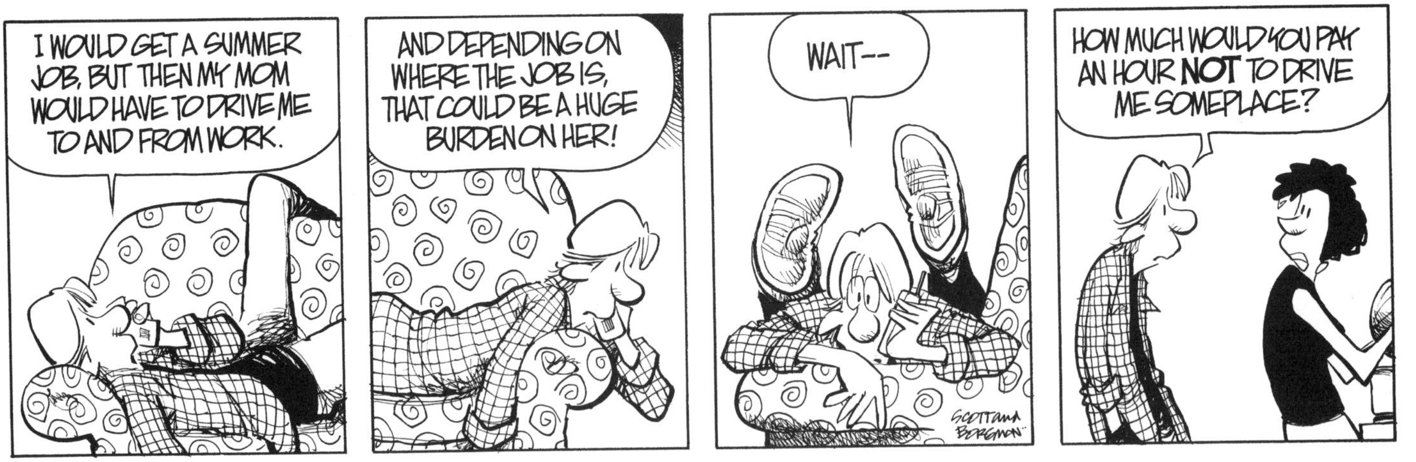
I WOULD GET A SUMMER JOB, BUT THEN MY MOM WOULD HAVE TO DRIVE ME TO AND FROM WORK.
AND DEPENDING ON WHERE THE JOB IS, THAT COULD BE A HUGE BURDEN ON HER!
WAIT--
HOW MUCH WOULD YOU PAY AN HOUR **NOT** TO DRIVE ME SOMEPLACE?

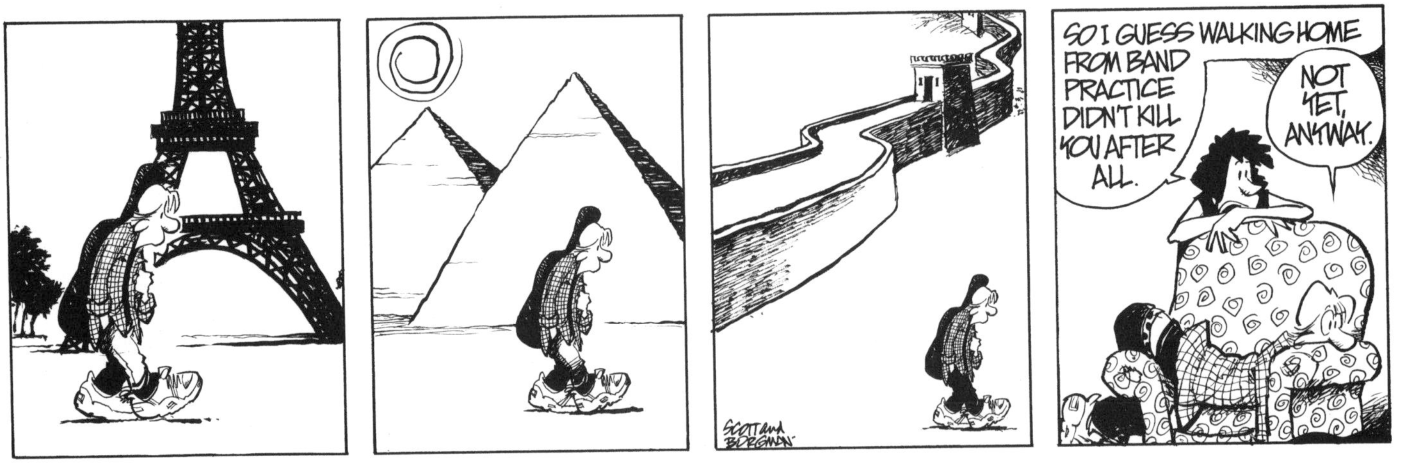
SO I GUESS WALKING HOME FROM BAND PRACTICE DIDN'T KILL YOU AFTER ALL.
NOT YET, ANYWAY.

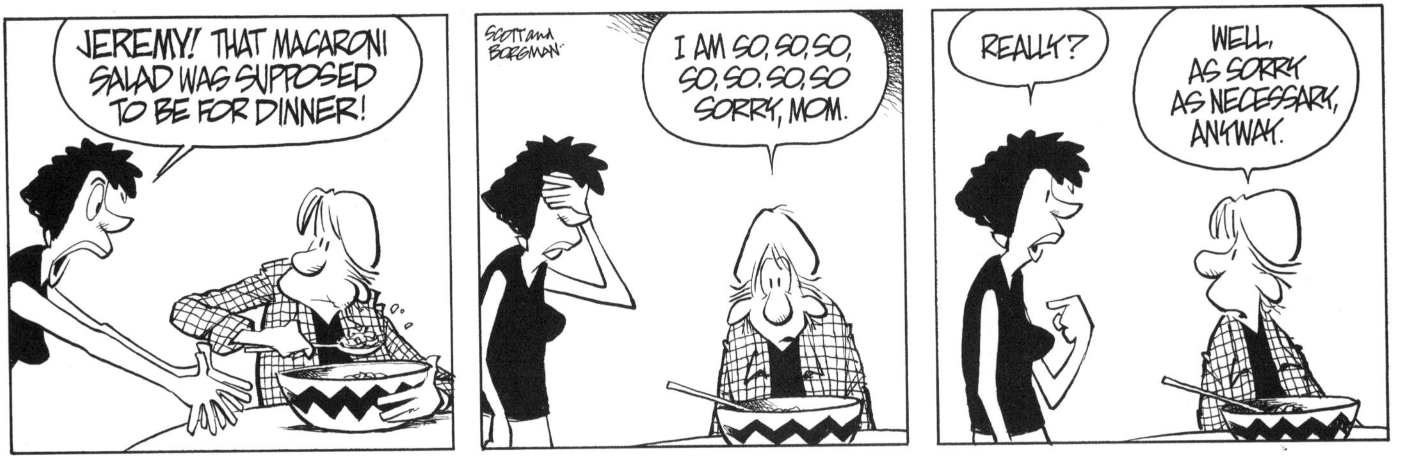
JEREMY! THAT MACARONI SALAD WAS SUPPOSED TO BE FOR DINNER!
I AM SO, SO, SO, SO, SO, SO, SO SORRY, MOM.
REALLY?
WELL, AS SORRY AS NECESSARY, ANYWAY.

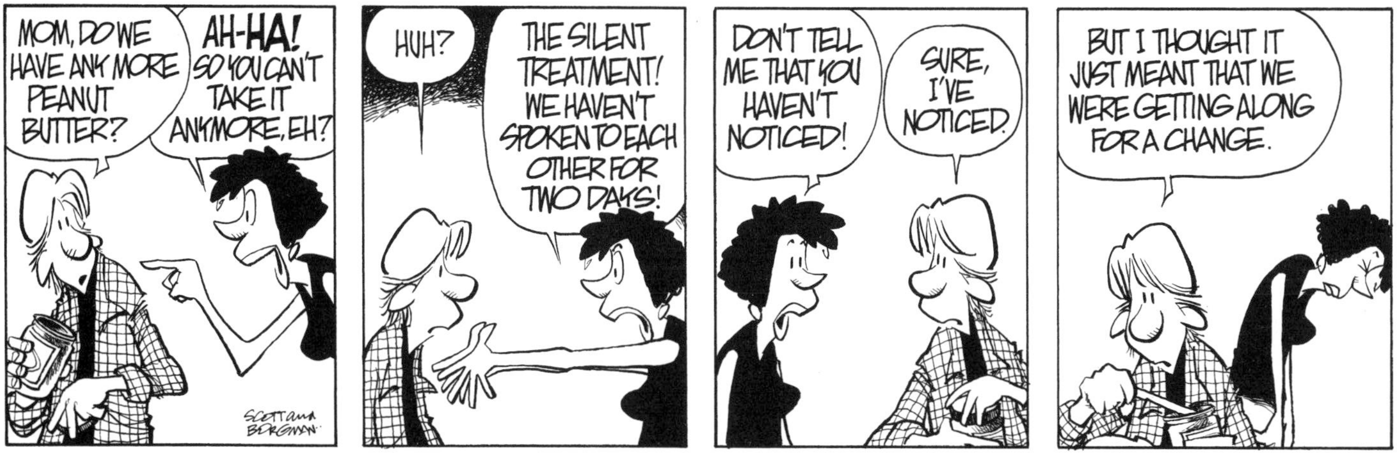
MOM, DO WE HAVE ANY MORE PEANUT BUTTER?
AH-HA! SO YOU CAN'T TAKE IT ANYMORE, EH?
SCOTT and BORGMAN
HUH?
THE SILENT TREATMENT! WE HAVEN'T SPOKEN TO EACH OTHER FOR TWO DAYS!
DON'T TELL ME THAT YOU HAVEN'T NOTICED!
SURE, I'VE NOTICED.
BUT I THOUGHT IT JUST MEANT THAT WE WERE GETTING ALONG FOR A CHANGE.

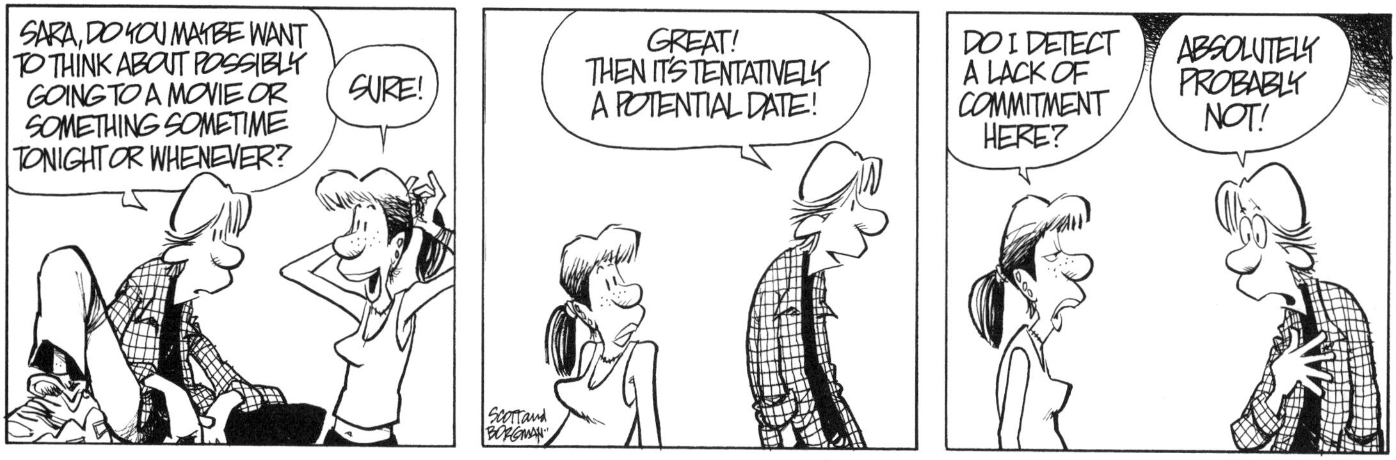
SARA, DO YOU MAYBE WANT TO THINK ABOUT POSSIBLY GOING TO A MOVIE OR SOMETHING SOMETIME TONIGHT OR WHENEVER?
SURE!
GREAT! THEN IT'S TENTATIVELY A POTENTIAL DATE!
SCOTT and BORGMAN
DO I DETECT A LACK OF COMMITMENT HERE?
ABSOLUTELY PROBABLY NOT!

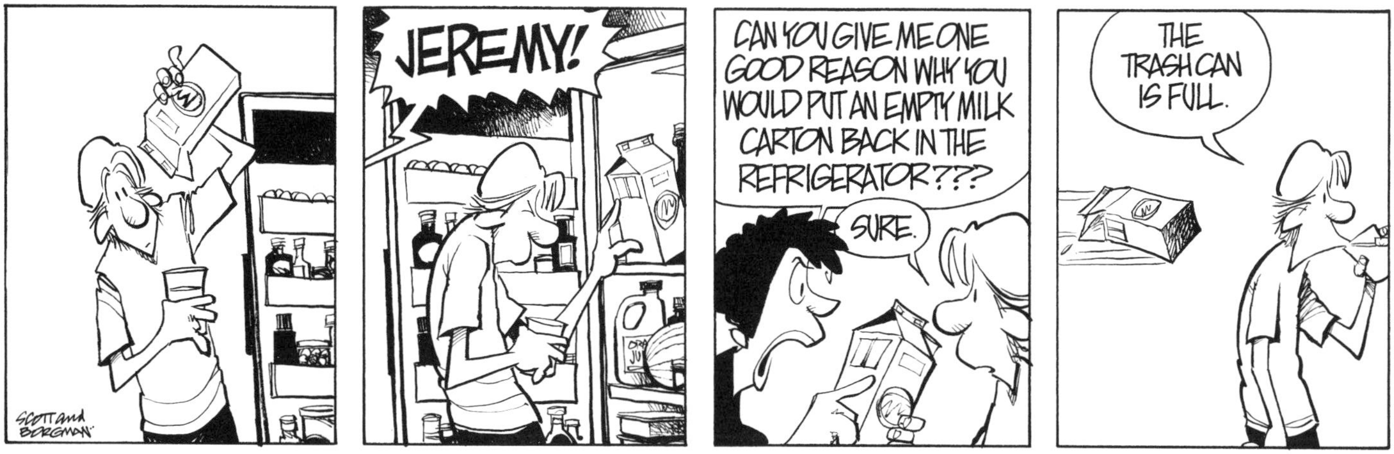
SCOTT and BORGMAN
JEREMY!
CAN YOU GIVE ME ONE GOOD REASON WHY YOU WOULD PUT AN EMPTY MILK CARTON BACK IN THE REFRIGERATOR???
SURE.
THE TRASH CAN IS FULL.

by
JERRY SCOTT and
JIM BORGMAN
Zits

ARE YOU READY TO GO, JEREMY?
GO WHERE?
SHOPPING! I TOLD YOU THAT I WANTED TO BUY YOU SOME NEW SHIRTS!
YOU DID?
WHEN?
THIS MORNING!!
SCOTT and BORGMAN
YOU WERE SITTING AT THE TABLE EATING A BOWL OF CEREAL AND LOOKING RIGHT AT ME!
AND THAT MADE YOU THINK THAT I WAS LISTENING?
I COULD USE SOME SHIRTS.

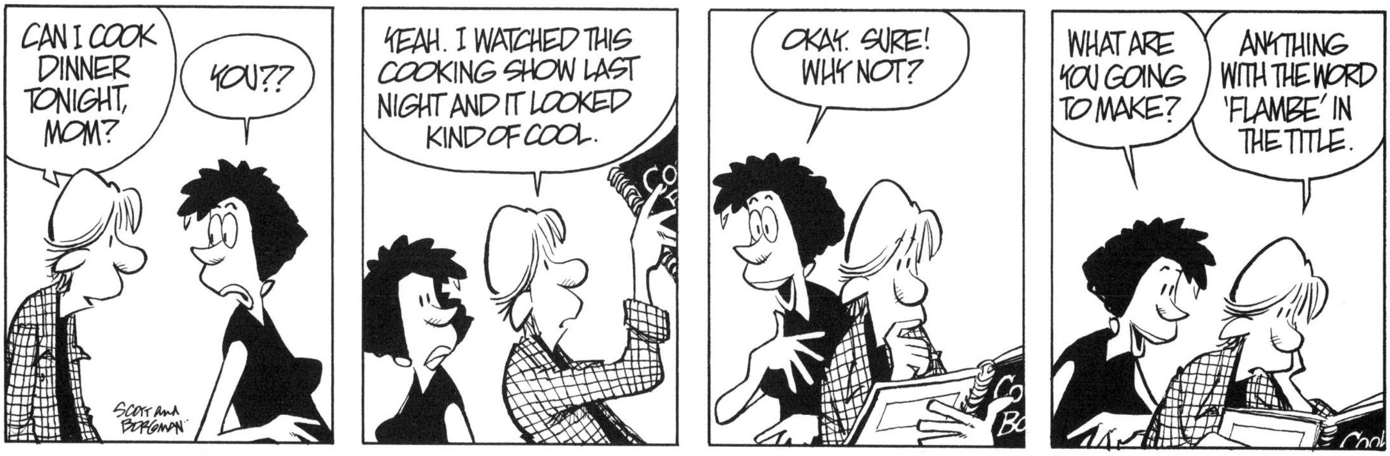
CAN I COOK DINNER TONIGHT, MOM?
YOU??
YEAH. I WATCHED THIS COOKING SHOW LAST NIGHT AND IT LOOKED KIND OF COOL.
OKAY. SURE! WHY NOT?
WHAT ARE YOU GOING TO MAKE?
ANYTHING WITH THE WORD 'FLAMBE' IN THE TITLE.

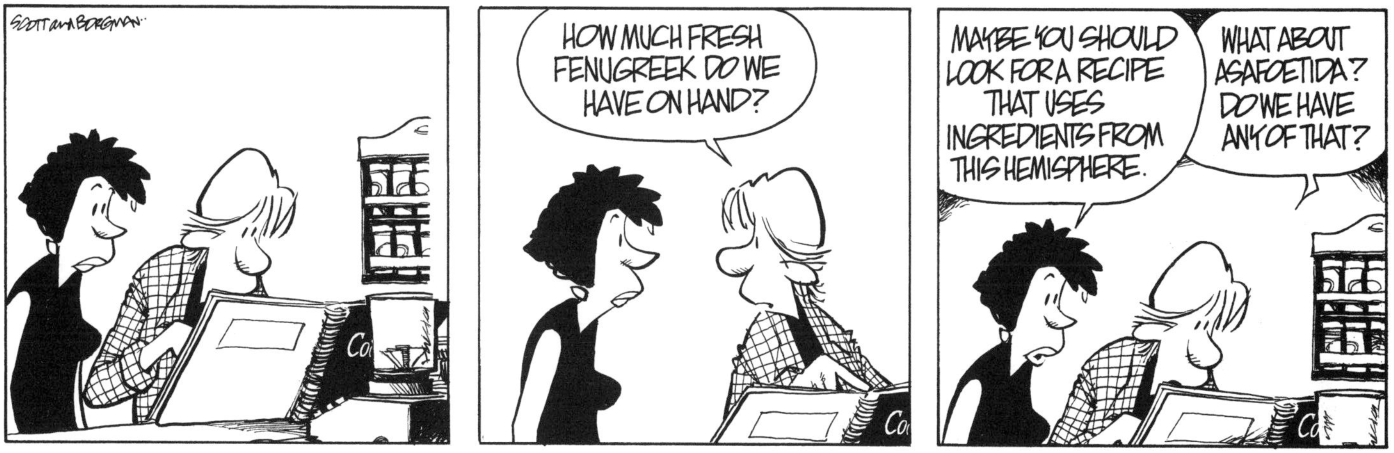
HOW MUCH FRESH FENUGREEK DO WE HAVE ON HAND?
MAYBE YOU SHOULD LOOK FOR A RECIPE THAT USES INGREDIENTS FROM THIS HEMISPHERE.
WHAT ABOUT ASAFOETIDA? DO WE HAVE ANY OF THAT?

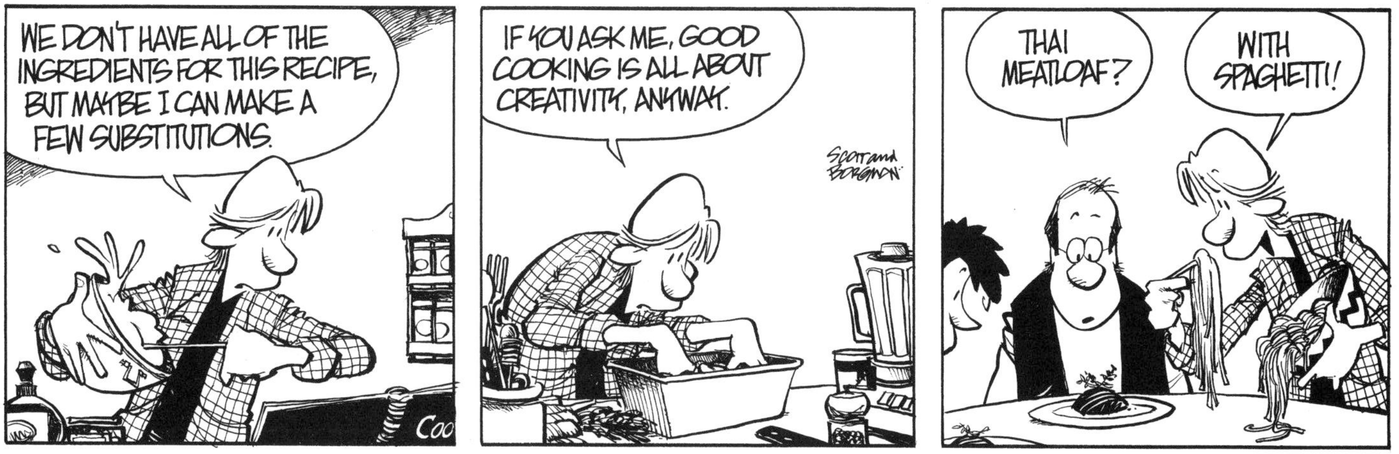
WE DON'T HAVE ALL OF THE INGREDIENTS FOR THIS RECIPE, BUT MAYBE I CAN MAKE A FEW SUBSTITUTIONS.
IF YOU ASK ME, GOOD COOKING IS ALL ABOUT CREATIVITY, ANYWAY.
THAI MEATLOAF?
WITH SPAGHETTI!

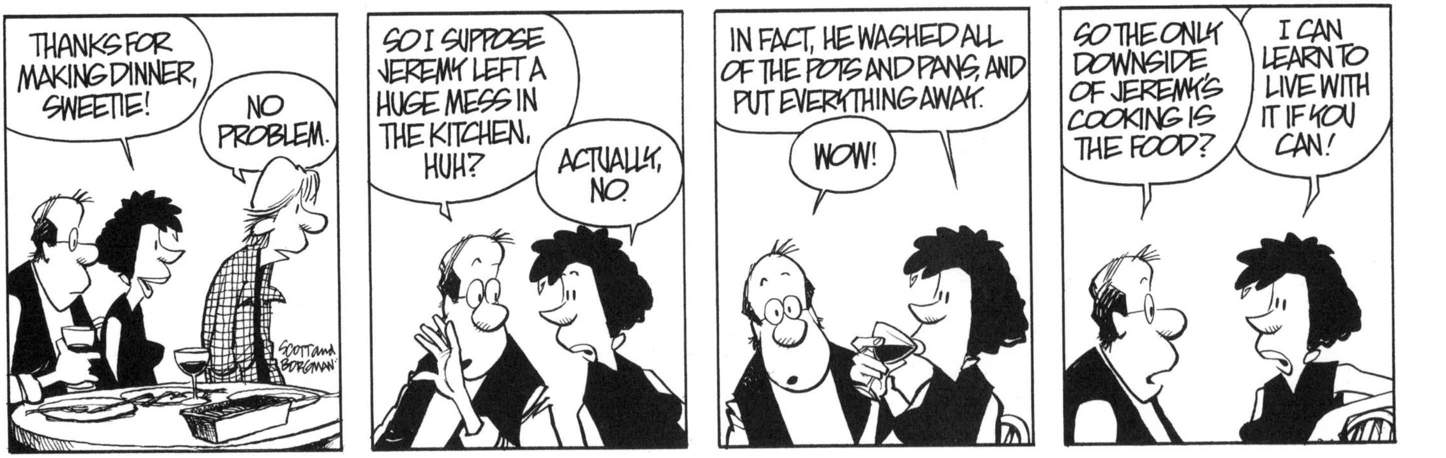
THANKS FOR MAKING DINNER, SWEETIE!
NO PROBLEM.
SO I SUPPOSE JEREMY LEFT A HUGE MESS IN THE KITCHEN, HUH?
ACTUALLY, NO.
IN FACT, HE WASHED ALL OF THE POTS AND PANS, AND PUT EVERYTHING AWAY.
WOW!
SO THE ONLY DOWNSIDE OF JEREMY'S COOKING IS THE FOOD?
I CAN LEARN TO LIVE WITH IT IF YOU CAN!

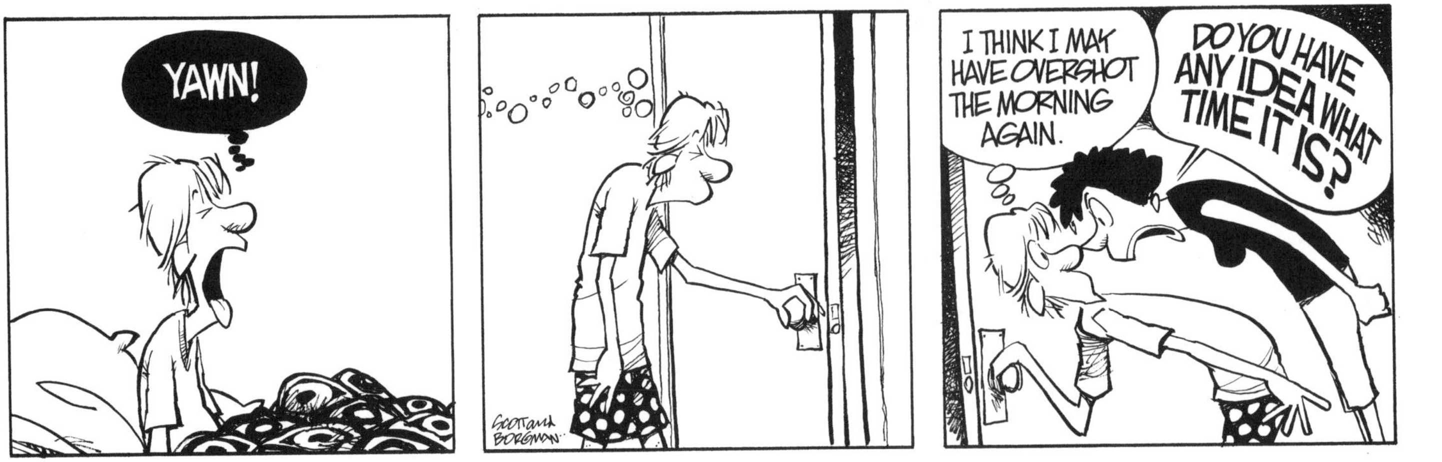
YAWN!
I THINK I MAY HAVE OVERSHOT THE MORNING AGAIN.
DO YOU HAVE ANY IDEA WHAT TIME IT IS?

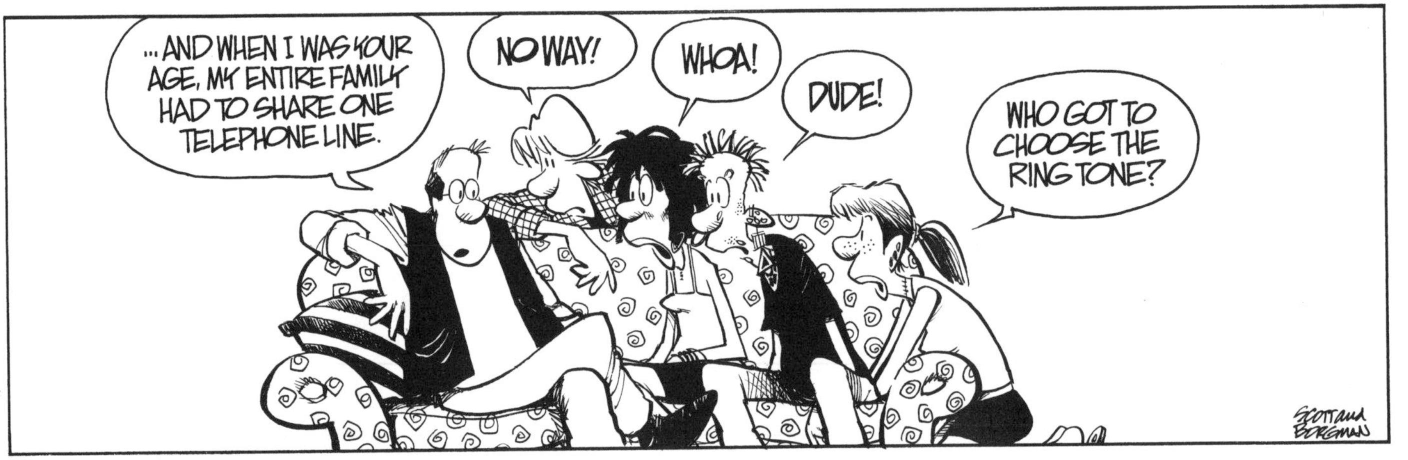
...AND WHEN I WAS YOUR AGE, MY ENTIRE FAMILY HAD TO SHARE ONE TELEPHONE LINE.
NO WAY!
WHOA!
DUDE!
WHO GOT TO CHOOSE THE RING TONE?

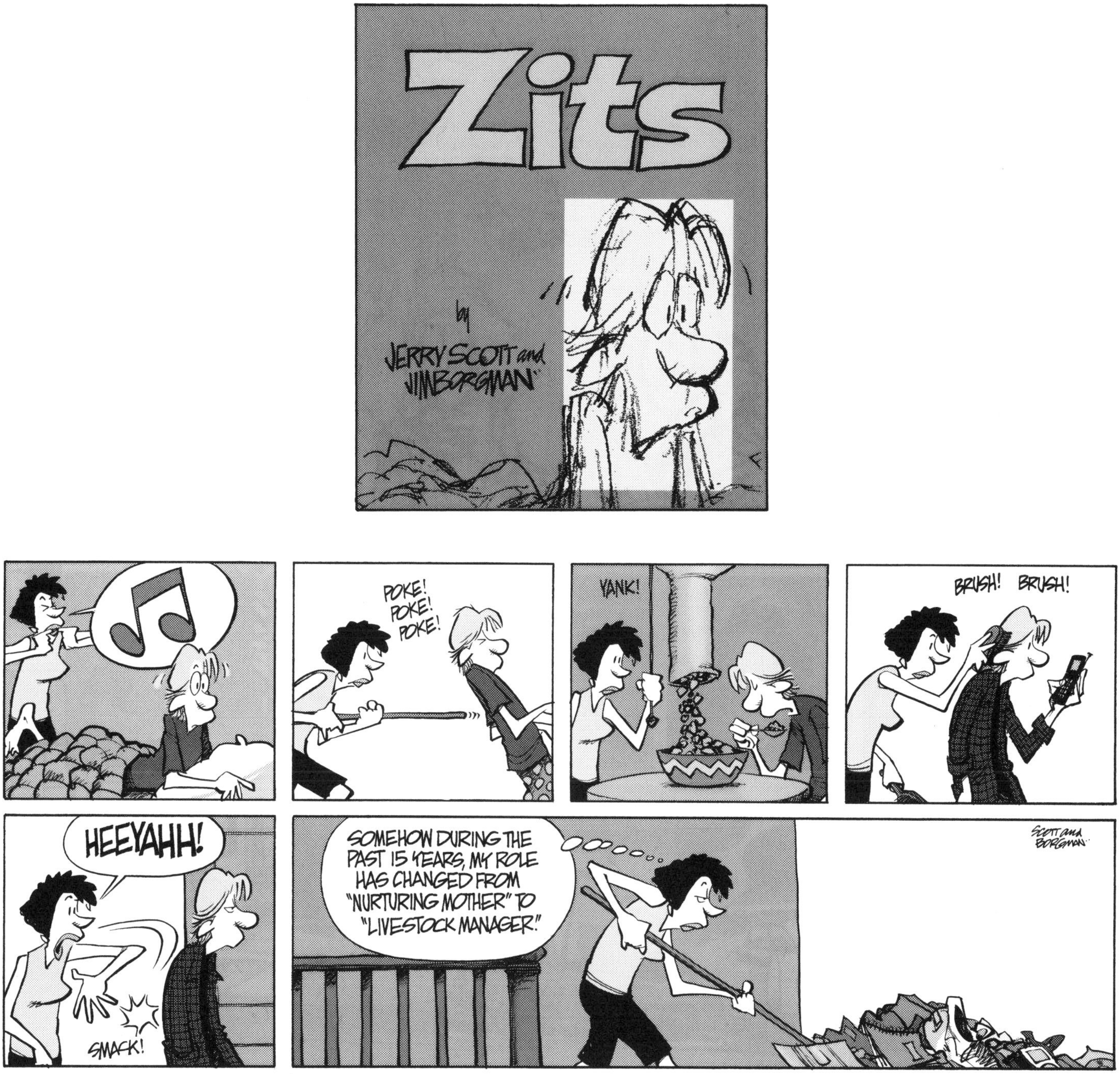
Zits
by
JERRY SCOTT and
JIM BORGMAN
POKE!
POKE!
POKE!
YANK!
BRUSH! BRUSH!
HEEYAHH!
SMACK!
SOMEHOW DURING THE PAST 15 YEARS, MY ROLE HAS CHANGED FROM "NURTURING MOTHER" TO "LIVESTOCK MANAGER."
SCOTT and BORGMAN

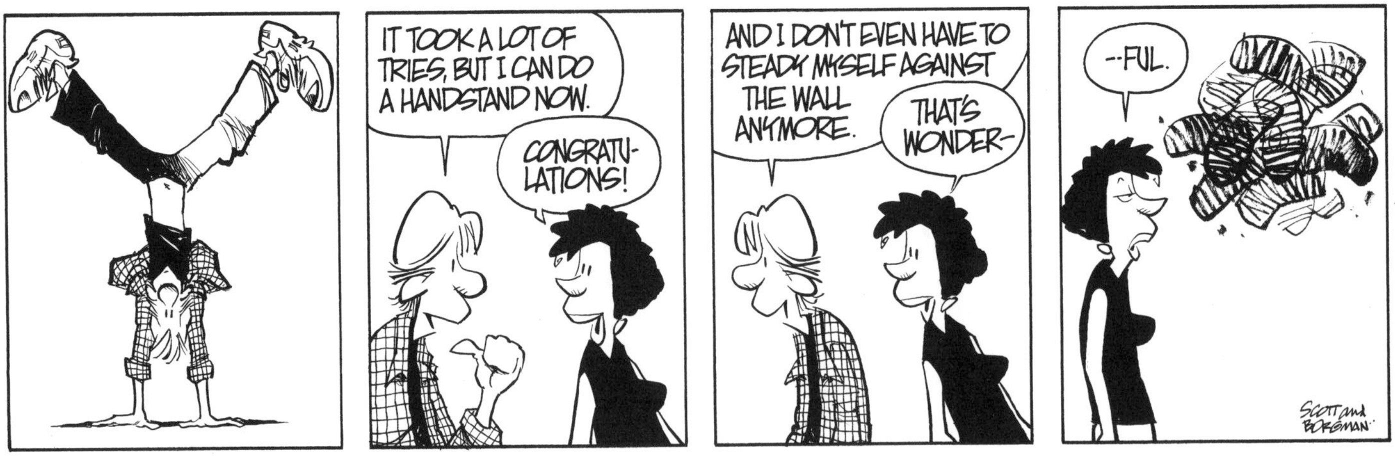
IT TOOK A LOT OF TRIES, BUT I CAN DO A HANDSTAND NOW.
CONGRATULATIONS!
AND I DON'T EVEN HAVE TO STEADY MYSELF AGAINST THE WALL ANYMORE.
THAT'S WONDER-
--FUL.
SCOTT and BORGMAN

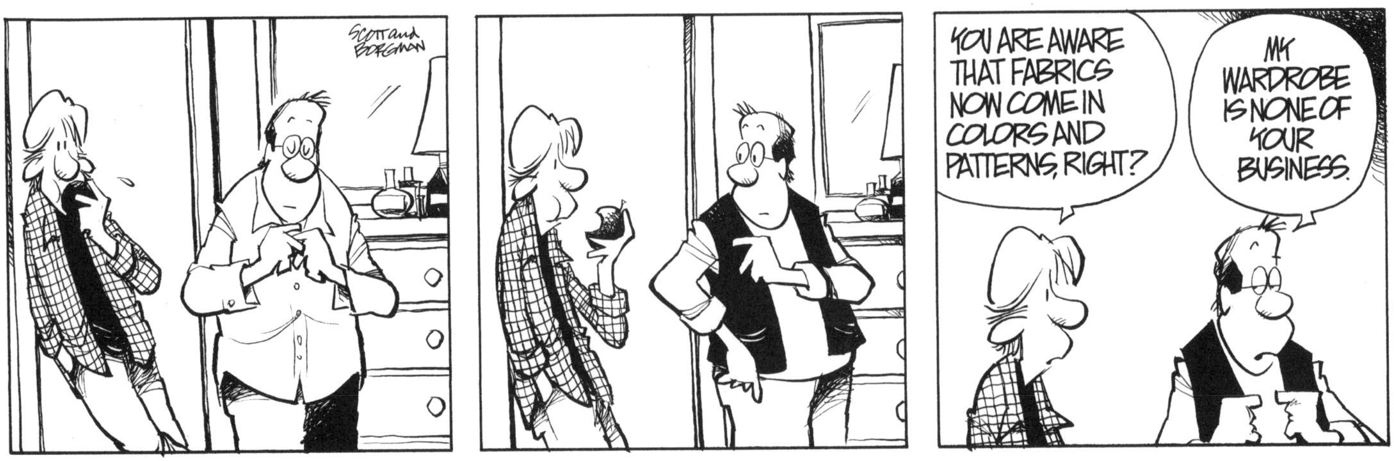
SCOTT and BORGMAN
YOU ARE AWARE THAT FABRICS NOW COME IN COLORS AND PATTERNS, RIGHT?
MY WARDROBE IS NONE OF YOUR BUSINESS.

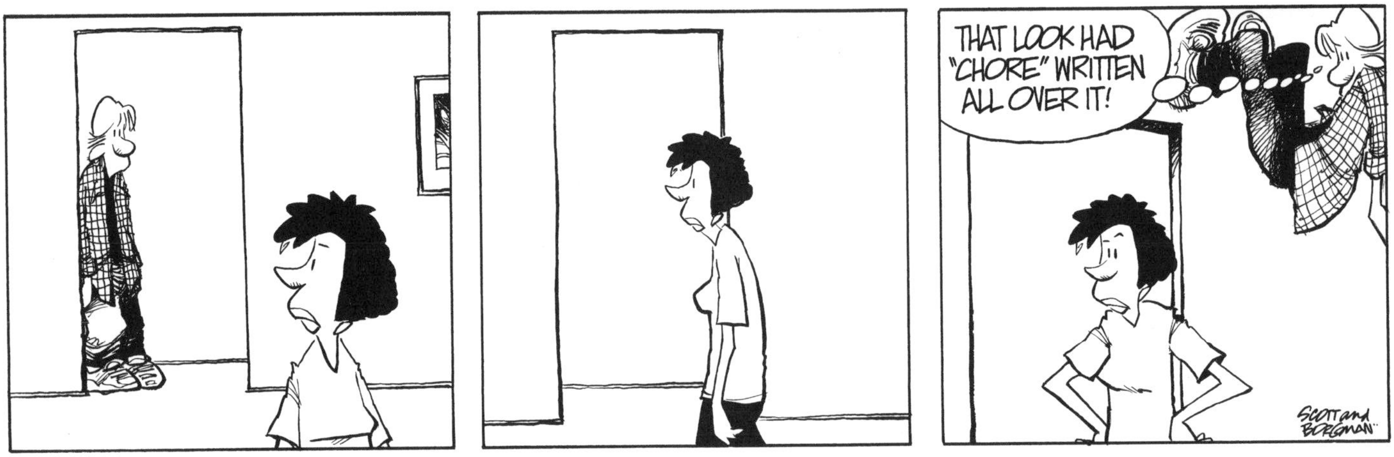
THAT LOOK HAD "CHORE" WRITTEN ALL OVER IT!
SCOTT and BORGMAN

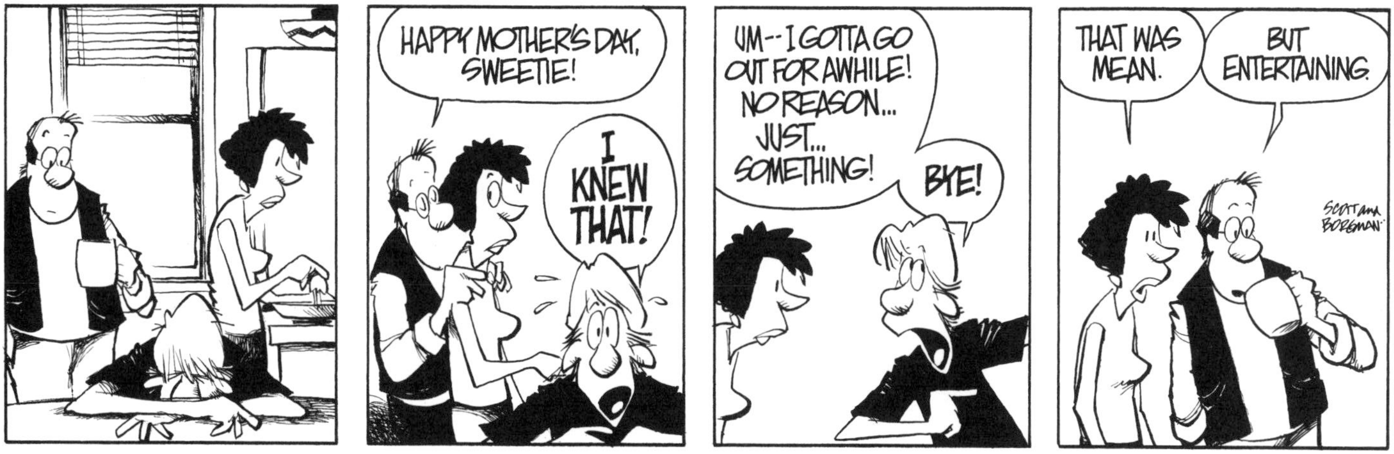
HAPPY MOTHER'S DAY, SWEETIE!
I KNEW THAT!
UM-- I GOTTA GO OUT FOR AWHILE! NO REASON... JUST... SOMETHING!
BYE!
THAT WAS MEAN.
BUT ENTERTAINING.

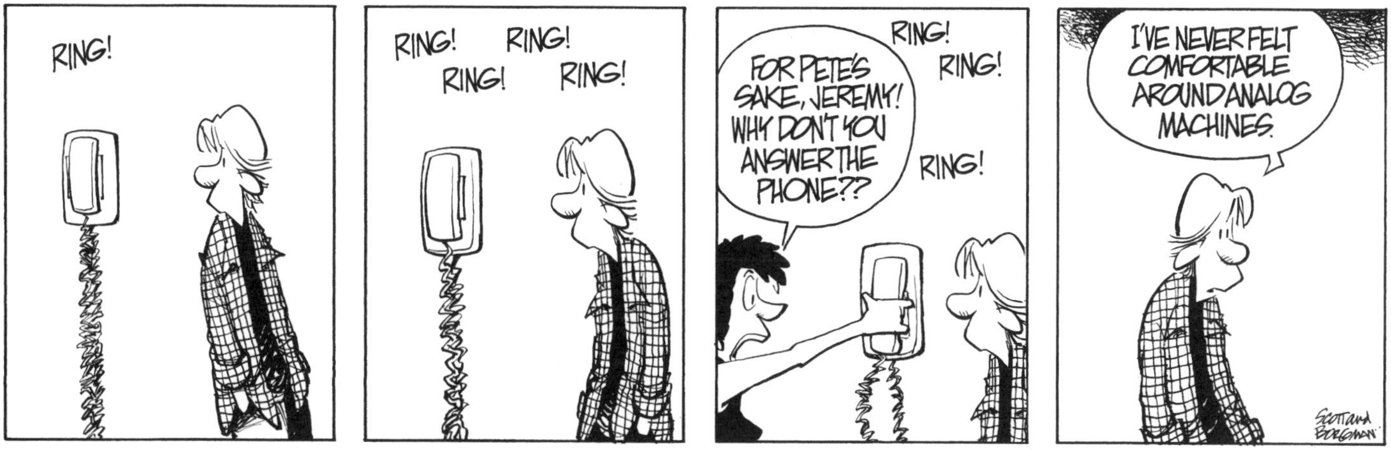
RING!
RING! RING!
RING! RING!
RING!
FOR PETE'S SAKE, JEREMY! WHY DON'T YOU ANSWER THE PHONE??
RING!
RING!
I'VE NEVER FELT COMFORTABLE AROUND ANALOG MACHINES.

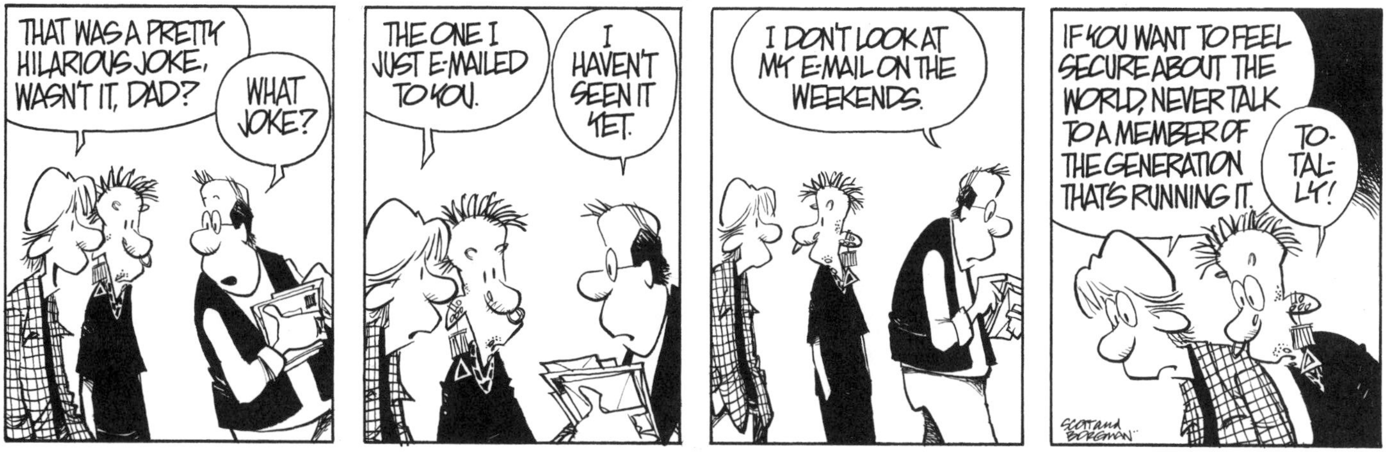
THAT WAS A PRETTY HILARIOUS JOKE, WASN'T IT, DAD?
WHAT JOKE?
THE ONE I JUST E-MAILED TO YOU.
I HAVEN'T SEEN IT YET.
I DON'T LOOK AT MY E-MAIL ON THE WEEKENDS.
IF YOU WANT TO FEEL SECURE ABOUT THE WORLD, NEVER TALK TO A MEMBER OF THE GENERATION THAT'S RUNNING IT.
TO-TAL-LY!

Zits
by
JERRY SCOTT and
JIM BORGMAN

YOU CAN FORGET ABOUT ME DRIVING YOU ANYWHERE UNTIL THE GARAGE IS CLEAN, JEREMY!
IT'S ABOUT TIME YOU LEARNED THAT THE UNIVERSE DOESN'T REVOLVE AROUND YOU!
MAYBE YOUR UNIVERSE.
SCOTT and BORGMAN

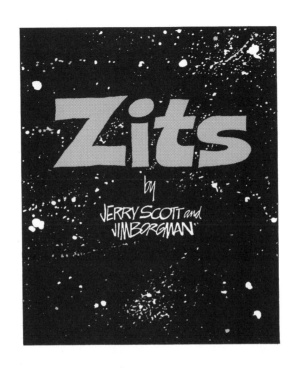

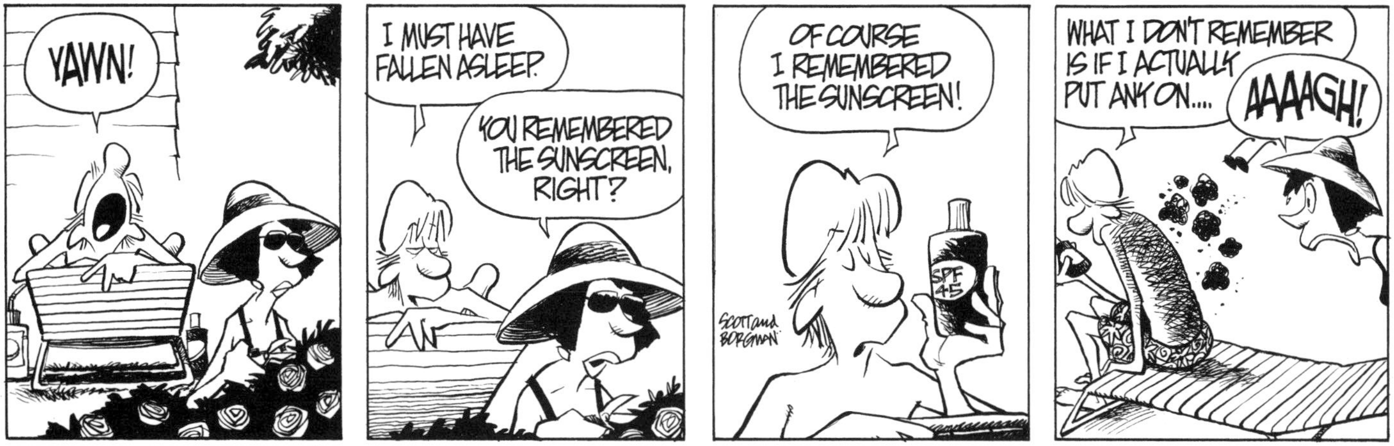
YAWN!
I MUST HAVE FALLEN ASLEEP.
YOU REMEMBERED THE SUNSCREEN, RIGHT?
OF COURSE I REMEMBERED THE SUNSCREEN!
SPF 45
SCOTT and BORGMAN
WHAT I DON'T REMEMBER IS IF I ACTUALLY PUT ANY ON....
AAAAGH!

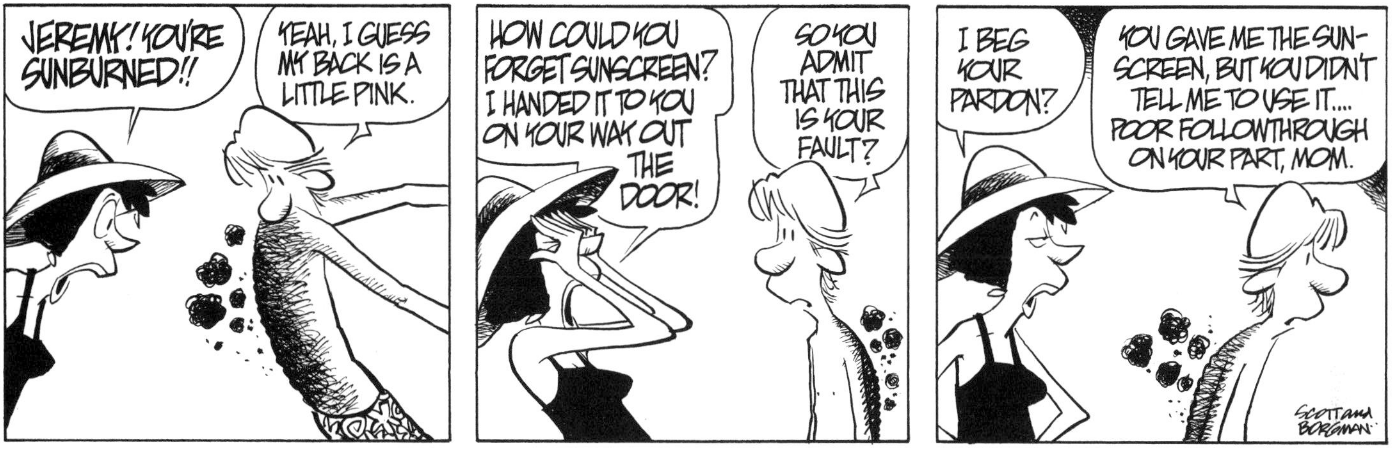
JEREMY! YOU'RE SUNBURNED!!
YEAH, I GUESS MY BACK IS A LITTLE PINK.
HOW COULD YOU FORGET SUNSCREEN? I HANDED IT TO YOU ON YOUR WAK OUT THE DOOR!
SO YOU ADMIT THAT THIS IS YOUR FAULT?
I BEG YOUR PARDON?
YOU GAVE ME THE SUN-SCREEN, BUT YOU DIDN'T TELL ME TO USE IT.... POOR FOLLOWTHROUGH ON YOUR PART, MOM.
SCOTT and BORGMAN

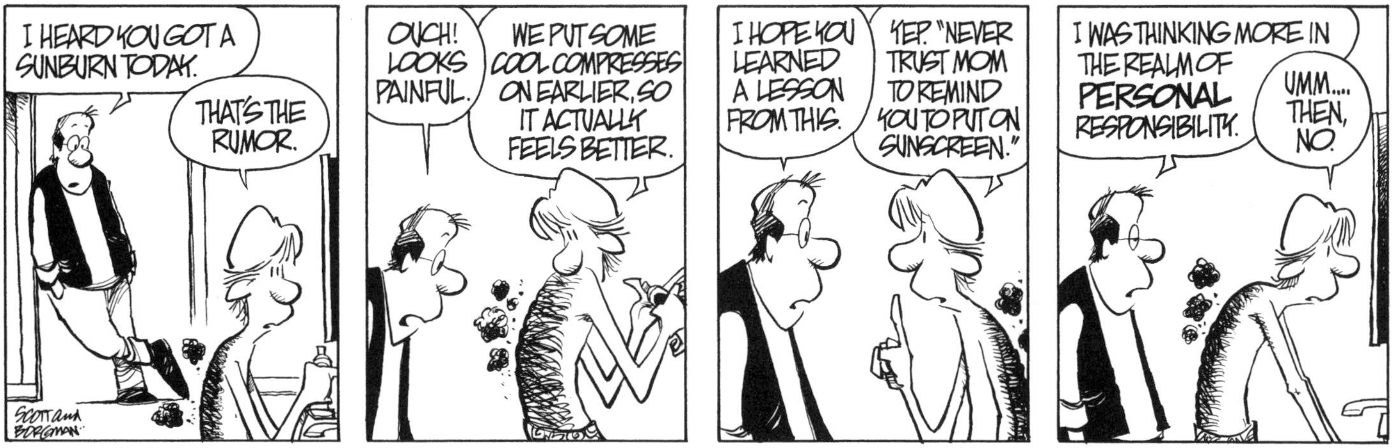
I HEARD YOU GOT A SUNBURN TODAY.
THAT'S THE RUMOR.
SCOTT and BORGMAN
OUCH! LOOKS PAINFUL.
WE PUT SOME COOL COMPRESSES ON EARLIER, SO IT ACTUALLY FEELS BETTER.
I HOPE YOU LEARNED A LESSON FROM THIS.
YEP. "NEVER TRUST MOM TO REMIND YOU TO PUT ON SUNSCREEN."
I WAS THINKING MORE IN THE REALM OF PERSONAL RESPONSIBILITY.
UMM.... THEN, NO.

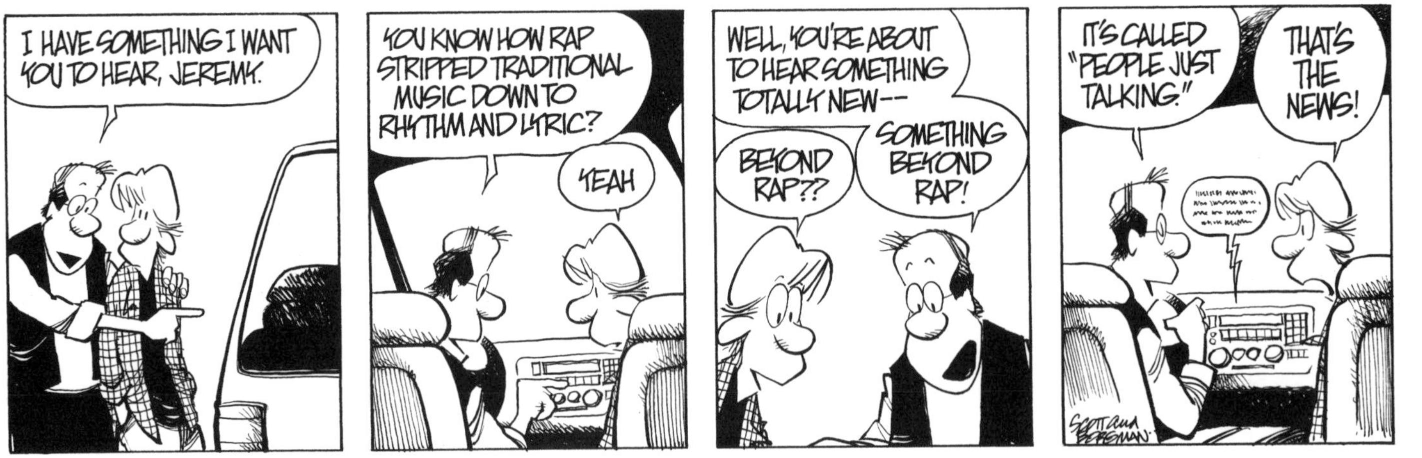
I HAVE SOMETHING I WANT YOU TO HEAR, JEREMY.
YOU KNOW HOW RAP STRIPPED TRADITIONAL MUSIC DOWN TO RHYTHM AND LYRIC?
YEAH
WELL, YOU'RE ABOUT TO HEAR SOMETHING TOTALLY NEW--
BEYOND RAP??
SOMETHING BEYOND RAP!
IT'S CALLED "PEOPLE JUST TALKING."
THAT'S THE NEWS!
SCOTT AND BORGMAN

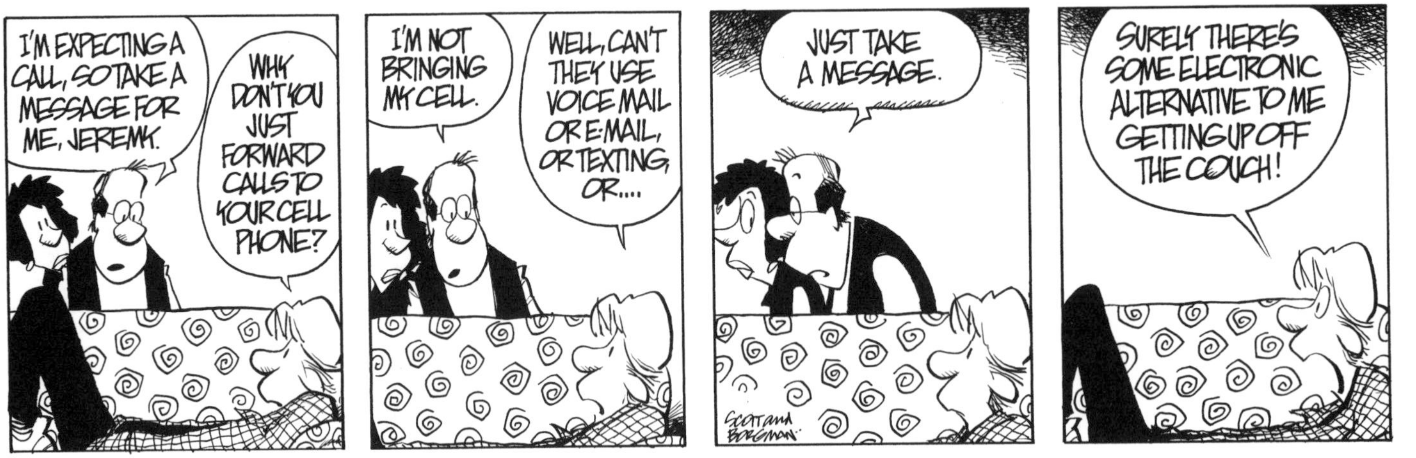
I'M EXPECTING A CALL, SO TAKE A MESSAGE FOR ME, JEREMY.
WHY DON'T YOU JUST FORWARD CALLS TO YOUR CELL PHONE?
I'M NOT BRINGING MY CELL.
WELL, CAN'T THEY USE VOICE MAIL OR E-MAIL, OR TEXTING, OR....
JUST TAKE A MESSAGE.
SCOTT AND BORGMAN
SURELY THERE'S SOME ELECTRONIC ALTERNATIVE TO ME GETTING UP OFF THE COUCH!

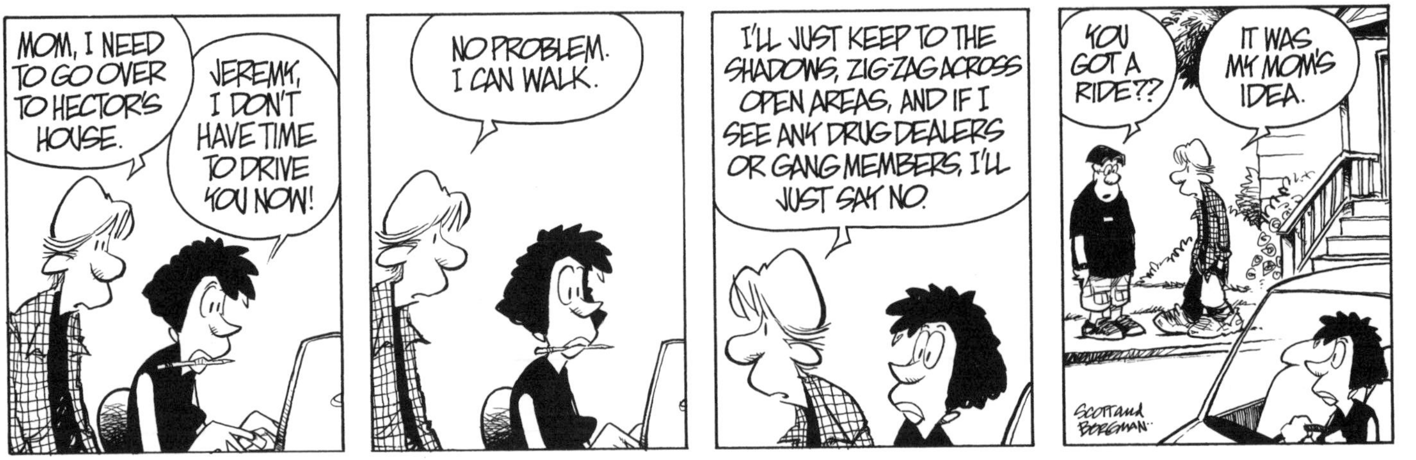
MOM, I NEED TO GO OVER TO HECTOR'S HOUSE.
JEREMY, I DON'T HAVE TIME TO DRIVE YOU NOW!
NO PROBLEM. I CAN WALK.
I'LL JUST KEEP TO THE SHADOWS, ZIG-ZAG ACROSS OPEN AREAS, AND IF I SEE ANY DRUG DEALERS OR GANG MEMBERS, I'LL JUST SAY NO.
YOU GOT A RIDE??
IT WAS MY MOM'S IDEA.
SCOTT AND BORGMAN

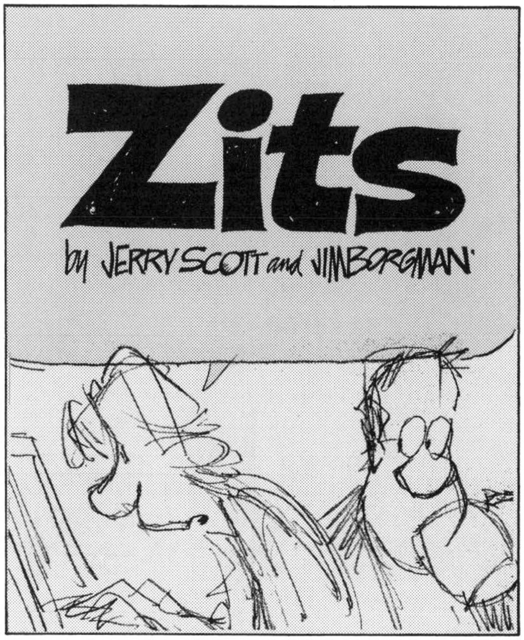
Zits
by JERRY SCOTT and JIM BORGMAN

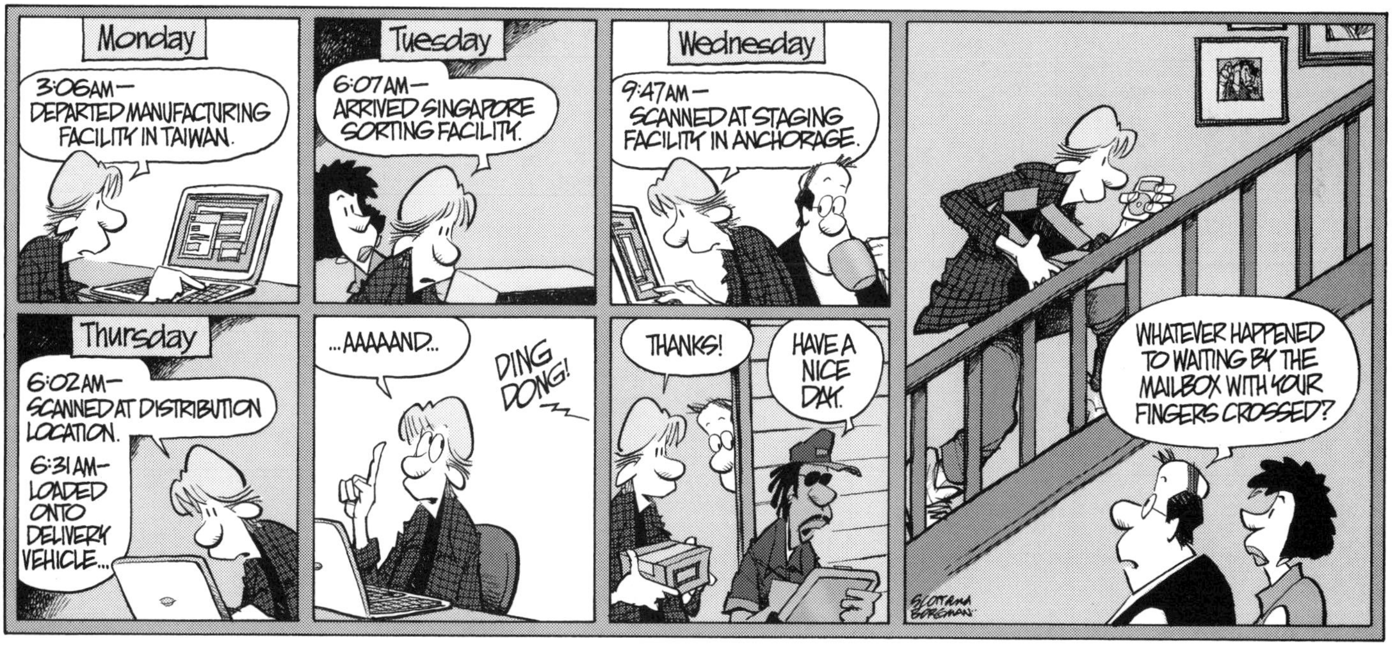
Monday
3:06 AM—
DEPARTED MANUFACTURING FACILITY IN TAIWAN.
Tuesday
6:07 AM—
ARRIVED SINGAPORE SORTING FACILITY.
Wednesday
9:47 AM—
SCANNED AT STAGING FACILITY IN ANCHORAGE.
Thursday
6:02 AM—
SCANNED AT DISTRIBUTION LOCATION.
6:31 AM—
LOADED ONTO DELIVERY VEHICLE...
...AAAAAND...
DING DONG!
THANKS!
HAVE A NICE DAY.
WHATEVER HAPPENED TO WAITING BY THE MAILBOX WITH YOUR FINGERS CROSSED?

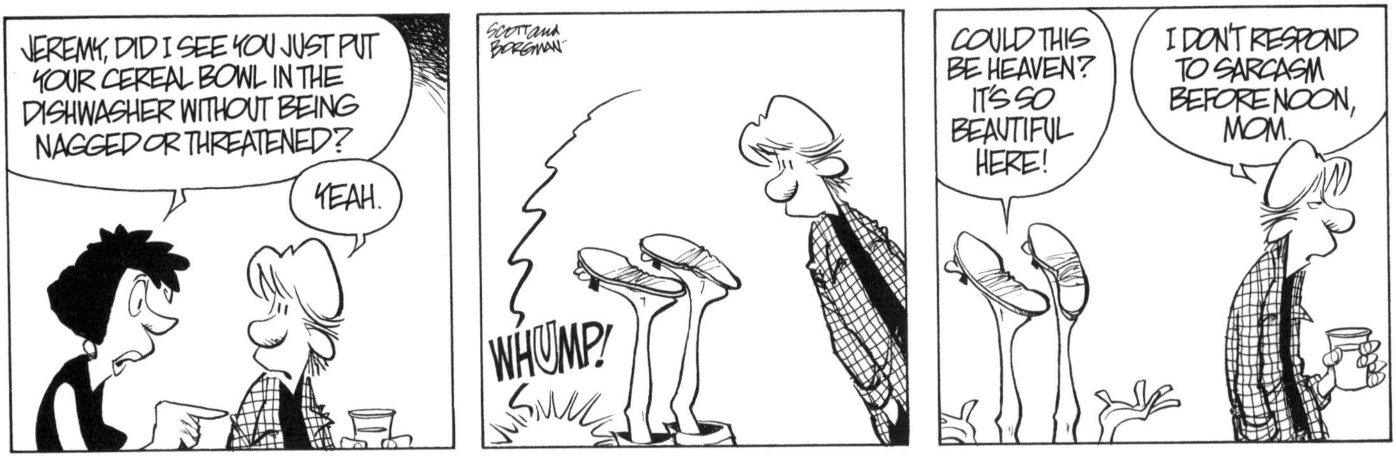
JEREMY, DID I SEE YOU JUST PUT YOUR CEREAL BOWL IN THE DISHWASHER WITHOUT BEING NAGGED OR THREATENED?
YEAH.
SCOTT and BORGMAN
WHUMP!
COULD THIS BE HEAVEN? IT'S SO BEAUTIFUL HERE!
I DON'T RESPOND TO SARCASM BEFORE NOON, MOM.

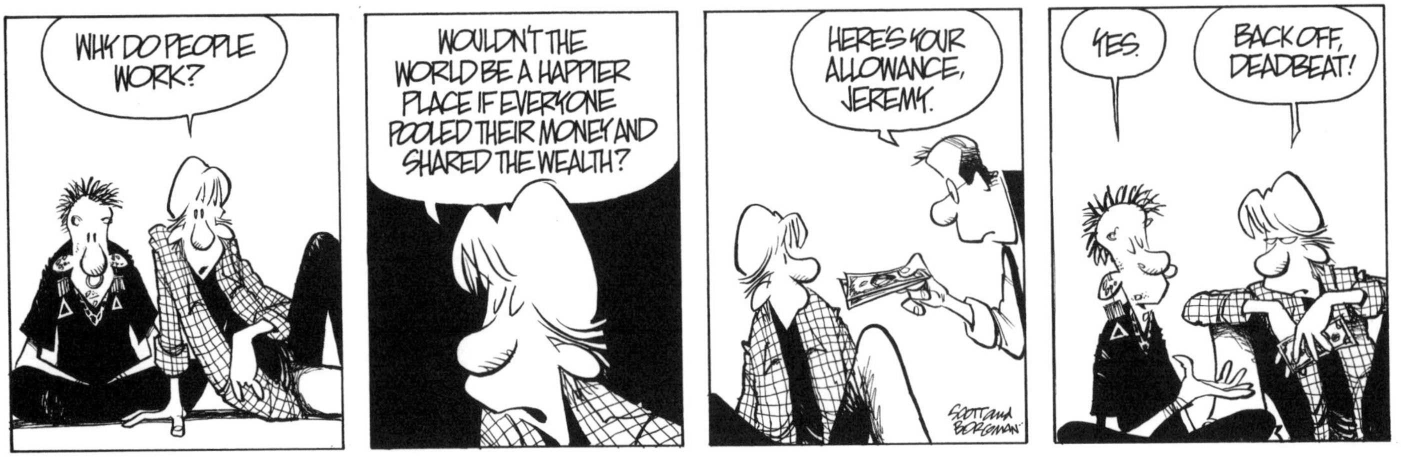
WHY DO PEOPLE WORK?
WOULDN'T THE WORLD BE A HAPPIER PLACE IF EVERYONE POOLED THEIR MONEY AND SHARED THE WEALTH?
HERE'S YOUR ALLOWANCE, JEREMY.
SCOTT and BORGMAN
YES.
BACK OFF, DEADBEAT!

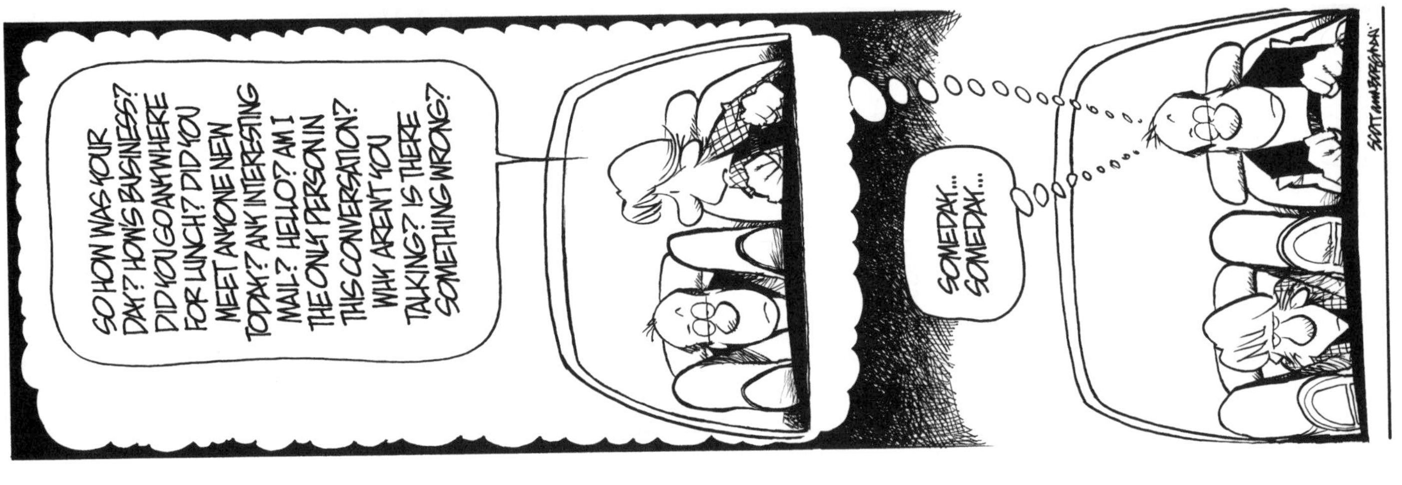
SO HOW WAS YOUR DAY? HOW'S BUSINESS? DID YOU GO ANYWHERE FOR LUNCH? DID YOU MEET ANYONE NEW TODAY? ANY INTERESTING MAIL? HELLO? AM I THE ONLY PERSON IN THIS CONVERSATION? WHY AREN'T YOU TALKING? IS THERE SOMETHING WRONG?
SOMEDAY... SOMEDAY...
SCOTT and BORGMAN

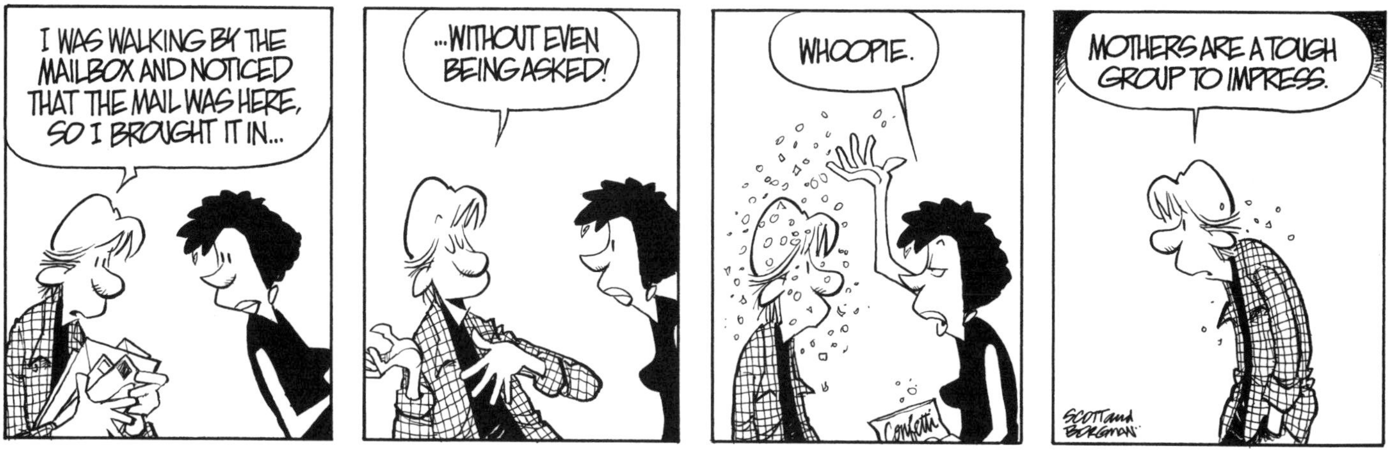
I WAS WALKING BY THE MAILBOX AND NOTICED THAT THE MAIL WAS HERE, SO I BROUGHT IT IN...
...WITHOUT EVEN BEING ASKED!
WHOOPIE.
Confetti
MOTHERS ARE A TOUGH GROUP TO IMPRESS.

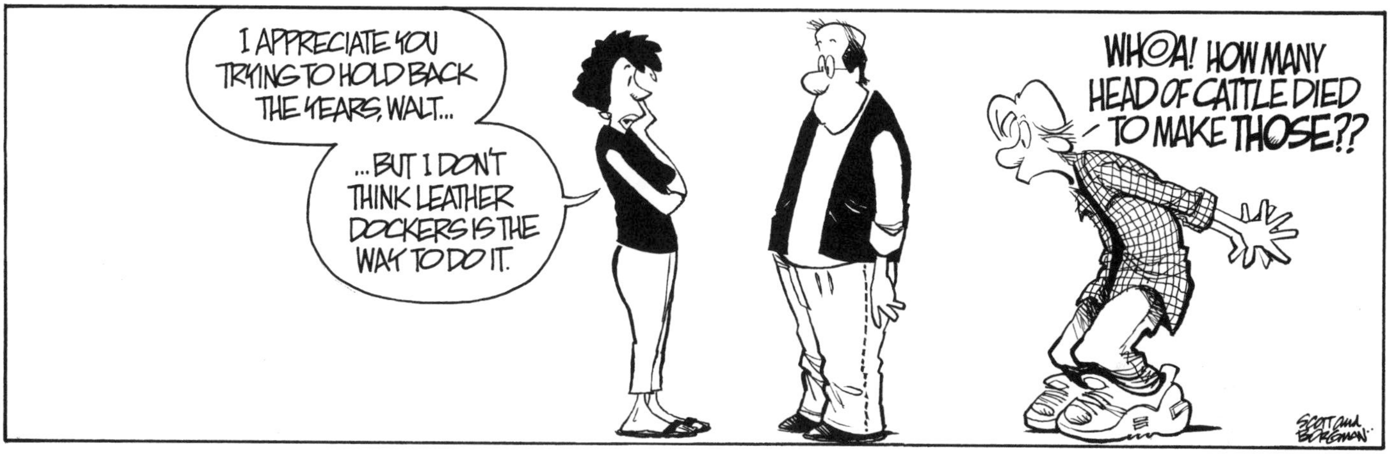
I APPRECIATE YOU TRYING TO HOLD BACK THE YEARS, WALT...
...BUT I DON'T THINK LEATHER DOCKERS IS THE WAY TO DO IT.
WHOA! HOW MANY HEAD OF CATTLE DIED TO MAKE THOSE??

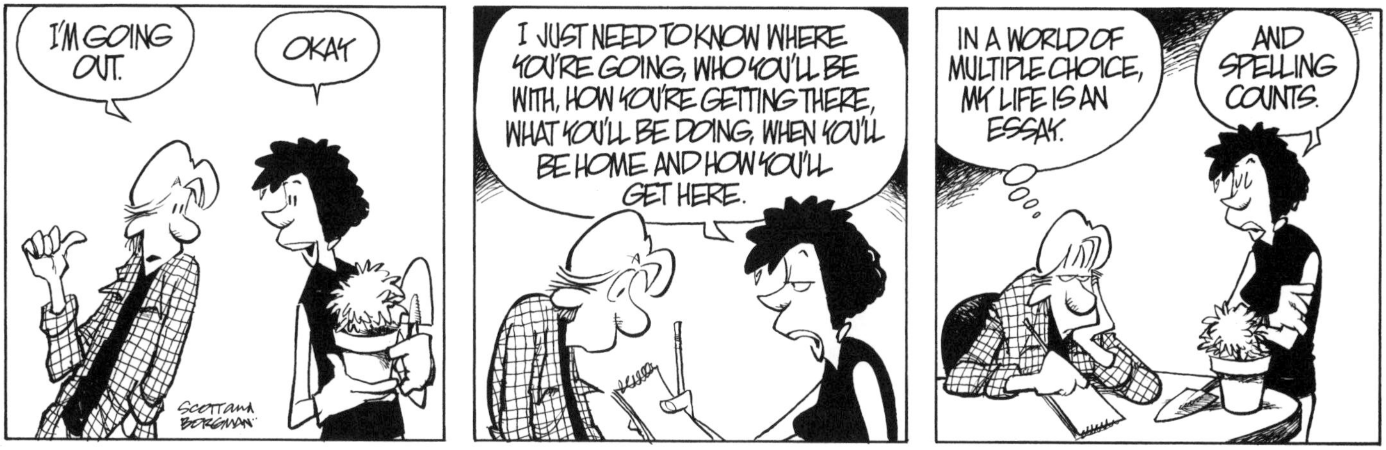
I'M GOING OUT.
OKAY
I JUST NEED TO KNOW WHERE YOU'RE GOING, WHO YOU'LL BE WITH, HOW YOU'RE GETTING THERE, WHAT YOU'LL BE DOING, WHEN YOU'LL BE HOME AND HOW YOU'LL GET HERE.
IN A WORLD OF MULTIPLE CHOICE, MY LIFE IS AN ESSAY.
AND SPELLING COUNTS.

Zits
by JERRY SCOTT and JIM BORGMAN

JEREMY, WE DON'T MAKE RULES TO RESTRICT YOU.... WE MAKE RULES TO KEEP YOU SAFE!
CURFEW
NO PARTIES
CHAPERONES
SCOTT and BORGMAN

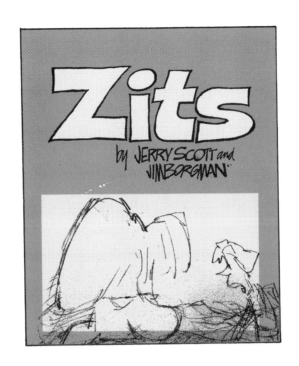

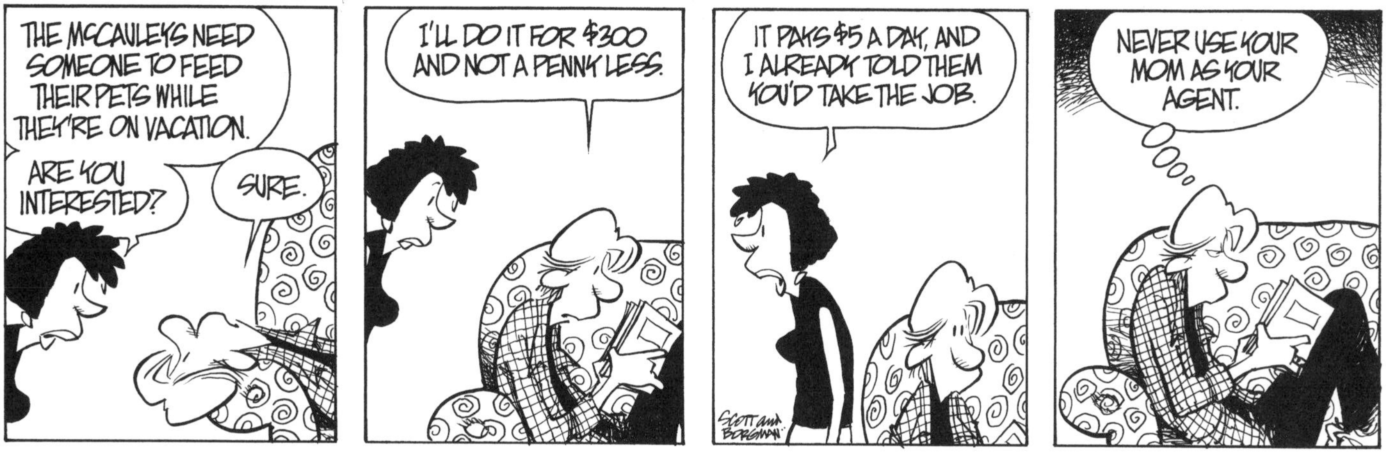
THE McCAULEYS NEED SOMEONE TO FEED THEIR PETS WHILE THEY'RE ON VACATION.
ARE YOU INTERESTED?
SURE.
I'LL DO IT FOR $300 AND NOT A PENNY LESS.
IT PAYS $5 A DAY, AND I ALREADY TOLD THEM YOU'D TAKE THE JOB.
NEVER USE YOUR MOM AS YOUR AGENT.

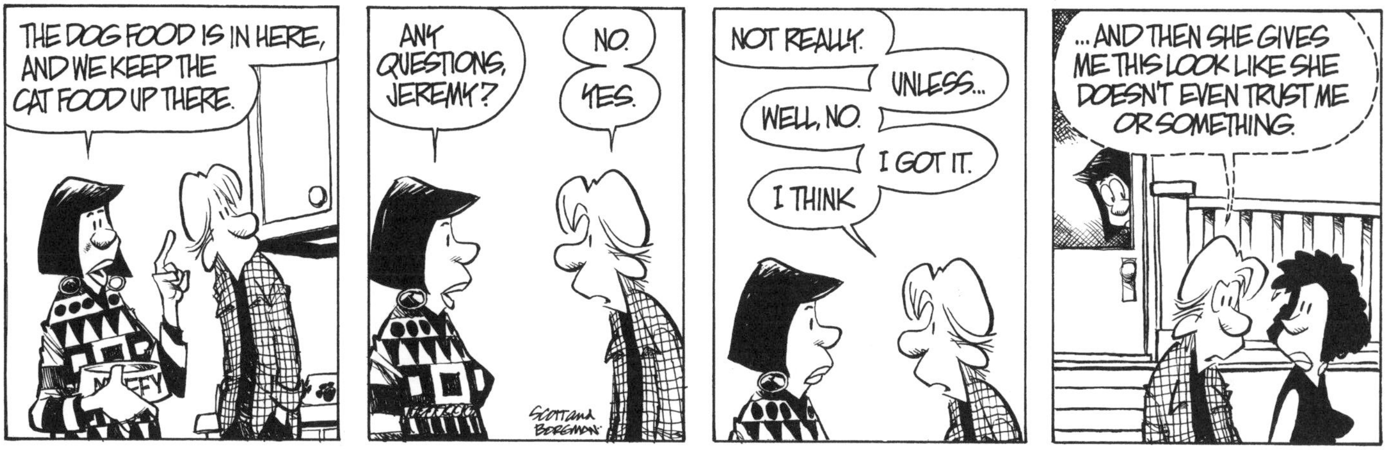
THE DOG FOOD IS IN HERE, AND WE KEEP THE CAT FOOD UP THERE.
ANY QUESTIONS, JEREMY?
NO.
YES.
NOT REALLY.
UNLESS...
WELL, NO.
I GOT IT.
I THINK
...AND THEN SHE GIVES ME THIS LOOK LIKE SHE DOESN'T EVEN TRUST ME OR SOMETHING.

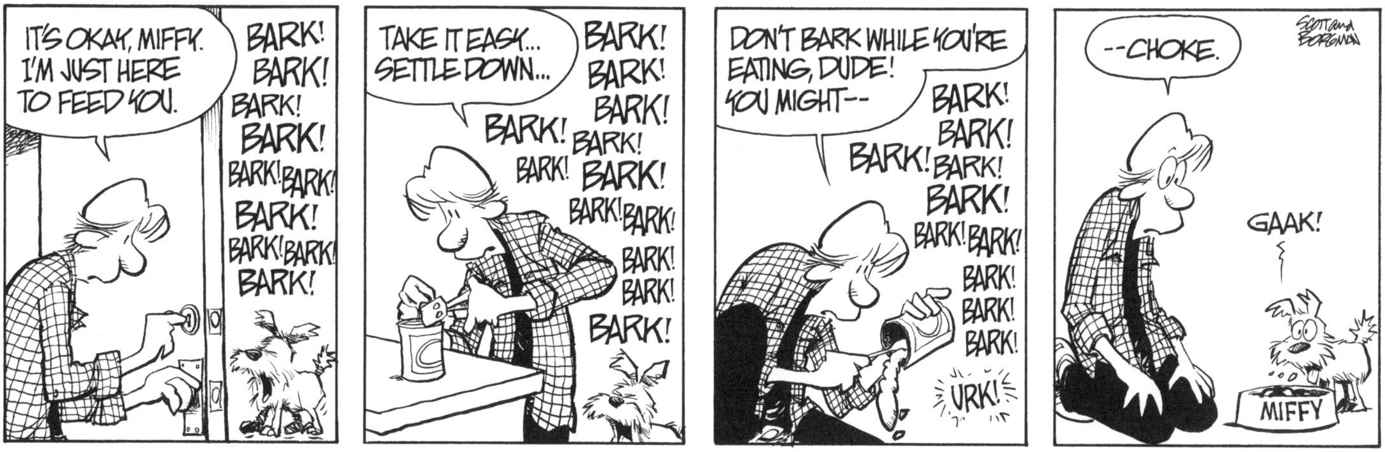
IT'S OKAY, MIFFY. I'M JUST HERE TO FEED YOU.
BARK! BARK! BARK! BARK! BARK! BARK! BARK! BARK! BARK! BARK!
TAKE IT EASY... SETTLE DOWN...
BARK! BARK! BARK! BARK! BARK! BARK! BARK! BARK! BARK! BARK! BARK!
DON'T BARK WHILE YOU'RE EATING, DUDE! YOU MIGHT--
BARK! BARK! BARK! BARK! BARK! BARK! BARK! BARK! BARK! BARK!
URK!
--CHOKE.
GAAK!
MIFFY

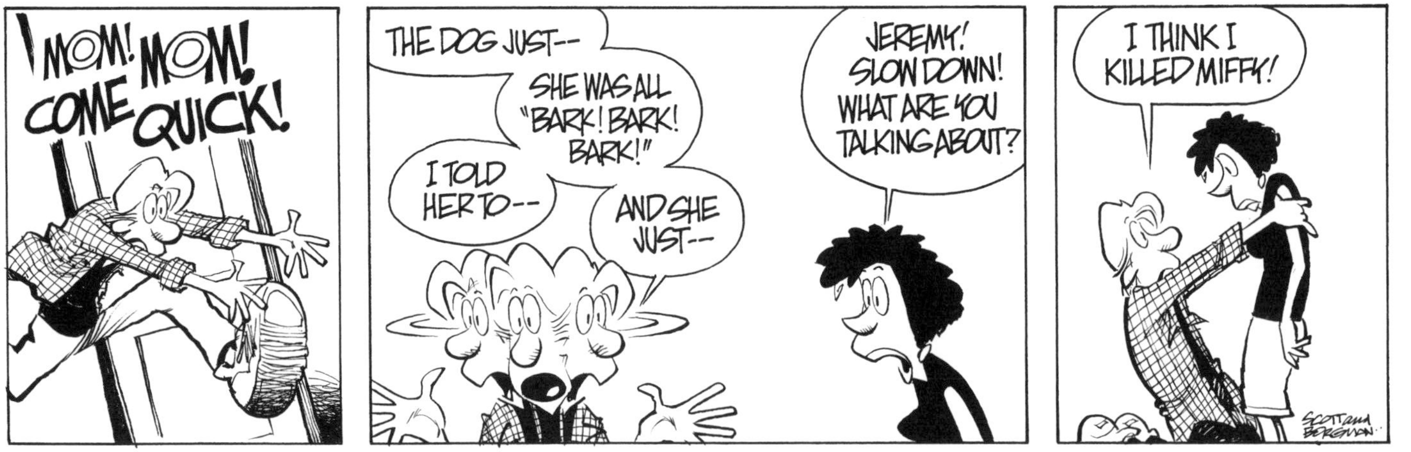
MOM! MOM! COME QUICK!
THE DOG JUST--
SHE WAS ALL "BARK! BARK! BARK!"
I TOLD HER TO--
AND SHE JUST--
JEREMY! SLOW DOWN! WHAT ARE YOU TALKING ABOUT?
I THINK I KILLED MIFFY!

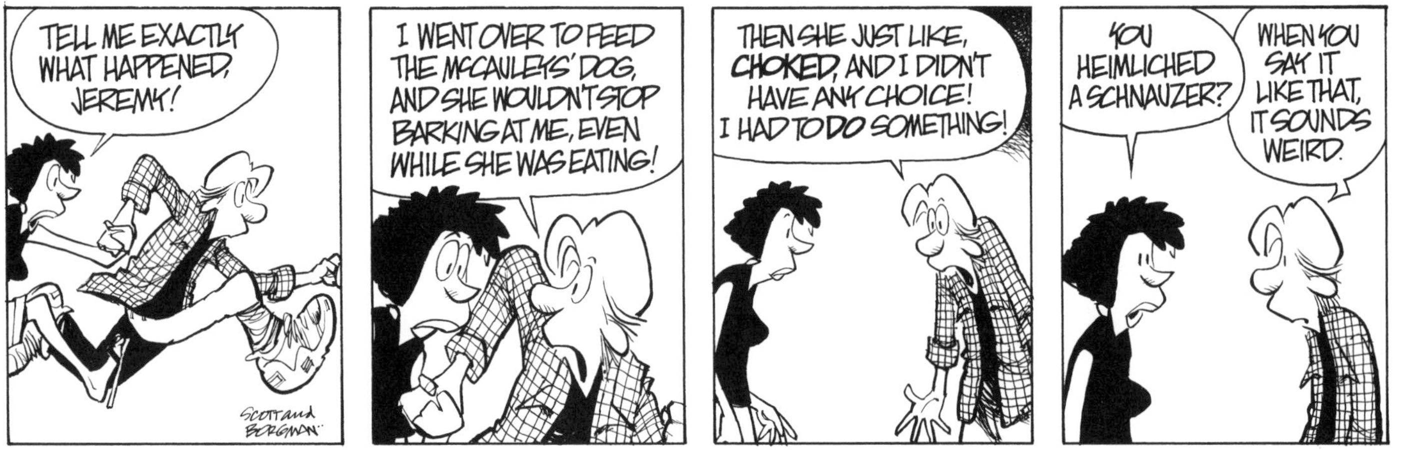
TELL ME EXACTLY WHAT HAPPENED, JEREMY!
I WENT OVER TO FEED THE McCAULEYS' DOG, AND SHE WOULDN'T STOP BARKING AT ME, EVEN WHILE SHE WAS EATING!
THEN SHE JUST LIKE, **CHOKED**, AND I DIDN'T HAVE ANY CHOICE! I HAD TO **DO** SOMETHING!
YOU HEIMLICHED A SCHNAUZER?
WHEN YOU SAY IT LIKE THAT, IT SOUNDS WEIRD.

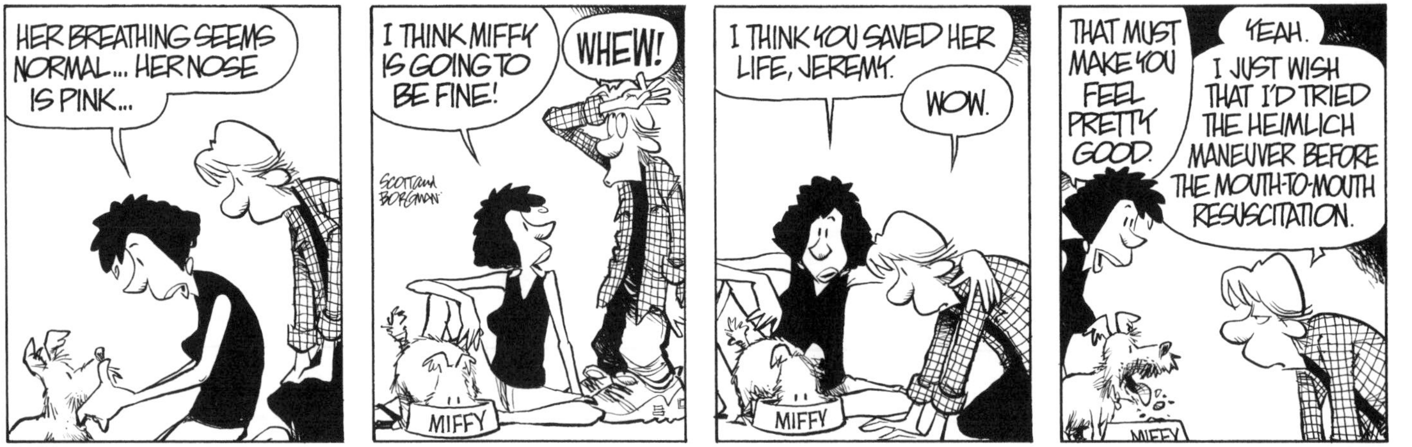
HER BREATHING SEEMS NORMAL... HER NOSE IS PINK...
I THINK MIFFY IS GOING TO BE FINE!
WHEW!
MIFFY
I THINK YOU SAVED HER LIFE, JEREMY.
WOW.
MIFFY
THAT MUST MAKE YOU FEEL PRETTY GOOD.
YEAH. I JUST WISH THAT I'D TRIED THE HEIMLICH MANEUVER BEFORE THE MOUTH-TO-MOUTH RESUSCITATION.

Zits
by
JERRY SCOTT and
JIM BORGMAN

WELL, YOU'D BETTER GET GOING.
YEAH...
WOW!
The End
WELL, YOU'D BETTER GET GOING.
YEAH

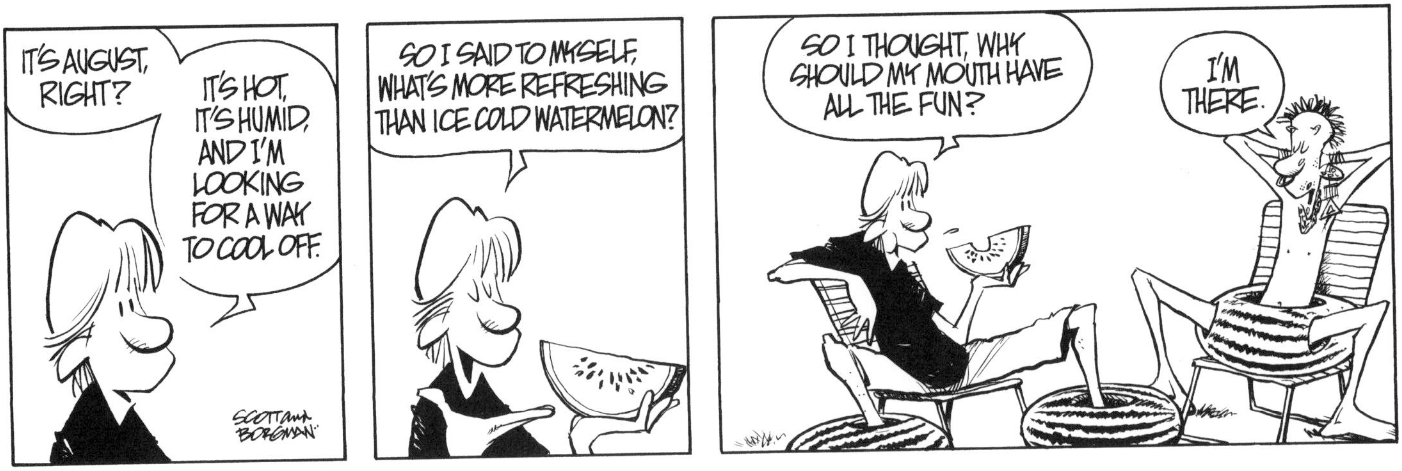
IT'S AUGUST, RIGHT?
IT'S HOT, IT'S HUMID, AND I'M LOOKING FOR A WAY TO COOL OFF.
SO I SAID TO MYSELF, WHAT'S MORE REFRESHING THAN ICE COLD WATERMELON?
SO I THOUGHT, WHY SHOULD MY MOUTH HAVE ALL THE FUN?
I'M THERE.
SCOTT and BORGMAN

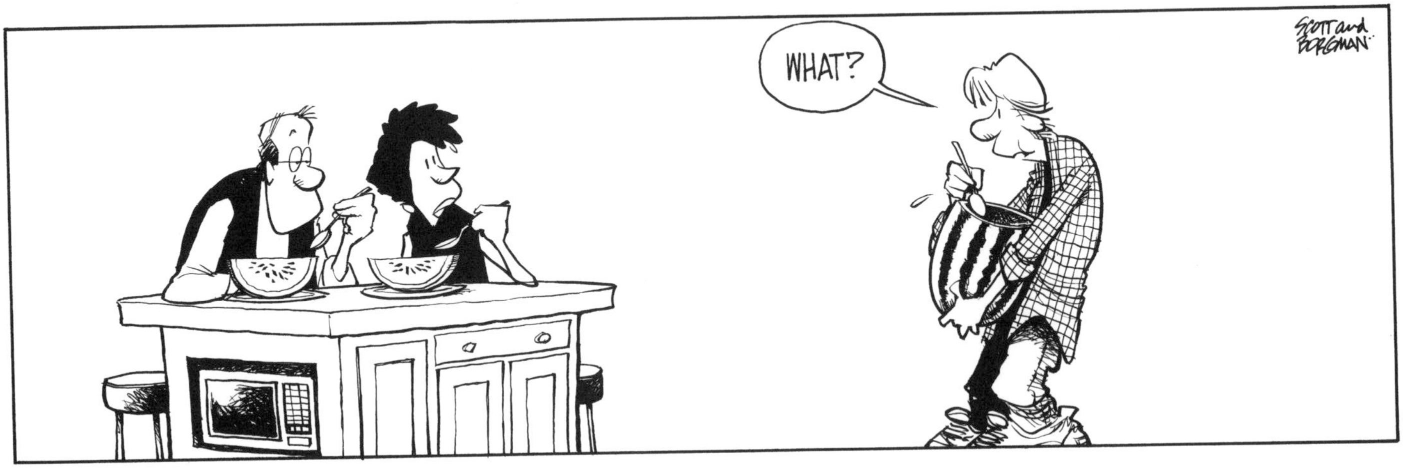
SCOTT and BORGMAN
WHAT?

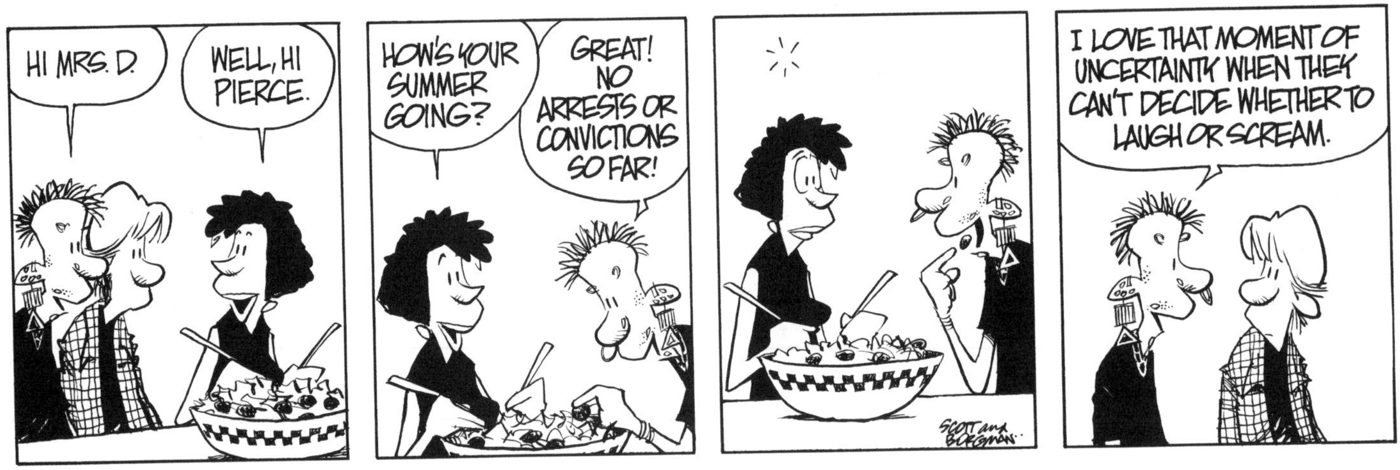
HI MRS. D.
WELL, HI PIERCE.
HOW'S YOUR SUMMER GOING?
GREAT! NO ARRESTS OR CONVICTIONS SO FAR!
SCOTT and BORGMAN
I LOVE THAT MOMENT OF UNCERTAINTY WHEN THEY CAN'T DECIDE WHETHER TO LAUGH OR SCREAM.

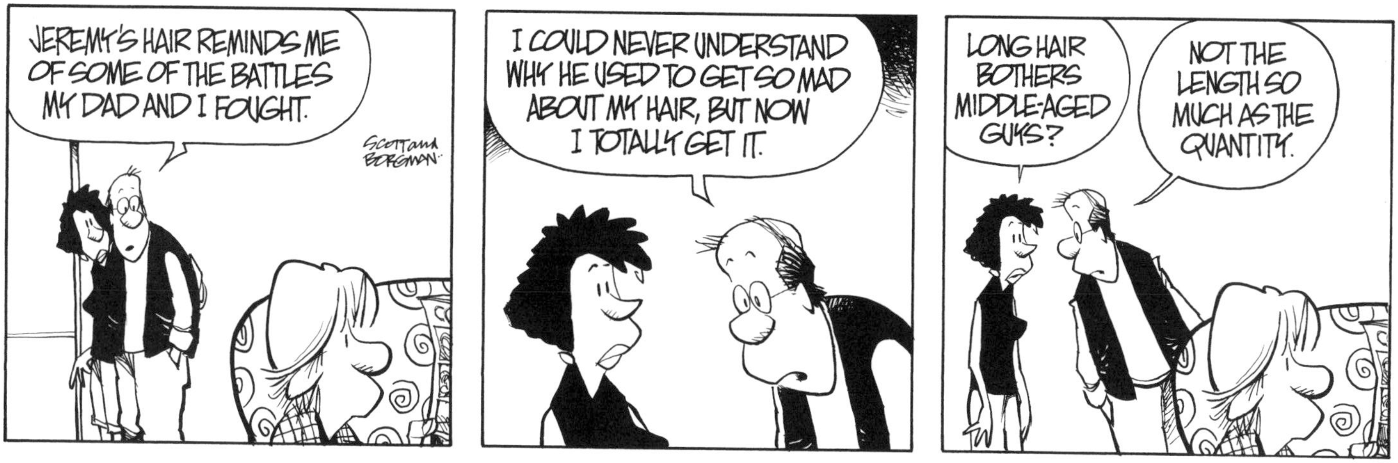
JEREMY'S HAIR REMINDS ME OF SOME OF THE BATTLES MY DAD AND I FOUGHT.
I COULD NEVER UNDERSTAND WHY HE USED TO GET SO MAD ABOUT MY HAIR, BUT NOW I TOTALLY GET IT.
LONG HAIR BOTHERS MIDDLE-AGED GUYS?
NOT THE LENGTH SO MUCH AS THE QUANTITY.

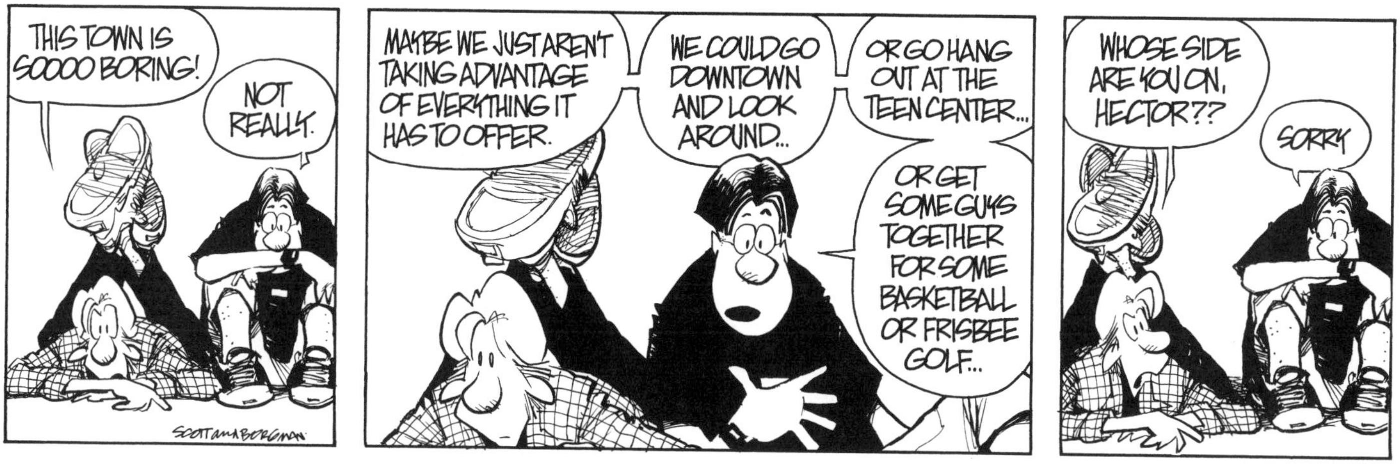
THIS TOWN IS SOOOO BORING!
NOT REALLY.
MAYBE WE JUST AREN'T TAKING ADVANTAGE OF EVERYTHING IT HAS TO OFFER.
WE COULD GO DOWNTOWN AND LOOK AROUND...
OR GO HANG OUT AT THE TEEN CENTER...
OR GET SOME GUYS TOGETHER FOR SOME BASKETBALL OR FRISBEE GOLF...
WHOSE SIDE ARE YOU ON, HECTOR??
SORRY

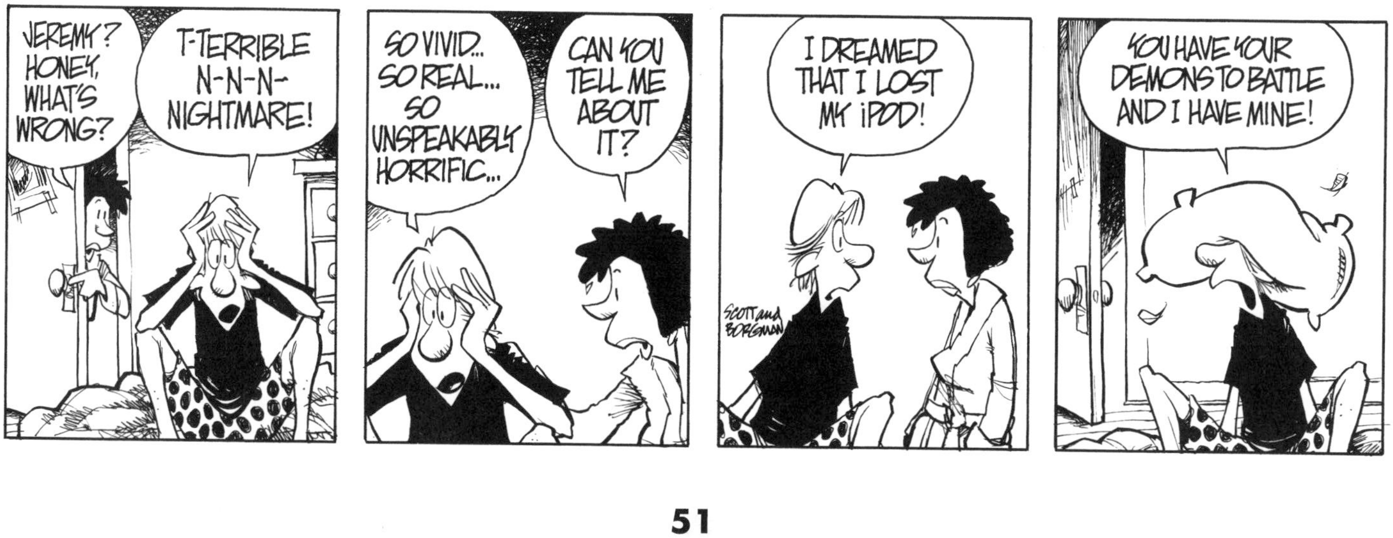
JEREMY? HONEY, WHAT'S WRONG?
T-TERRIBLE N-N-N-NIGHTMARE!
SO VIVID... SO REAL... SO UNSPEAKABLY HORRIFIC...
CAN YOU TELL ME ABOUT IT?
I DREAMED THAT I LOST MY iPOD!
YOU HAVE YOUR DEMONS TO BATTLE AND I HAVE MINE!

Zits
by JERRY SCOTT and JIM BORGMAN

HAVE A NICE NIGHT, DUDE.
THANKS
SCOTT and BORGMAN
WAIT-
WAS THIS FOR EVERYBODY?

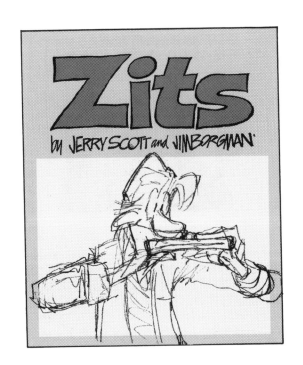

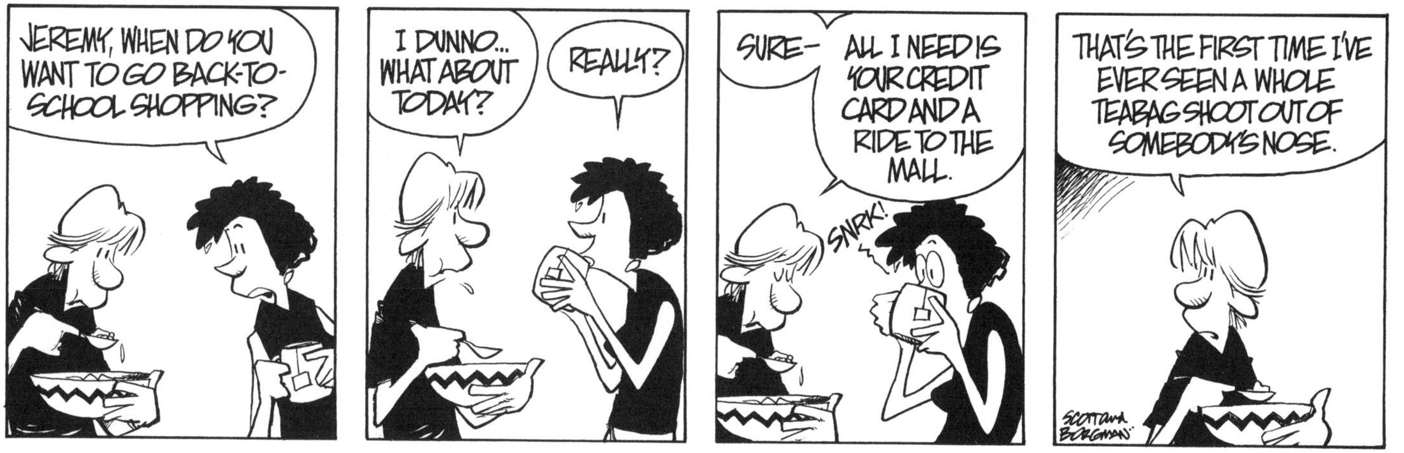
JEREMY, WHEN DO YOU WANT TO GO BACK-TO-SCHOOL SHOPPING?
I DUNNO... WHAT ABOUT TODAY?
REALLY?
SURE-
ALL I NEED IS YOUR CREDIT CARD AND A RIDE TO THE MALL.
SNRK!
THAT'S THE FIRST TIME I'VE EVER SEEN A WHOLE TEABAG SHOOT OUT OF SOMEBODY'S NOSE.

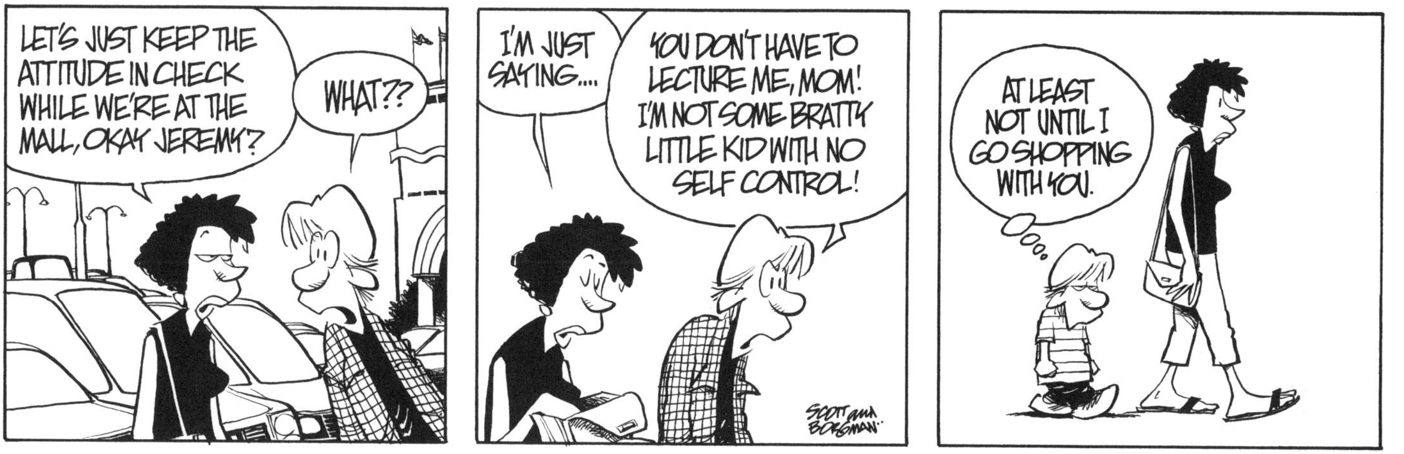
LET'S JUST KEEP THE ATTITUDE IN CHECK WHILE WE'RE AT THE MALL, OKAY JEREMY?
WHAT??
I'M JUST SAYING....
YOU DON'T HAVE TO LECTURE ME, MOM! I'M NOT SOME BRATTY LITTLE KID WITH NO SELF CONTROL!
AT LEAST NOT UNTIL I GO SHOPPING WITH YOU.

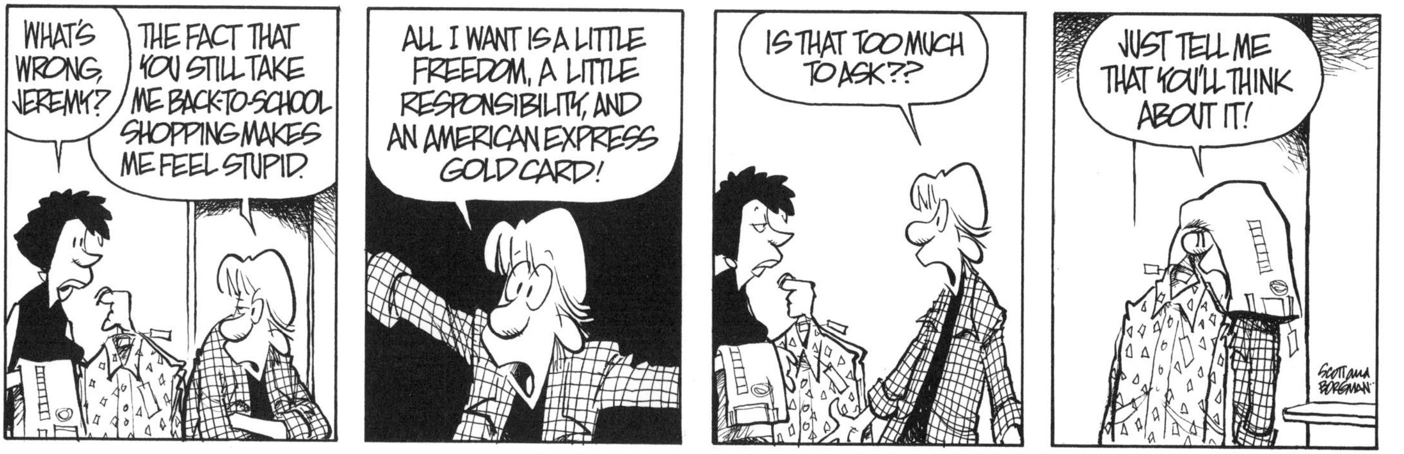
WHAT'S WRONG, JEREMY?
THE FACT THAT YOU STILL TAKE ME BACK-TO-SCHOOL SHOPPING MAKES ME FEEL STUPID.
ALL I WANT IS A LITTLE FREEDOM, A LITTLE RESPONSIBILITY, AND AN AMERICAN EXPRESS GOLD CARD!
IS THAT TOO MUCH TO ASK??
JUST TELL ME THAT YOU'LL THINK ABOUT IT!

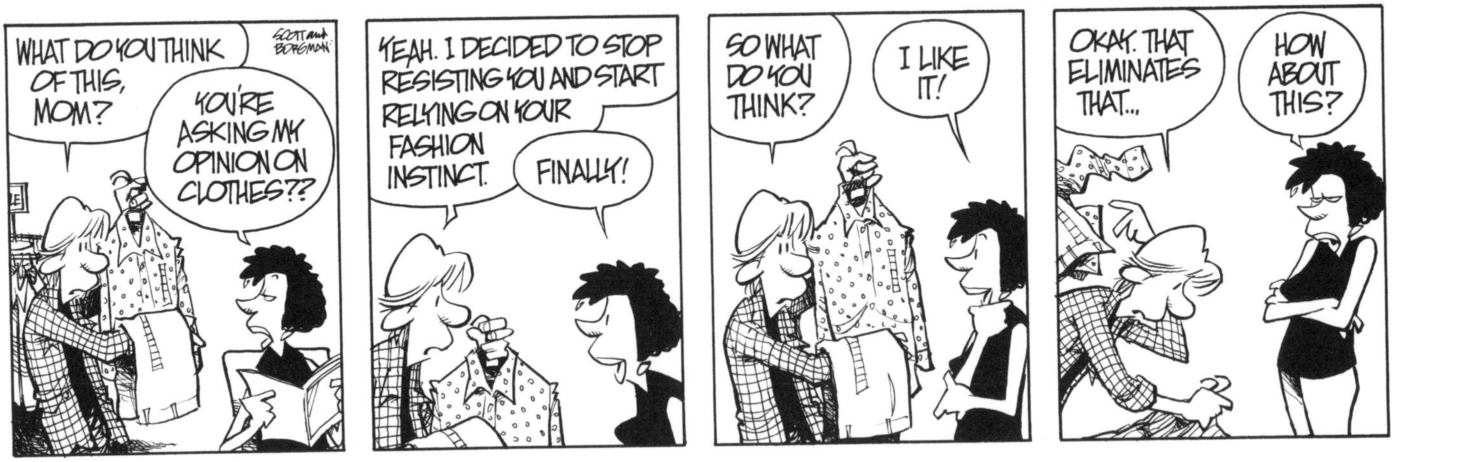
SCOTT and BORGMAN
WHAT DO YOU THINK OF THIS, MOM?
YOU'RE ASKING MY OPINION ON CLOTHES??
YEAH. I DECIDED TO STOP RESISTING YOU AND START RELYING ON YOUR FASHION INSTINCT.
FINALLY!
SO WHAT DO YOU THINK?
I LIKE IT!
OKAY. THAT ELIMINATES THAT...
HOW ABOUT THIS?

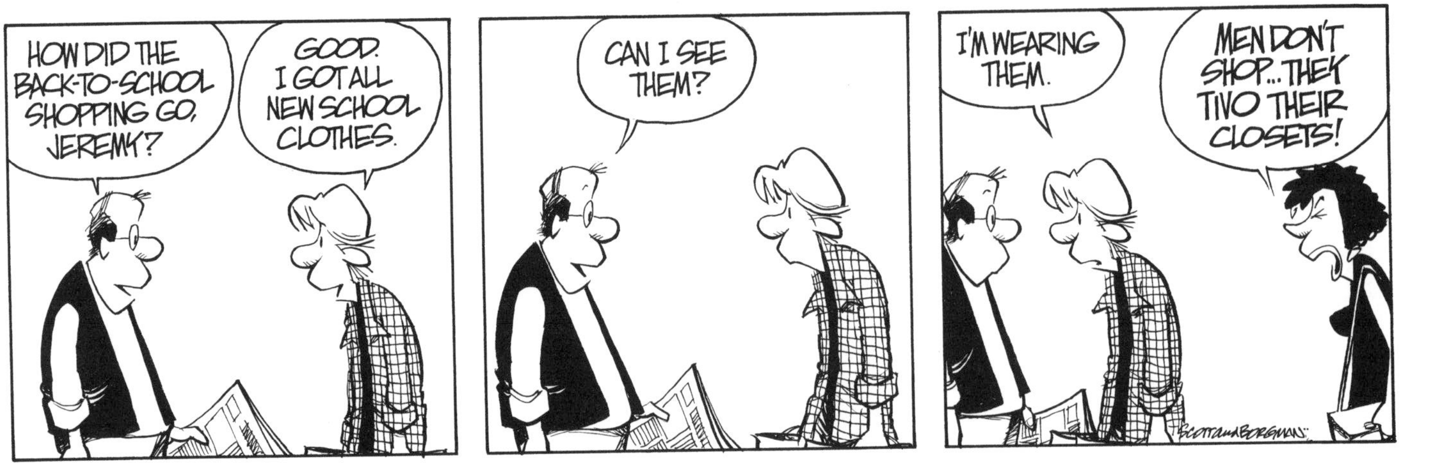
HOW DID THE BACK-TO-SCHOOL SHOPPING GO, JEREMY?
GOOD. I GOT ALL NEW SCHOOL CLOTHES.
CAN I SEE THEM?
I'M WEARING THEM.
MEN DON'T SHOP... THEY TIVO THEIR CLOSETS!
SCOTT and BORGMAN

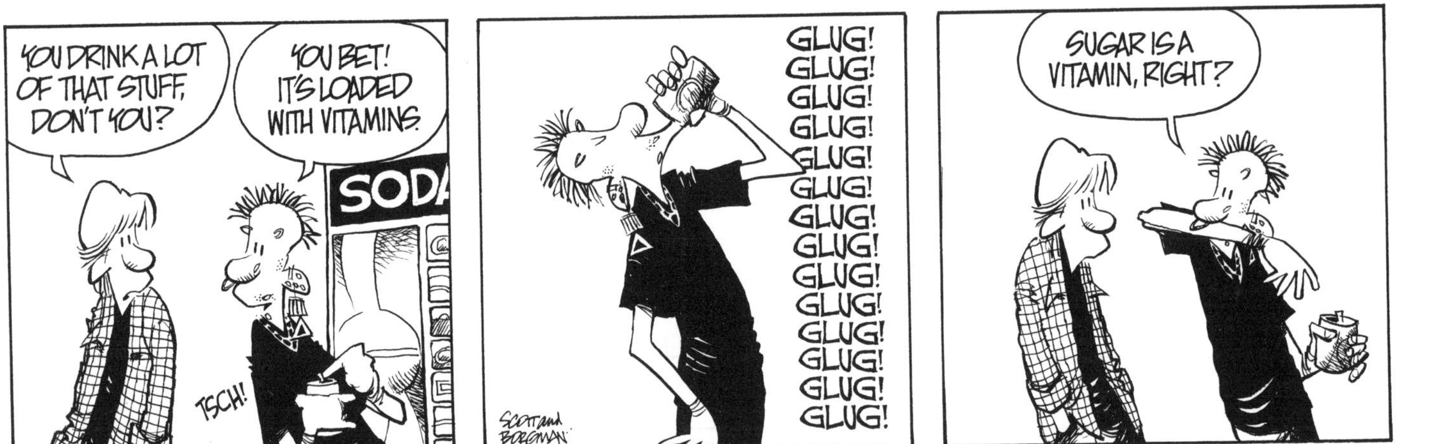
YOU DRINK A LOT OF THAT STUFF, DON'T YOU?
YOU BET! IT'S LOADED WITH VITAMINS.
SODA
TSCH!
GLUG! GLUG! GLUG! GLUG! GLUG! GLUG! GLUG! GLUG! GLUG! GLUG! GLUG! GLUG! GLUG! GLUG!
SCOTT and BORGMAN
SUGAR IS A VITAMIN, RIGHT?

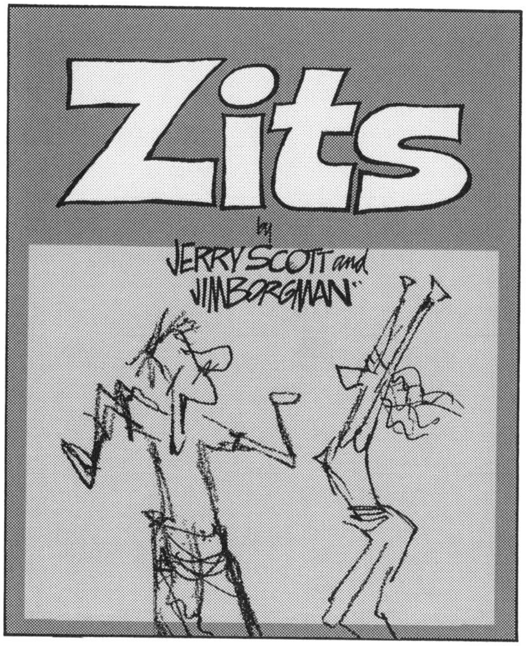
Zits
by
JERRY SCOTT and
JIM BORGMAN

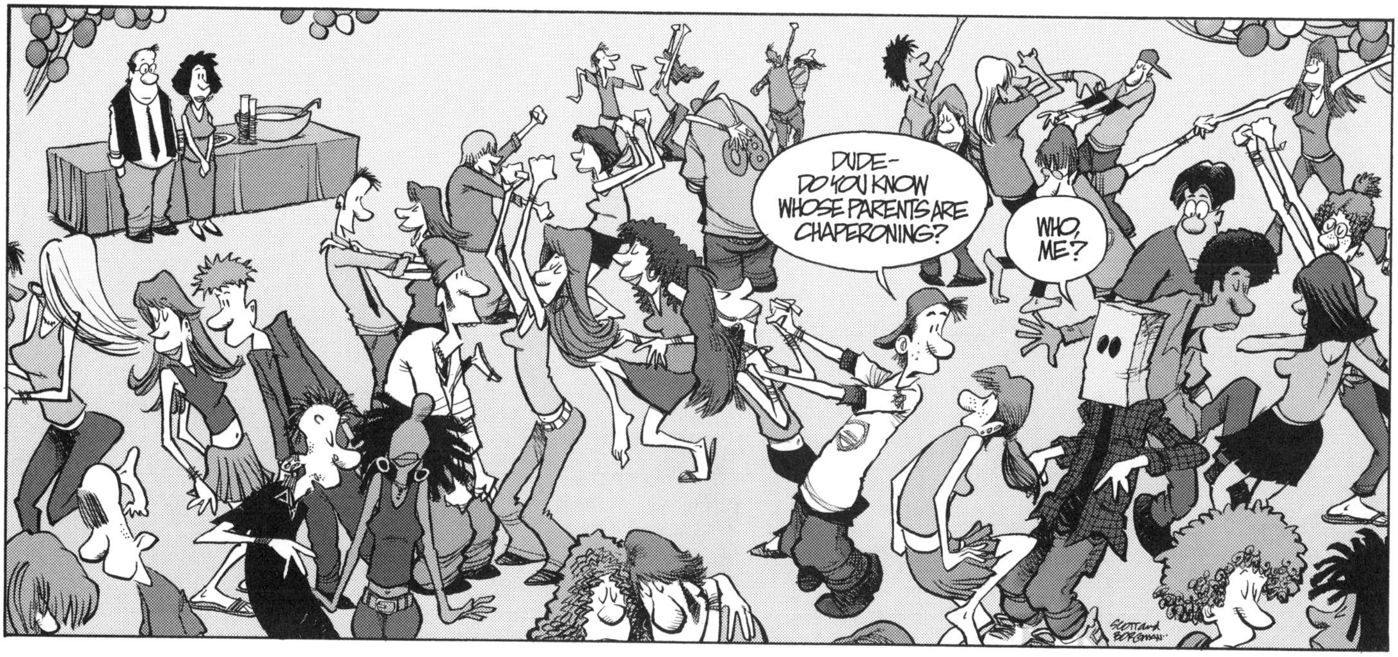
DUDE-
DO YOU KNOW
WHOSE PARENTS ARE
CHAPERONING?
WHO,
ME?
SCOTT and BORGMAN

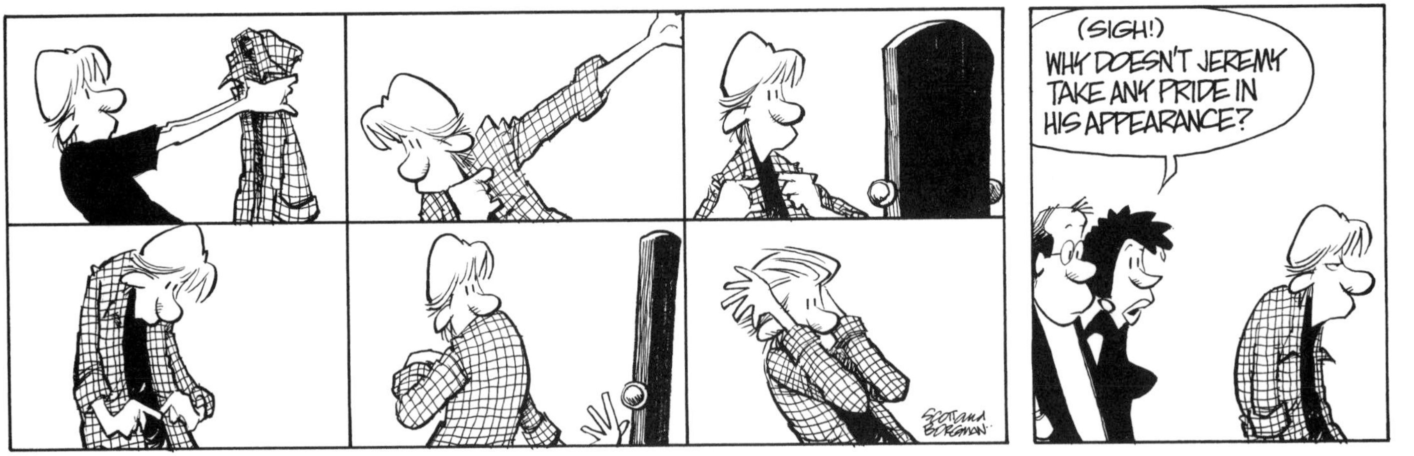
(SIGH!)
WHY DOESN'T JEREMY TAKE ANY PRIDE IN HIS APPEARANCE?

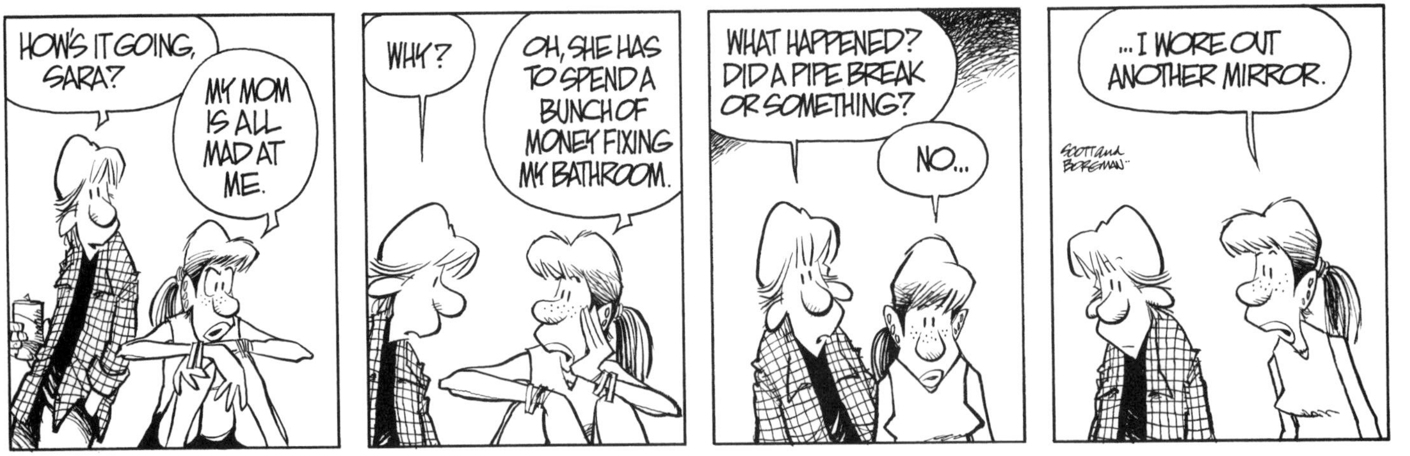
HOW'S IT GOING, SARA?
MY MOM IS ALL MAD AT ME.
WHY?
OH, SHE HAS TO SPEND A BUNCH OF MONEY FIXING MY BATHROOM.
WHAT HAPPENED? DID A PIPE BREAK OR SOMETHING?
NO...
...I WORE OUT ANOTHER MIRROR.

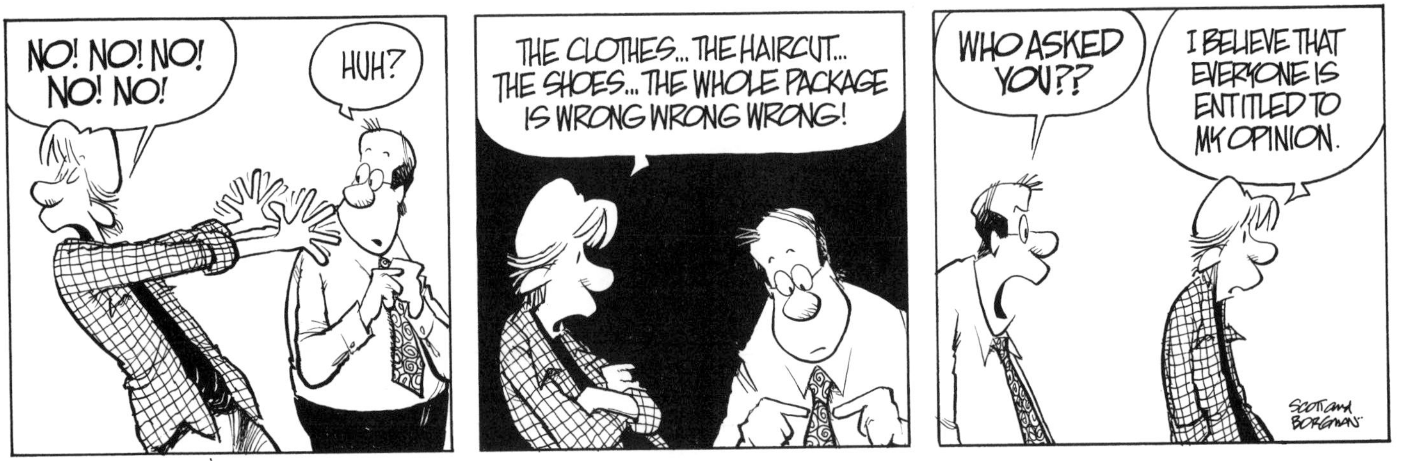
NO! NO! NO! NO! NO!
HUH?
THE CLOTHES... THE HAIRCUT... THE SHOES... THE WHOLE PACKAGE IS WRONG WRONG WRONG!
WHO ASKED YOU??
I BELIEVE THAT EVERYONE IS ENTITLED TO MY OPINION.

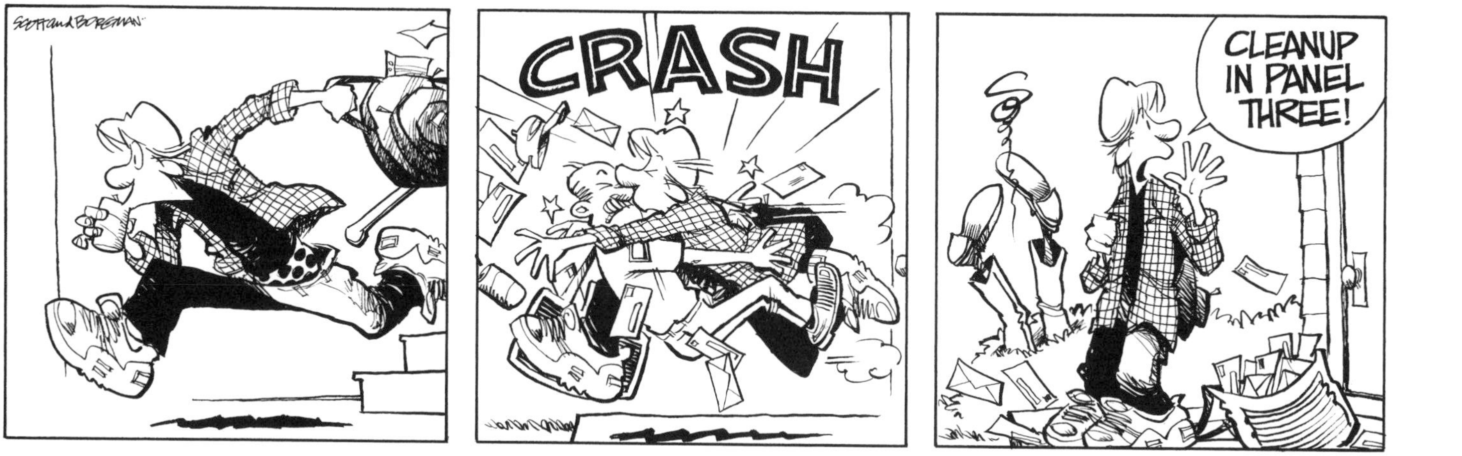
SCOTT and BORGMAN
CRASH
CLEANUP IN PANEL THREE!

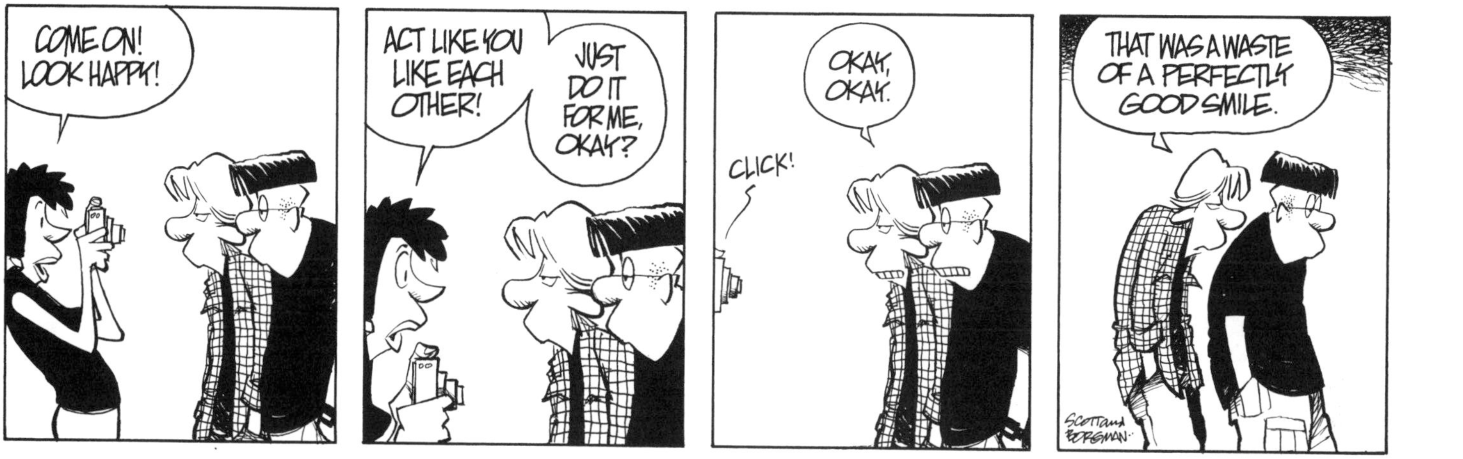
COME ON! LOOK HAPPY!
ACT LIKE YOU LIKE EACH OTHER!
JUST DO IT FOR ME, OKAY?
CLICK!
OKAY, OKAY.
THAT WAS A WASTE OF A PERFECTLY GOOD SMILE.
SCOTT and BORGMAN

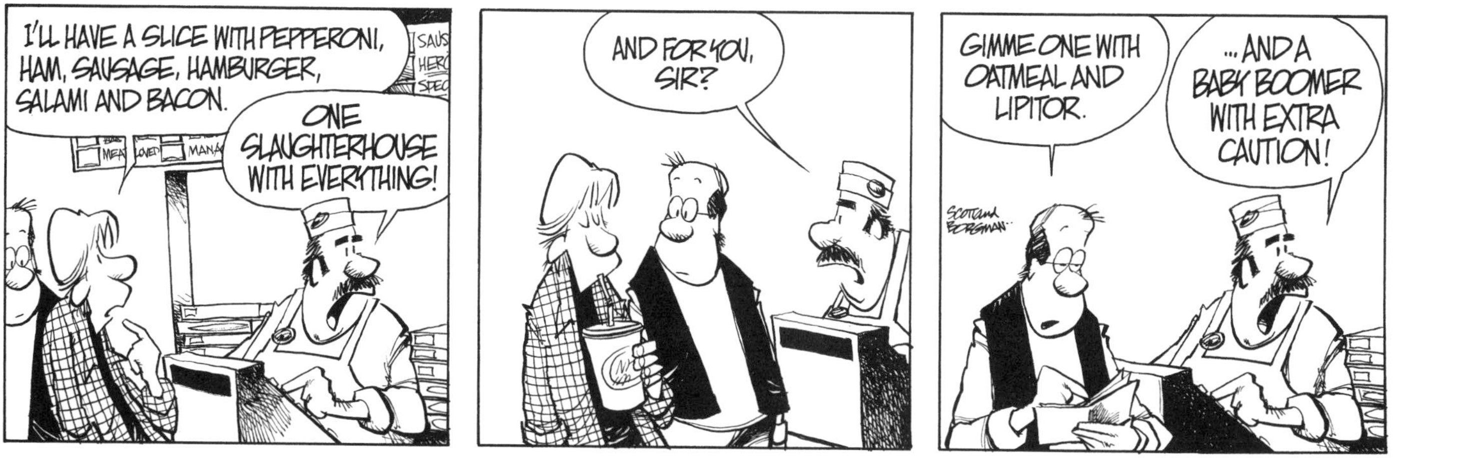
I'LL HAVE A SLICE WITH PEPPERONI, HAM, SAUSAGE, HAMBURGER, SALAMI AND BACON.
ONE SLAUGHTERHOUSE WITH EVERYTHING!
AND FOR YOU, SIR?
GIMME ONE WITH OATMEAL AND LIPITOR.
...AND A BABY BOOMER WITH EXTRA CAUTION!
SCOTT and BORGMAN

Zits
by JERRY SCOTT and JIM BORGMAN

Backpack Geology
STRATA AND FORMATIONS
RECENT ADDITIONS:
50% CHANCE OF RECOVERY IF RETRIEVED WITHIN THREE HOURS
FIRST LEVEL OF COMPACTION:
SEARCH AND RECOVERY SOMETIMES YIELDS RESULTS
PERMACRUD:
NO OBJECT BELOW HERE HAS EVER BEEN RECOVERED BY A PARENT
LOST ZONE:
PURELY THEORETICAL
DEEP COMPACTION:
MATERIAL AT THIS DEPTH CHANGES ON A MOLECULAR LEVEL AND BECOMES PART OF THE BACKPACK STRUCTURE
JEREMY, YOUR TEACHER SAYS SHE SENT THE FORM HOME WITH YOU.... CAN I CHECK YOUR BACKPACK?
HELP YOURSELF.
SCOTT AND BORGMAN

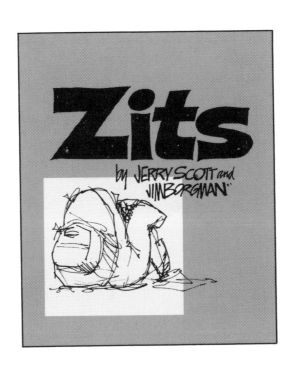

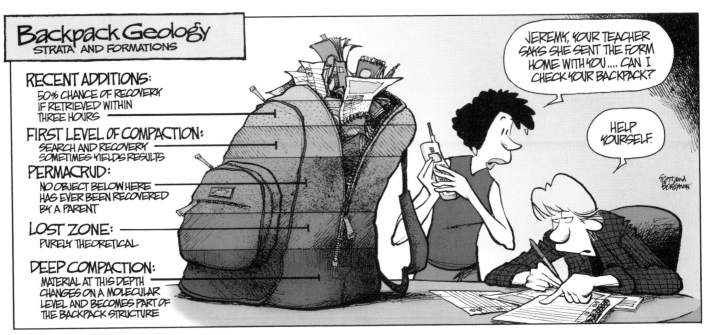

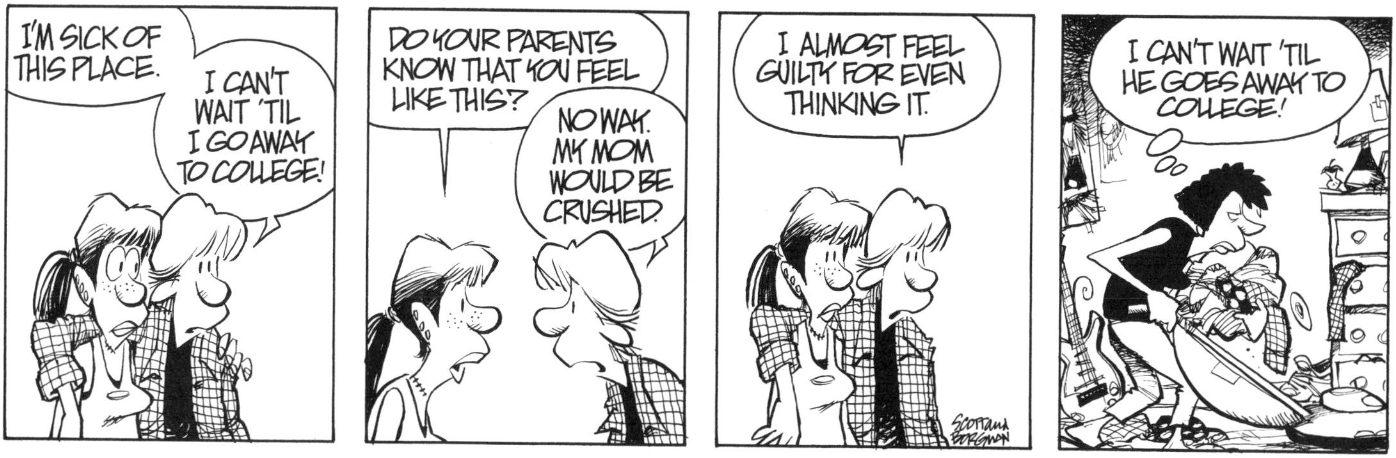
I'M SICK OF THIS PLACE.
I CAN'T WAIT 'TIL I GO AWAY TO COLLEGE!
DO YOUR PARENTS KNOW THAT YOU FEEL LIKE THIS?
NO WAY. MY MOM WOULD BE CRUSHED.
I ALMOST FEEL GUILTY FOR EVEN THINKING IT.
I CAN'T WAIT 'TIL HE GOES AWAY TO COLLEGE!

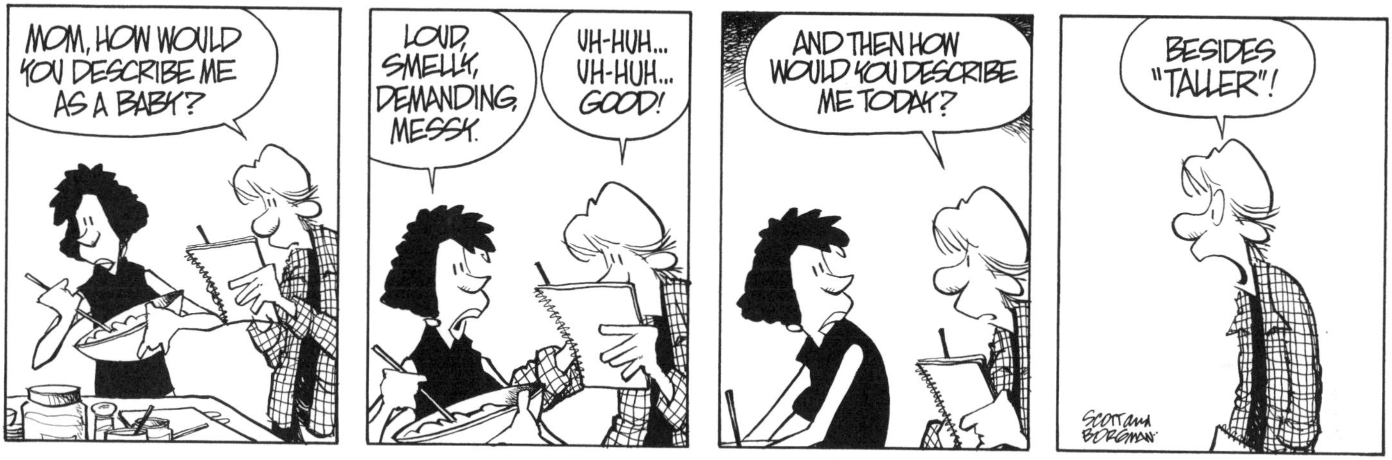
MOM, HOW WOULD YOU DESCRIBE ME AS A BABY?
LOUD, SMELLY, DEMANDING, MESSY.
UH-HUH... UH-HUH... GOOD!
AND THEN HOW WOULD YOU DESCRIBE ME TODAY?
BESIDES "TALLER"!

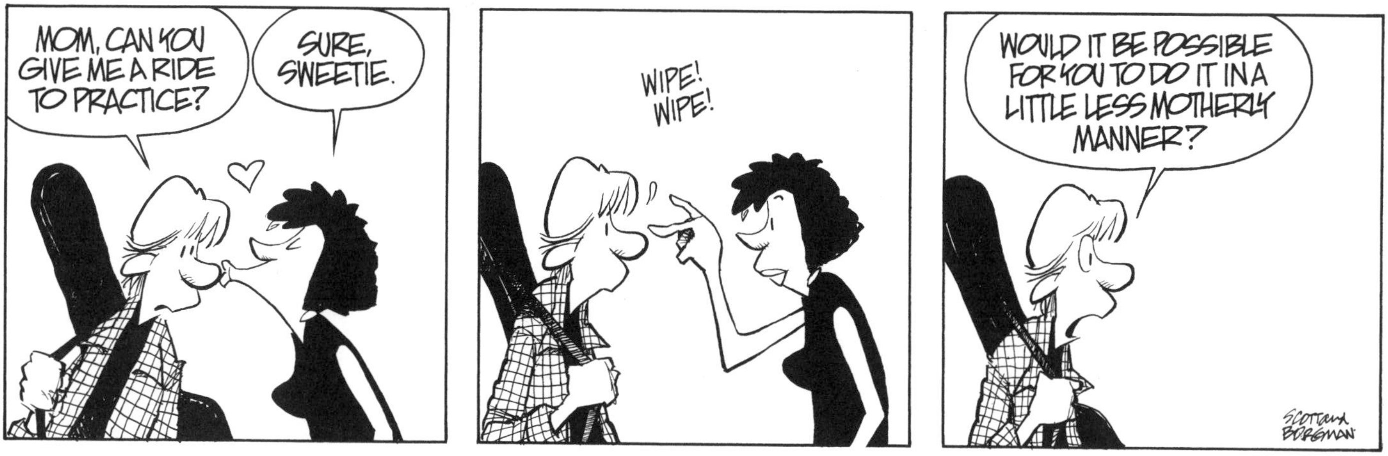
MOM, CAN YOU GIVE ME A RIDE TO PRACTICE?
SURE, SWEETIE.
WIPE! WIPE!
WOULD IT BE POSSIBLE FOR YOU TO DO IT IN A LITTLE LESS MOTHERLY MANNER?

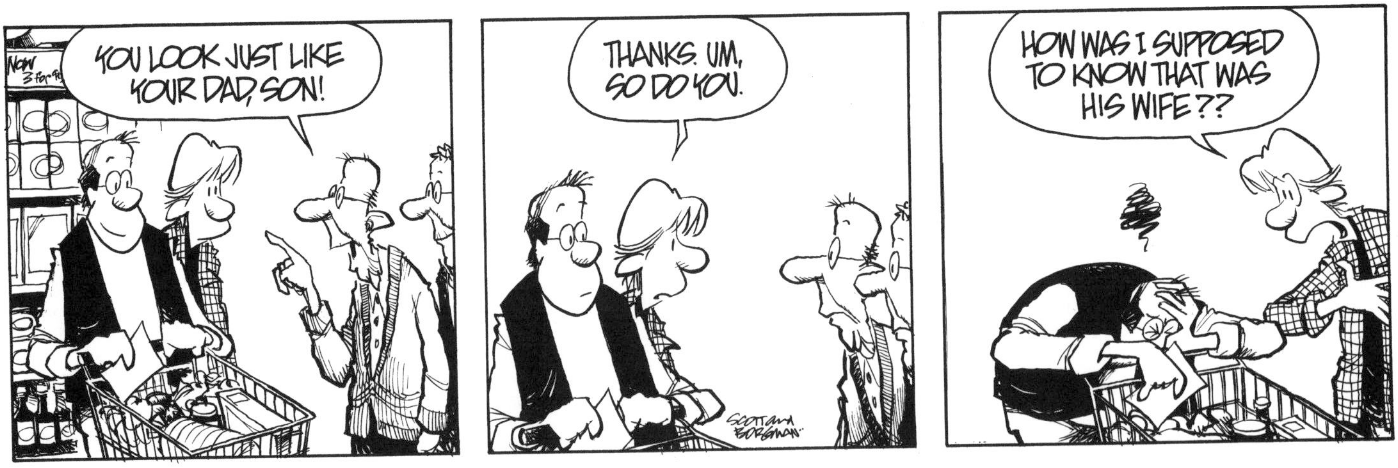
YOU LOOK JUST LIKE YOUR DAD, SON!
THANKS. UM, SO DO YOU.
HOW WAS I SUPPOSED TO KNOW THAT WAS HIS WIFE??

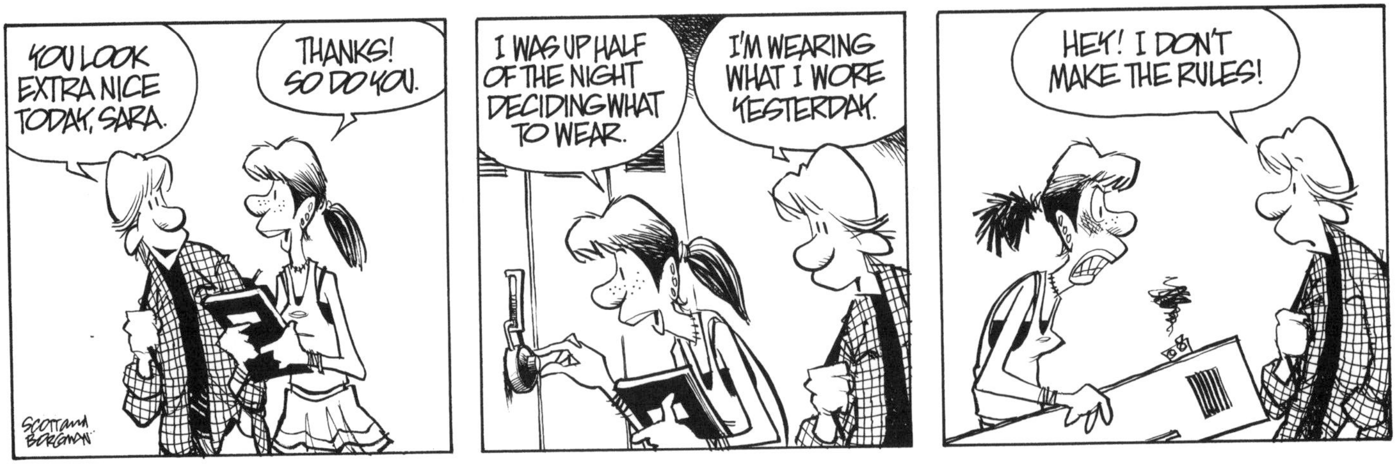
YOU LOOK EXTRA NICE TODAY, SARA.
THANKS! SO DO YOU.
I WAS UP HALF OF THE NIGHT DECIDING WHAT TO WEAR.
I'M WEARING WHAT I WORE YESTERDAY.
HEY! I DON'T MAKE THE RULES!

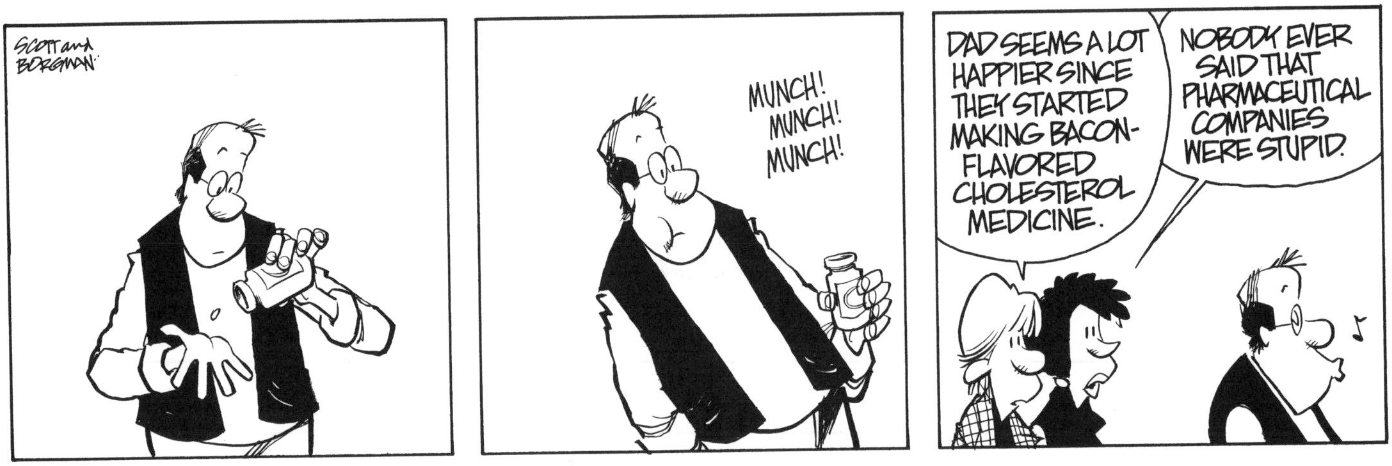
MUNCH! MUNCH! MUNCH!
DAD SEEMS A LOT HAPPIER SINCE THEY STARTED MAKING BACON-FLAVORED CHOLESTEROL MEDICINE.
NOBODY EVER SAID THAT PHARMACEUTICAL COMPANIES WERE STUPID.

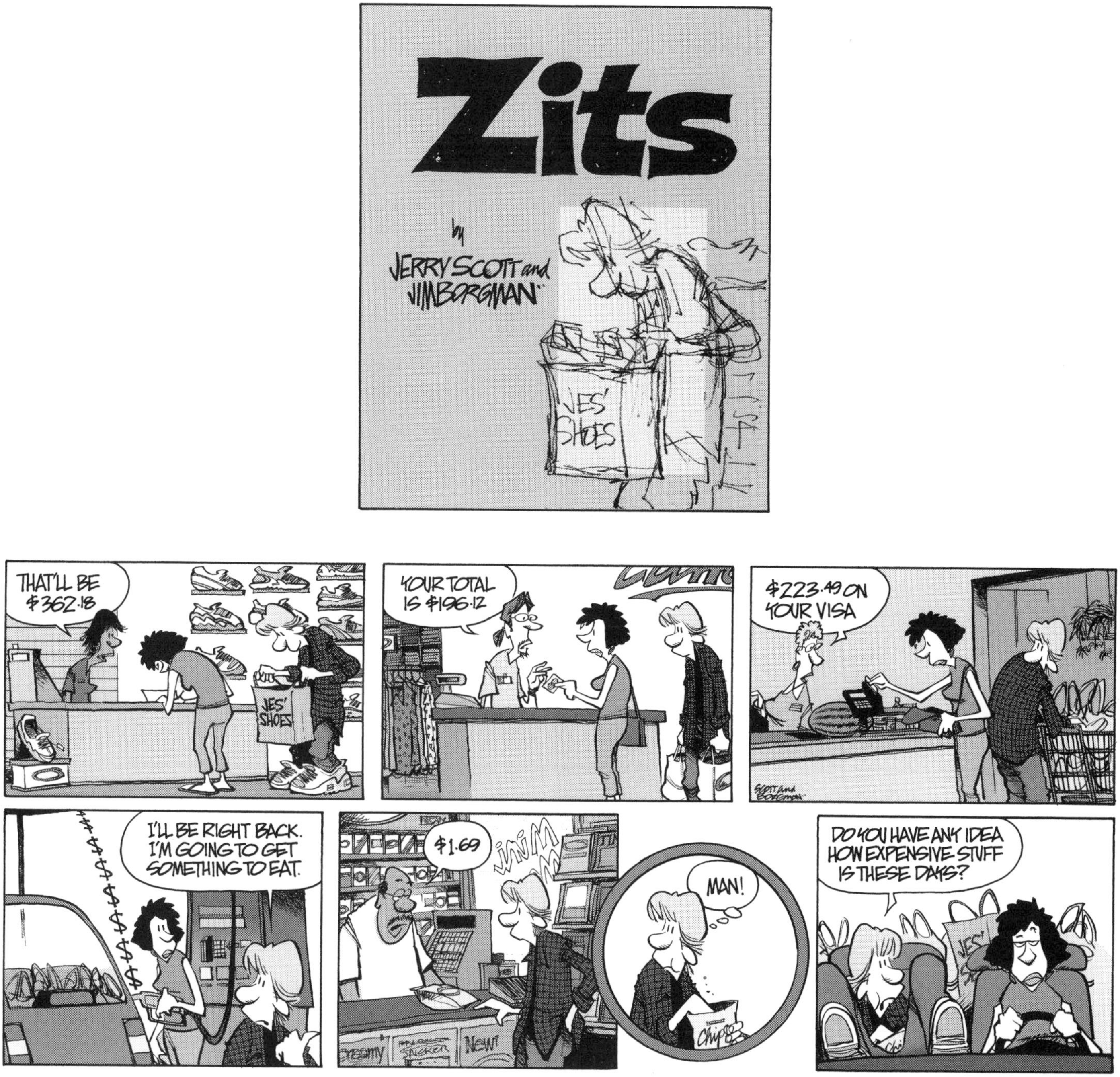
Zits
by
JERRY SCOTT and
JIM BORGMAN
JES' SHOES
THAT'LL BE $362.18
JES' SHOES
YOUR TOTAL IS $196.12
$223.49 ON YOUR VISA
SCOTT and BORGMAN
I'LL BE RIGHT BACK. I'M GOING TO GET SOMETHING TO EAT.
$1.69
MAN!
Chips
DO YOU HAVE ANY IDEA HOW EXPENSIVE STUFF IS THESE DAYS?
JES'

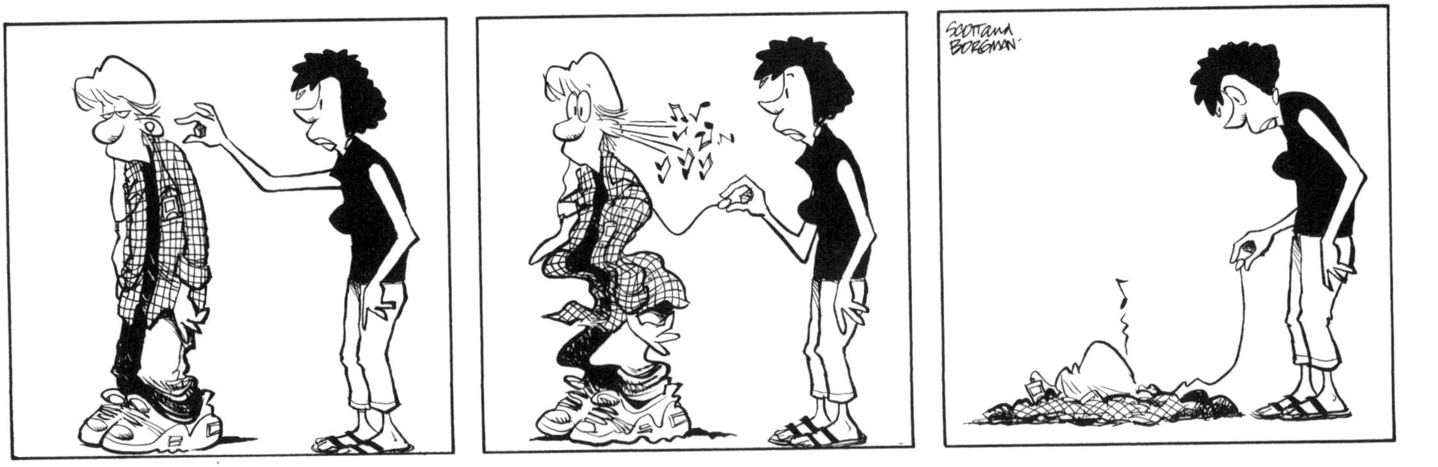

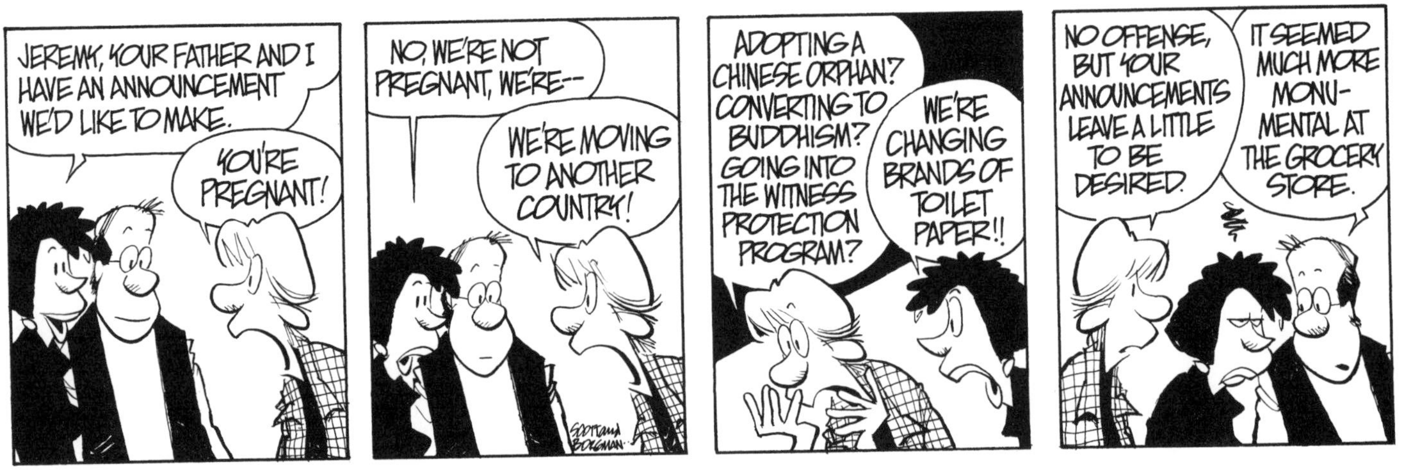

JEREMY, YOUR FATHER AND I HAVE AN ANNOUNCEMENT WE'D LIKE TO MAKE.
YOU'RE PREGNANT!
NO, WE'RE NOT PREGNANT, WE'RE--
WE'RE MOVING TO ANOTHER COUNTRY!
ADOPTING A CHINESE ORPHAN? CONVERTING TO BUDDHISM? GOING INTO THE WITNESS PROTECTION PROGRAM?
WE'RE CHANGING BRANDS OF TOILET PAPER!!
NO OFFENSE, BUT YOUR ANNOUNCEMENTS LEAVE A LITTLE TO BE DESIRED.
IT SEEMED MUCH MORE MONU-MENTAL AT THE GROCERY STORE.

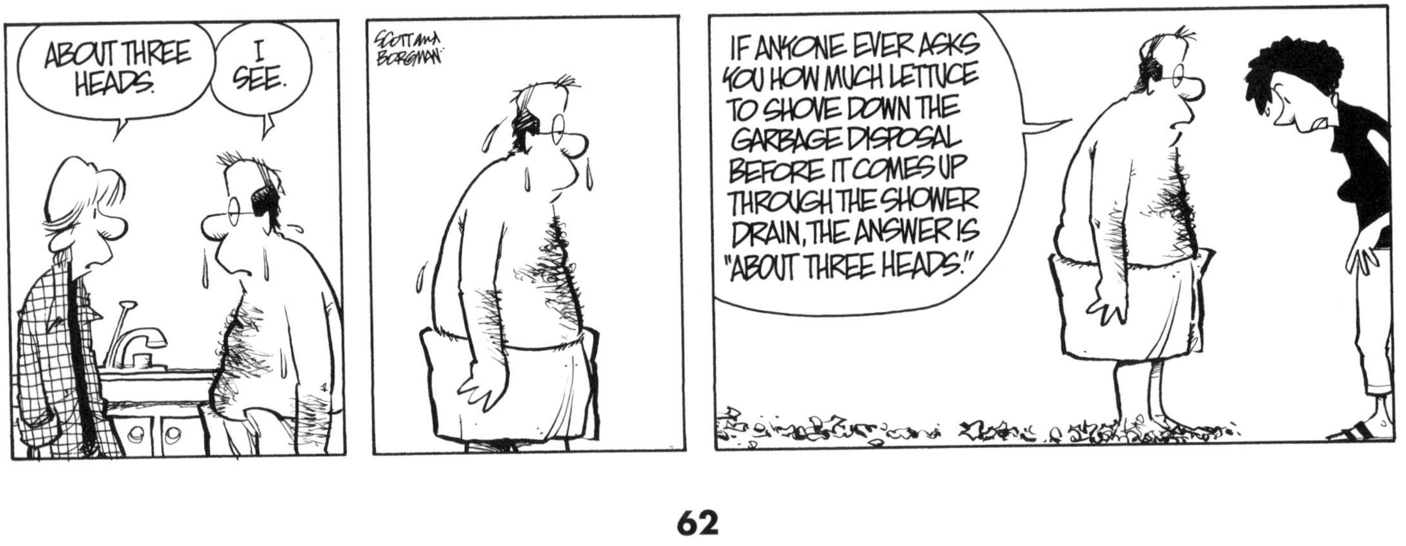

ABOUT THREE HEADS.
I SEE.
IF ANYONE EVER ASKS YOU HOW MUCH LETTUCE TO SHOVE DOWN THE GARBAGE DISPOSAL BEFORE IT COMES UP THROUGH THE SHOWER DRAIN, THE ANSWER IS "ABOUT THREE HEADS."

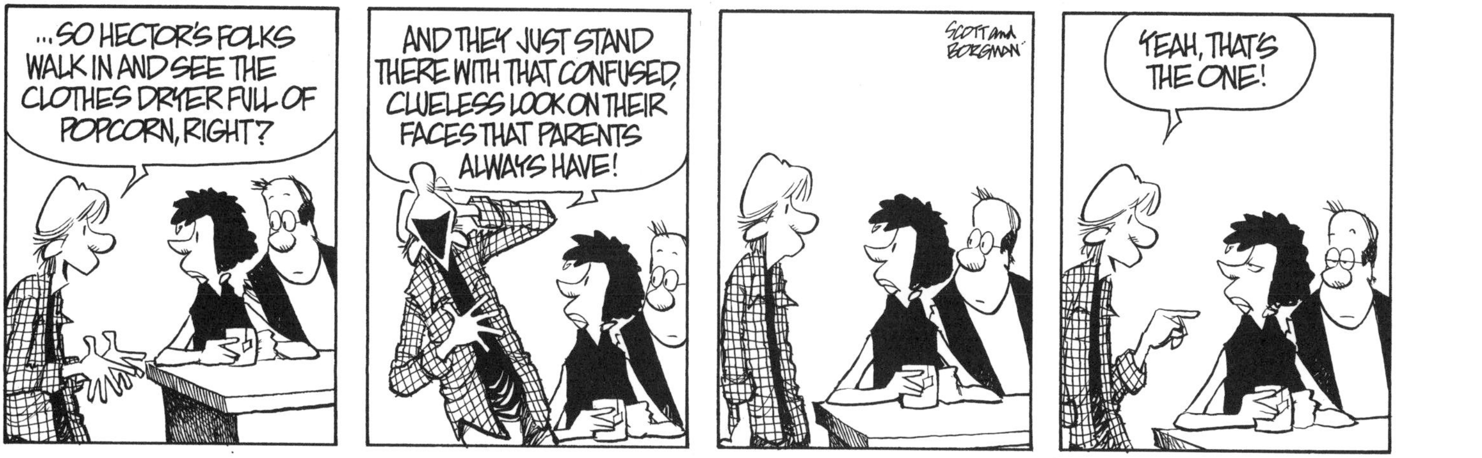
...SO HECTOR'S FOLKS WALK IN AND SEE THE CLOTHES DRYER FULL OF POPCORN, RIGHT?
AND THEY JUST STAND THERE WITH THAT CONFUSED, CLUELESS LOOK ON THEIR FACES THAT PARENTS ALWAYS HAVE!
SCOTT AND BORGMAN
YEAH, THAT'S THE ONE!

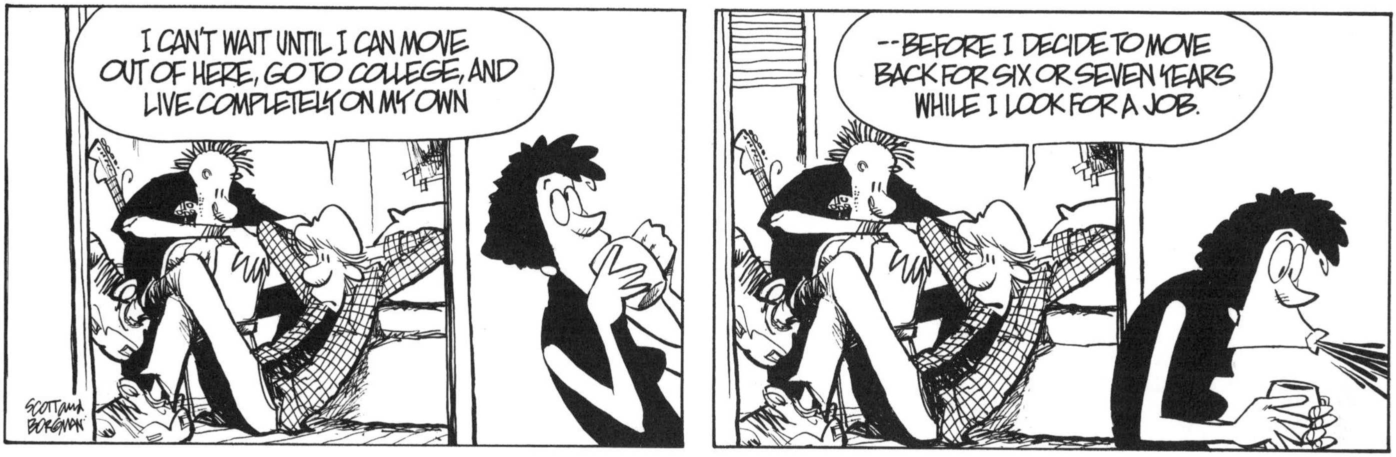
I CAN'T WAIT UNTIL I CAN MOVE OUT OF HERE, GO TO COLLEGE, AND LIVE COMPLETELY ON MY OWN
SCOTT AND BORGMAN
--BEFORE I DECIDE TO MOVE BACK FOR SIX OR SEVEN YEARS WHILE I LOOK FOR A JOB.

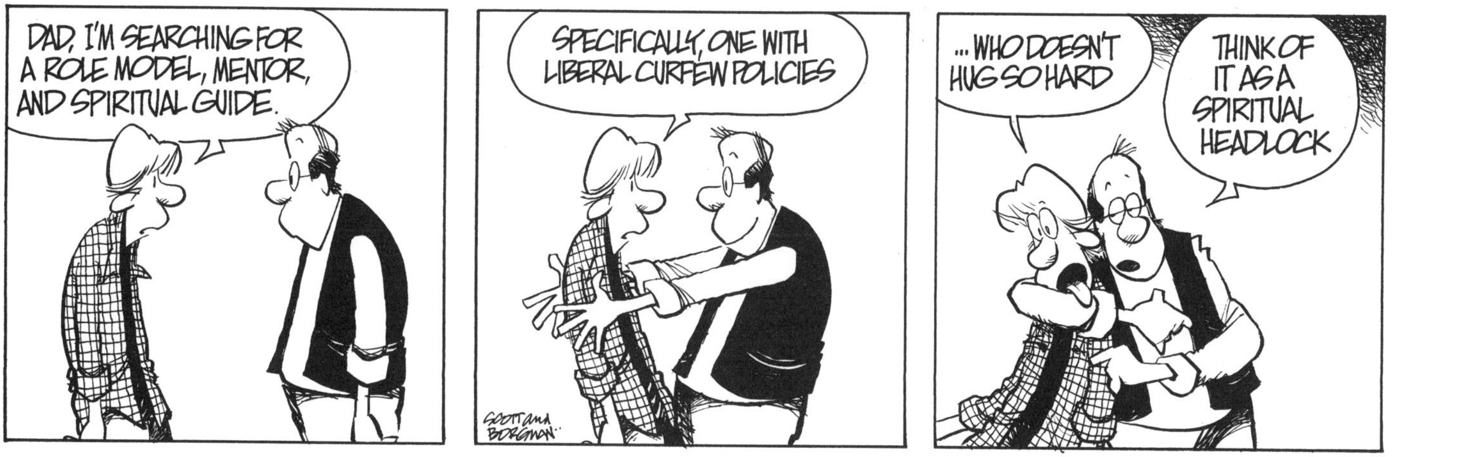
DAD, I'M SEARCHING FOR A ROLE MODEL, MENTOR, AND SPIRITUAL GUIDE.
SPECIFICALLY, ONE WITH LIBERAL CURFEW POLICIES
SCOTT AND BORGMAN
...WHO DOESN'T HUG SO HARD
THINK OF IT AS A SPIRITUAL HEADLOCK

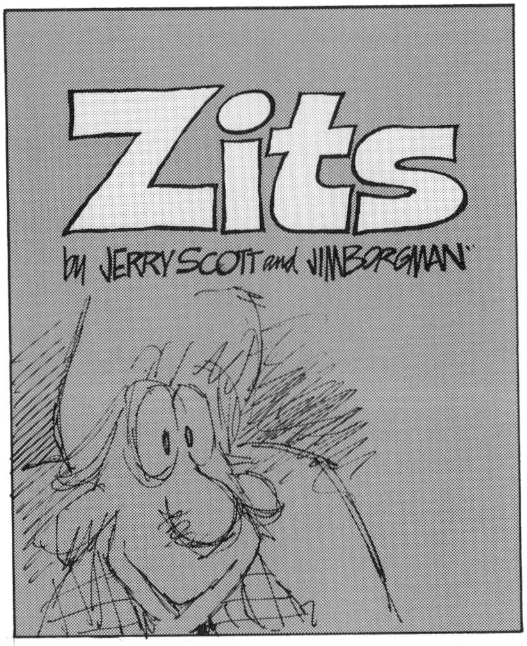
Zits
by JERRY SCOTT and JIM BORGMAN

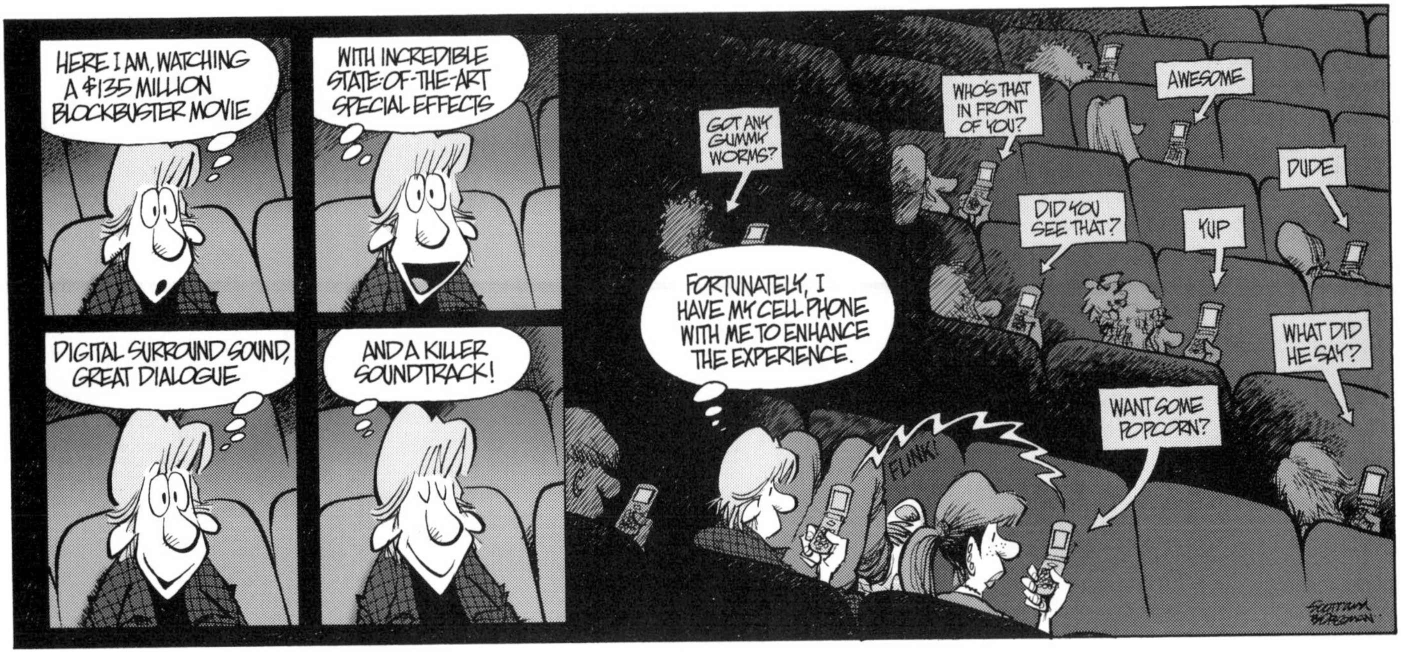
HERE I AM, WATCHING A $135 MILLION BLOCKBUSTER MOVIE
WITH INCREDIBLE STATE-OF-THE-ART SPECIAL EFFECTS
DIGITAL SURROUND SOUND, GREAT DIALOGUE
AND A KILLER SOUNDTRACK!
FORTUNATELY, I HAVE MY CELL PHONE WITH ME TO ENHANCE THE EXPERIENCE.
GOT ANY GUMMY WORMS?
WHO'S THAT IN FRONT OF YOU?
AWESOME
DUDE
DID YOU SEE THAT?
YUP
WHAT DID HE SAY?
WANT SOME POPCORN?
FLINK!

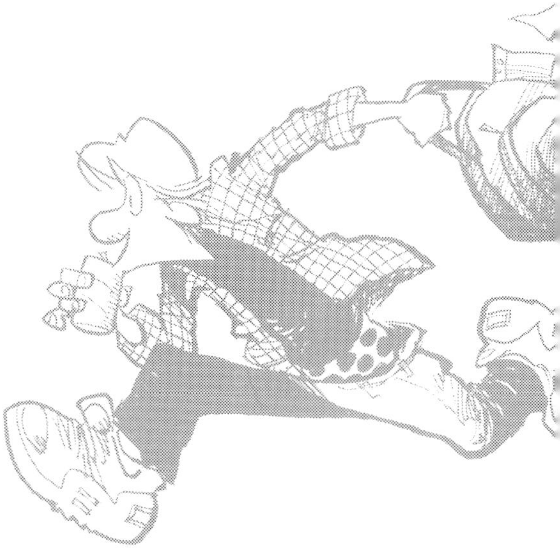

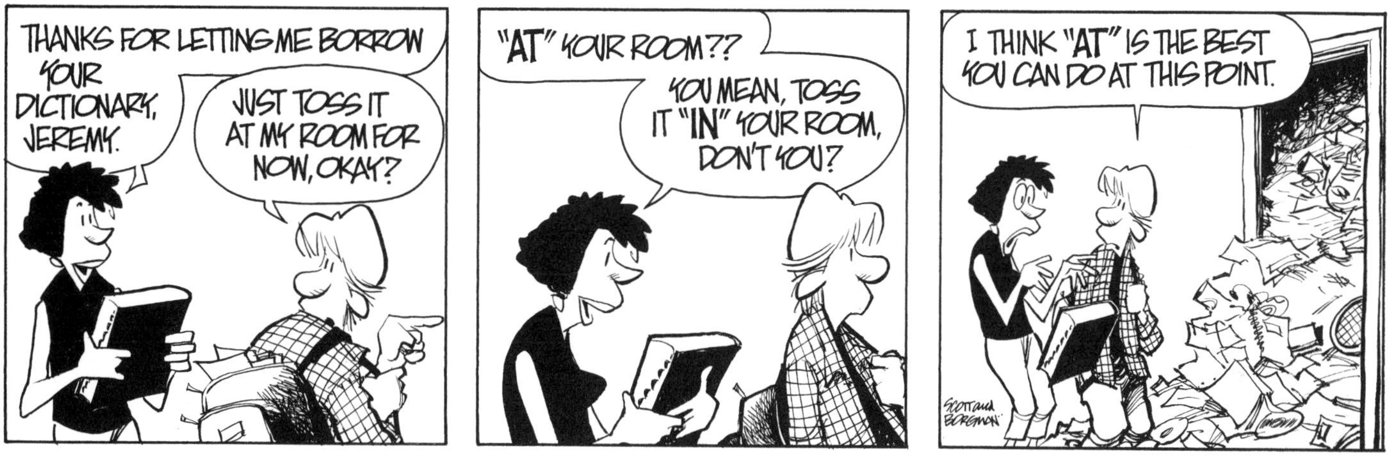
THANKS FOR LETTING ME BORROW YOUR DICTIONARY, JEREMY.
JUST TOSS IT AT MY ROOM FOR NOW, OKAY?
"AT" YOUR ROOM??
YOU MEAN, TOSS IT "IN" YOUR ROOM, DON'T YOU?
I THINK "AT" IS THE BEST YOU CAN DO AT THIS POINT.
SCOTT and BORGMAN

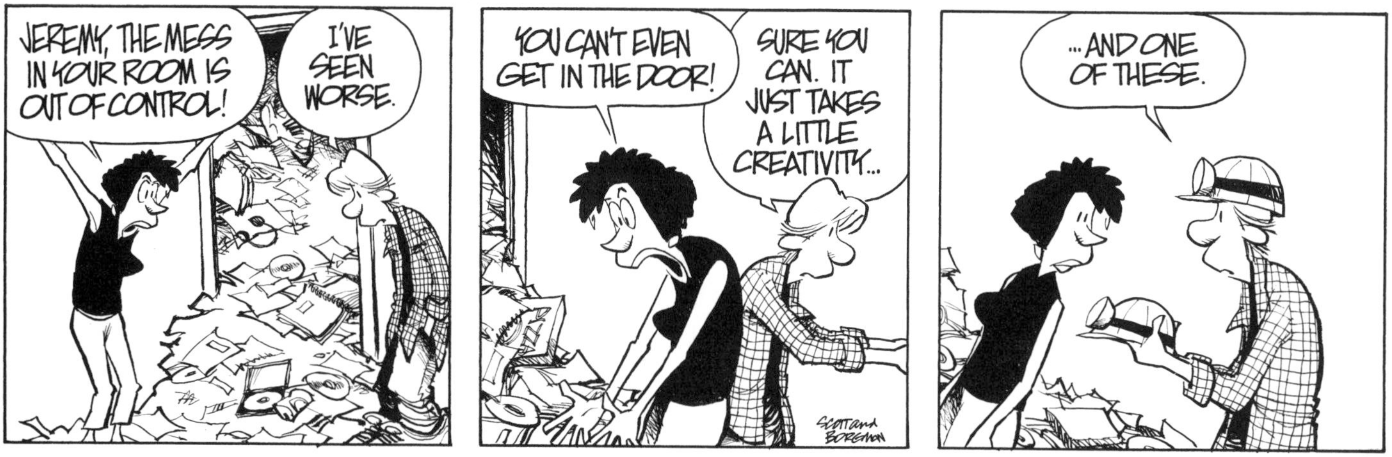
JEREMY, THE MESS IN YOUR ROOM IS OUT OF CONTROL!
I'VE SEEN WORSE.
YOU CAN'T EVEN GET IN THE DOOR!
SURE YOU CAN. IT JUST TAKES A LITTLE CREATIVITY...
SCOTT and BORGMAN
...AND ONE OF THESE.

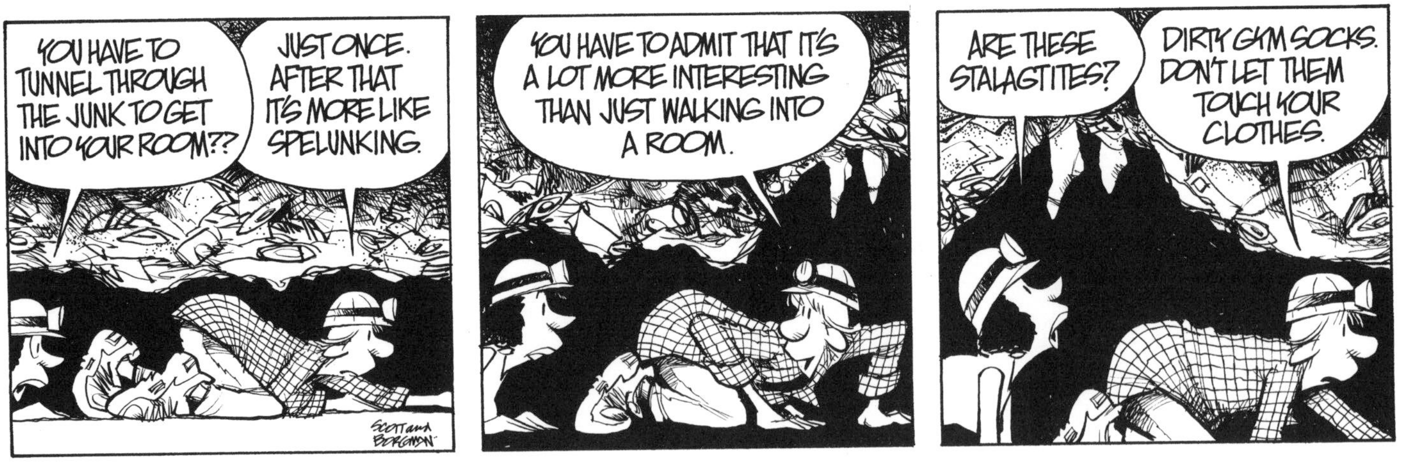
YOU HAVE TO TUNNEL THROUGH THE JUNK TO GET INTO YOUR ROOM??
JUST ONCE. AFTER THAT IT'S MORE LIKE SPELUNKING.
YOU HAVE TO ADMIT THAT IT'S A LOT MORE INTERESTING THAN JUST WALKING INTO A ROOM.
ARE THESE STALAGTITES?
DIRTY GYM SOCKS. DON'T LET THEM TOUCH YOUR CLOTHES.

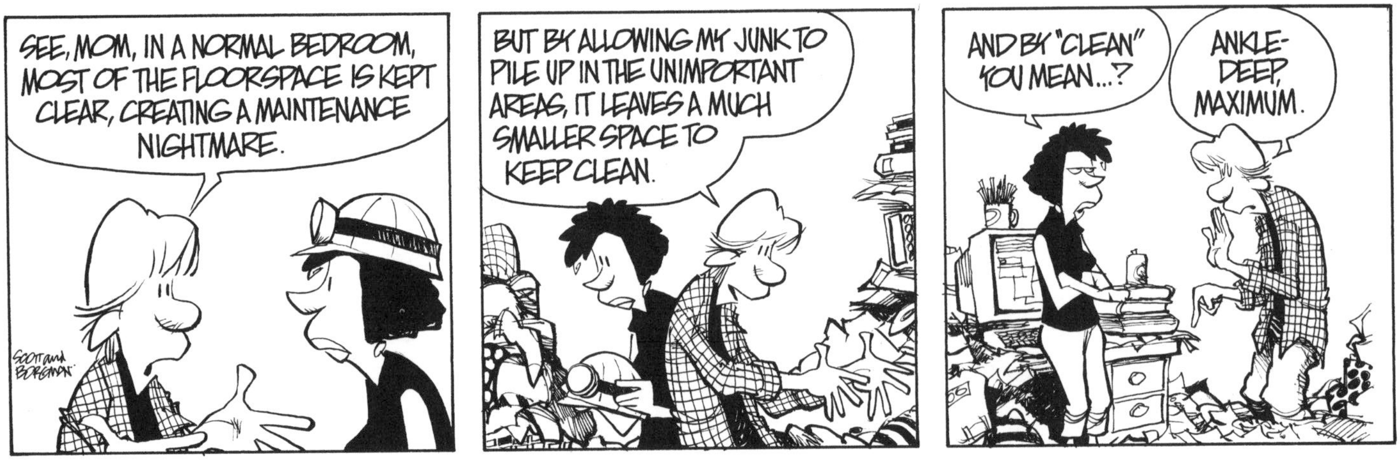
SEE, MOM, IN A NORMAL BEDROOM, MOST OF THE FLOORSPACE IS KEPT CLEAR, CREATING A MAINTENANCE NIGHTMARE.
BUT BY ALLOWING MY JUNK TO PILE UP IN THE UNIMPORTANT AREAS, IT LEAVES A MUCH SMALLER SPACE TO KEEP CLEAN.
AND BY "CLEAN" YOU MEAN...?
ANKLE-DEEP, MAXIMUM.

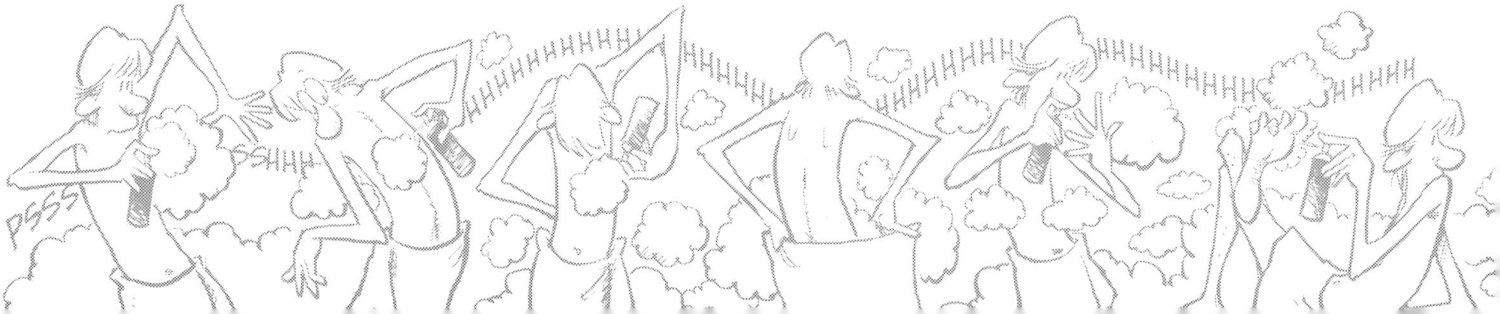

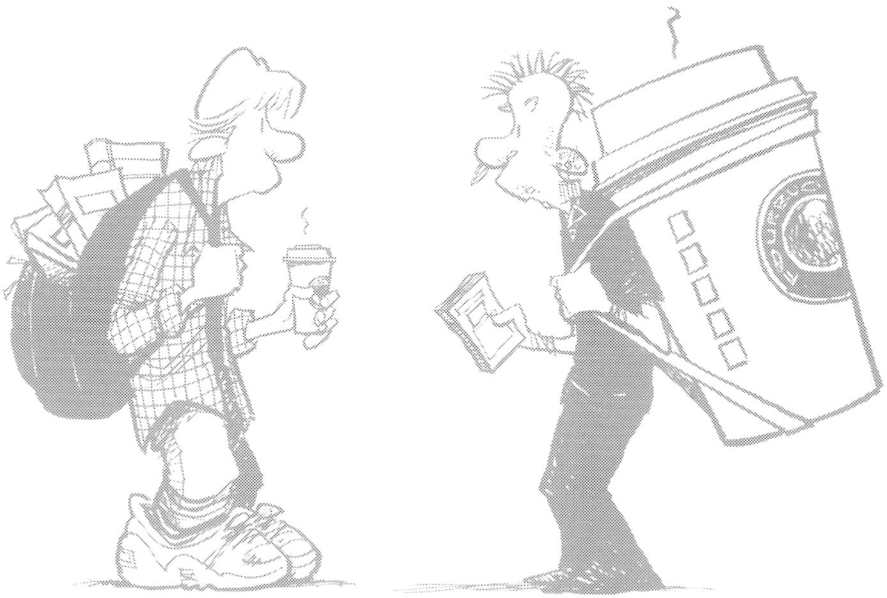

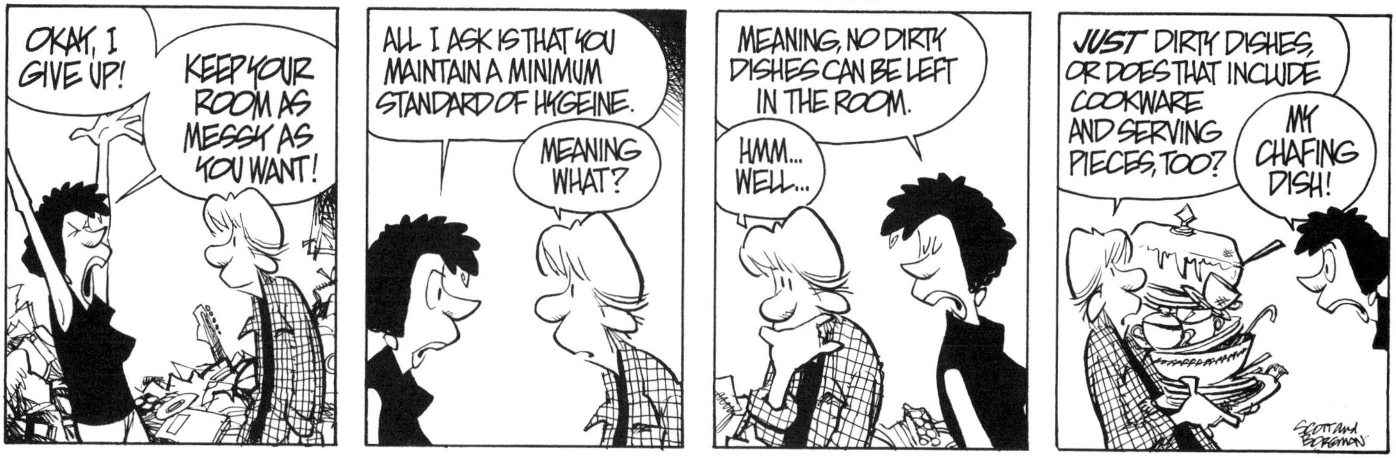

OKAY, I GIVE UP!
KEEP YOUR ROOM AS MESSY AS YOU WANT!
ALL I ASK IS THAT YOU MAINTAIN A MINIMUM STANDARD OF HYGEINE.
MEANING WHAT?
MEANING, NO DIRTY DISHES CAN BE LEFT IN THE ROOM.
HMM... WELL...
JUST DIRTY DISHES, OR DOES THAT INCLUDE COOKWARE AND SERVING PIECES, TOO?
MY CHAFING DISH!

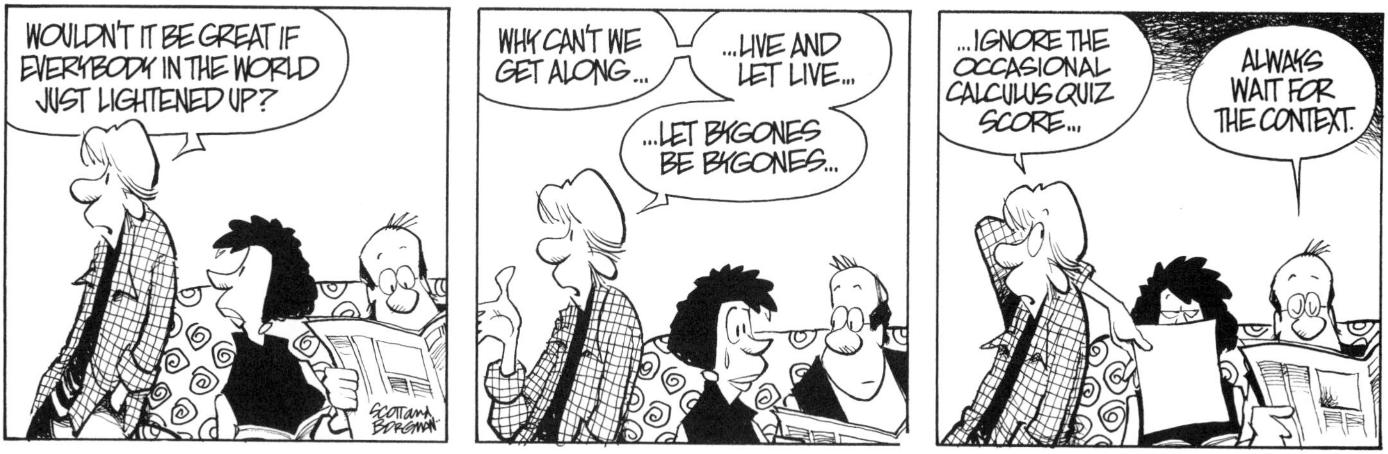

WOULDN'T IT BE GREAT IF EVERYBODY IN THE WORLD JUST LIGHTENED UP?
WHY CAN'T WE GET ALONG...
...LIVE AND LET LIVE...
...LET BYGONES BE BYGONES...
...IGNORE THE OCCASIONAL CALCULUS QUIZ SCORE...
ALWAYS WAIT FOR THE CONTEXT.

Zits
by JERRY SCOTT and JIM BORGMAN

JEREMY? ARE YOU OKAY?
I'M FINE. JUST WARMING UP.
WARMING UP FOR WHAT?
I'M HOME!
HEY DOOD! WHAT UP?
OH.

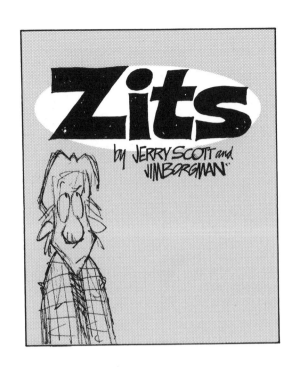

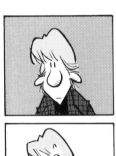

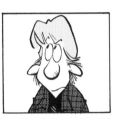

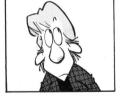

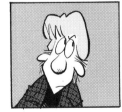

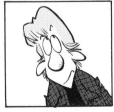

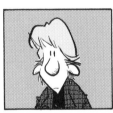

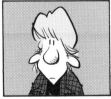

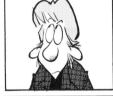

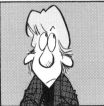

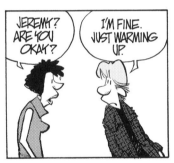

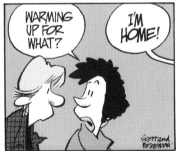

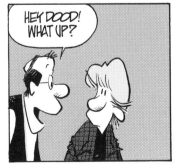

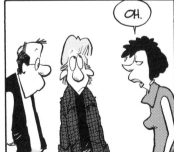

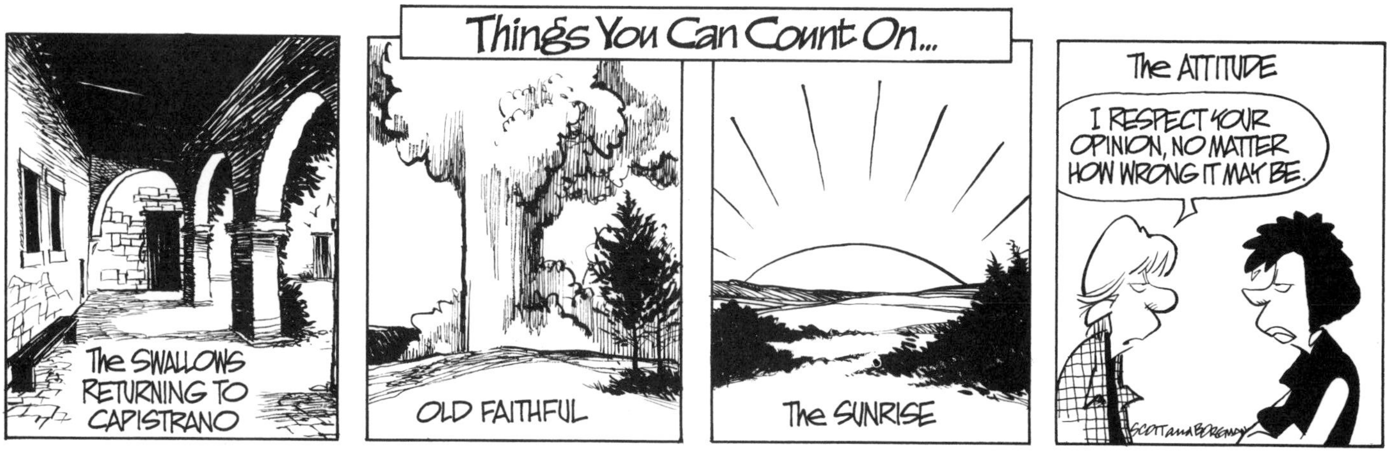
Things You Can Count On...
The SWALLOWS RETURNING TO CAPISTRANO
OLD FAITHFUL
The SUNRISE
The ATTITUDE
I RESPECT YOUR OPINION, NO MATTER HOW WRONG IT MAY BE.

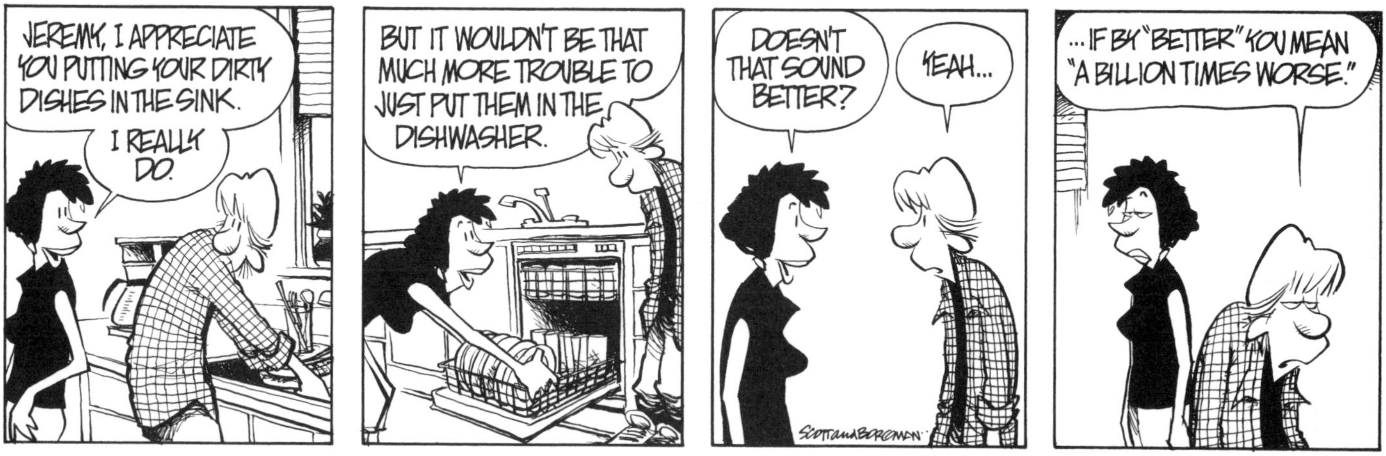
JEREMY, I APPRECIATE YOU PUTTING YOUR DIRTY DISHES IN THE SINK.
I REALLY DO.
BUT IT WOULDN'T BE THAT MUCH MORE TROUBLE TO JUST PUT THEM IN THE DISHWASHER.
DOESN'T THAT SOUND BETTER?
YEAH...
... IF BY "BETTER" YOU MEAN "A BILLION TIMES WORSE."

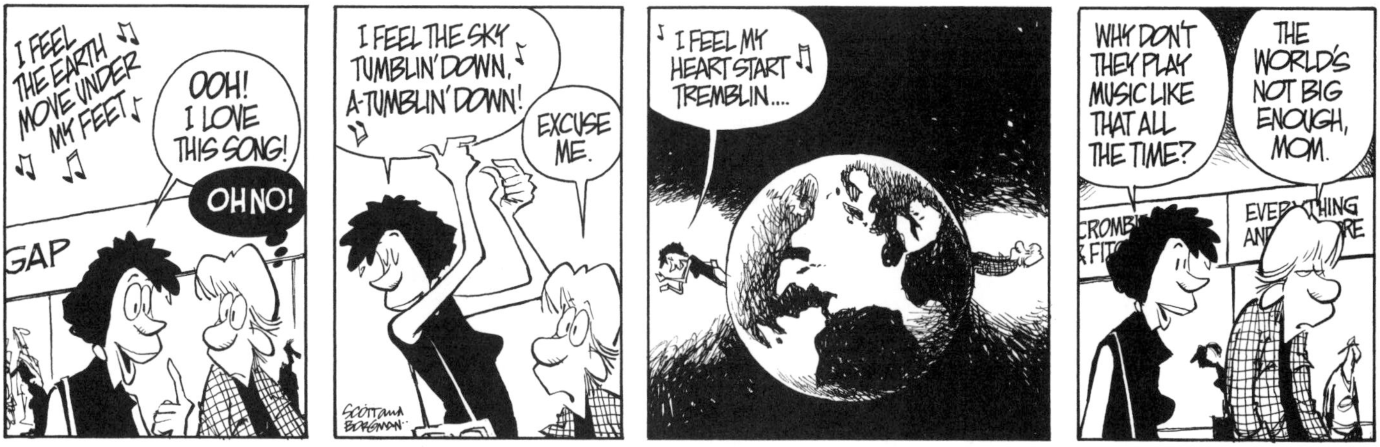
I FEEL THE EARTH MOVE UNDER MY FEET
OOH! I LOVE THIS SONG!
OH NO!
GAP
I FEEL THE SKY TUMBLIN' DOWN, A-TUMBLIN' DOWN!
EXCUSE ME.
I FEEL MY HEART START TREMBLIN....
WHY DON'T THEY PLAY MUSIC LIKE THAT ALL THE TIME?
THE WORLD'S NOT BIG ENOUGH, MOM.

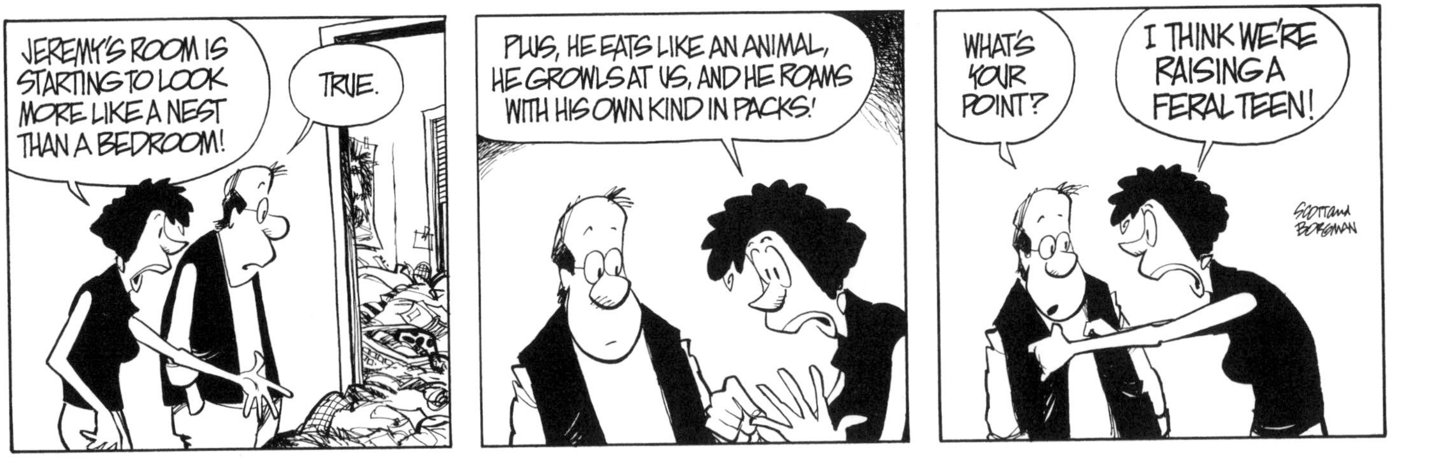
JEREMY'S ROOM IS STARTING TO LOOK MORE LIKE A NEST THAN A BEDROOM!
TRUE.
PLUS, HE EATS LIKE AN ANIMAL, HE GROWLS AT US, AND HE ROAMS WITH HIS OWN KIND IN PACKS!
WHAT'S YOUR POINT?
I THINK WE'RE RAISING A FERAL TEEN!

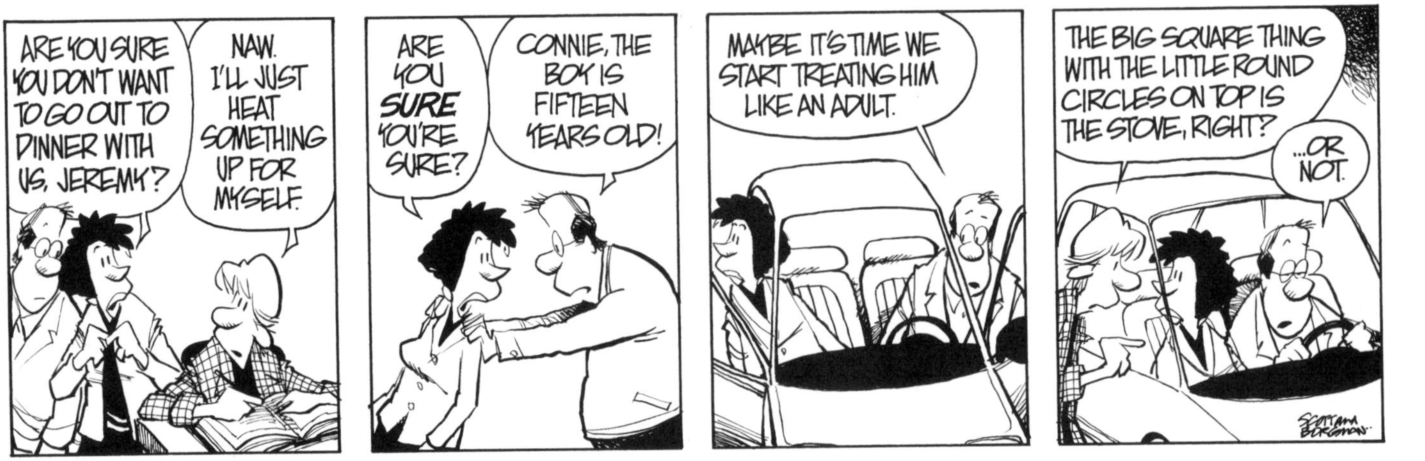
ARE YOU SURE YOU DON'T WANT TO GO OUT TO DINNER WITH US, JEREMY?
NAW. I'LL JUST HEAT SOMETHING UP FOR MYSELF.
ARE YOU **SURE** YOU'RE SURE?
CONNIE, THE BOY IS FIFTEEN YEARS OLD!
MAYBE IT'S TIME WE START TREATING HIM LIKE AN ADULT.
THE BIG SQUARE THING WITH THE LITTLE ROUND CIRCLES ON TOP IS THE STOVE, RIGHT?
...OR NOT.

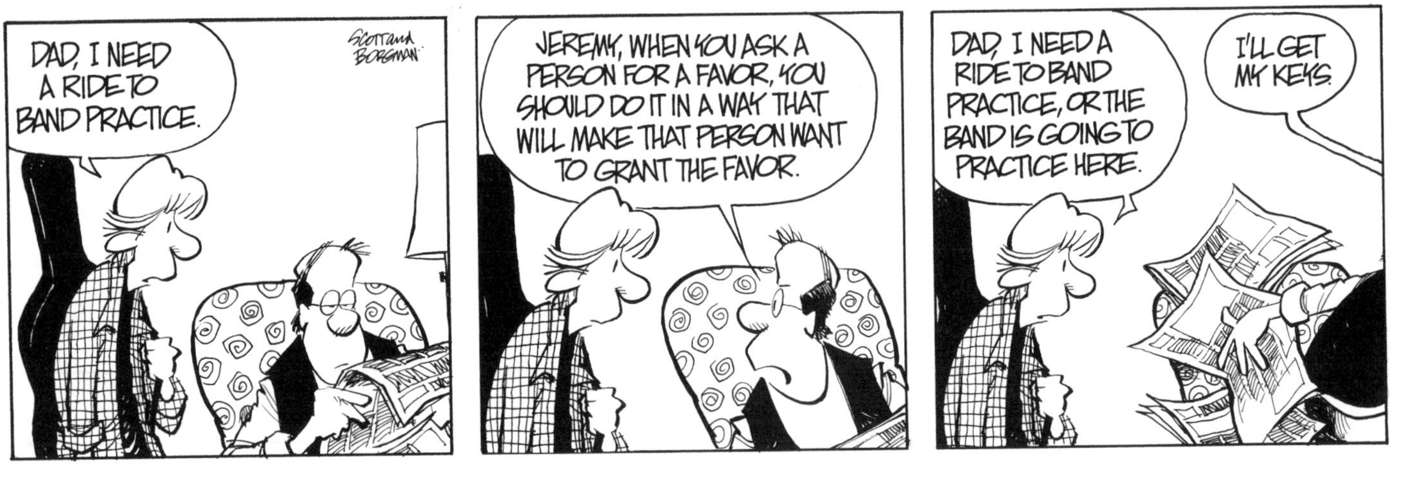
DAD, I NEED A RIDE TO BAND PRACTICE.
JEREMY, WHEN YOU ASK A PERSON FOR A FAVOR, YOU SHOULD DO IT IN A WAY THAT WILL MAKE THAT PERSON WANT TO GRANT THE FAVOR.
DAD, I NEED A RIDE TO BAND PRACTICE, OR THE BAND IS GOING TO PRACTICE HERE.
I'LL GET MY KEYS.

FLEEDLE! FLEEDLE! FLEEDLE!

HOLD ON, GUYS

HI MOM. FINE.

UH-HUH. JUST KIND OF UM, STUDYING WITH JEREMY.

SUBJECT? OH, YOU KNOW... REGULAR SCHOOL SUB-ECTS.

MOM?

CAN YOU HEAR ME? HELLO?

I CAN'T HEAR YOU. HAVE TO MOVE TO ALL ON-OU JACK.

FLINK!

THAT WAS IMPRESSIVE.

NOT BEING A GOOD LIAR HAS FORCED ME TO DEVELOP OTHER SURVIVAL SKILLS.

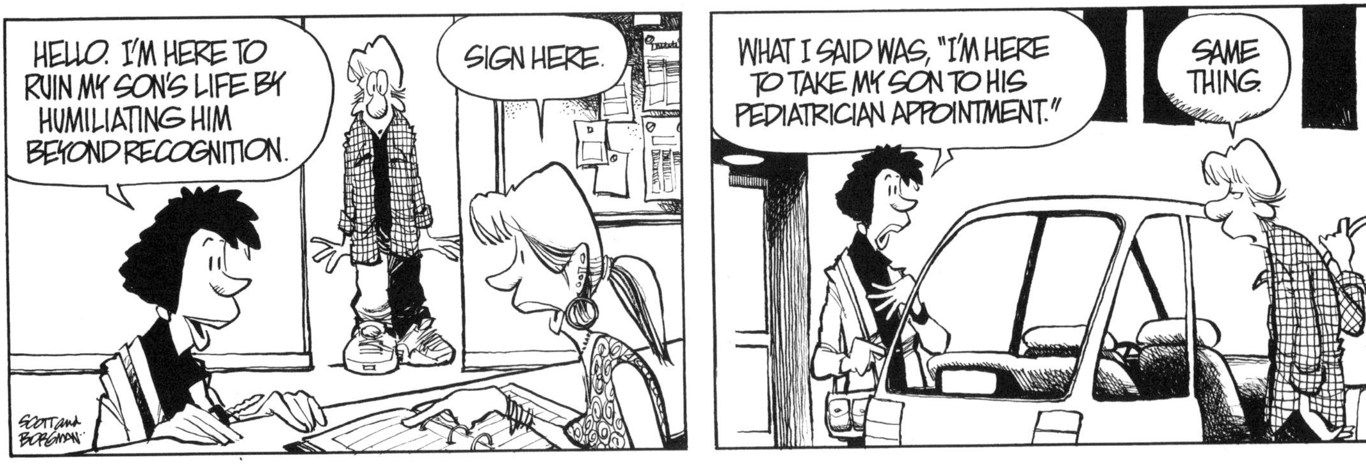
HELLO. I'M HERE TO RUIN MY SON'S LIFE BY HUMILIATING HIM BEYOND RECOGNITION.
SIGN HERE.
WHAT I SAID WAS, "I'M HERE TO TAKE MY SON TO HIS PEDIATRICIAN APPOINTMENT."
SAME THING.

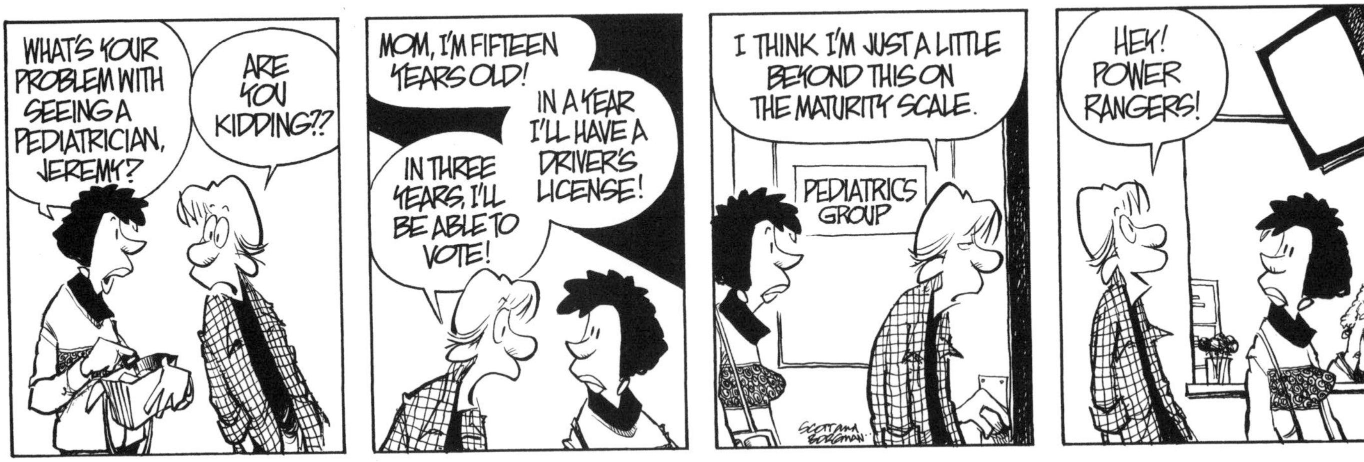
WHAT'S YOUR PROBLEM WITH SEEING A PEDIATRICIAN, JEREMY?
ARE YOU KIDDING?!?
MOM, I'M FIFTEEN YEARS OLD!
IN A YEAR I'LL HAVE A DRIVER'S LICENSE!
IN THREE YEARS, I'LL BE ABLE TO VOTE!
I THINK I'M JUST A LITTLE BEYOND THIS ON THE MATURITY SCALE.
PEDIATRICS GROUP
HEY! POWER RANGERS!

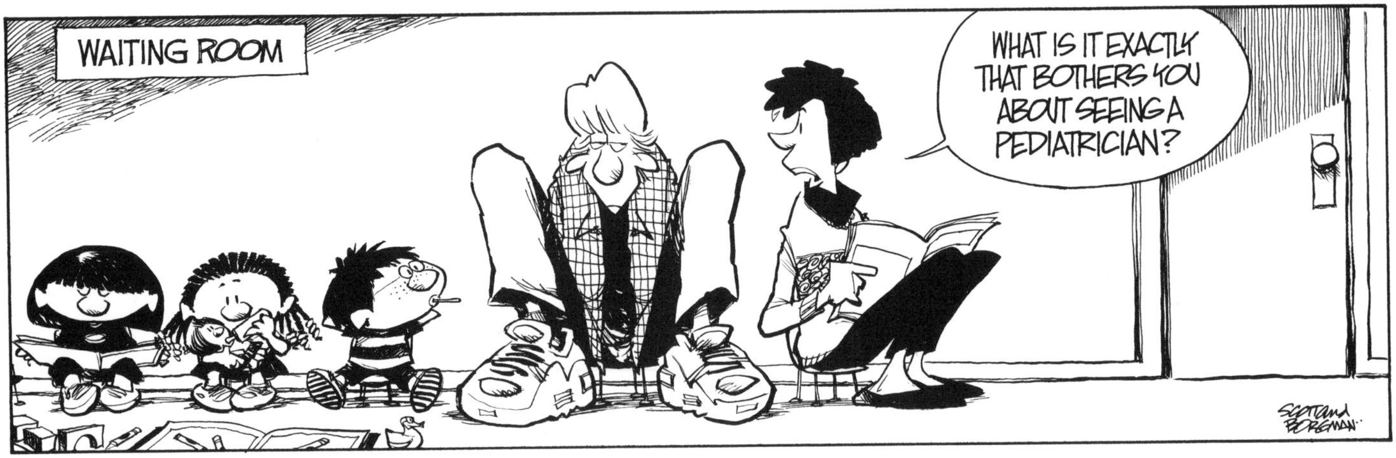
WAITING ROOM
WHAT IS IT EXACTLY THAT BOTHERS YOU ABOUT SEEING A PEDIATRICIAN?

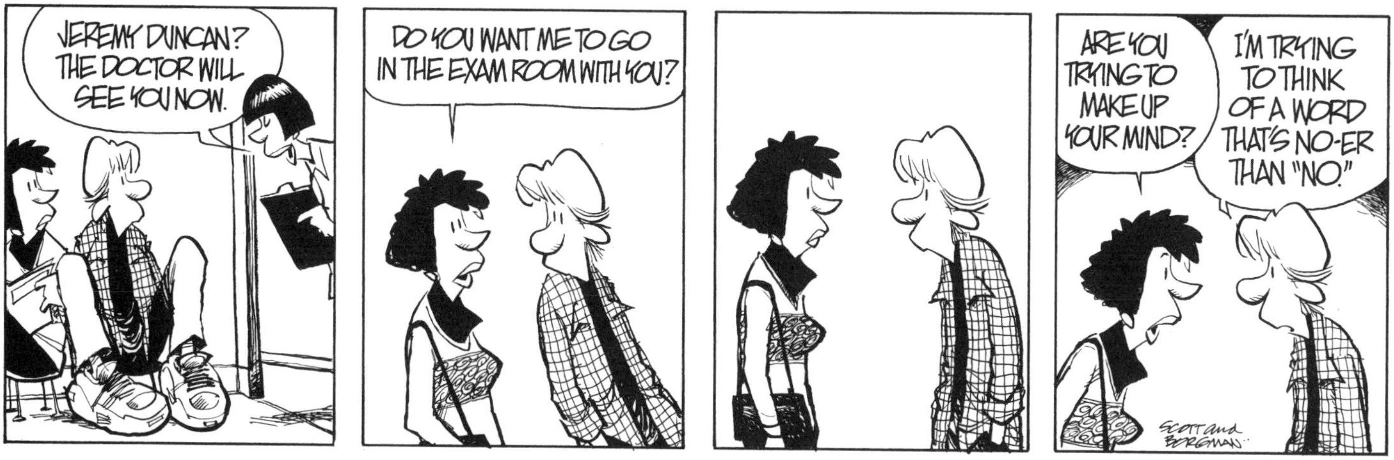
JEREMY DUNCAN? THE DOCTOR WILL SEE YOU NOW.
DO YOU WANT ME TO GO IN THE EXAM ROOM WITH YOU?
ARE YOU TRYING TO MAKE UP YOUR MIND?
I'M TRYING TO THINK OF A WORD THAT'S NO-ER THAN "NO."
SCOTT and BORGMAN

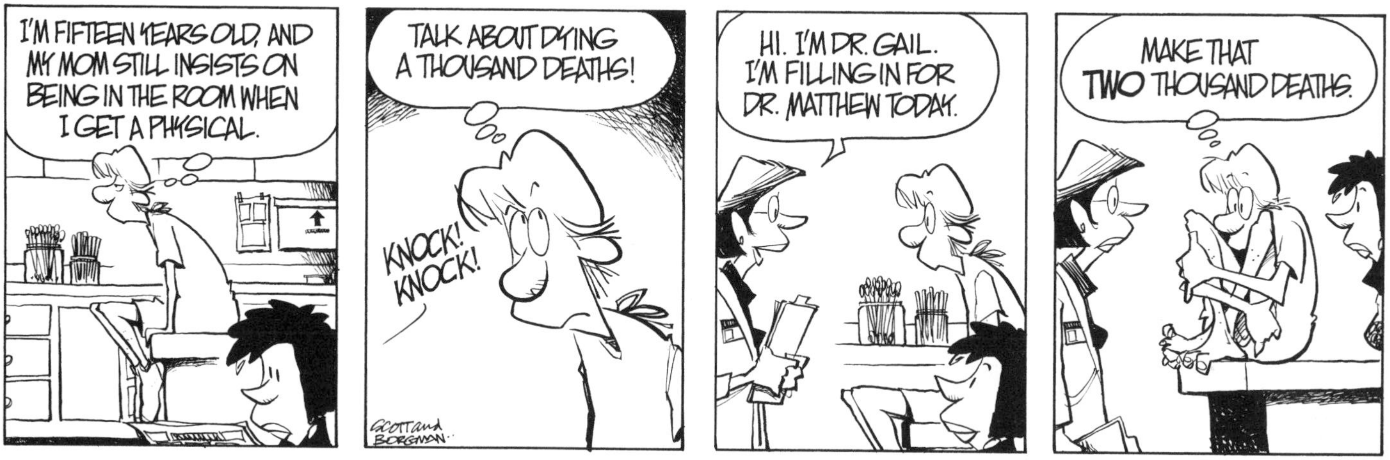
I'M FIFTEEN YEARS OLD, AND MY MOM STILL INSISTS ON BEING IN THE ROOM WHEN I GET A PHYSICAL.
TALK ABOUT DYING A THOUSAND DEATHS!
KNOCK! KNOCK!
SCOTT and BORGMAN
HI. I'M DR. GAIL. I'M FILLING IN FOR DR. MATTHEW TODAY.
MAKE THAT TWO THOUSAND DEATHS.

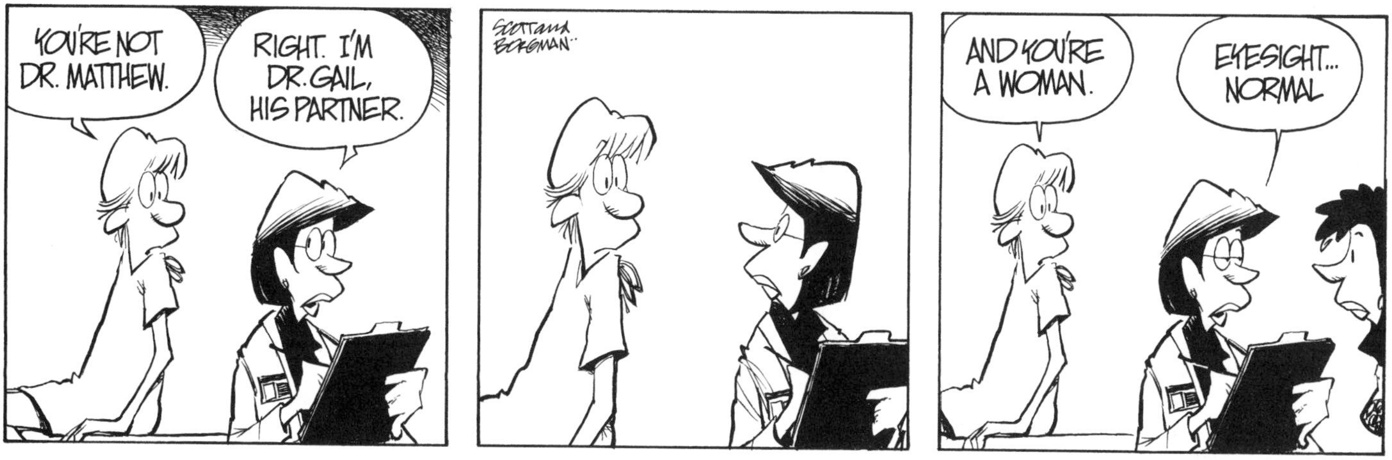
YOU'RE NOT DR. MATTHEW.
RIGHT. I'M DR. GAIL, HIS PARTNER.
SCOTT and BORGMAN
AND YOU'RE A WOMAN.
EYESIGHT... NORMAL

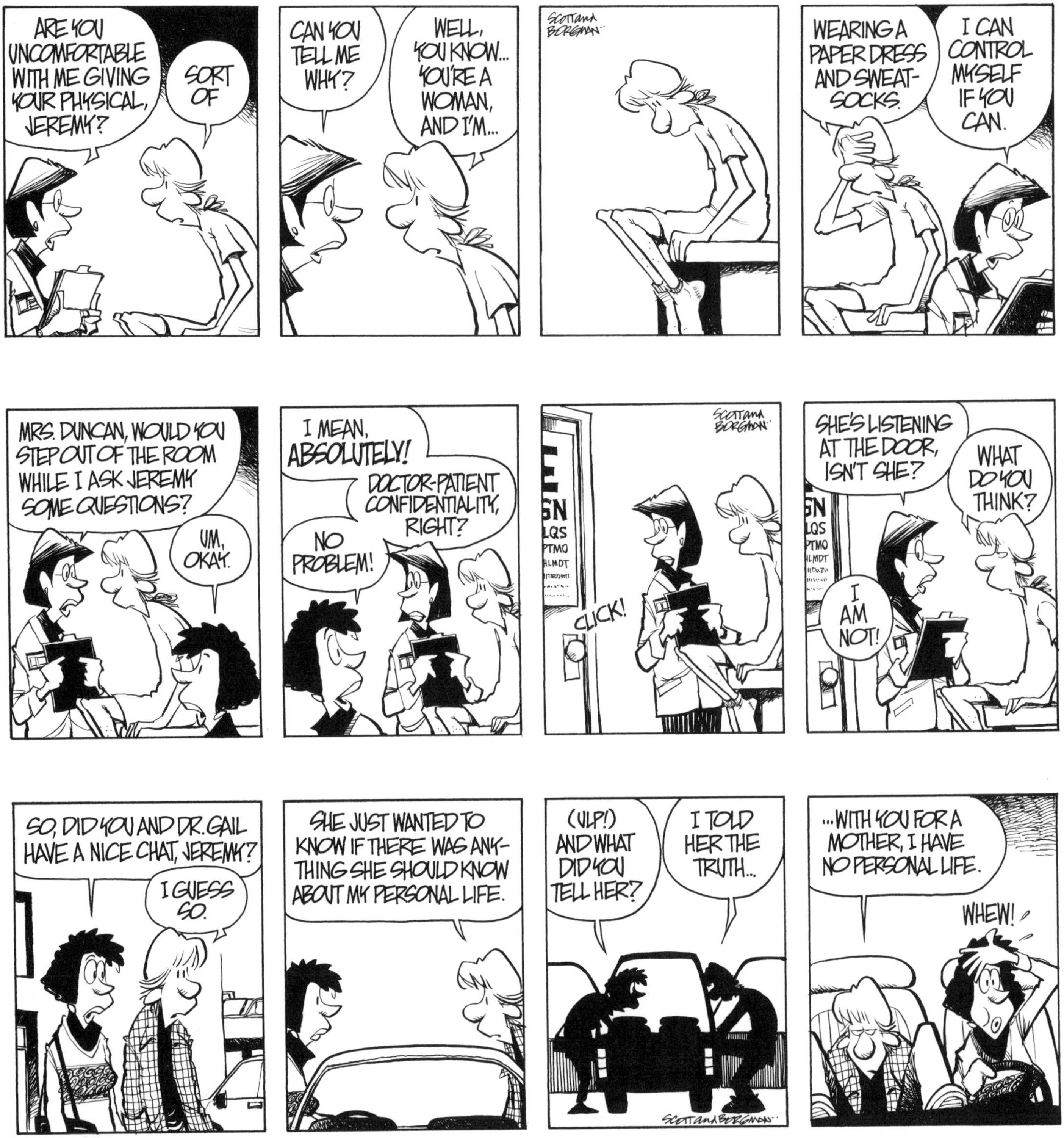
ARE YOU UNCOMFORTABLE WITH ME GIVING YOUR PHYSICAL, JEREMY?
SORT OF
CAN YOU TELL ME WHY?
WELL, YOU KNOW... YOU'RE A WOMAN, AND I'M...
WEARING A PAPER DRESS AND SWEAT-SOCKS.
I CAN CONTROL MYSELF IF YOU CAN.
MRS. DUNCAN, WOULD YOU STEP OUT OF THE ROOM WHILE I ASK JEREMY SOME QUESTIONS?
UM, OKAY.
I MEAN, ABSOLUTELY!
DOCTOR-PATIENT CONFIDENTIALITY, RIGHT?
NO PROBLEM!
CLICK!
SHE'S LISTENING AT THE DOOR, ISN'T SHE?
WHAT DO YOU THINK?
I AM NOT!
SO, DID YOU AND DR. GAIL HAVE A NICE CHAT, JEREMY?
I GUESS SO.
SHE JUST WANTED TO KNOW IF THERE WAS ANY-THING SHE SHOULD KNOW ABOUT MY PERSONAL LIFE.
(ULP!) AND WHAT DID YOU TELL HER?
I TOLD HER THE TRUTH...
...WITH YOU FOR A MOTHER, I HAVE NO PERSONAL LIFE.
WHEW!

Zits
by JERRY SCOTT and JIM BORGMAN

WHAT'S THE MATTER, MOM?
NOTHING IS THE MATTER... I GUESS I'M JUST HAPPY!
ABOUT WHAT?
WELL, I'M HAPPY ABOUT THE WAY DINNER IS TURNING OUT, AND I'M HAPPY THAT WE'RE GOING TO SIT DOWN AS A FAMILY TO EAT IT.
THAT, MY SON, IS WHAT YOU CALL MARITAL BLISS.
REALLY?
I WAS GOING TO GUESS DELIRIUM.

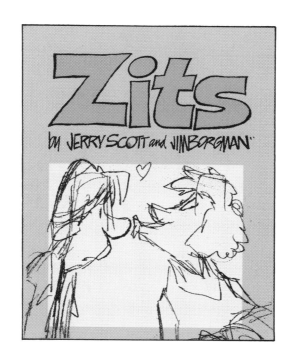

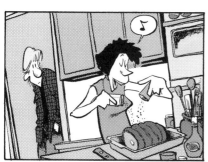

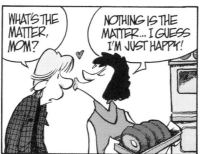

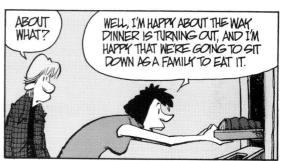

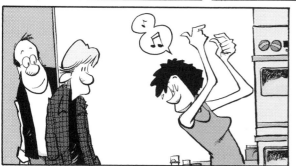

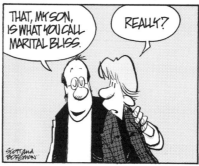

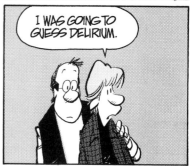

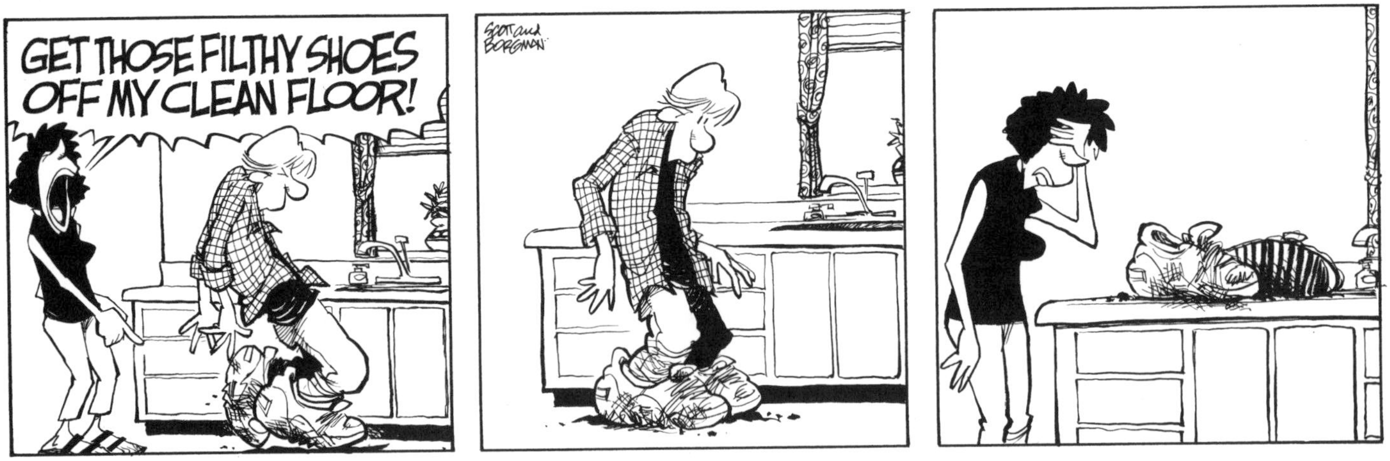
GET THOSE FILTHY SHOES OFF MY CLEAN FLOOR!

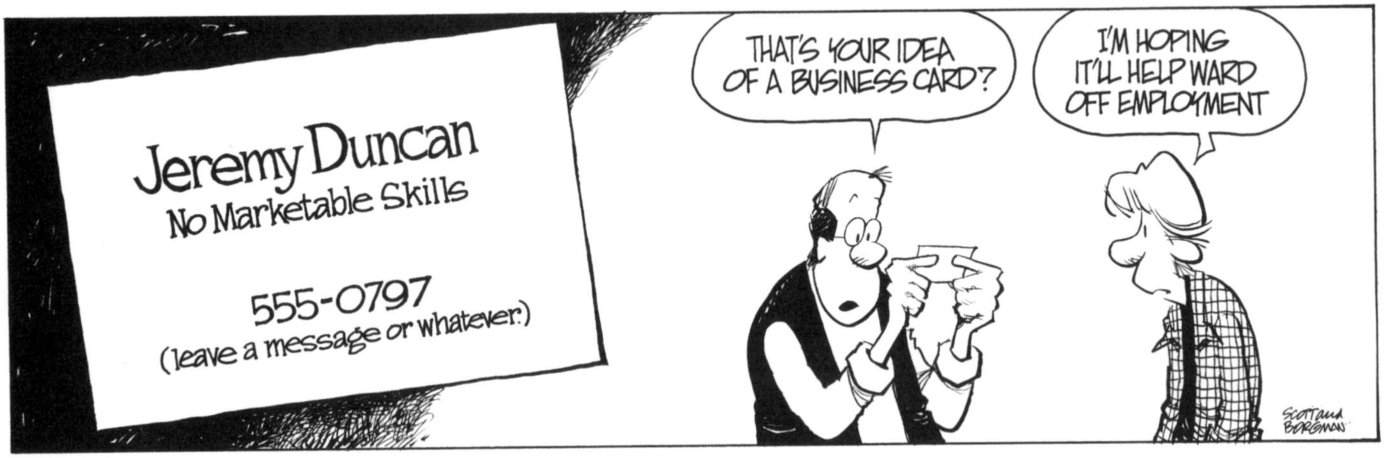
Jeremy Duncan
No Marketable Skills
555-0797
(leave a message or whatever.)
THAT'S YOUR IDEA OF A BUSINESS CARD?
I'M HOPING IT'LL HELP WARD OFF EMPLOYMENT

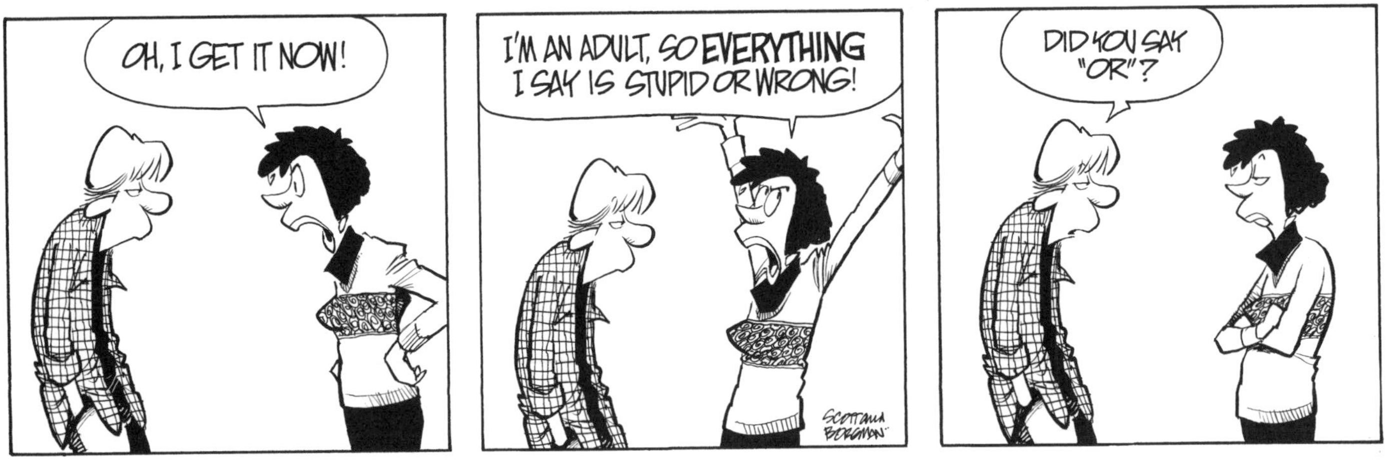
OH, I GET IT NOW!
I'M AN ADULT, SO EVERYTHING I SAY IS STUPID OR WRONG!
DID YOU SAY "OR"?

Zits
by
JERRY SCOTT and JIM BORGMAN

'MORNING, DEAR
GOOD MORNING
YAWN!
I WAS THINKING ABOUT MAKING BACON AND EGGS THIS MORNING. DOES THAT SOUND GOOD?
YOU BET!
NOTHING STARTS THE DAY OUT RIGHT LIKE INGESTING A COUPLE OF UNBORN CHICKENS AND A PILE OF MOLECULARLY-ALTERED PIG FAT.
GULP!
MUNCH! MUNCH! MUNCH!
I THINK FIRST PERIOD BIOLOGY IS RUINING JEREMY'S APPETITE.
CAN I HAVE MY UNBORN CHICKENS SCRAMBLED?

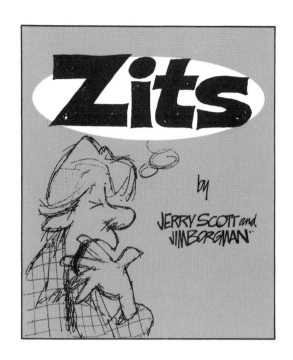

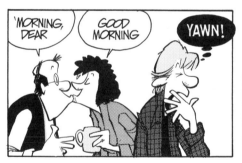

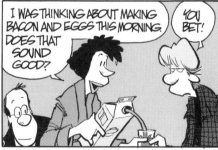

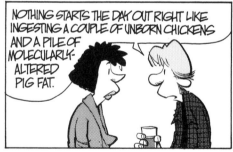

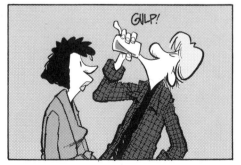

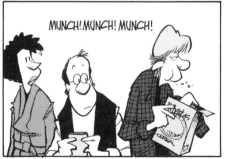

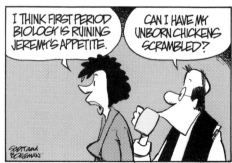

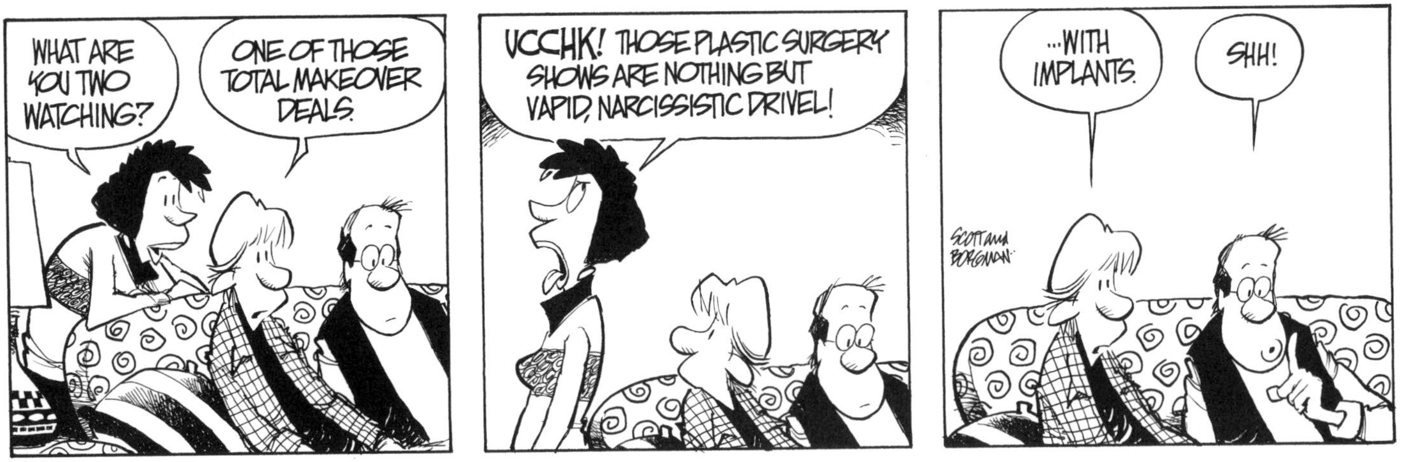
WHAT ARE YOU TWO WATCHING?
ONE OF THOSE TOTAL MAKEOVER DEALS.
UCCHK! THOSE PLASTIC SURGERY SHOWS ARE NOTHING BUT VAPID, NARCISSISTIC DRIVEL!
...WITH IMPLANTS.
SHH!
SCOTT and BORGMAN

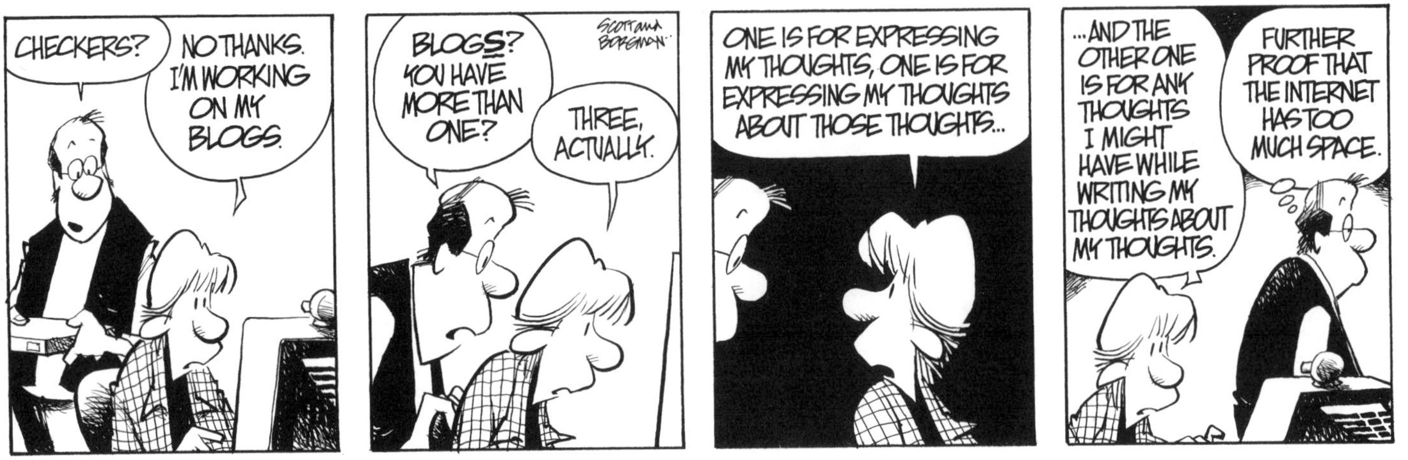
CHECKERS?
NO THANKS. I'M WORKING ON MY BLOGS.
BLOGS? YOU HAVE MORE THAN ONE?
THREE, ACTUALLY.
SCOTT and BORGMAN
ONE IS FOR EXPRESSING MY THOUGHTS, ONE IS FOR EXPRESSING MY THOUGHTS ABOUT THOSE THOUGHTS...
...AND THE OTHER ONE IS FOR ANY THOUGHTS I MIGHT HAVE WHILE WRITING MY THOUGHTS ABOUT MY THOUGHTS.
FURTHER PROOF THAT THE INTERNET HAS TOO MUCH SPACE.

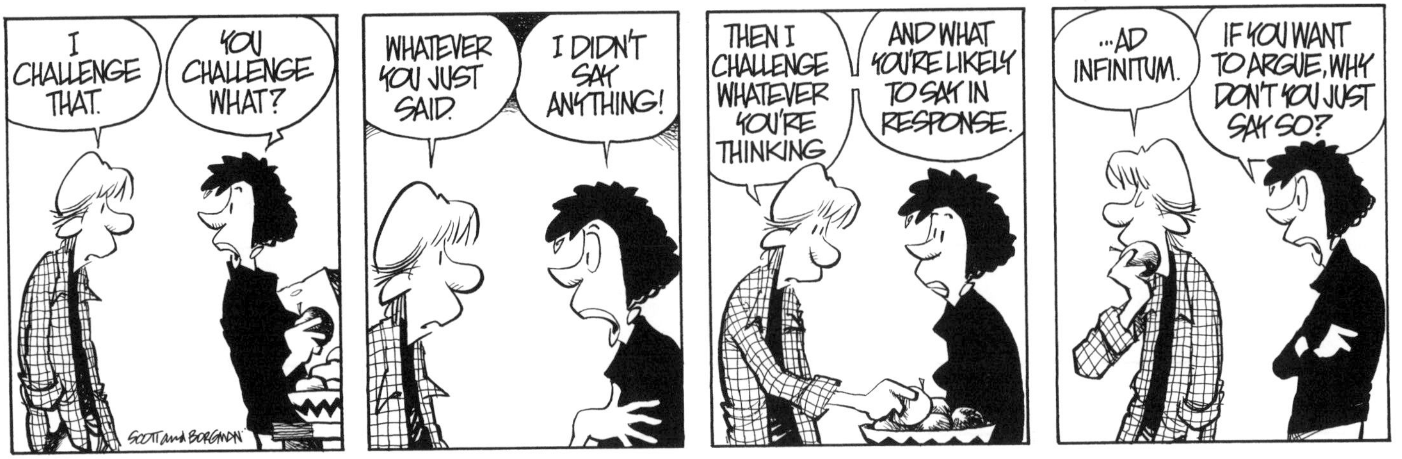
I CHALLENGE THAT.
YOU CHALLENGE WHAT?
SCOTT and BORGMAN
WHATEVER YOU JUST SAID.
I DIDN'T SAY ANYTHING!
THEN I CHALLENGE WHATEVER YOU'RE THINKING
AND WHAT YOU'RE LIKELY TO SAY IN RESPONSE.
...AD INFINITUM.
IF YOU WANT TO ARGUE, WHY DON'T YOU JUST SAY SO?

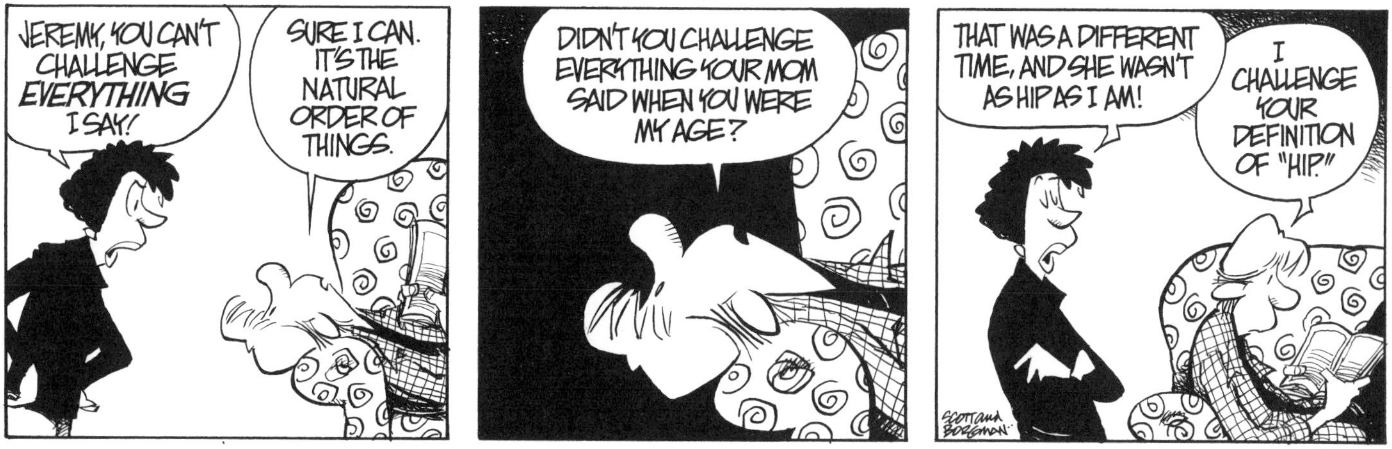
JEREMY, YOU CAN'T CHALLENGE **EVERYTHING** I SAY!
SURE I CAN. IT'S THE NATURAL ORDER OF THINGS.
DIDN'T YOU CHALLENGE EVERYTHING YOUR MOM SAID WHEN YOU WERE MY AGE?
THAT WAS A DIFFERENT TIME, AND SHE WASN'T AS HIP AS I AM!
I CHALLENGE YOUR DEFINITION OF "HIP."

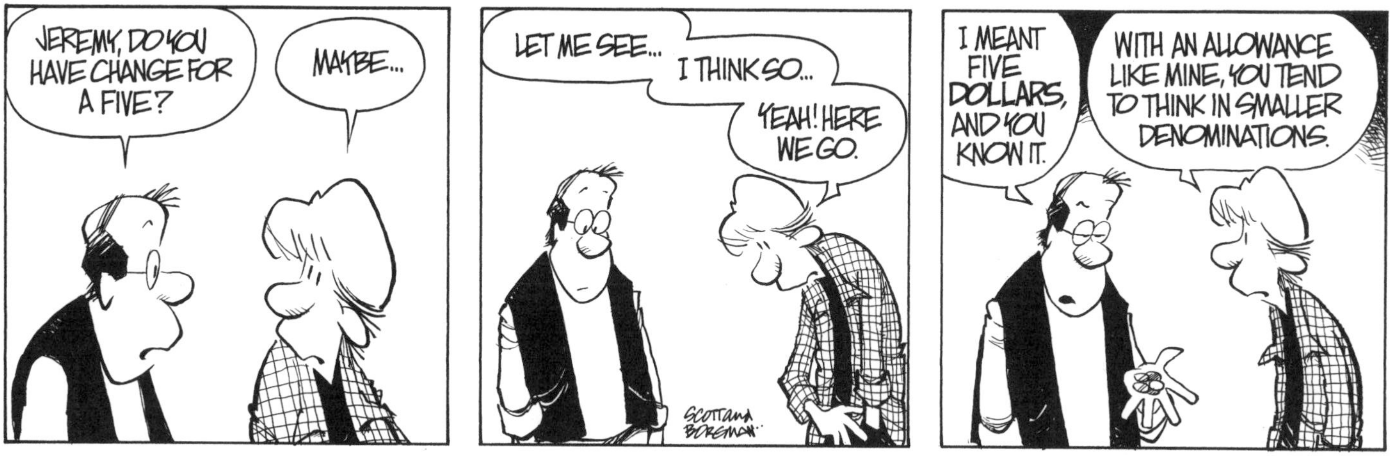
JEREMY, DO YOU HAVE CHANGE FOR A FIVE?
MAYBE...
LET ME SEE...
I THINK SO...
YEAH! HERE WE GO.
I MEANT FIVE **DOLLARS**, AND YOU KNOW IT.
WITH AN ALLOWANCE LIKE MINE, YOU TEND TO THINK IN SMALLER DENOMINATIONS.

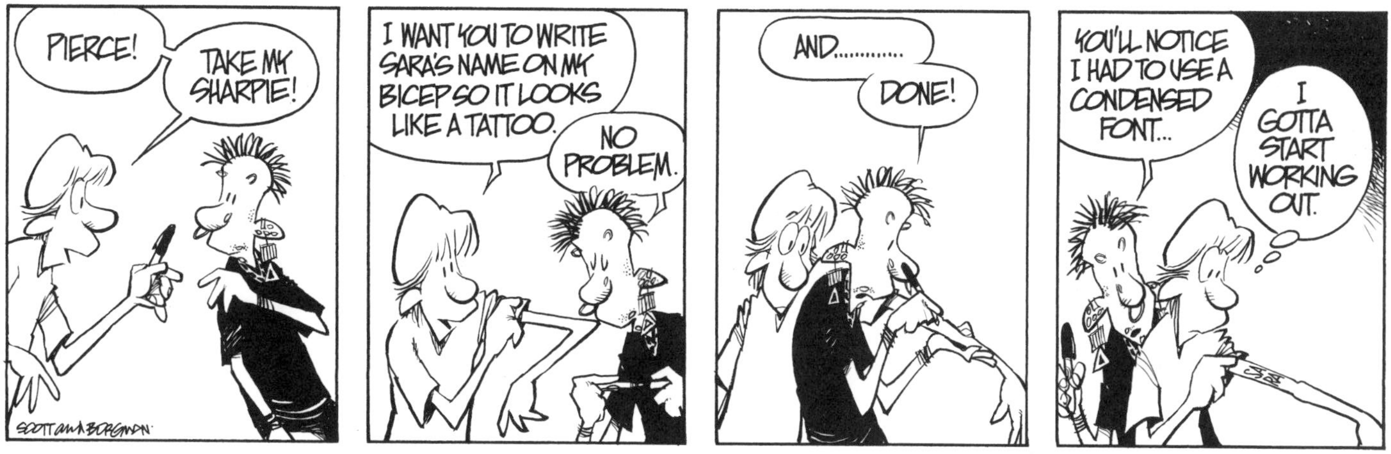
PIERCE!
TAKE MY SHARPIE!
I WANT YOU TO WRITE SARA'S NAME ON MY BICEP SO IT LOOKS LIKE A TATTOO.
NO PROBLEM.
AND............
DONE!
YOU'LL NOTICE I HAD TO USE A CONDENSED FONT...
I GOTTA START WORKING OUT.

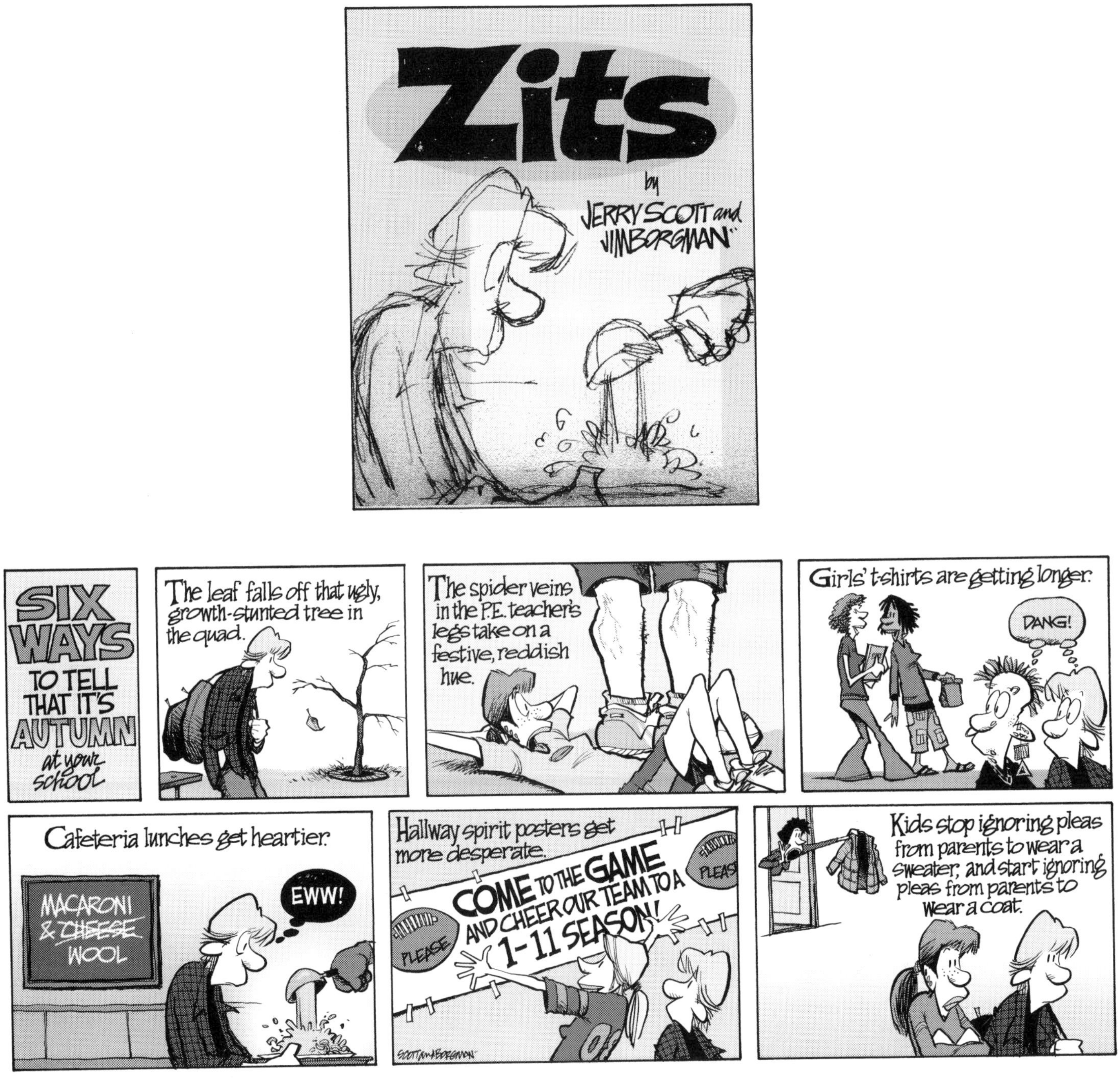
Zits
by
JERRY SCOTT and
JIM BORGMAN
SIX WAYS TO TELL THAT IT'S AUTUMN at your school
The leaf falls off that ugly, growth-stunted tree in the quad.
The spider veins in the P.E. teacher's legs take on a festive, reddish hue.
Girls' t-shirts are getting longer.
DANG!
Cafeteria lunches get heartier.
MACARONI & CHEESE WOOL
EWW!
Hallway spirit posters get more desperate.
COME TO THE GAME AND CHEER OUR TEAM TO A 1-11 SEASON!
PLEASE
PLEASE
Kids stop ignoring pleas from parents to wear a sweater, and start ignoring pleas from parents to wear a coat.

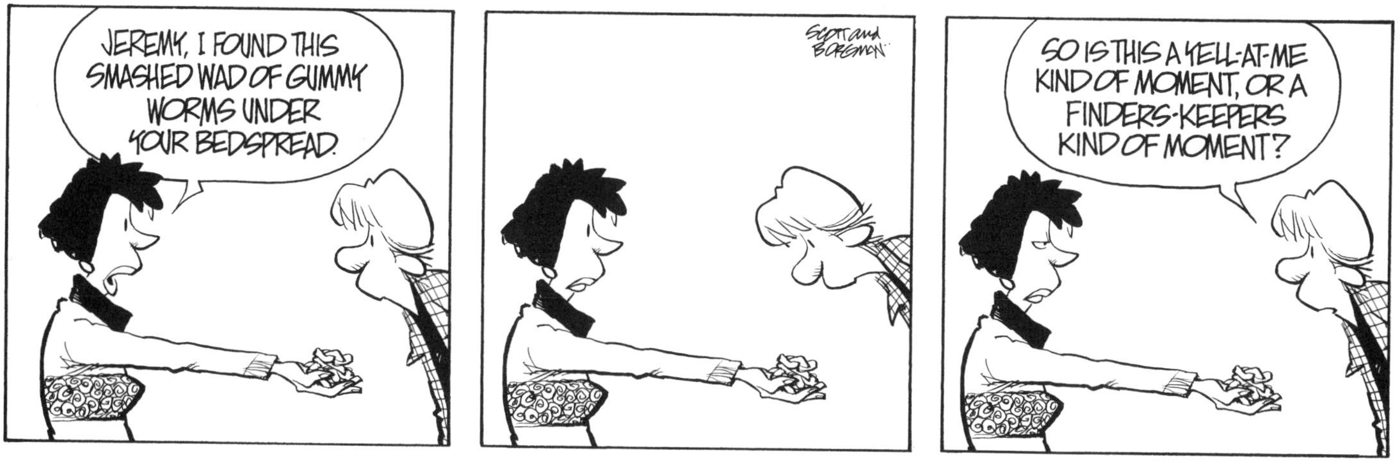
JEREMY, I FOUND THIS SMASHED WAD OF GUMMY WORMS UNDER YOUR BEDSPREAD.
SCOTT and BORGMAN
SO IS THIS A YELL-AT-ME KIND OF MOMENT, OR A FINDERS-KEEPERS KIND OF MOMENT?

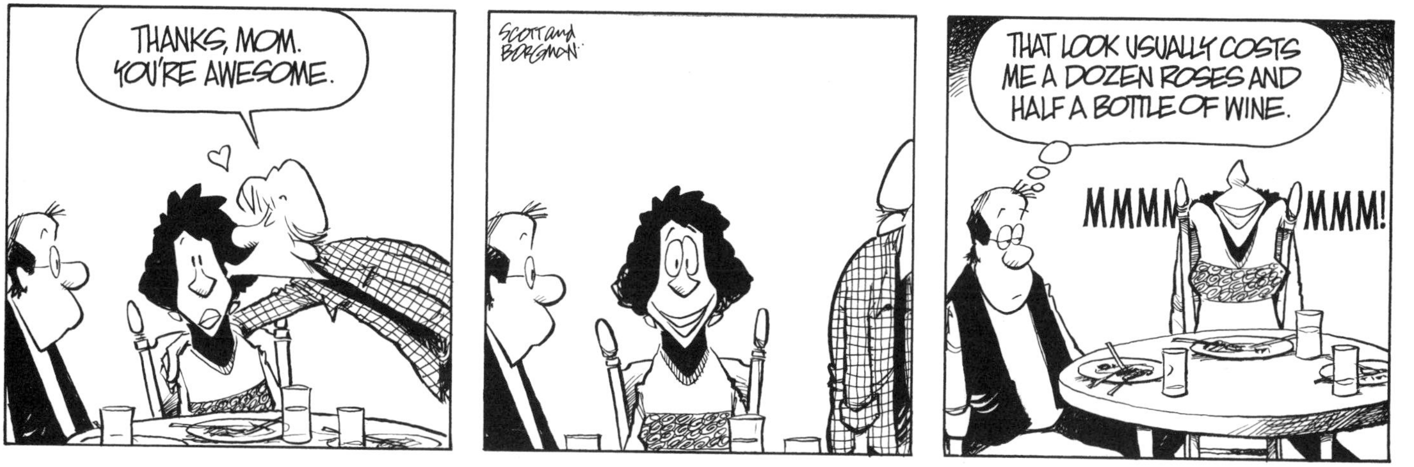
THANKS, MOM. YOU'RE AWESOME.
SCOTT and BORGMAN
THAT LOOK USUALLY COSTS ME A DOZEN ROSES AND HALF A BOTTLE OF WINE.
MMMM
MMM!

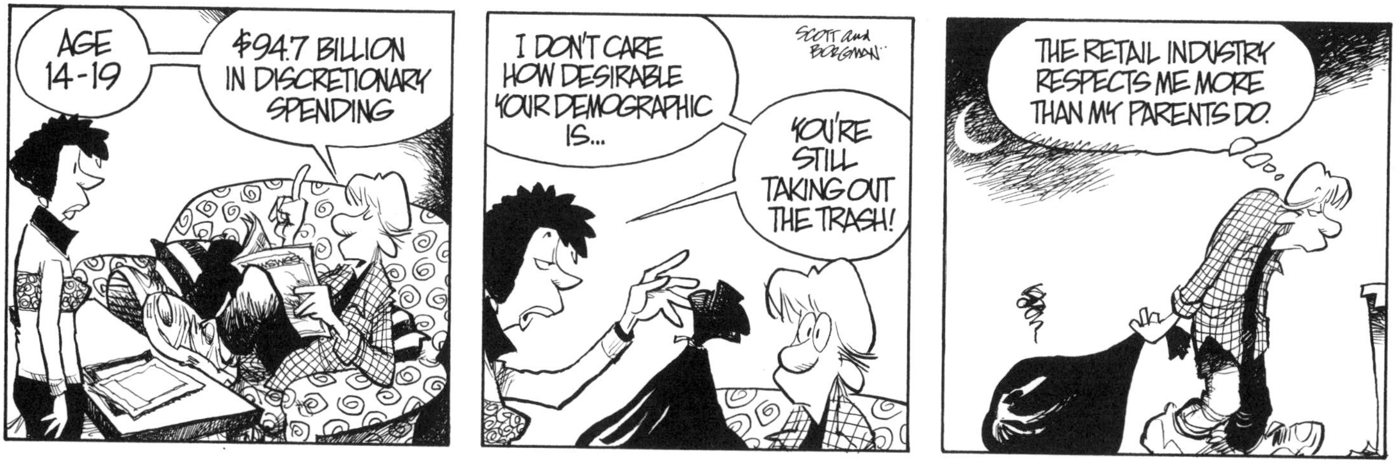
AGE 14-19
$94.7 BILLION IN DISCRETIONARY SPENDING
I DON'T CARE HOW DESIRABLE YOUR DEMOGRAPHIC IS...
YOU'RE STILL TAKING OUT THE TRASH!
SCOTT and BORGMAN
THE RETAIL INDUSTRY RESPECTS ME MORE THAN MY PARENTS DO.

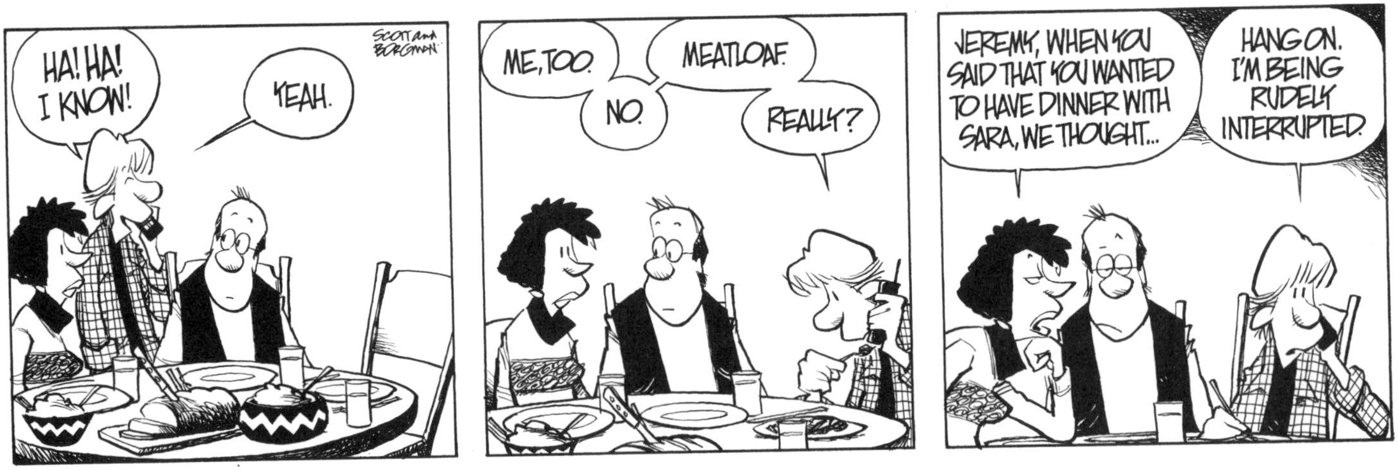
HA! HA! I KNOW!
YEAH.
ME, TOO.
NO.
MEATLOAF.
REALLY?
JEREMY, WHEN YOU SAID THAT YOU WANTED TO HAVE DINNER WITH SARA, WE THOUGHT...
HANG ON. I'M BEING RUDELY INTERRUPTED.

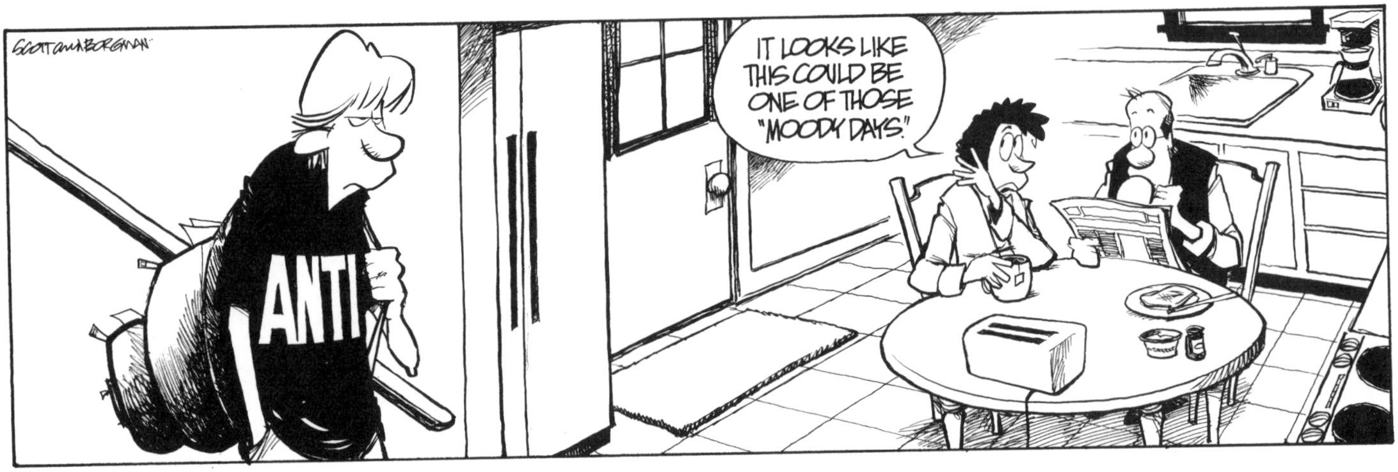
ANTI
IT LOOKS LIKE THIS COULD BE ONE OF THOSE "MOODY DAYS."

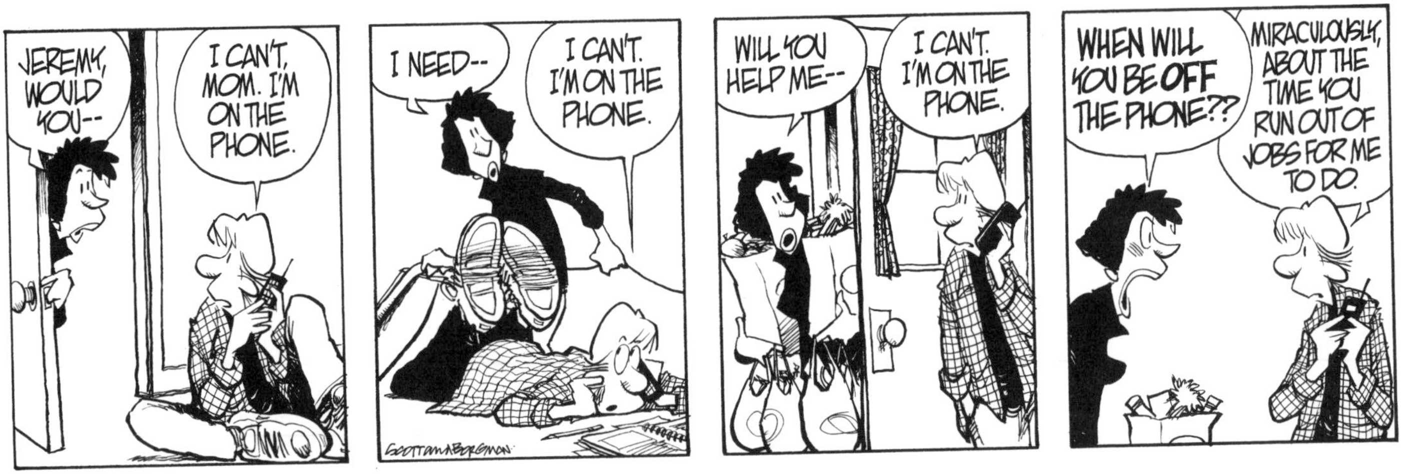
JEREMY, WOULD YOU--
I CAN'T, MOM. I'M ON THE PHONE.
I NEED--
I CAN'T. I'M ON THE PHONE.
WILL YOU HELP ME--
I CAN'T. I'M ON THE PHONE.
WHEN WILL YOU BE OFF THE PHONE??
MIRACULOUSLY, ABOUT THE TIME YOU RUN OUT OF JOBS FOR ME TO DO.

Zits

by JERRY SCOTT and JIM BORGMAN

7 SCARIER THINGS to say on HALLOWEEN than "TRICK OR TREAT" (TEEN EDITION)

IN THREE YEARS I'LL BE GETTING COLLEGE LOANS SUBSIDIZED BY YOUR TAX DOLLARS.

AAAGH!

I'M WORKING UP THE COURAGE TO ASK YOUR DAUGHTER OUT.

YEEEP!

REALLY? ME, TOO.

HE JUST GOT HIS DRIVER'S PERMIT.

YAAAHH!

PEOPLE MY AGE BASICALLY CONTROL WHAT YOU SEE ON TV AND AT THE MOVIES.

NOOO!

WHEN I TURN EIGHTEEN, I MIGHT VOTE.

AAACK!

YOUR FUTURE SOCIAL SECURITY CHECK DEPENDS ON US LANDING HIGH-PAYING JOBS.

GASP!

TWO WORDS: BOOMERANG GENERATION

TAKE IT ALL!

NOW GO AWAY!

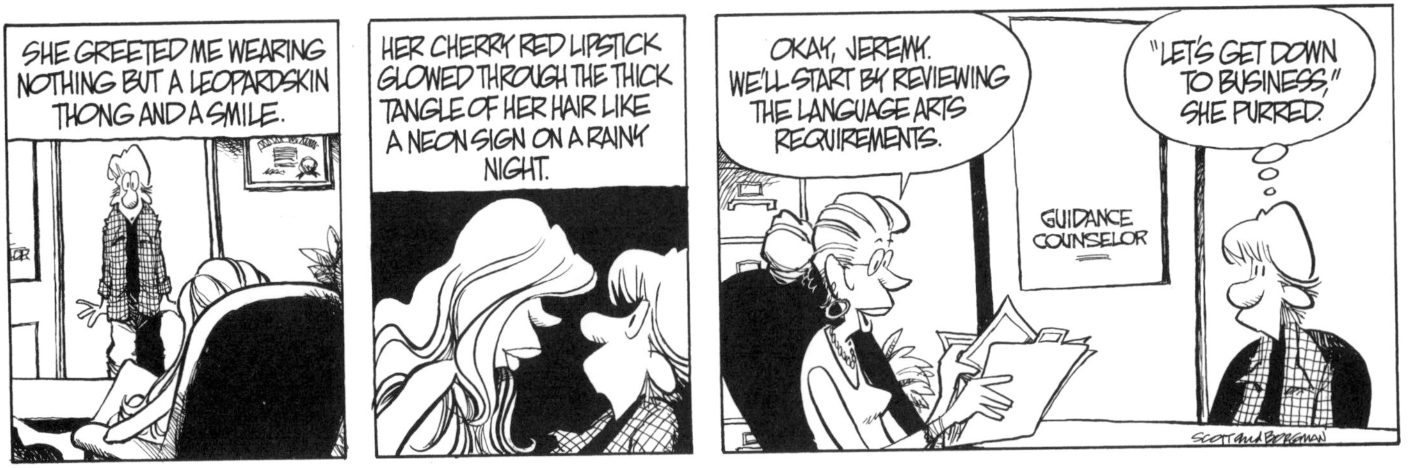
SHE GREETED ME WEARING NOTHING BUT A LEOPARDSKIN THONG AND A SMILE.
HER CHERRY RED LIPSTICK GLOWED THROUGH THE THICK TANGLE OF HER HAIR LIKE A NEON SIGN ON A RAINY NIGHT.
OKAY, JEREMY. WE'LL START BY REVIEWING THE LANGUAGE ARTS REQUIREMENTS.
GUIDANCE COUNSELOR
"LET'S GET DOWN TO BUSINESS," SHE PURRED.
SCOTT and BORGMAN

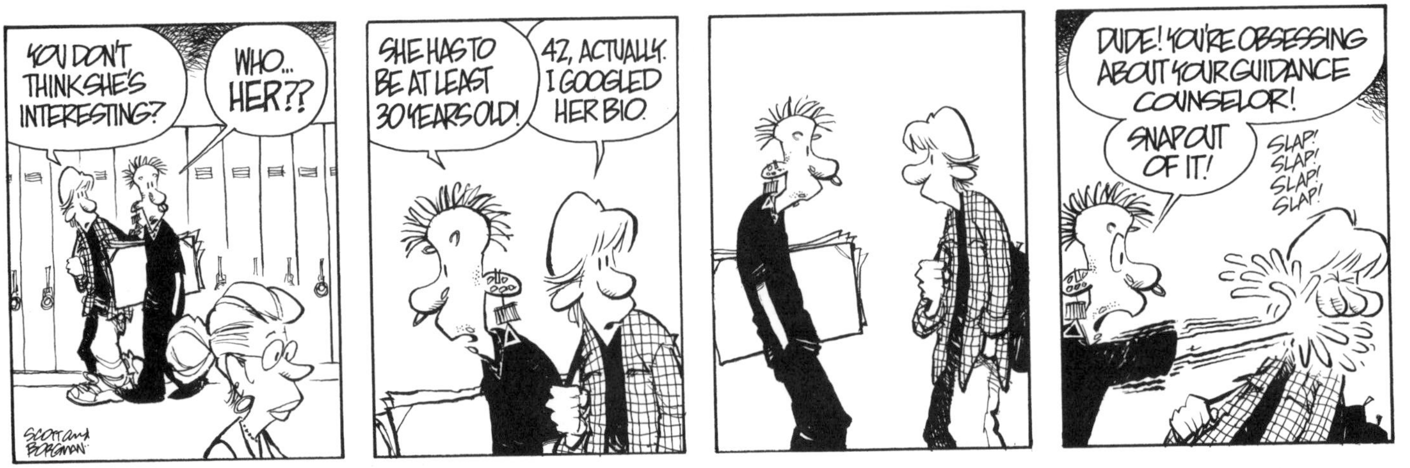
YOU DON'T THINK SHE'S INTERESTING?
WHO... HER??
SCOTT and BORGMAN
SHE HAS TO BE AT LEAST 30 YEARS OLD!
42, ACTUALLY. I GOOGLED HER BIO.
DUDE! YOU'RE OBSESSING ABOUT YOUR GUIDANCE COUNSELOR!
SNAP OUT OF IT!
SLAP! SLAP! SLAP! SLAP!

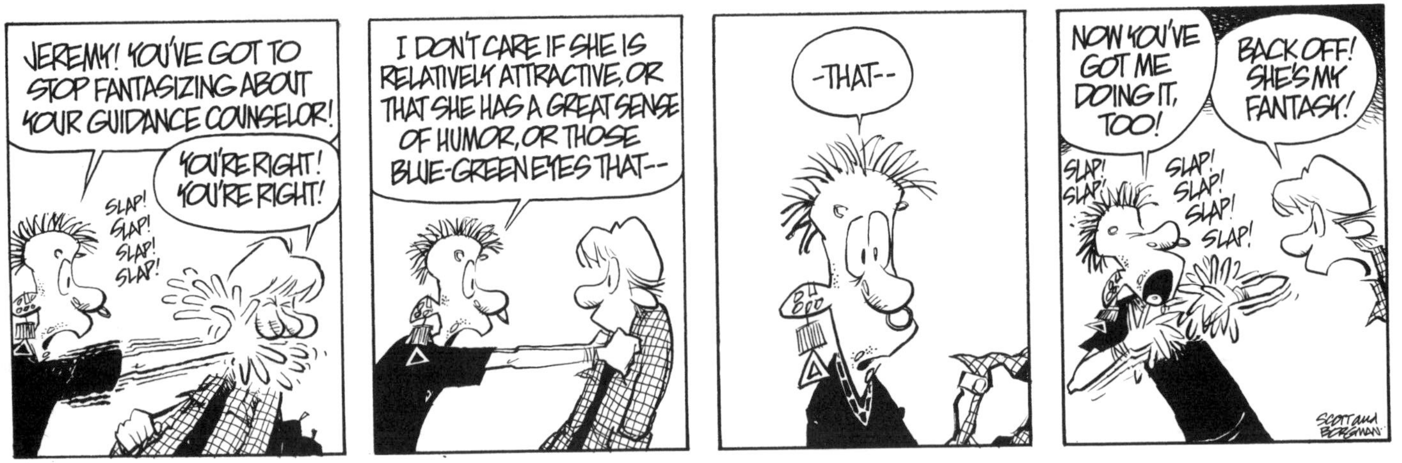
JEREMY! YOU'VE GOT TO STOP FANTASIZING ABOUT YOUR GUIDANCE COUNSELOR!
SLAP! SLAP! SLAP! SLAP!
YOU'RE RIGHT! YOU'RE RIGHT!
I DON'T CARE IF SHE IS RELATIVELY ATTRACTIVE, OR THAT SHE HAS A GREAT SENSE OF HUMOR, OR THOSE BLUE-GREEN EYES THAT--
-THAT--
NOW YOU'VE GOT ME DOING IT, TOO!
SLAP! SLAP!
SLAP! SLAP! SLAP! SLAP!
BACK OFF! SHE'S MY FANTASY!
SCOTT and BORGMAN

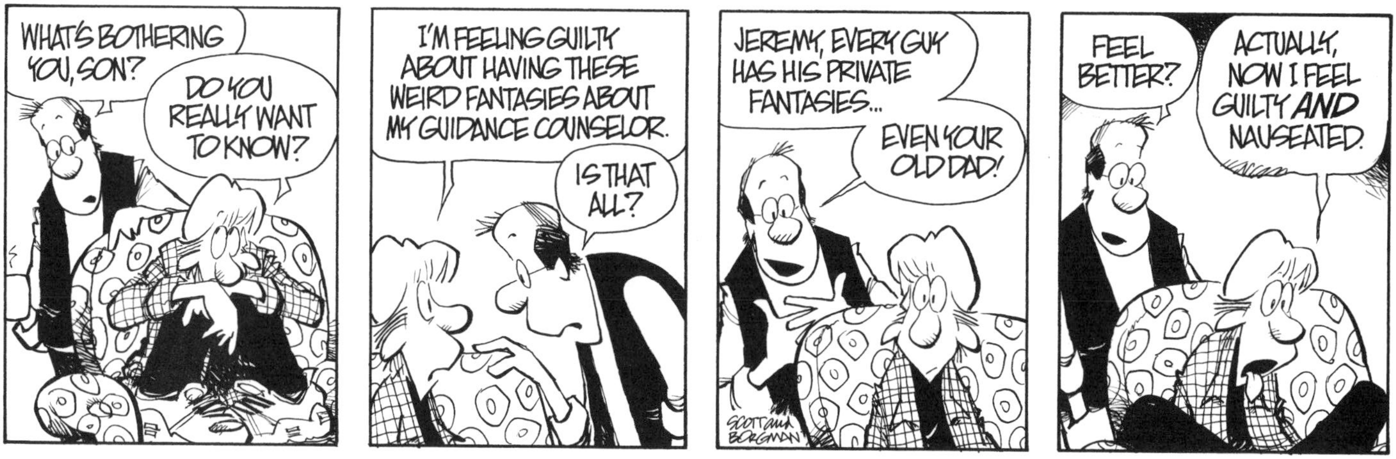
WHAT'S BOTHERING YOU, SON?
DO YOU REALLY WANT TO KNOW?
I'M FEELING GUILTY ABOUT HAVING THESE WEIRD FANTASIES ABOUT MY GUIDANCE COUNSELOR.
IS THAT ALL?
JEREMY, EVERY GUY HAS HIS PRIVATE FANTASIES...
EVEN YOUR OLD DAD!
SCOTT and BORGMAN
FEEL BETTER?
ACTUALLY, NOW I FEEL GUILTY **AND** NAUSEATED.

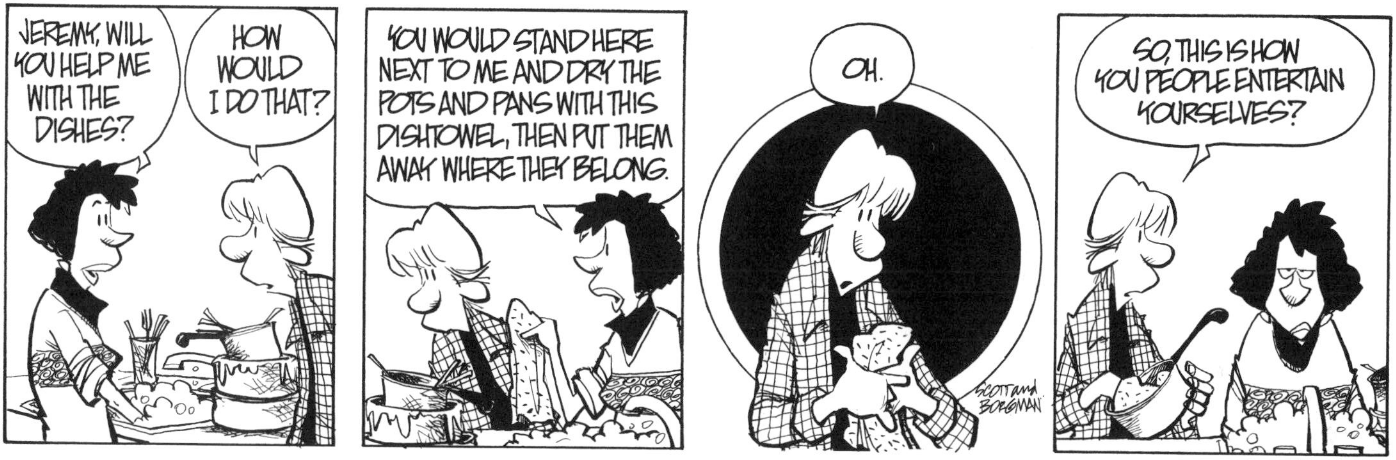
JEREMY, WILL YOU HELP ME WITH THE DISHES?
HOW WOULD I DO THAT?
YOU WOULD STAND HERE NEXT TO ME AND DRY THE POTS AND PANS WITH THIS DISHTOWEL, THEN PUT THEM AWAY WHERE THEY BELONG.
OH.
SCOTT and BORGMAN
SO, THIS IS HOW YOU PEOPLE ENTERTAIN YOURSELVES?

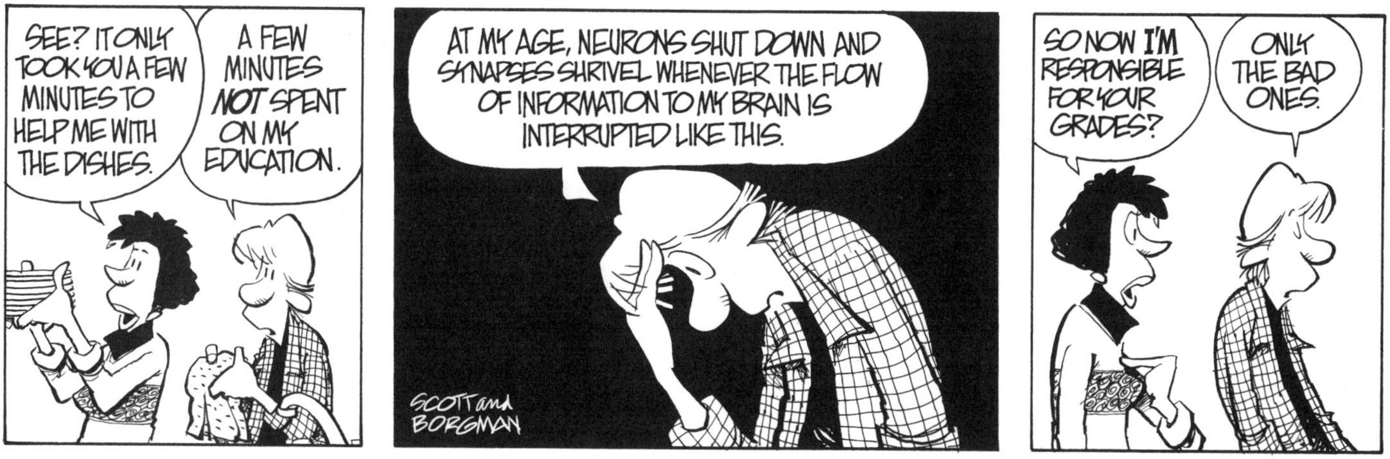
SEE? IT ONLY TOOK YOU A FEW MINUTES TO HELP ME WITH THE DISHES.
A FEW MINUTES **NOT** SPENT ON MY EDUCATION.
AT MY AGE, NEURONS SHUT DOWN AND SYNAPSES SHRIVEL WHENEVER THE FLOW OF INFORMATION TO MY BRAIN IS INTERRUPTED LIKE THIS.
SCOTT and BORGMAN
SO NOW **I'M** RESPONSIBLE FOR YOUR GRADES?
ONLY THE BAD ONES.

Zits
by JERRY SCOTT and JIM BORGMAN

JEREMY? IT'S TIME TO GET UP...
TAP! TAP!
Z
JEREMY!
IT'S 7:15
KNOCK! KNOCK!
Z
RISE AND SHINE!
KNOCK! KNOCK! KNOCK! KNOCK! KNOCK!
Z
LET'S GO! LET'S GO!
BAM! BAM! BAM!
Z
KRASH!
Z
GET UP!
I DON'T MEAN TO BE CRITICAL, BUT IF YOU'D GET ME UP EARLIER, WE WOULDN'T HAVE TO RACE TO SCHOOL LIKE THIS EVERY DAY.

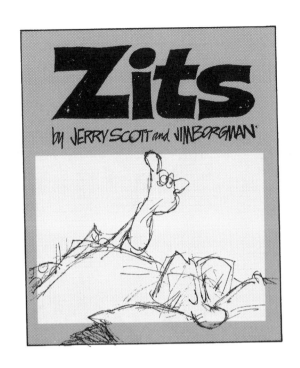

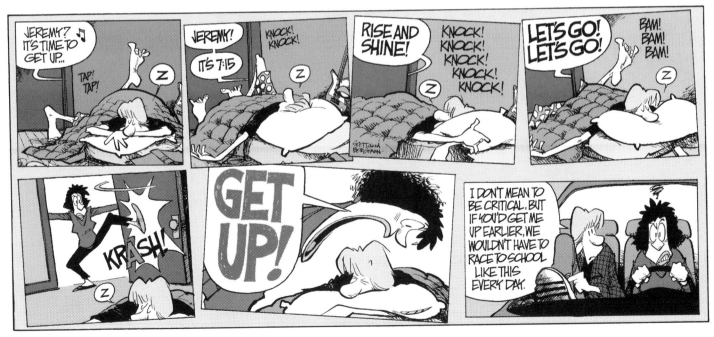

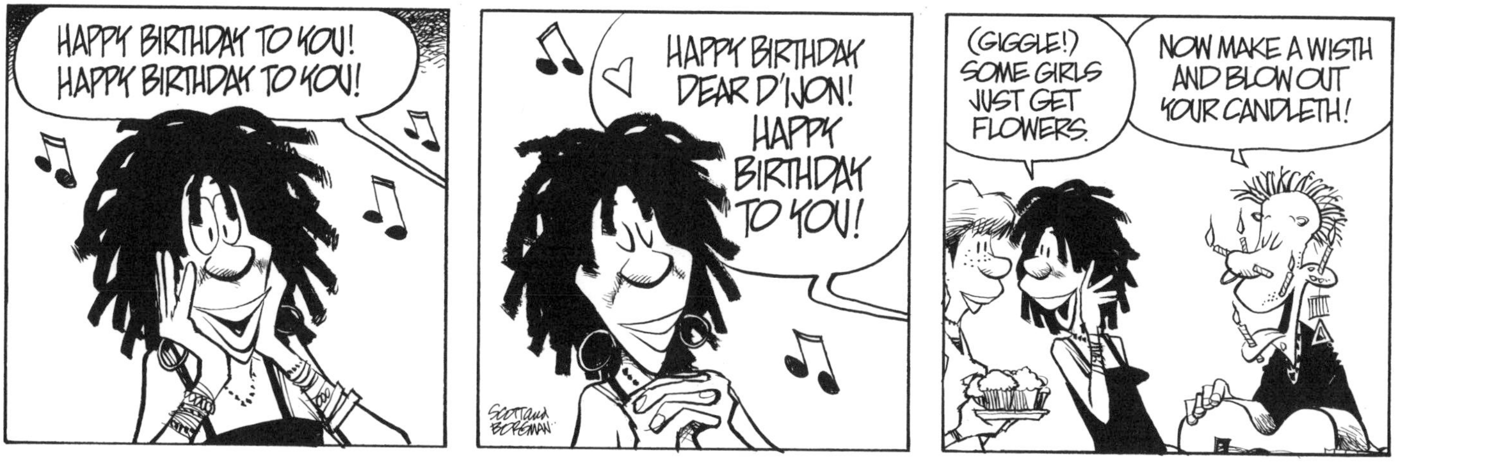
HAPPY BIRTHDAY TO YOU! HAPPY BIRTHDAY TO YOU!
HAPPY BIRTHDAY DEAR D'IJON! HAPPY BIRTHDAY TO YOU!
(GIGGLE!) SOME GIRLS JUST GET FLOWERS.
NOW MAKE A WISTH AND BLOW OUT YOUR CANDLETH!

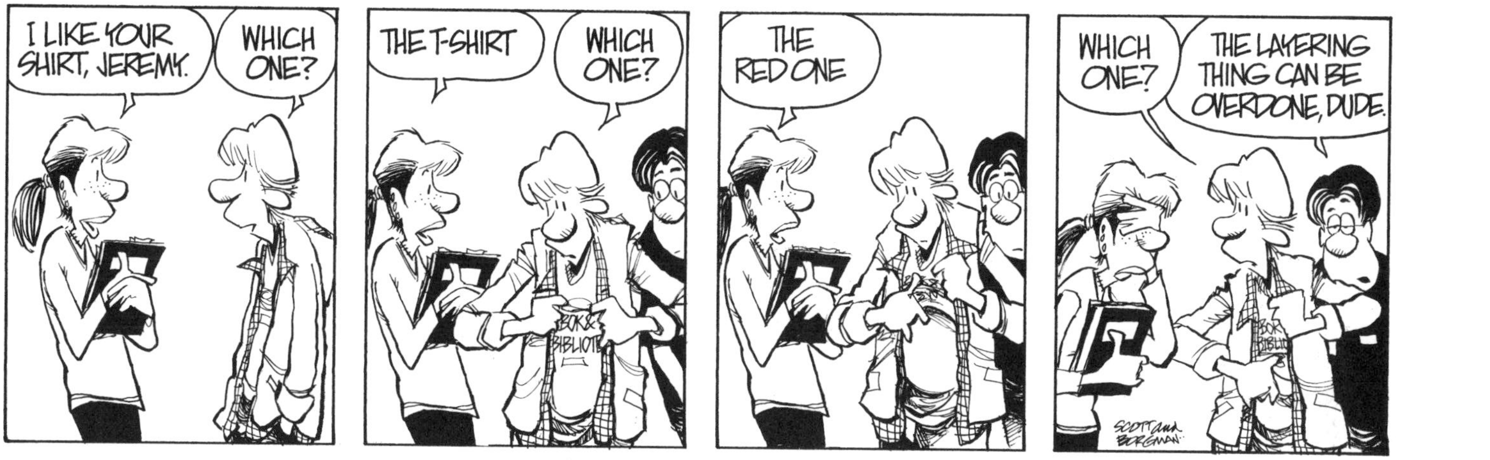
I LIKE YOUR SHIRT, JEREMY.
WHICH ONE?
THE T-SHIRT
WHICH ONE?
THE RED ONE
WHICH ONE?
THE LAYERING THING CAN BE OVERDONE, DUDE.

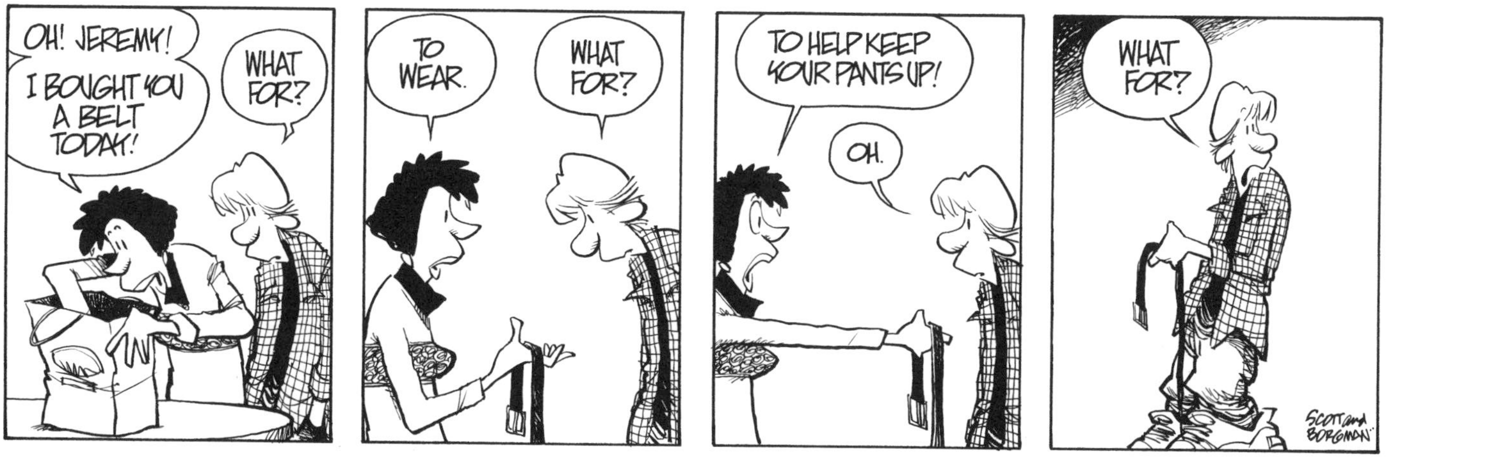
OH! JEREMY!
I BOUGHT YOU A BELT TODAY!
WHAT FOR?
TO WEAR.
WHAT FOR?
TO HELP KEEP YOUR PANTS UP!
OH.
WHAT FOR?

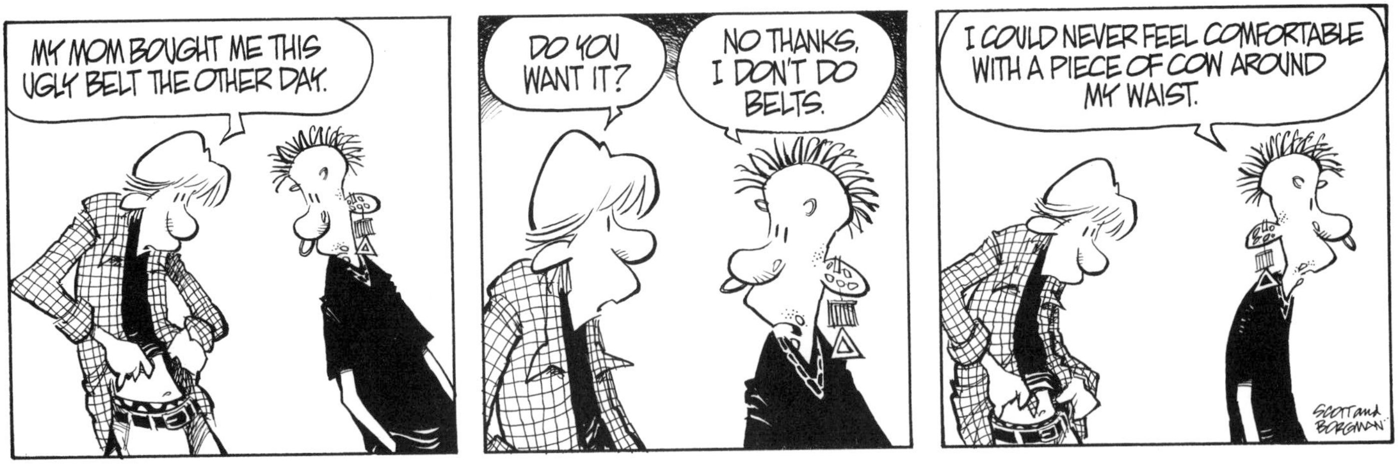
MY MOM BOUGHT ME THIS UGLY BELT THE OTHER DAY.
DO YOU WANT IT?
NO THANKS, I DON'T DO BELTS.
I COULD NEVER FEEL COMFORTABLE WITH A PIECE OF COW AROUND MY WAIST.
SCOTT and BORGMAN

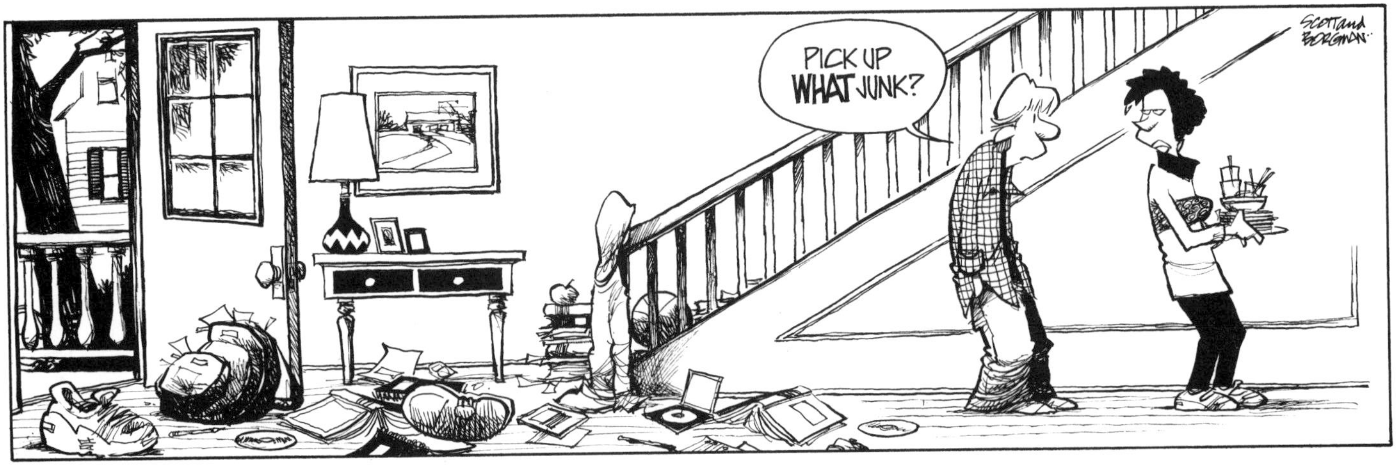
SCOTT and BORGMAN
PICK UP **WHAT** JUNK?

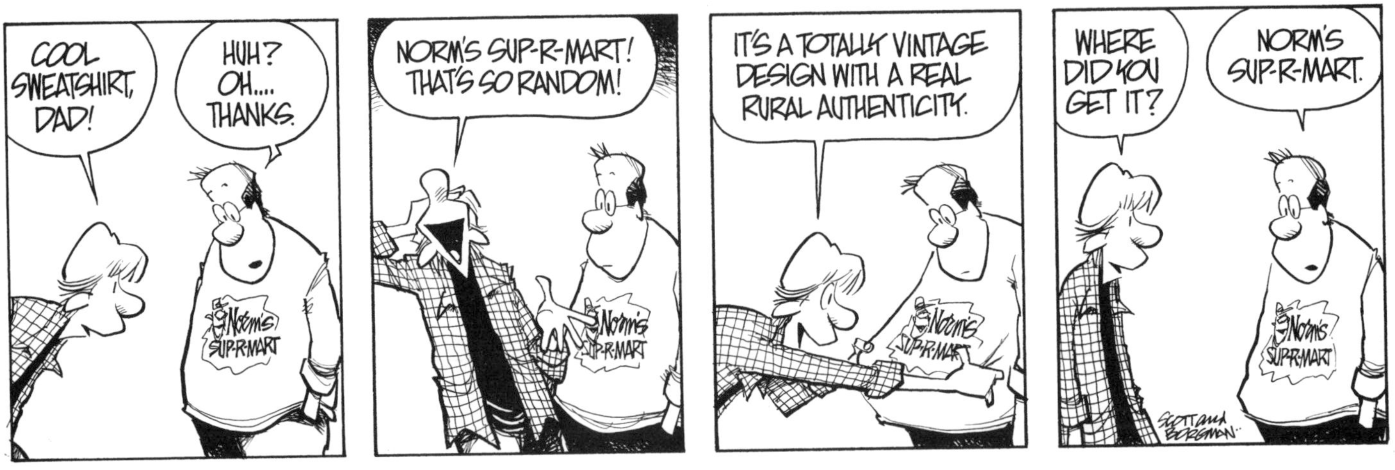
COOL SWEATSHIRT, DAD!
HUH? OH.... THANKS.
Norm's SUP-R-MART
NORM'S SUP-R-MART! THAT'S SO RANDOM!
IT'S A TOTALLY VINTAGE DESIGN WITH A REAL RURAL AUTHENTICITY.
SCOTT and BORGMAN
WHERE DID YOU GET IT?
NORM'S SUP-R-MART.

Zits
by JERRY SCOTT and JIM BORGMAN

DOINK!
IS HIGH SCHOOL
HEY! HEY!
COME ON, KIDS! WE KNOW YOU'RE TIRED! SLEEP-DEPRIVED AND UNINSPIRED!
BUT TOSS THAT TRASH RESPONSIBLY AND KEEP OUR CAMPUS LITTER-FREE!
SCOTT and BORGMAN
WOO!
YEAH!
YIP! YIP!
IF YOU ASK ME, THERE CAN BE SUCH A THING AS TOO MUCH SCHOOL SPIRIT.

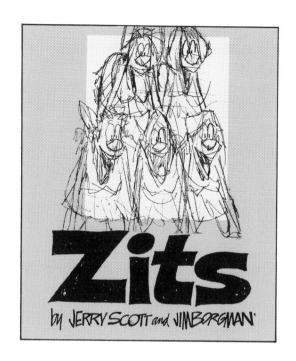

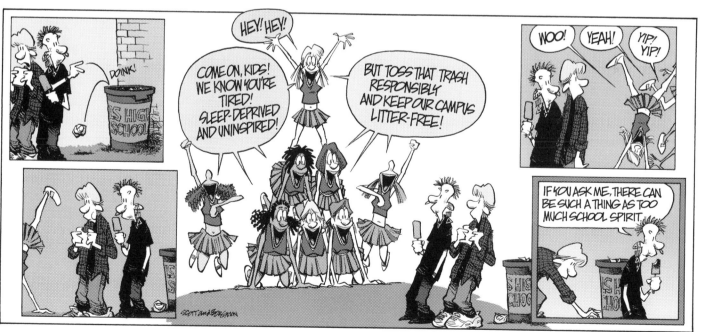

GUESS WHAT!

UH-OH

YOU DON'T HAVE TO LUG THAT HEAVY BACKPACK TO SCHOOL ANYMORE, BECAUSE I BOUGHT YOU **THIS NIFTY ROLLING BACKPACK!**

SCOTT AND BORGMAN

DID I DO GOOD!?

DOES THE TERM "ASSISTED SOCIAL SUICIDE" MEAN ANYTHING TO YOU?

MOM, I CAN'T TAKE A ROLLING BACKPACK TO SCHOOL!

CAN YOU IMAGINE WHAT WOULD HAPPEN IF I START PULLING THAT THING DOWN THE HALLWAY?

SCOTT AND BORGMAN

BETTER POSTURE?

WORSE THAN THAT! I'D BE MOCKED!

JEREMY, YOUR BACKPACK WEIGHS FORTY-THREE POUNDS!

MOM...

WOULDN'T IT MAKE MORE SENSE TO USE THIS CONVENIENT ROLLING BACKPACK INSTEAD OF LUGGING YOUR OLD ONE AROUND ON YOUR SHOULDER?

MOM!

SCOTT AND BORGMAN

NOW, IF IT'S THE FABRIC YOU DON'T LIKE, I COULD SEW A LITTLE SLIPCOVER FOR IT...

WHAT PART OF "ROLLING-BACKPACK-MAKES-YOU-A-DORK" DON'T YOU UNDERSTAND?

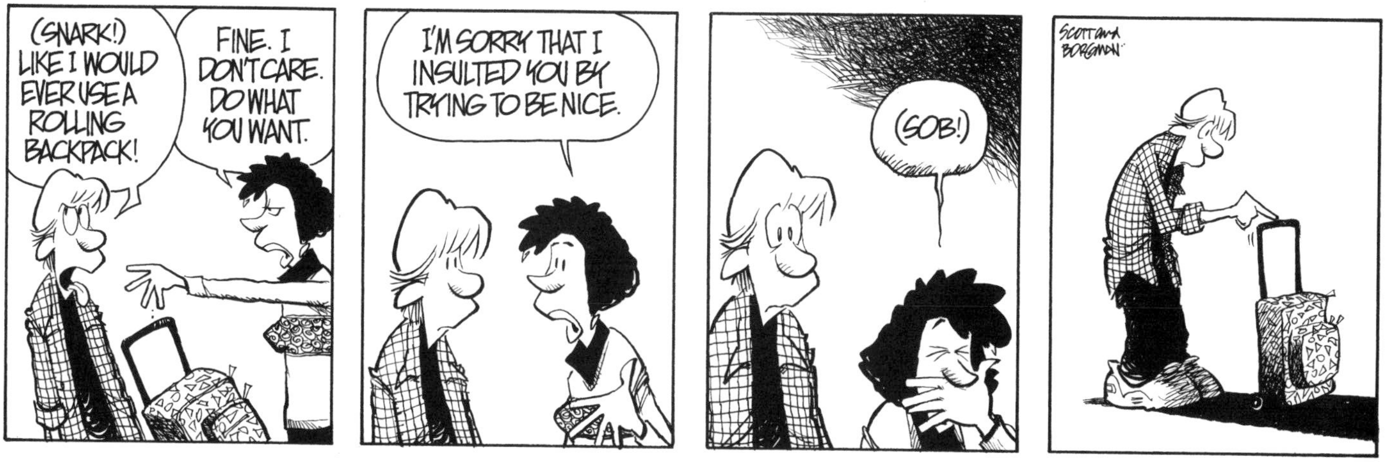
(SNARK!) LIKE I WOULD EVER USE A ROLLING BACKPACK!
FINE. I DON'T CARE. DO WHAT YOU WANT.
I'M SORRY THAT I INSULTED YOU BY TRYING TO BE NICE.
(SOB!)
SCOTT AND BORGMAN

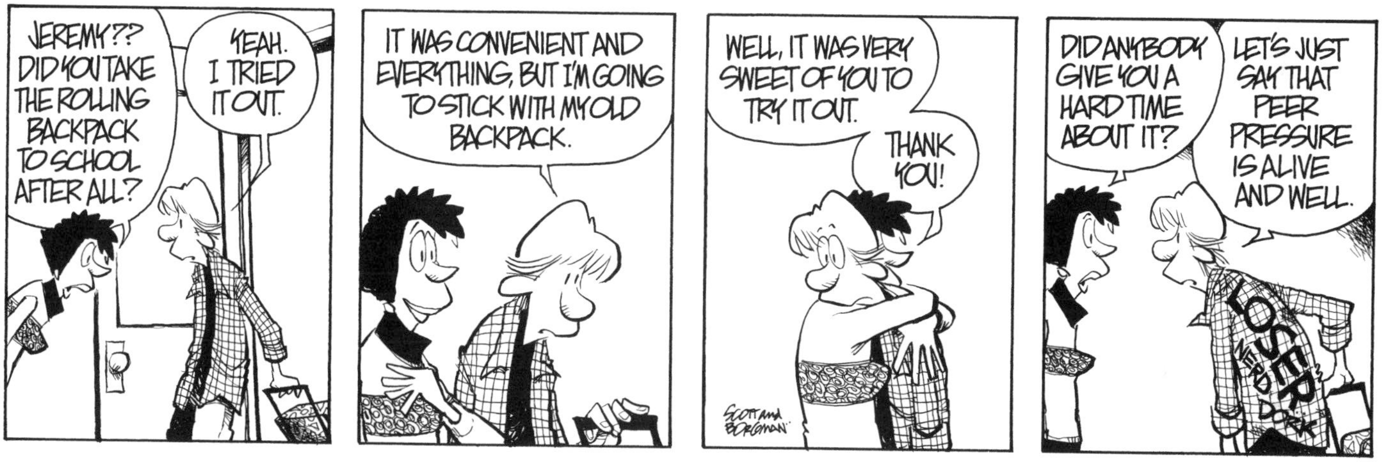
JEREMY?? DID YOU TAKE THE ROLLING BACKPACK TO SCHOOL AFTER ALL?
YEAH. I TRIED IT OUT.
IT WAS CONVENIENT AND EVERYTHING, BUT I'M GOING TO STICK WITH MY OLD BACKPACK.
WELL, IT WAS VERY SWEET OF YOU TO TRY IT OUT.
THANK YOU!
SCOTT AND BORGMAN
DID ANYBODY GIVE YOU A HARD TIME ABOUT IT?
LET'S JUST SAY THAT PEER PRESSURE IS ALIVE AND WELL.
LOSER
NERD
DORK

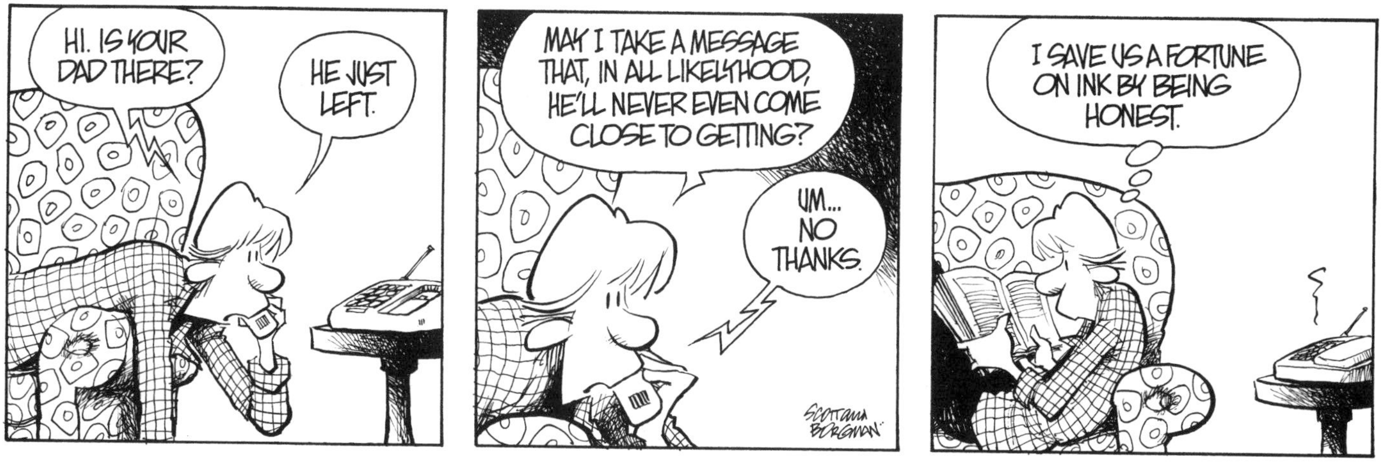
HI. IS YOUR DAD THERE?
HE JUST LEFT.
MAY I TAKE A MESSAGE THAT, IN ALL LIKELYHOOD, HE'LL NEVER EVEN COME CLOSE TO GETTING?
UM... NO THANKS.
SCOTT AND BORGMAN
I SAVE US A FORTUNE ON INK BY BEING HONEST.

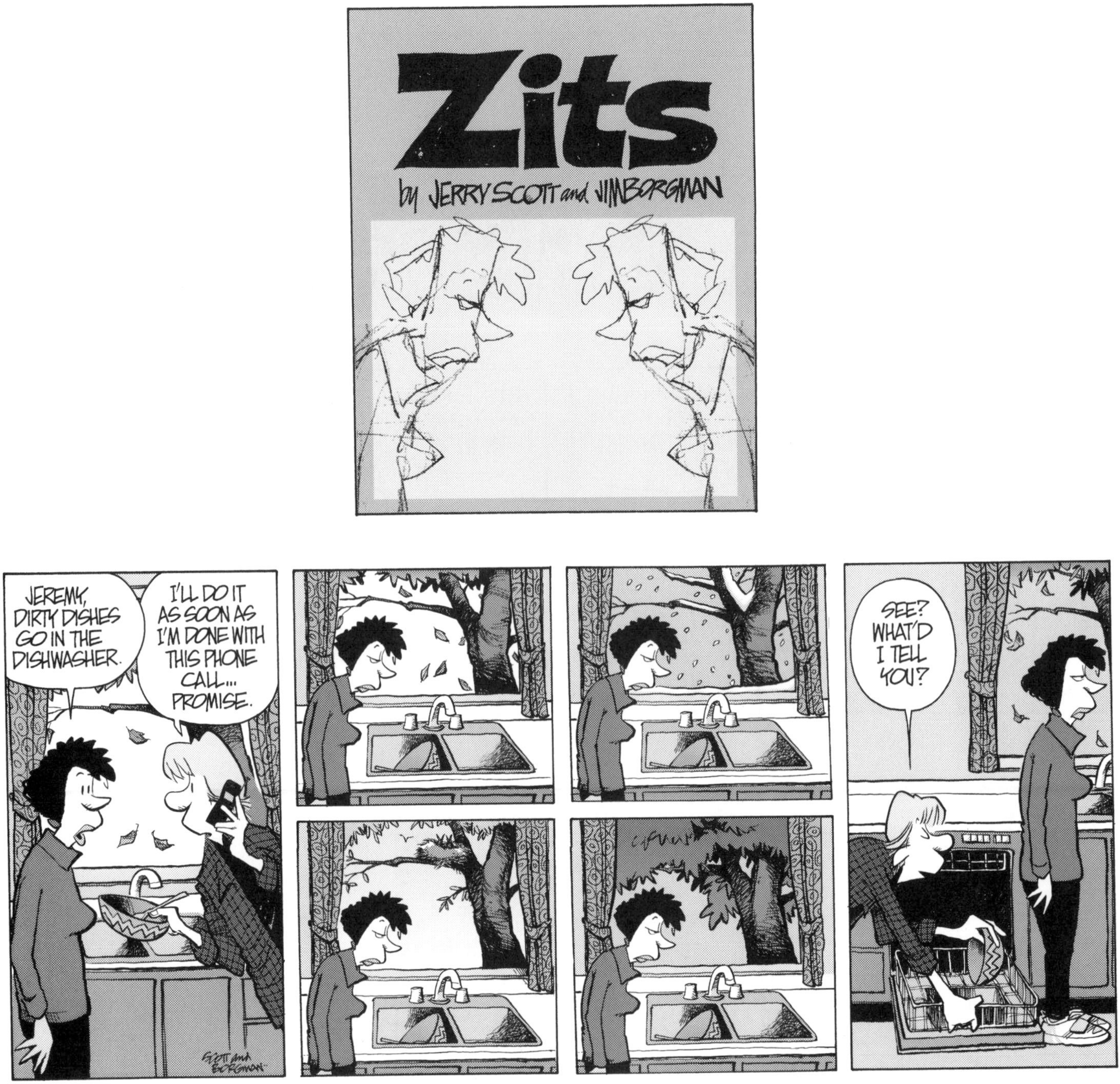
Zits
by JERRY SCOTT and JIM BORGMAN
JEREMY, DIRTY DISHES GO IN THE DISHWASHER.
I'LL DO IT AS SOON AS I'M DONE WITH THIS PHONE CALL... PROMISE.
SEE? WHAT'D I TELL YOU?

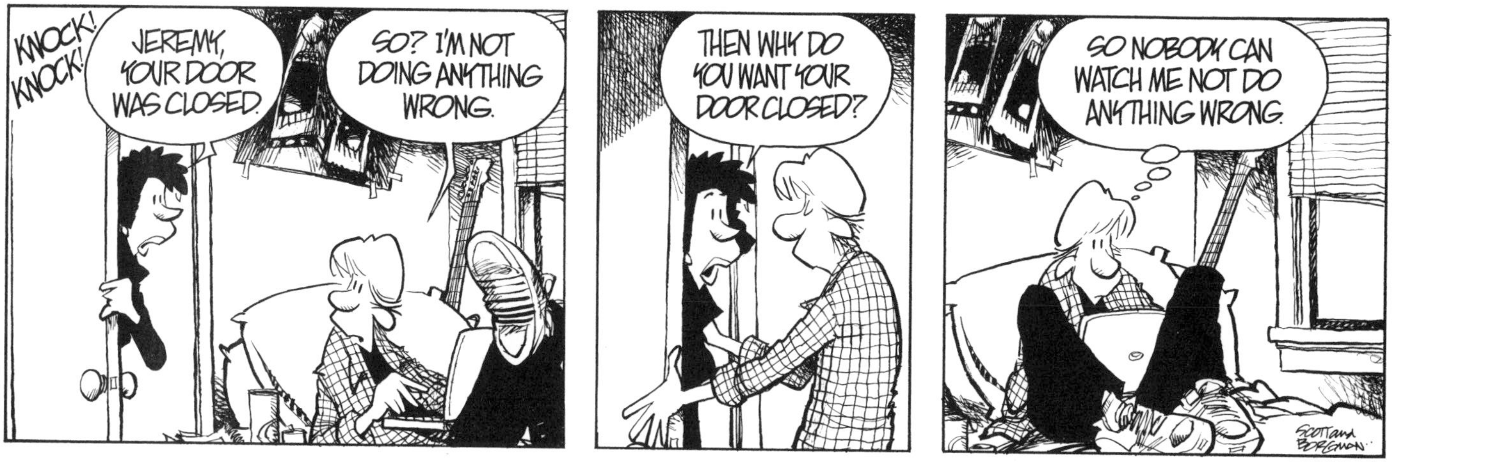
KNOCK! KNOCK!
JEREMY, YOUR DOOR WAS CLOSED.
SO? I'M NOT DOING ANYTHING WRONG.
THEN WHY DO YOU WANT YOUR DOOR CLOSED?
SO NOBODY CAN WATCH ME NOT DO ANYTHING WRONG.

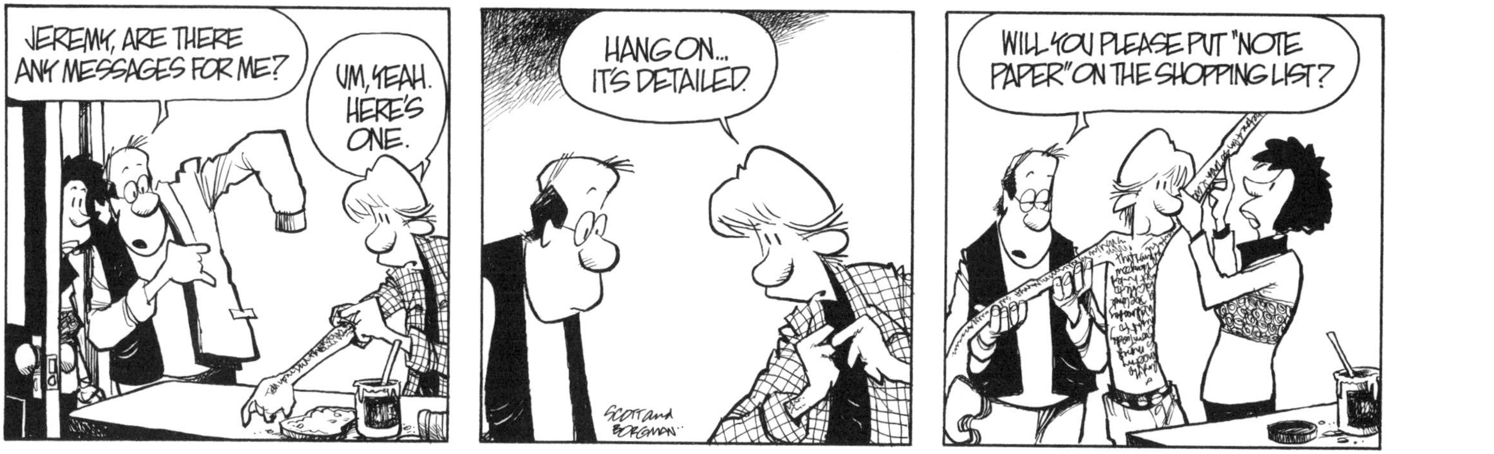
JEREMY, ARE THERE ANY MESSAGES FOR ME?
UM, YEAH. HERE'S ONE.
HANG ON... IT'S DETAILED.
WILL YOU PLEASE PUT "NOTE PAPER" ON THE SHOPPING LIST?

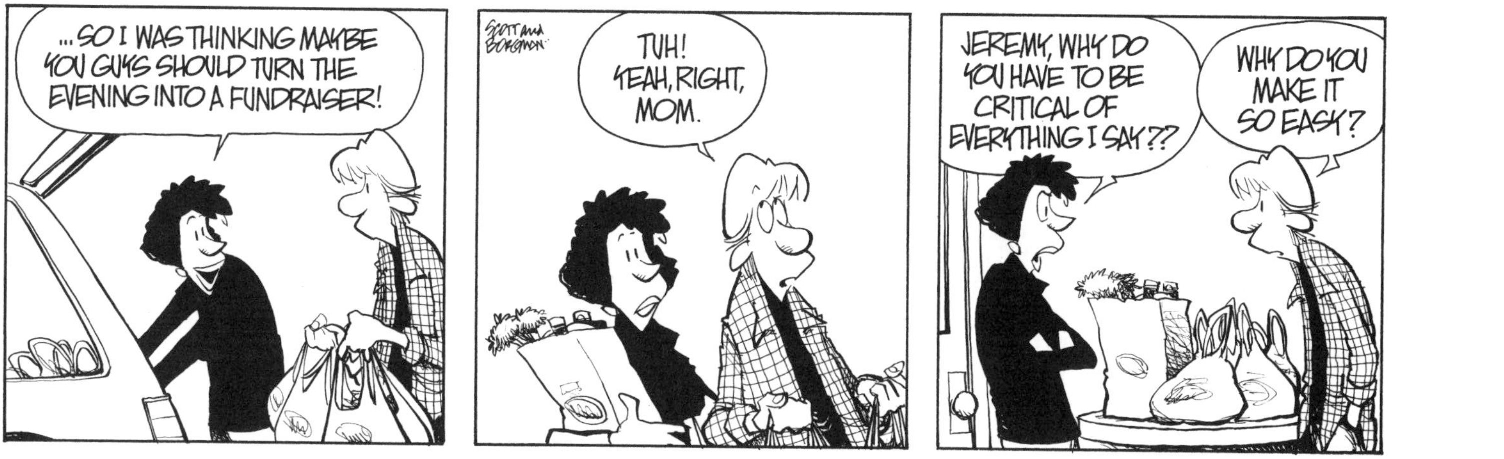
...SO I WAS THINKING MAYBE YOU GUYS SHOULD TURN THE EVENING INTO A FUNDRAISER!
TUH! YEAH, RIGHT, MOM.
JEREMY, WHY DO YOU HAVE TO BE CRITICAL OF EVERYTHING I SAY??
WHY DO YOU MAKE IT SO EASY?

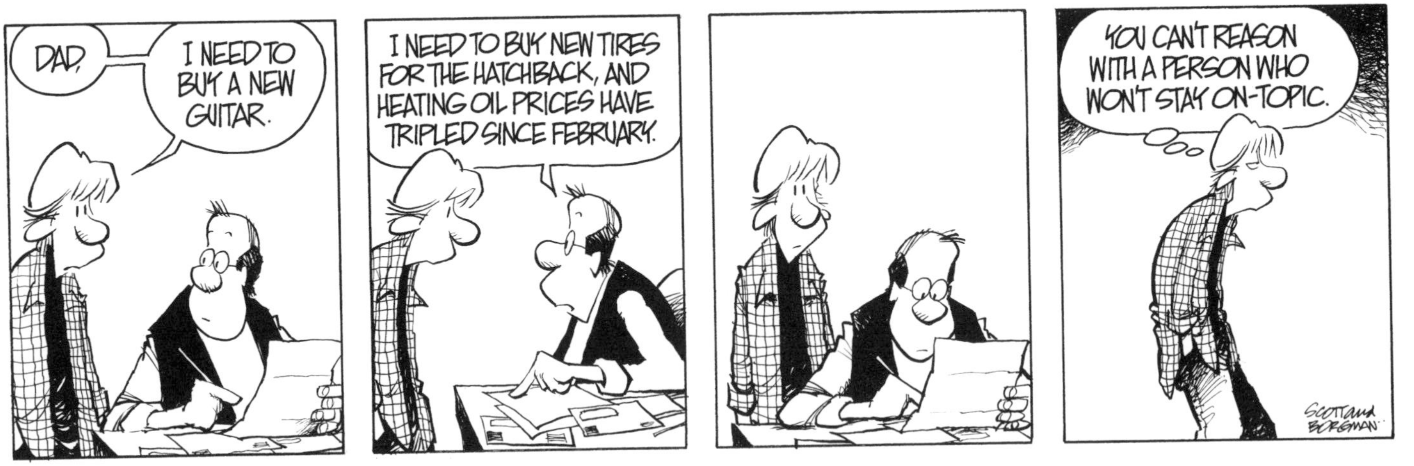
DAD,
I NEED TO BUY A NEW GUITAR.
I NEED TO BUY NEW TIRES FOR THE HATCHBACK, AND HEATING OIL PRICES HAVE TRIPLED SINCE FEBRUARY.
YOU CAN'T REASON WITH A PERSON WHO WON'T STAY ON-TOPIC.
SCOTT and BORGMAN

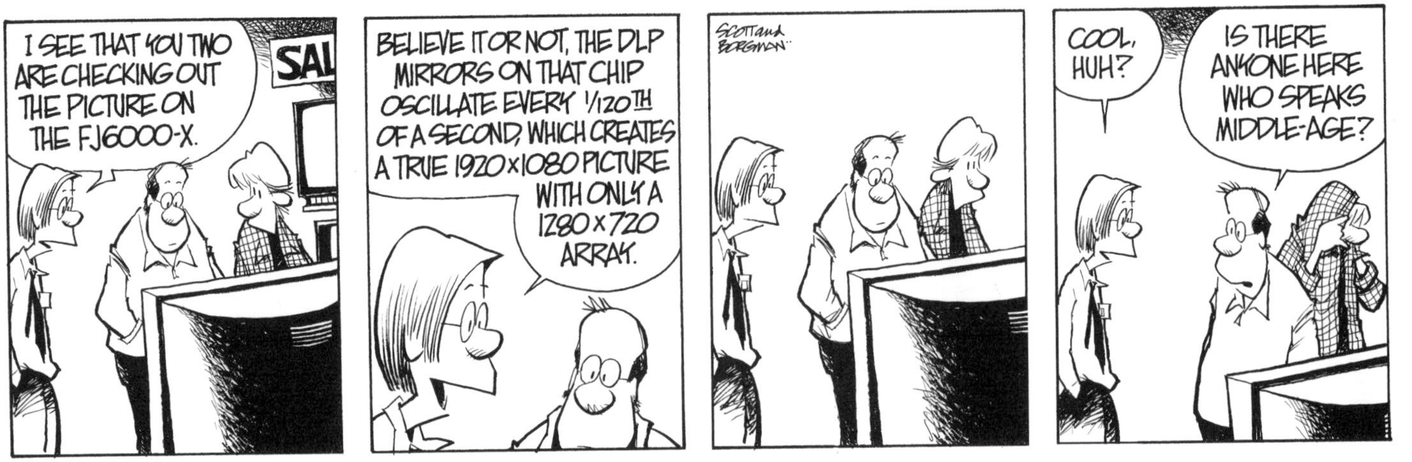
SAL
I SEE THAT YOU TWO ARE CHECKING OUT THE PICTURE ON THE FJ6000-X.
BELIEVE IT OR NOT, THE DLP MIRRORS ON THAT CHIP OSCILLATE EVERY 1/120TH OF A SECOND, WHICH CREATES A TRUE 1920 x 1080 PICTURE WITH ONLY A 1280 x 720 ARRAY.
SCOTT and BORGMAN
COOL, HUH?
IS THERE ANYONE HERE WHO SPEAKS MIDDLE-AGE?

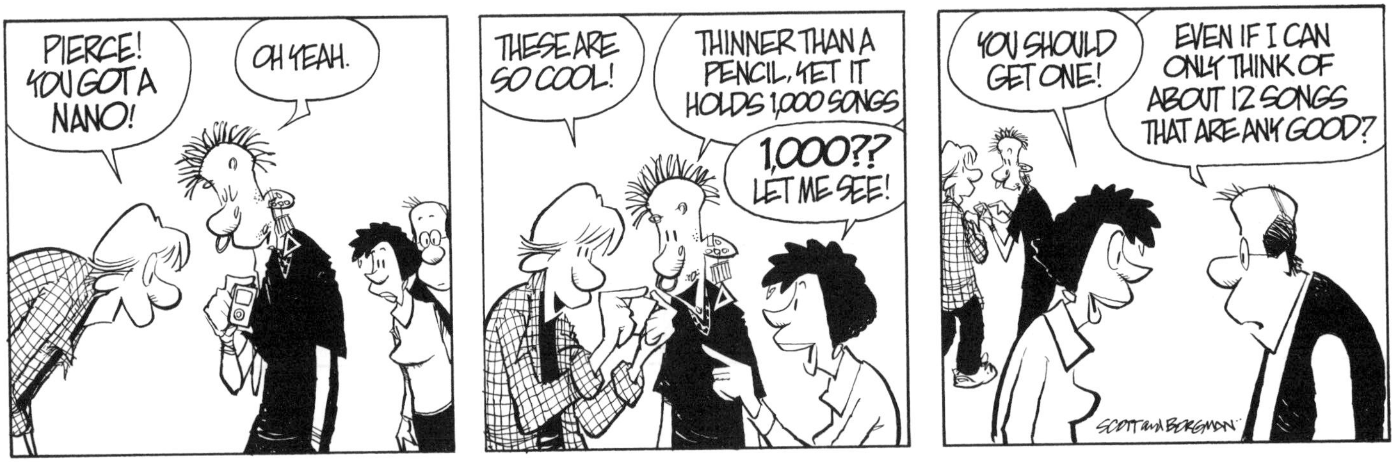
PIERCE! YOU GOT A NANO!
OH YEAH.
THESE ARE SO COOL!
THINNER THAN A PENCIL, YET IT HOLDS 1,000 SONGS
1,000?? LET ME SEE!
YOU SHOULD GET ONE!
EVEN IF I CAN ONLY THINK OF ABOUT 12 SONGS THAT ARE ANY GOOD?
SCOTT and BORGMAN

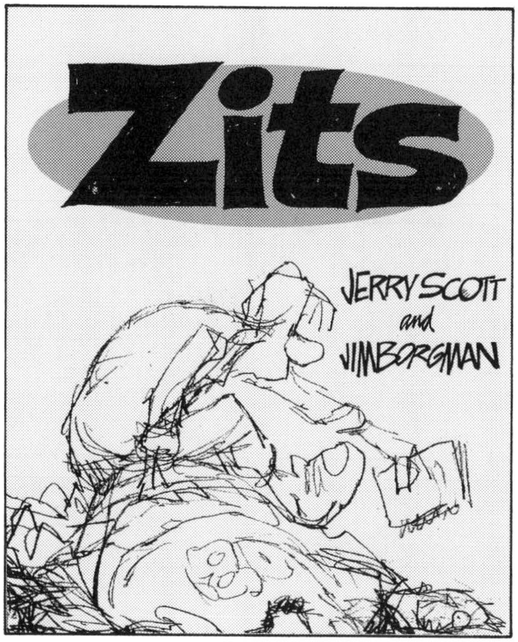
Zits
JERRY SCOTT
and
JIM BORGMAN

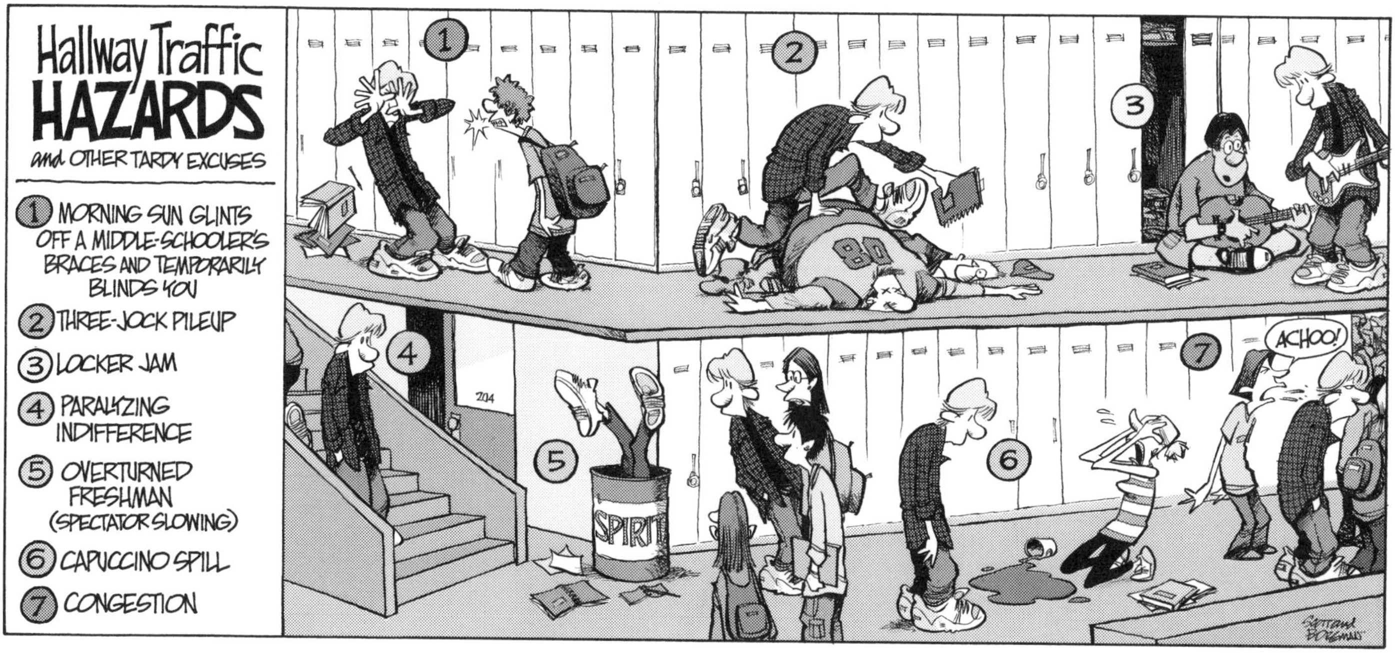
Hallway Traffic
HAZARDS
and OTHER TARDY EXCUSES
1 MORNING SUN GLINTS OFF A MIDDLE-SCHOOLER'S BRACES AND TEMPORARILY BLINDS YOU
2 THREE-JOCK PILEUP
3 LOCKER JAM
4 PARALYZING INDIFFERENCE
5 OVERTURNED FRESHMAN (SPECTATOR SLOWING)
6 CAPUCCINO SPILL
7 CONGESTION
1
2
3
4
204
5
SPIRIT
6
7
ACHOO!

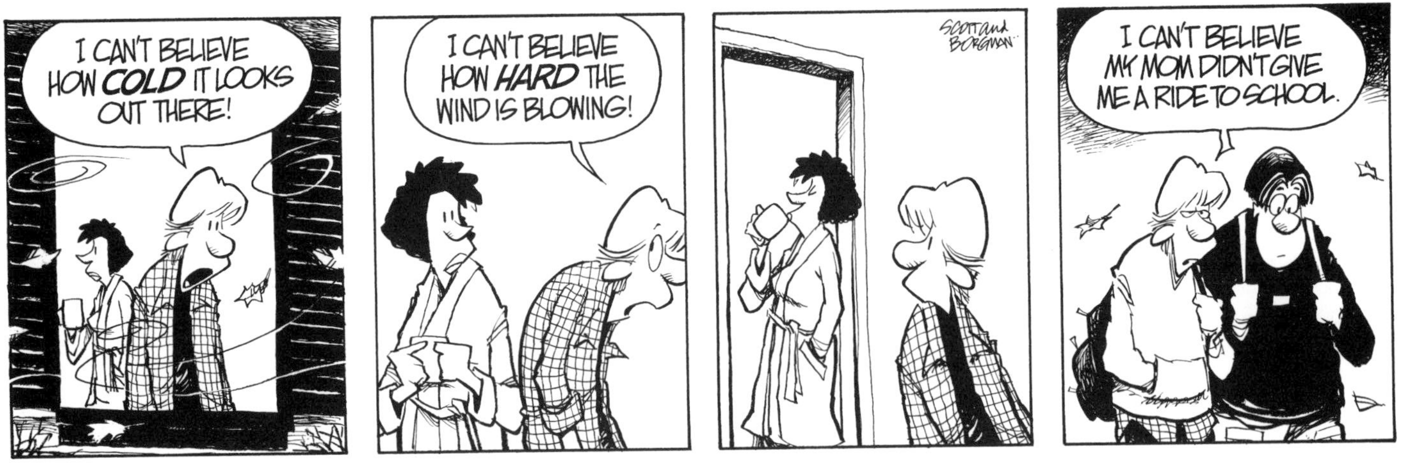
I CAN'T BELIEVE HOW COLD IT LOOKS OUT THERE!
I CAN'T BELIEVE HOW HARD THE WIND IS BLOWING!
I CAN'T BELIEVE MY MOM DIDN'T GIVE ME A RIDE TO SCHOOL.

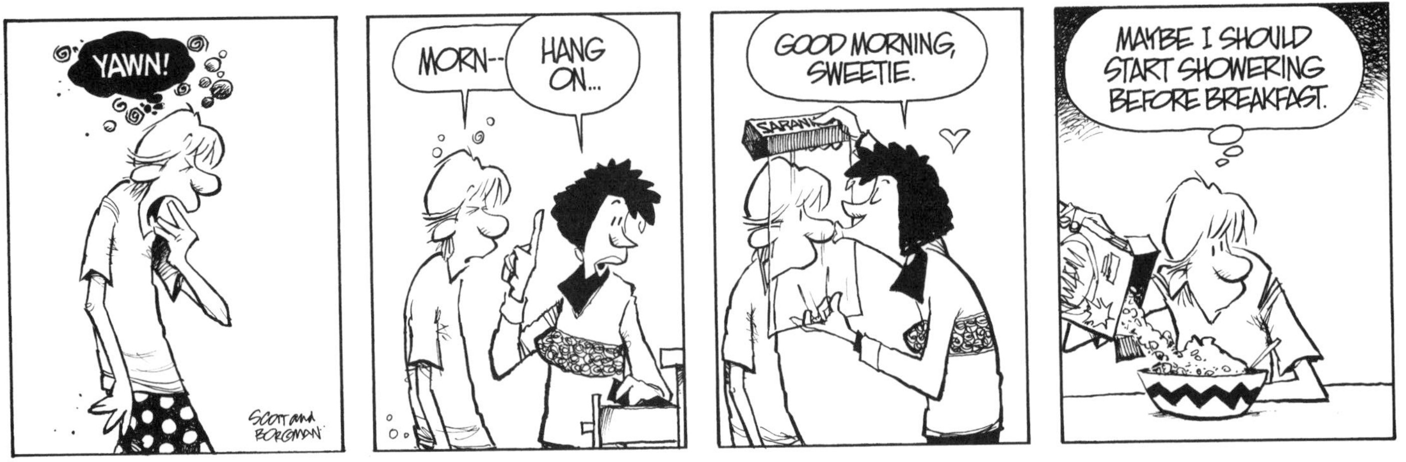
YAWN!
MORN--
HANG ON...
GOOD MORNING, SWEETIE.
MAYBE I SHOULD START SHOWERING BEFORE BREAKFAST.

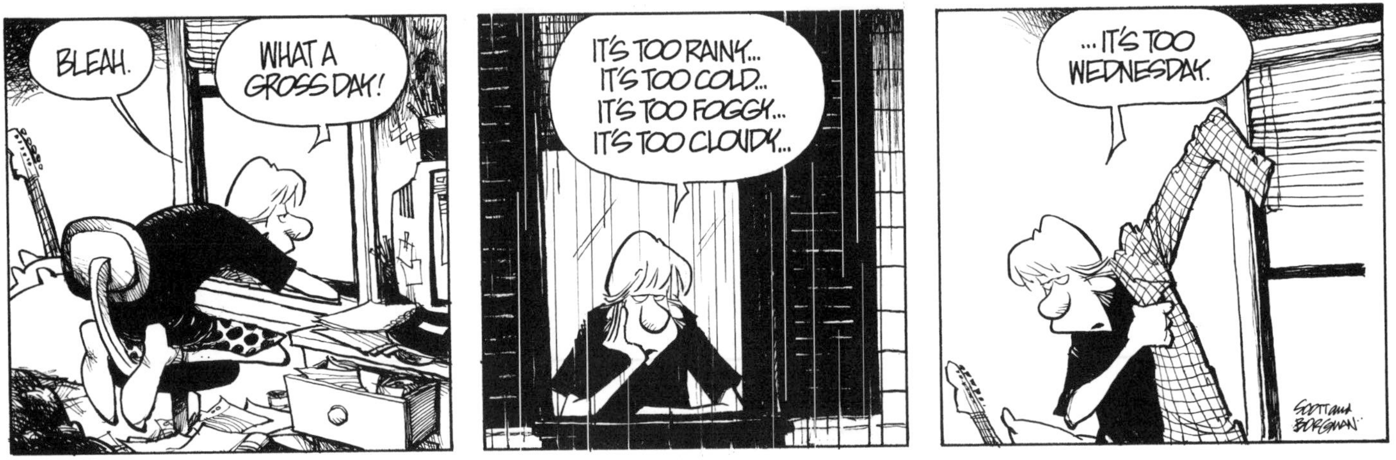
BLEAH.
WHAT A GROSS DAY!
IT'S TOO RAINY... IT'S TOO COLD... IT'S TOO FOGGY... IT'S TOO CLOUDY...
...IT'S TOO WEDNESDAY.

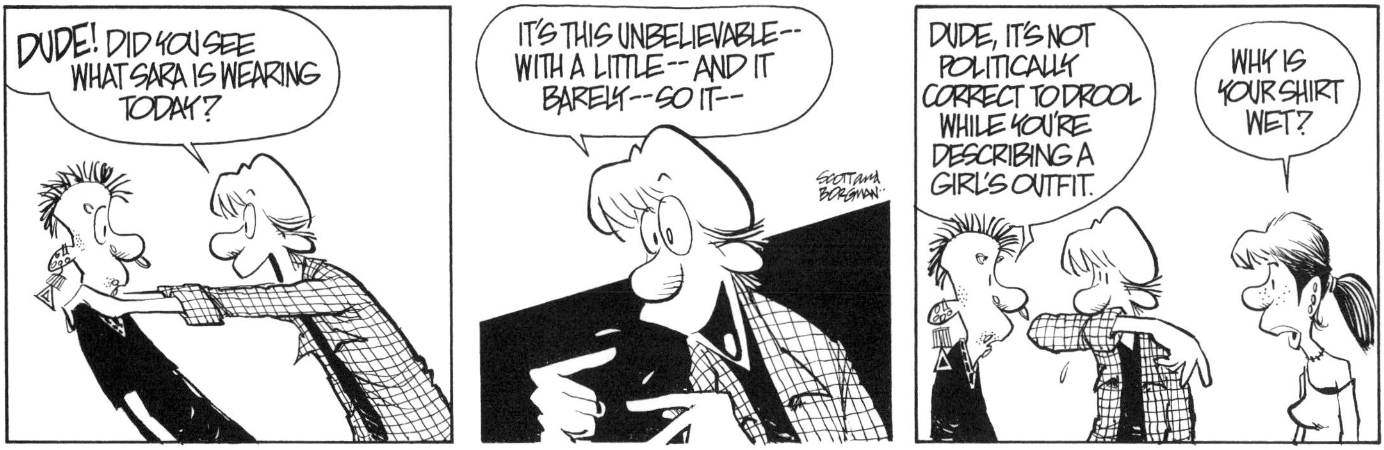
DUDE! DID YOU SEE WHAT SARA IS WEARING TODAY?
IT'S THIS UNBELIEVABLE-- WITH A LITTLE-- AND IT BARELY-- SO IT--
DUDE, IT'S NOT POLITICALLY CORRECT TO DROOL WHILE YOU'RE DESCRIBING A GIRL'S OUTFIT.
WHY IS YOUR SHIRT WET?

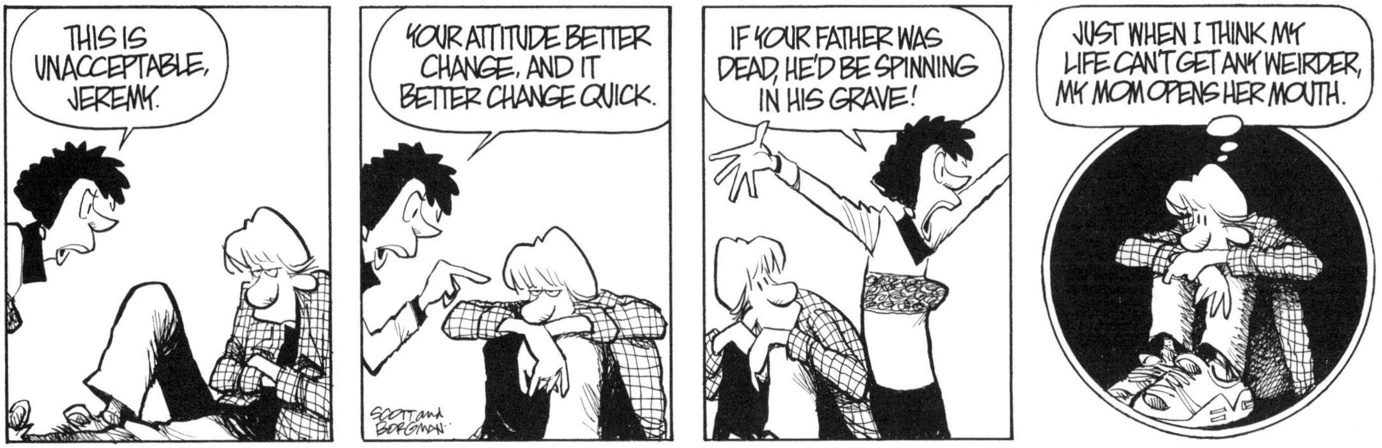
THIS IS UNACCEPTABLE, JEREMY.
YOUR ATTITUDE BETTER CHANGE, AND IT BETTER CHANGE QUICK.
IF YOUR FATHER WAS DEAD, HE'D BE SPINNING IN HIS GRAVE!
JUST WHEN I THINK MY LIFE CAN'T GET ANY WEIRDER, MY MOM OPENS HER MOUTH.

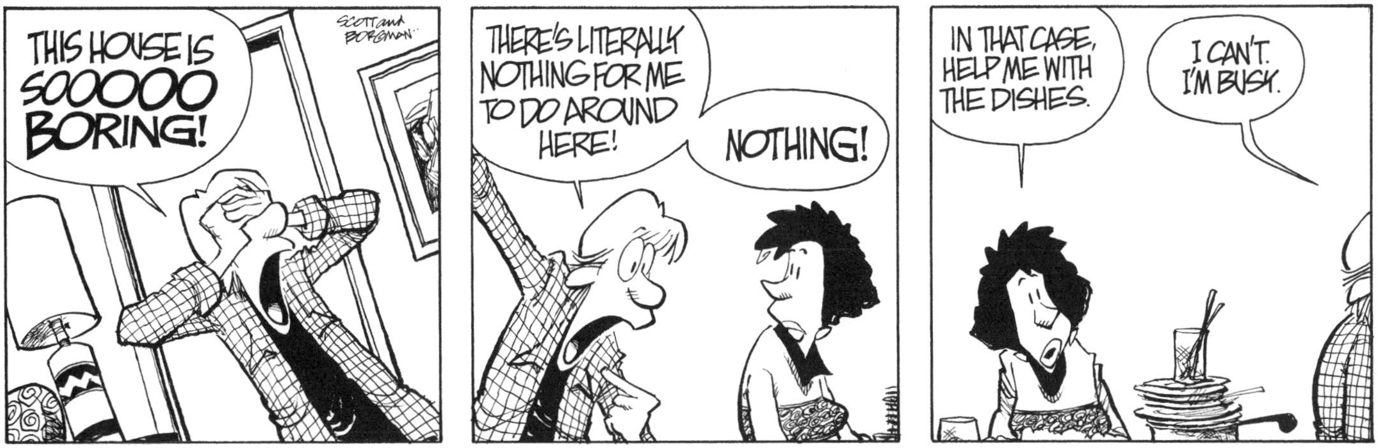
THIS HOUSE IS SOOOOO BORING!
THERE'S LITERALLY NOTHING FOR ME TO DO AROUND HERE!
NOTHING!
IN THAT CASE, HELP ME WITH THE DISHES.
I CAN'T. I'M BUSY.

Zits
by JERRY SCOTT and JIM BORGMAN

HA! HA! NO WAY!
SERIOUSLY! SO THEN I BEEP
HANG ON, PIERCE. I HAVE ANOTHER CALL.
SCOTT and BORGMAN
HI JEREMY. IT'S ME.
HEY! HI SARA. I WAS GOING TO CALL Y--
JEREMY! TELEPHONE!
HANG ON.
AMIGO!
HECTOR! HI! HANG ON! THERE'S SOMEONE AT THE DOOR.
DING DONG!
HOW LONG ARE YOU PLANNING TO KEEP ME ON HOLD?

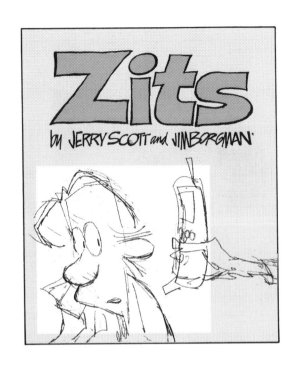

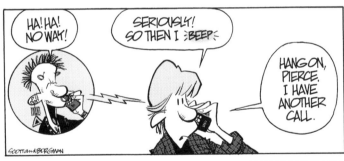

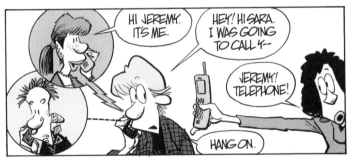

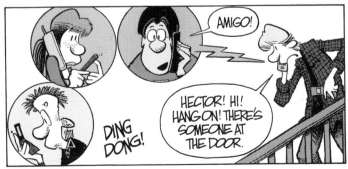

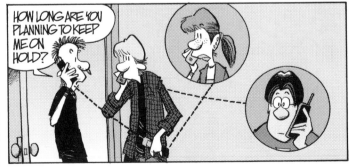

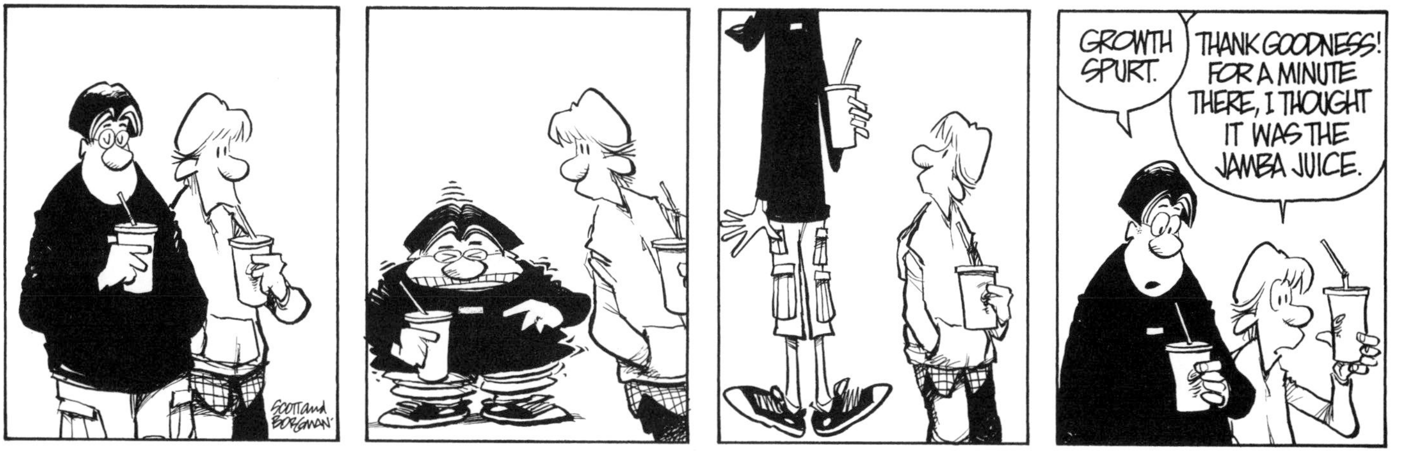
GROWTH SPURT.
THANK GOODNESS! FOR A MINUTE THERE, I THOUGHT IT WAS THE JAMBA JUICE.

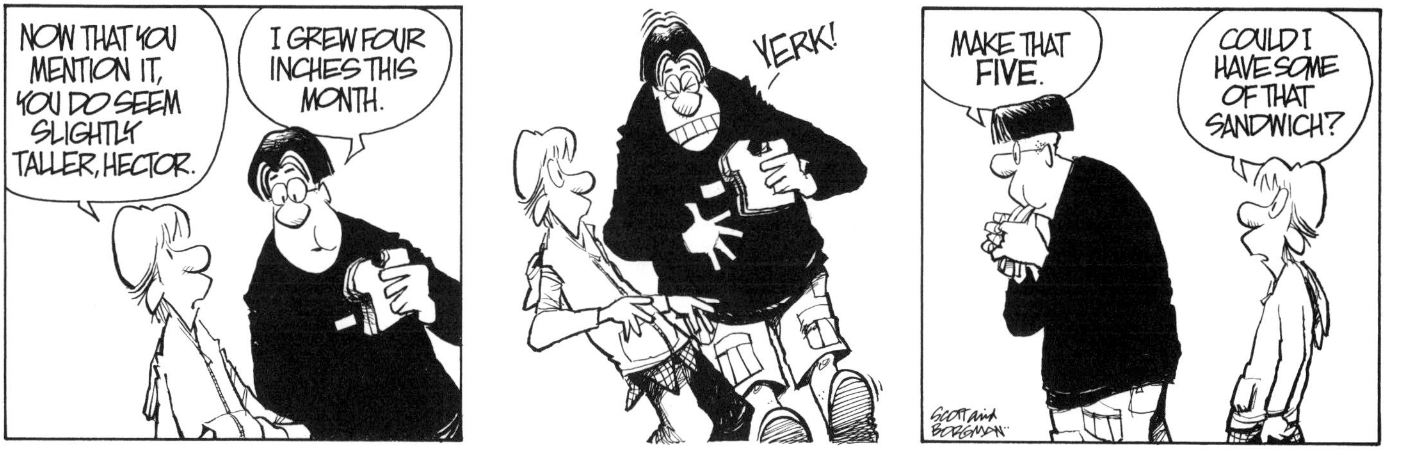
NOW THAT YOU MENTION IT, YOU DO SEEM SLIGHTLY TALLER, HECTOR.
I GREW FOUR INCHES THIS MONTH.
YERK!
MAKE THAT FIVE.
COULD I HAVE SOME OF THAT SANDWICH?

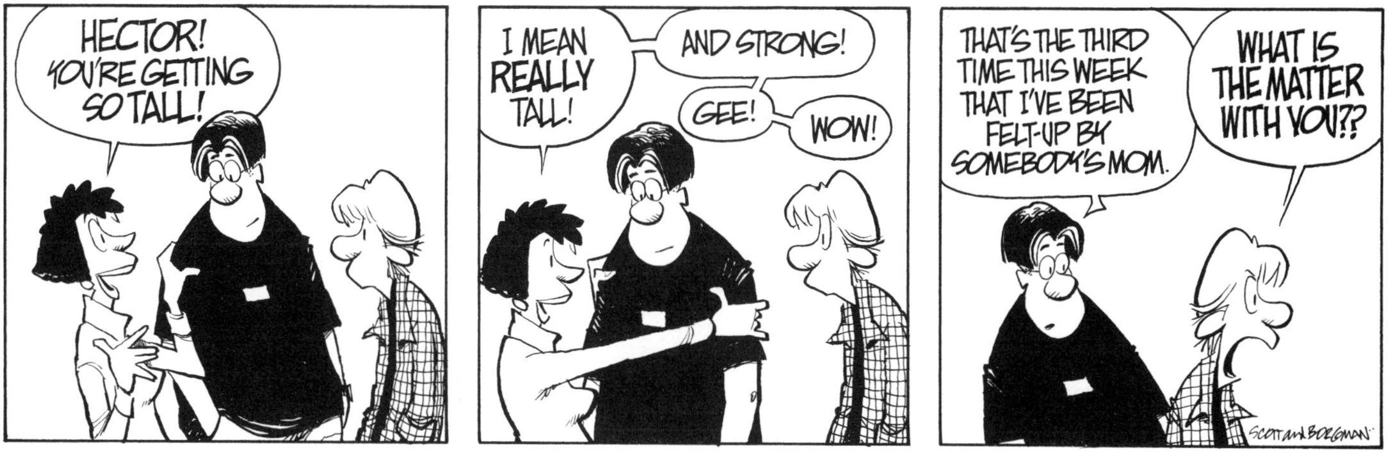
HECTOR! YOU'RE GETTING SO TALL!
I MEAN REALLY TALL!
AND STRONG!
GEE!
WOW!
THAT'S THE THIRD TIME THIS WEEK THAT I'VE BEEN FELT-UP BY SOMEBODY'S MOM.
WHAT IS THE MATTER WITH YOU??

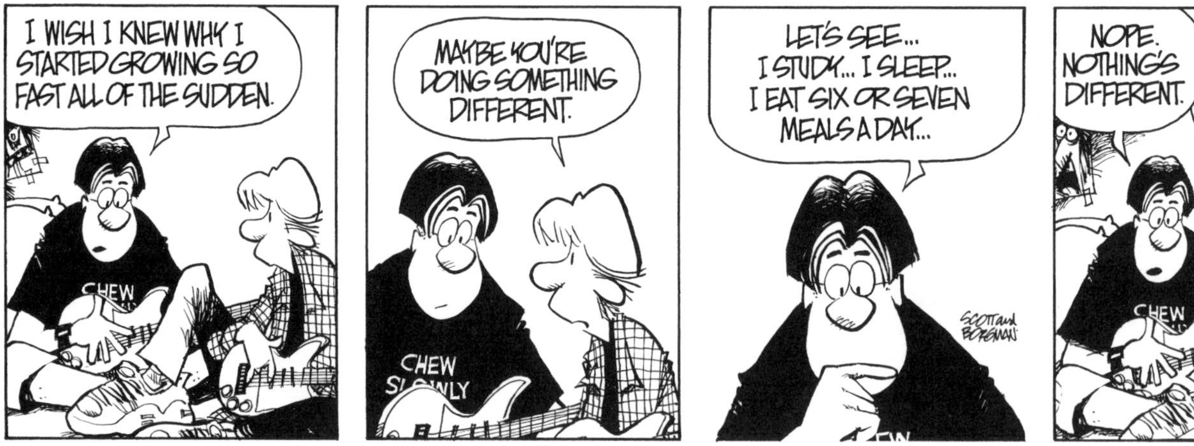
I WISH I KNEW WHY I STARTED GROWING SO FAST ALL OF THE SUDDEN.
CHEW
MAYBE YOU'RE DOING SOMETHING DIFFERENT.
CHEW SLOWLY
LET'S SEE... I STUDY... I SLEEP... I EAT SIX OR SEVEN MEALS A DAY...
SCOTT and BORGMAN
NOPE. NOTHING'S DIFFERENT.
YOU GET BY ON ONLY SIX OR SEVEN MEALS A DAY?
CHEW

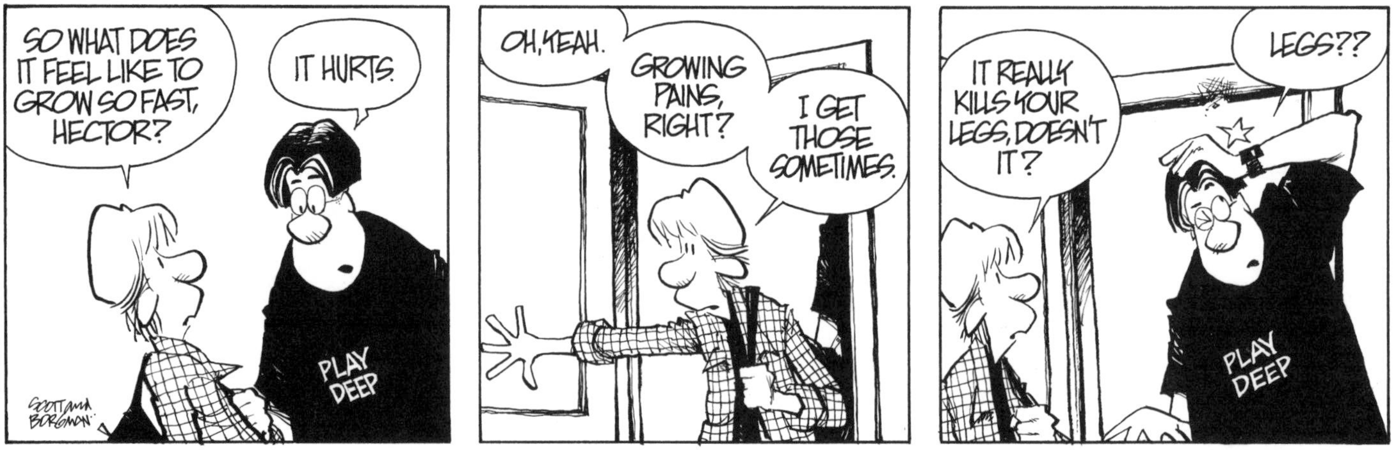
SO WHAT DOES IT FEEL LIKE TO GROW SO FAST, HECTOR?
IT HURTS.
PLAY DEEP
SCOTT and BORGMAN
OH, YEAH.
GROWING PAINS, RIGHT?
I GET THOSE SOMETIMES.
IT REALLY KILLS YOUR LEGS, DOESN'T IT?
LEGS??
PLAY DEEP

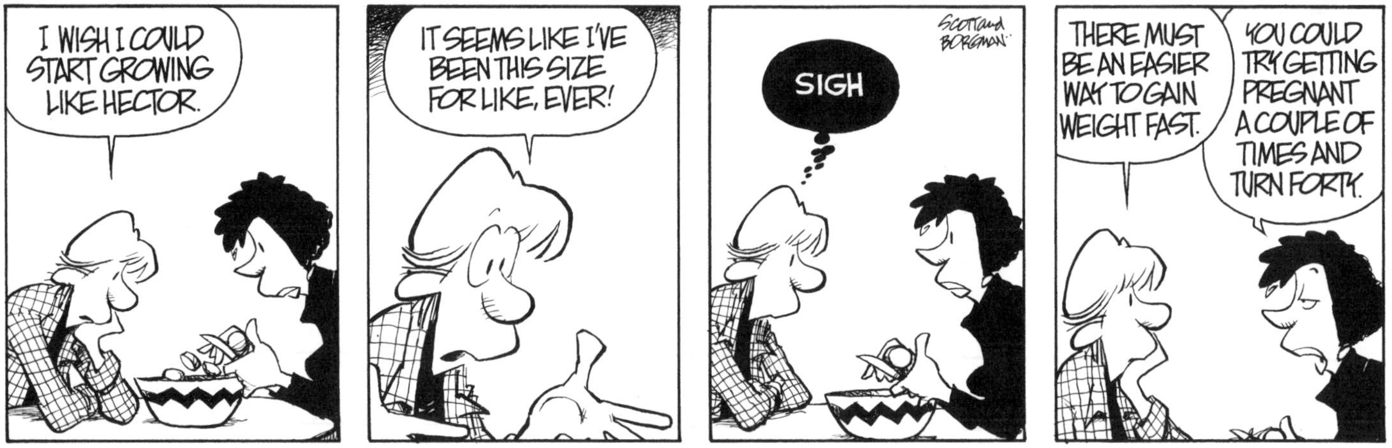
I WISH I COULD START GROWING LIKE HECTOR.
IT SEEMS LIKE I'VE BEEN THIS SIZE FOR LIKE, EVER!
SCOTT and BORGMAN
SIGH
THERE MUST BE AN EASIER WAY TO GAIN WEIGHT FAST.
YOU COULD TRY GETTING PREGNANT A COUPLE OF TIMES AND TURN FORTY.

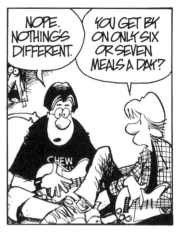

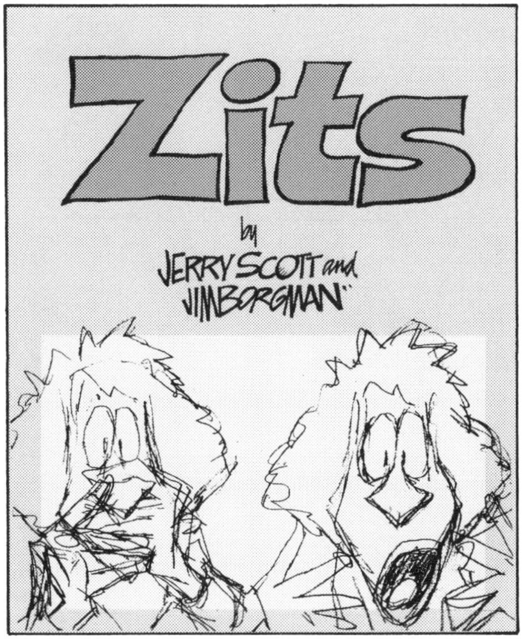
Zits
by
JERRY SCOTT and
JIM BORGMAN

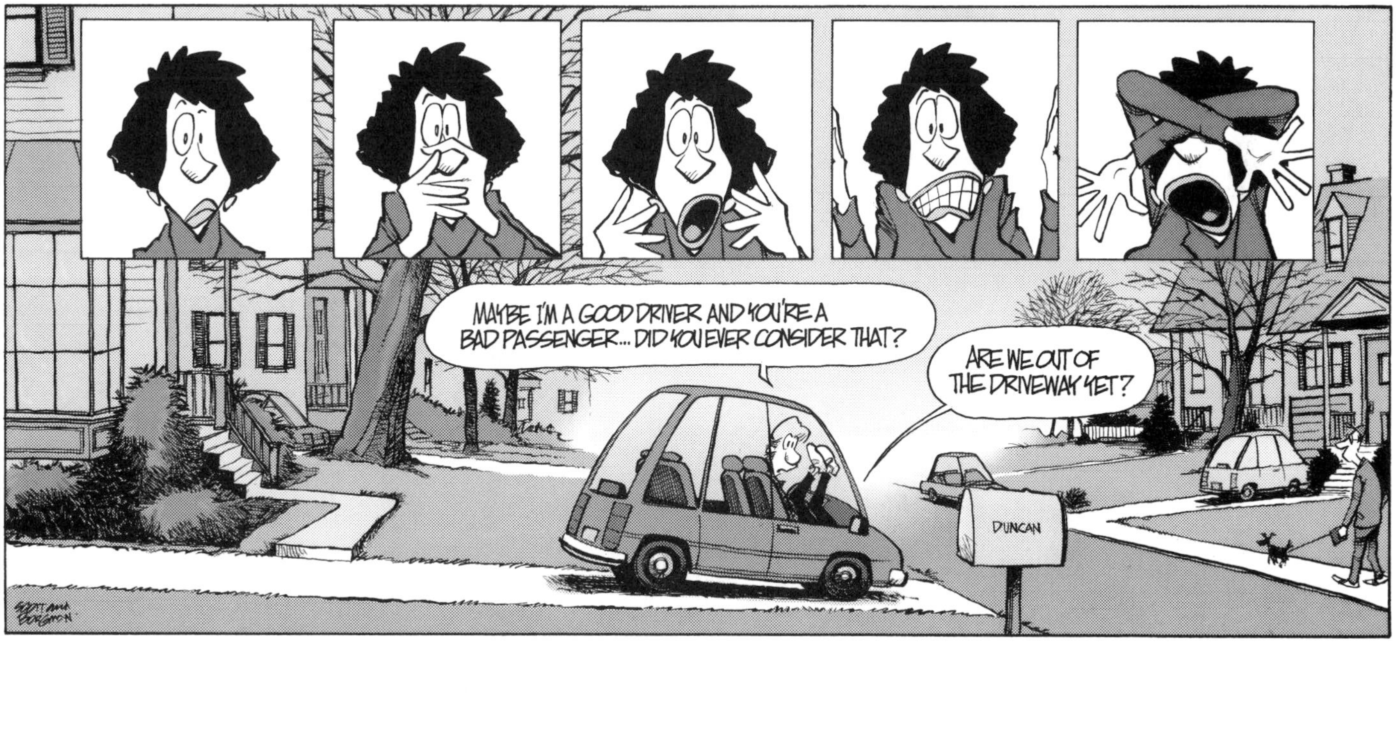
MAYBE I'M A GOOD DRIVER AND YOU'RE A BAD PASSENGER... DID YOU EVER CONSIDER THAT?
ARE WE OUT OF THE DRIVEWAY YET?
DUNCAN

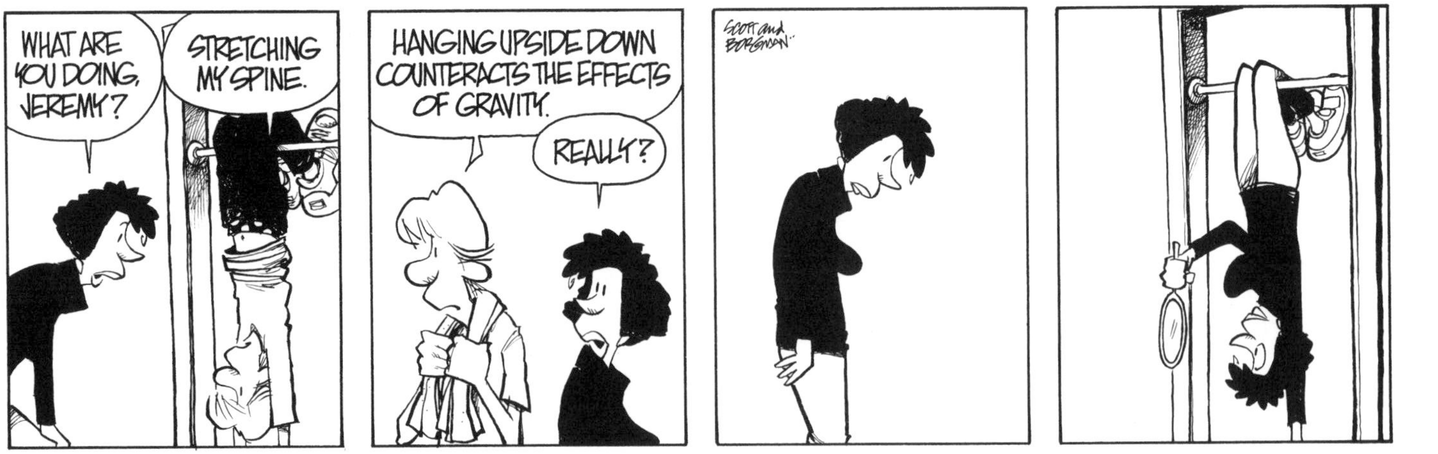
WHAT ARE YOU DOING, JEREMY?
STRETCHING MY SPINE.
HANGING UPSIDE DOWN COUNTERACTS THE EFFECTS OF GRAVITY.
REALLY?

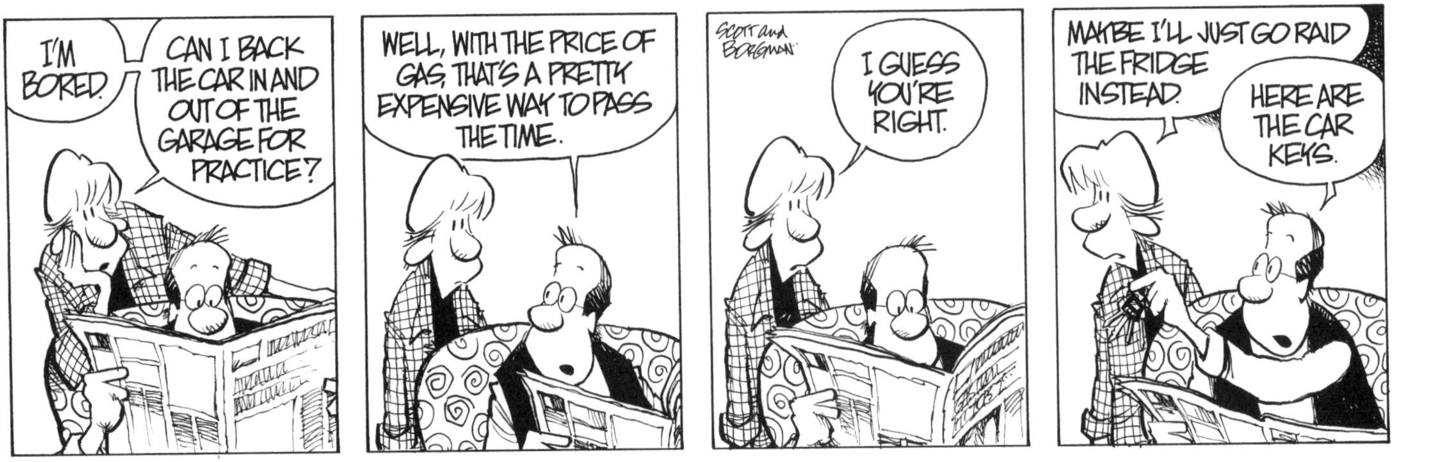
I'M BORED.
CAN I BACK THE CAR IN AND OUT OF THE GARAGE FOR PRACTICE?
WELL, WITH THE PRICE OF GAS, THAT'S A PRETTY EXPENSIVE WAY TO PASS THE TIME.
I GUESS YOU'RE RIGHT.
MAYBE I'LL JUST GO RAID THE FRIDGE INSTEAD.
HERE ARE THE CAR KEYS.

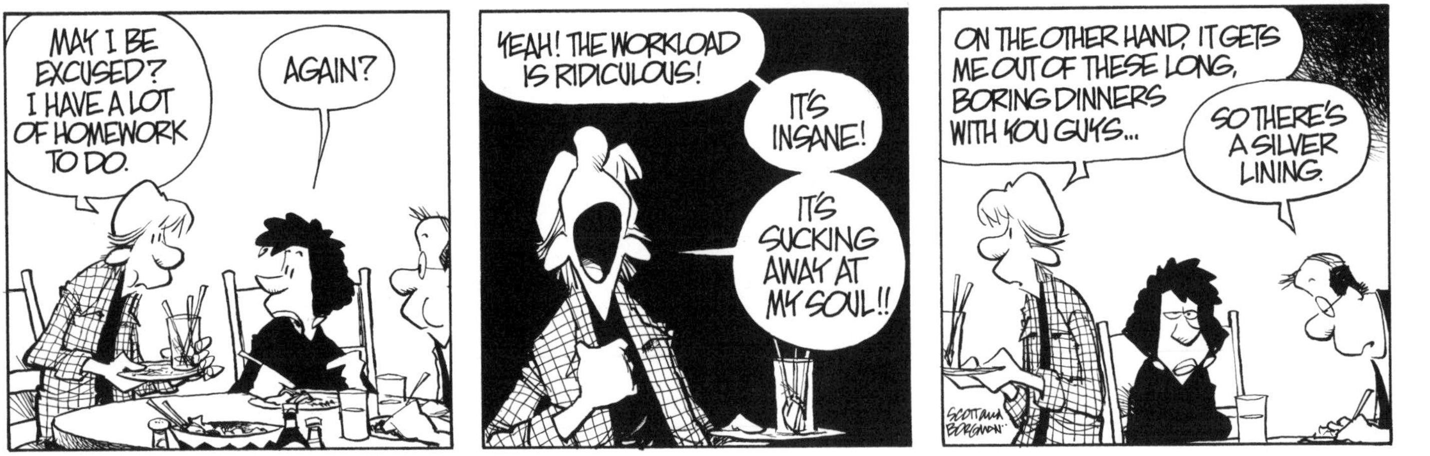
MAY I BE EXCUSED? I HAVE A LOT OF HOMEWORK TO DO.
AGAIN?
YEAH! THE WORKLOAD IS RIDICULOUS!
IT'S INSANE!
IT'S SUCKING AWAY AT MY SOUL!!
ON THE OTHER HAND, IT GETS ME OUT OF THESE LONG, BORING DINNERS WITH YOU GUYS...
SO THERE'S A SILVER LINING.

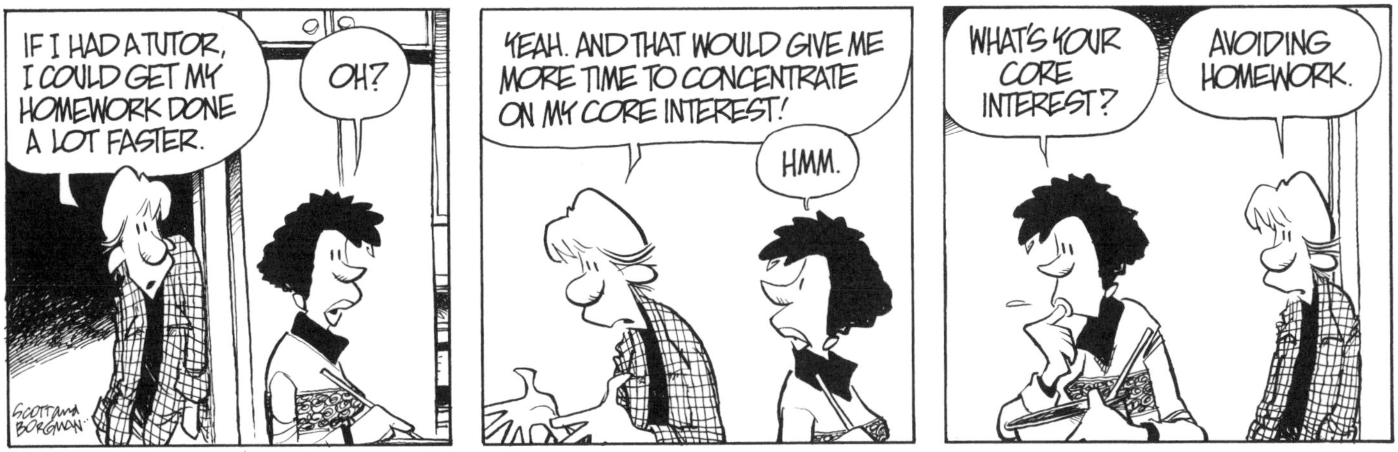
IF I HAD A TUTOR, I COULD GET MY HOMEWORK DONE A LOT FASTER.
OH?
YEAH. AND THAT WOULD GIVE ME MORE TIME TO CONCENTRATE ON MY CORE INTEREST!
HMM.
WHAT'S YOUR CORE INTEREST?
AVOIDING HOMEWORK.

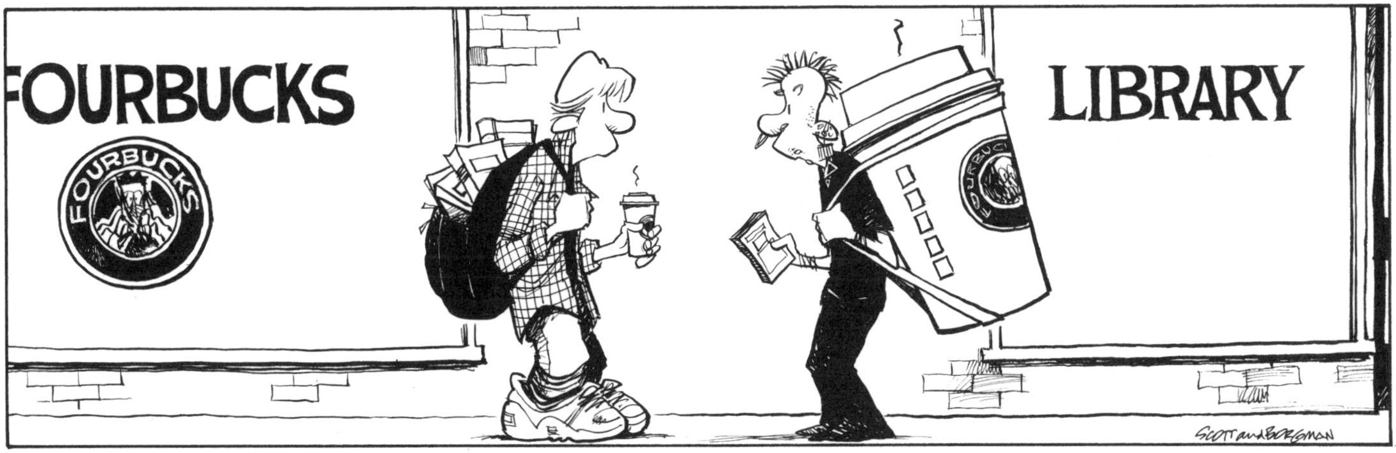
FOURBUCKS
FOURBUCKS
LIBRARY

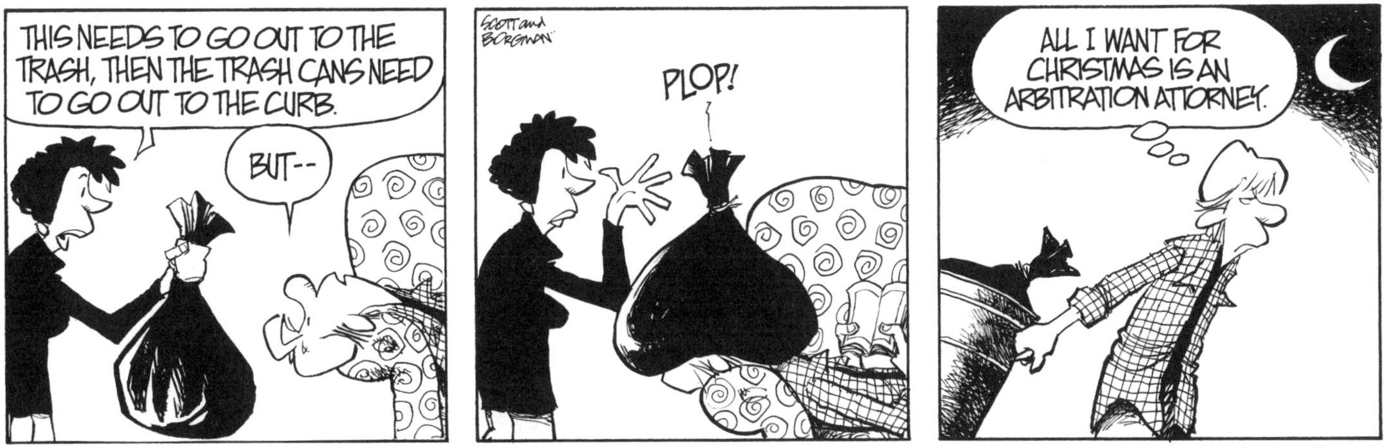
THIS NEEDS TO GO OUT TO THE TRASH, THEN THE TRASH CANS NEED TO GO OUT TO THE CURB.
BUT--
PLOP!
ALL I WANT FOR CHRISTMAS IS AN ARBITRATION ATTORNEY.

Zits
by JERRY SCOTT and JIM BORGMAN

Z-Z-Z-ZIP!
SCOTT and BORGMAN
ZIP!
SIGH.
TALK TO HER, DAD! SHE'S BEEN STARING AT ME AND SIGHING LIKE THAT ALL AFTERNOON!

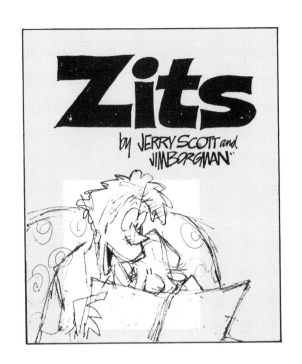

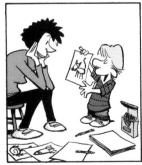

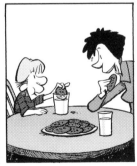

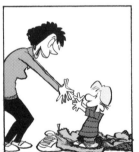

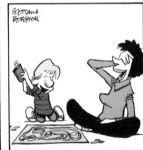

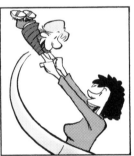

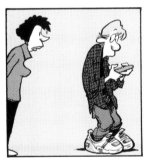

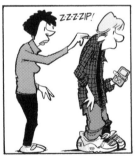

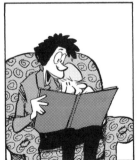

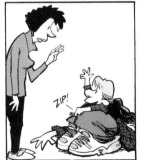

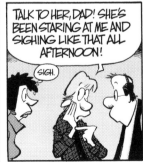

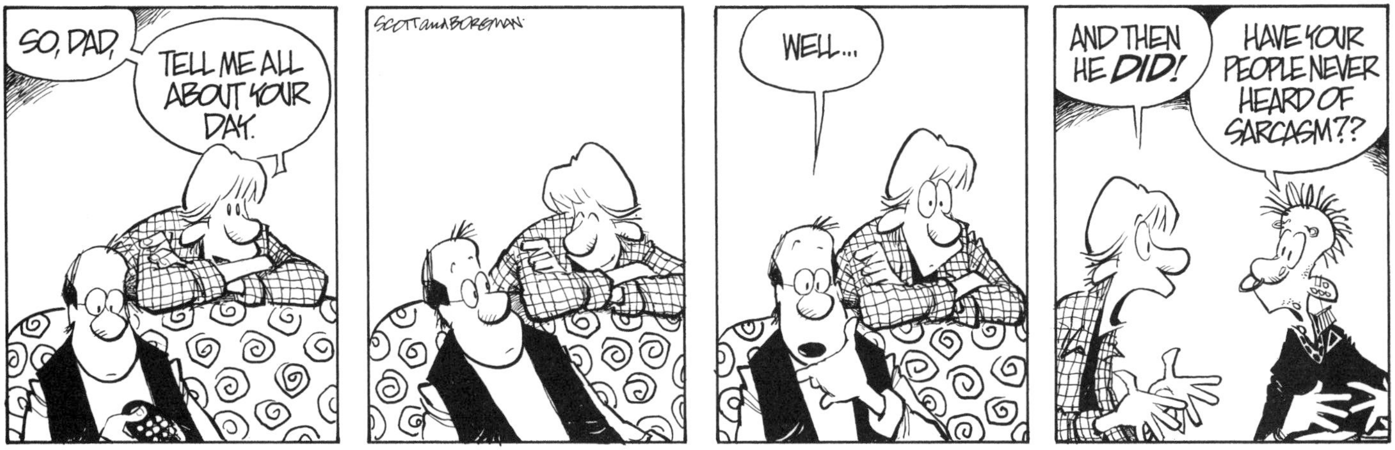
SO, DAD,
TELL ME ALL ABOUT YOUR DAY.
SCOTT and BORGMAN
WELL...
AND THEN HE *DID*!
HAVE YOUR PEOPLE NEVER HEARD OF SARCASM??

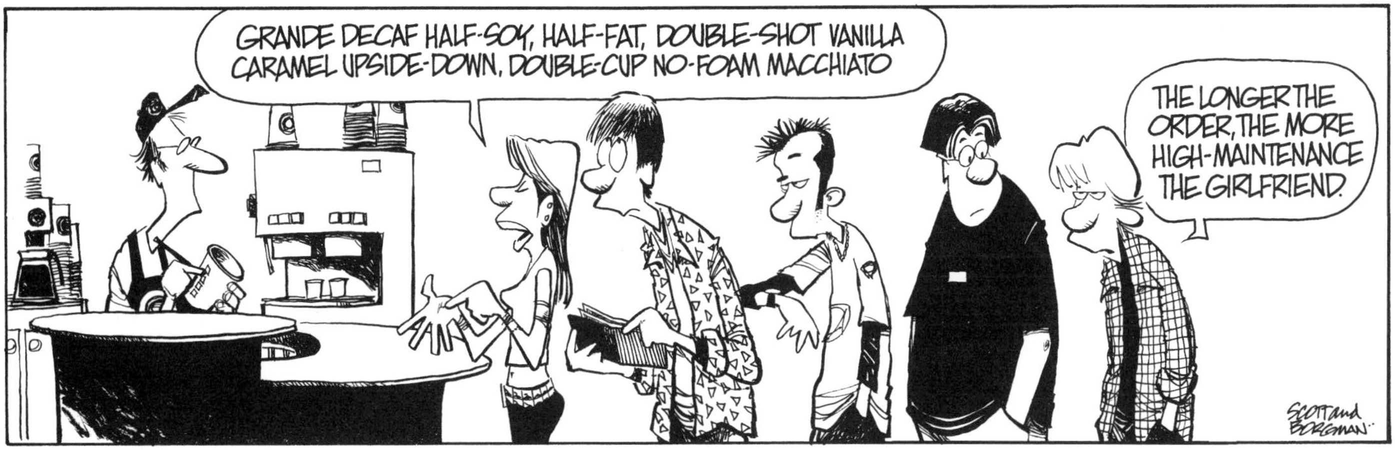
GRANDE DECAF HALF-SOY, HALF-FAT, DOUBLE-SHOT VANILLA CARAMEL UPSIDE-DOWN, DOUBLE-CUP NO-FOAM MACCHIATO
THE LONGER THE ORDER, THE MORE HIGH-MAINTENANCE THE GIRLFRIEND.
SCOTT and BORGMAN

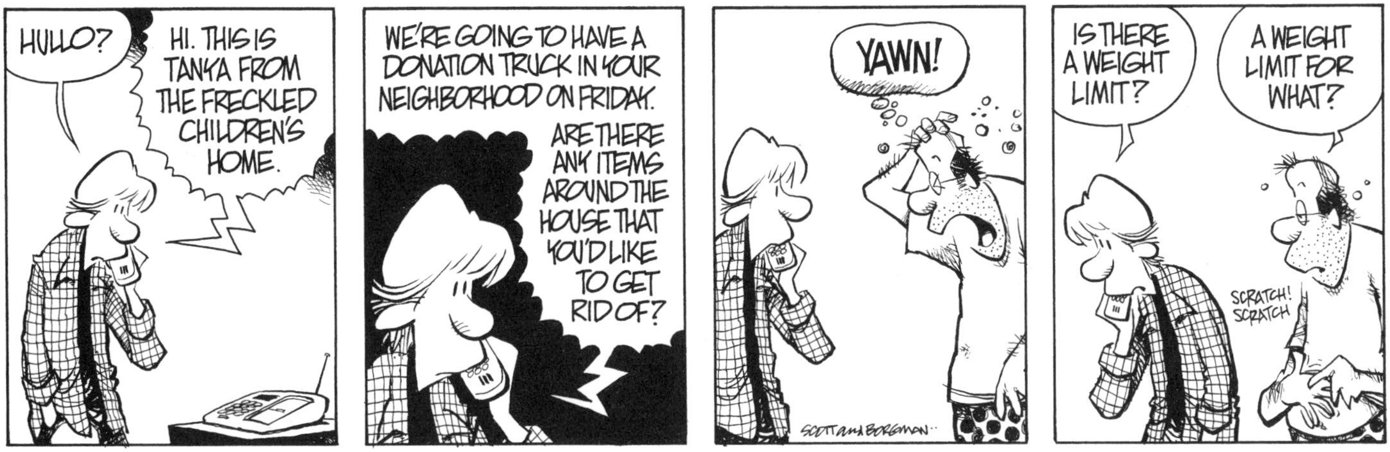
HULLO?
HI. THIS IS TANYA FROM THE FRECKLED CHILDREN'S HOME.
WE'RE GOING TO HAVE A DONATION TRUCK IN YOUR NEIGHBORHOOD ON FRIDAY.
ARE THERE ANY ITEMS AROUND THE HOUSE THAT YOU'D LIKE TO GET RID OF?
YAWN!
SCOTT and BORGMAN
IS THERE A WEIGHT LIMIT?
A WEIGHT LIMIT FOR WHAT?
SCRATCH! SCRATCH

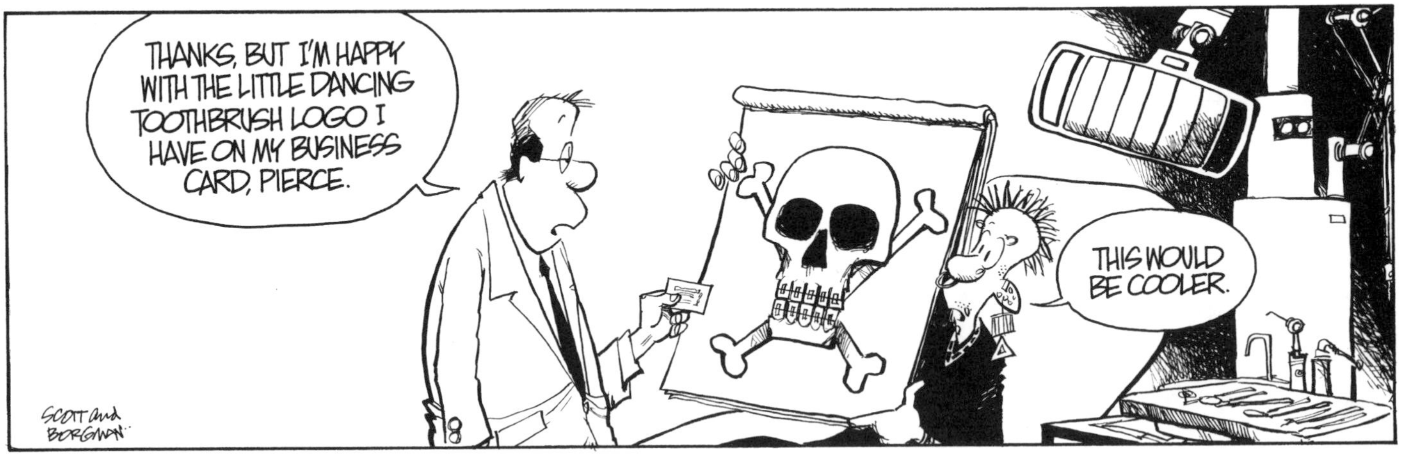
THANKS, BUT I'M HAPPY WITH THE LITTLE DANCING TOOTHBRUSH LOGO I HAVE ON MY BUSINESS CARD, PIERCE.
THIS WOULD BE COOLER.
SCOTT and BORGMAN

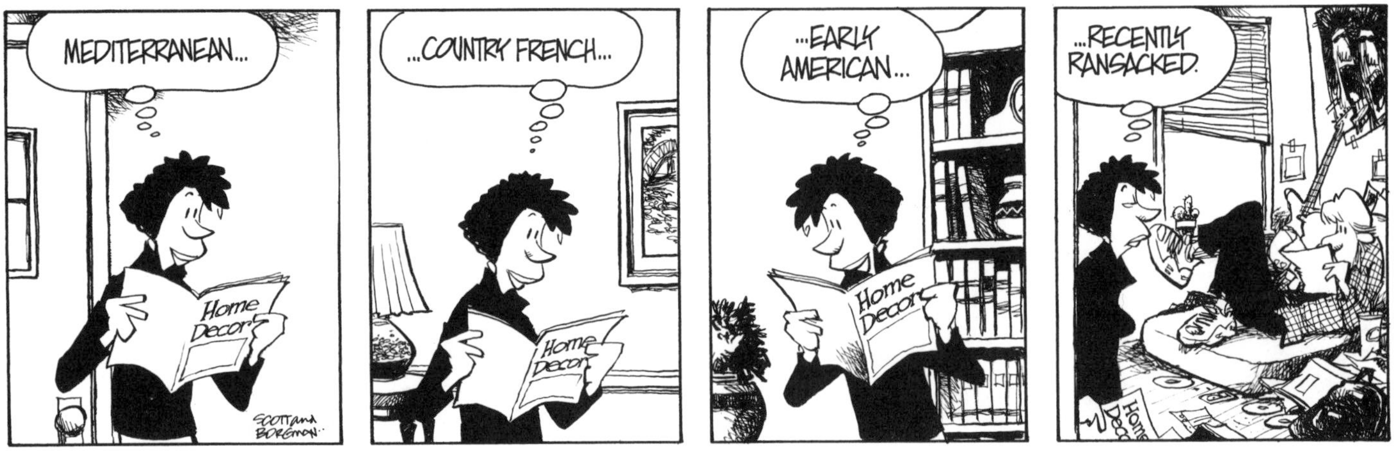
MEDITERRANEAN...
Home Decor
SCOTT and BORGMAN
...COUNTRY FRENCH...
Home Decor
...EARLY AMERICAN...
Home Decor
...RECENTLY RANSACKED.
Home Decor

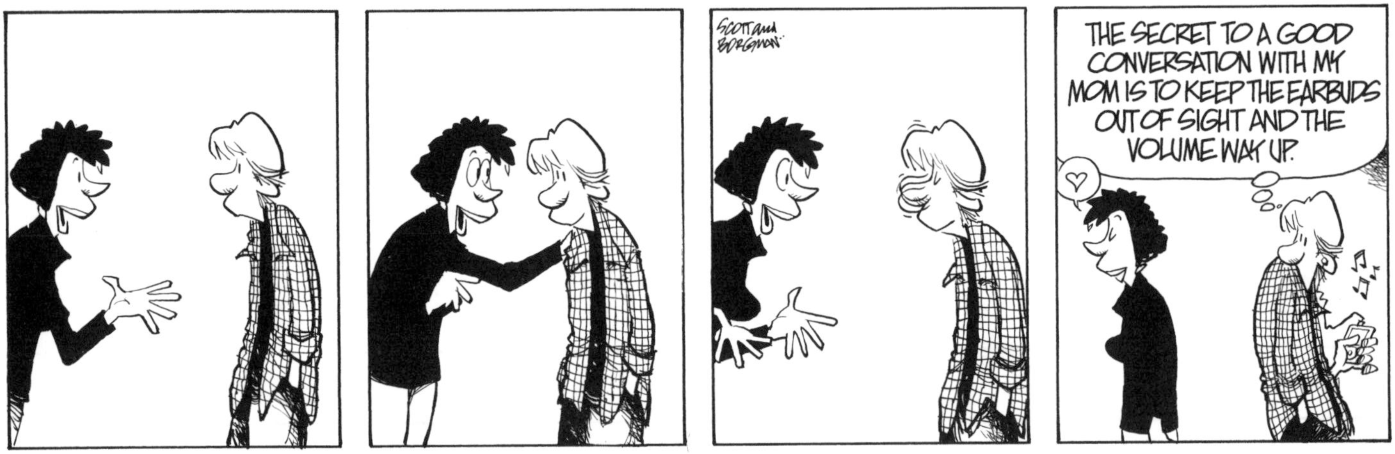
SCOTT and BORGMAN
THE SECRET TO A GOOD CONVERSATION WITH MY MOM IS TO KEEP THE EARBUDS OUT OF SIGHT AND THE VOLUME WAY UP.

JERRY SCOTT and JIM BORGMAN
Zits

Cheap LAST-MINUTE
GIFT CARDS
that YOUR PARENTS WILL LOVE!
JUST CLIP 'EM OUT, TAPE 'EM TO THE BATHROOM MIRROR, AND YOU'RE DONE!
THIS ENTITLES THE BEARER TO ONE
SARCASM-FREE MEAL *
*LIMITED TO 30 MINUTES
THIS ENTITLES THE BEARER TO ONE
DRIVING-FREE SATURDAY
THIS ENTITLES THE BEARER TO ONE
COMPLETE RESPONSE to the QUESTION, "HOW WAS SCHOOL TODAY?"
THREE-SENTENCE MINIMUM, EXCLUDING SIGHS, GROANS AND "I DON'T KNOW'S"
THIS ENTITLES THE BEARER TO ONE
HUG
USING AT LEAST ONE ARM
(NON-EYE ROLLING)
THIS ENTITLES THE BEARER TO ONE
CONVERSATION WITH ME FACING IN YOUR GENERAL DIRECTION
BONUS – NO EAR BUDS!

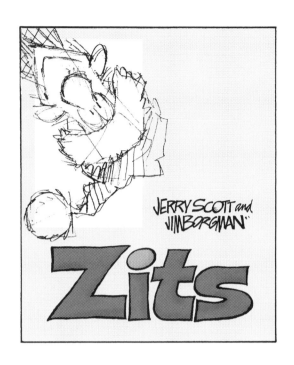

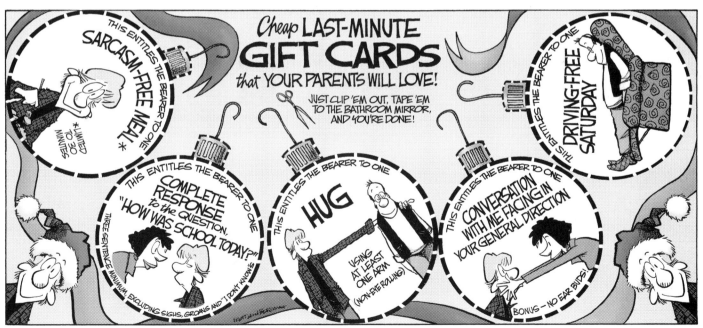

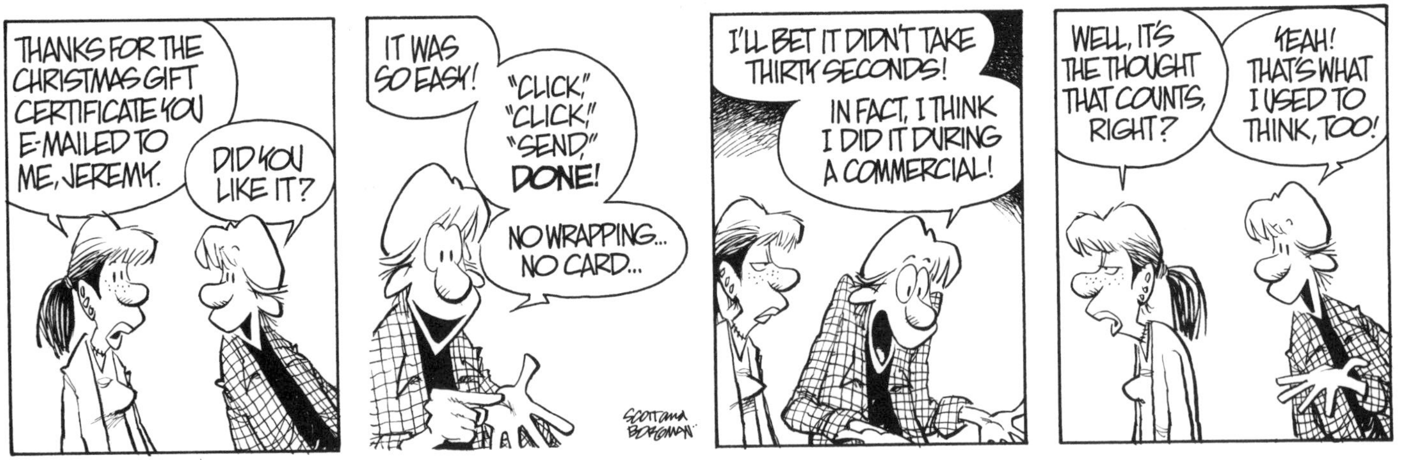
THANKS FOR THE CHRISTMAS GIFT CERTIFICATE YOU E-MAILED TO ME, JEREMY.
DID YOU LIKE IT?
IT WAS SO EASY!
"CLICK," "CLICK," "SEND," DONE!
NO WRAPPING... NO CARD...
I'LL BET IT DIDN'T TAKE THIRTY SECONDS!
IN FACT, I THINK I DID IT DURING A COMMERCIAL!
WELL, IT'S THE THOUGHT THAT COUNTS, RIGHT?
YEAH! THAT'S WHAT I USED TO THINK, TOO!

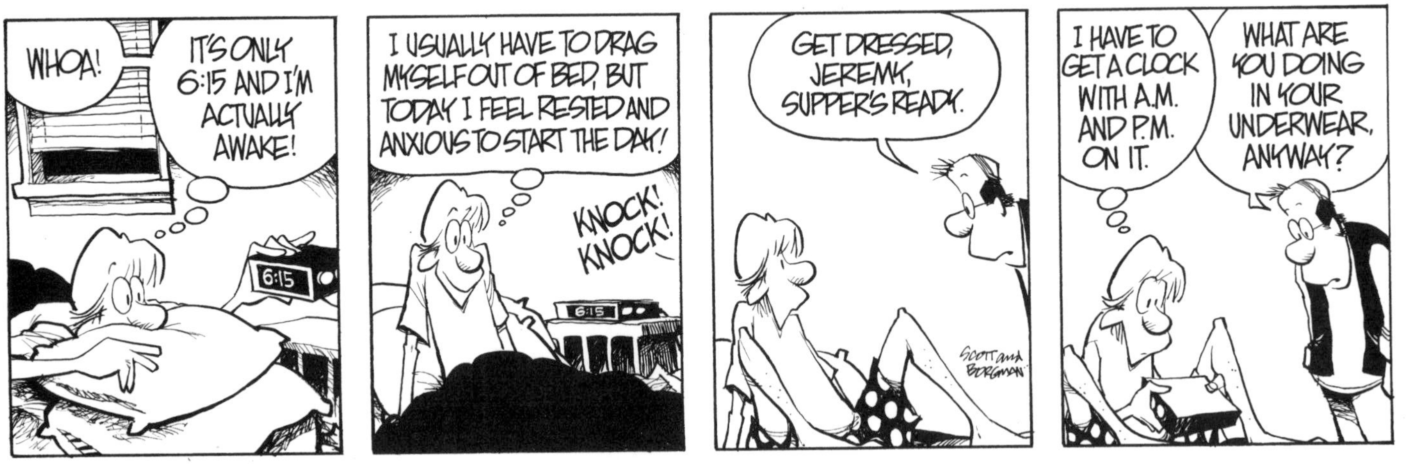
WHOA!
IT'S ONLY 6:15 AND I'M ACTUALLY AWAKE!
6:15
I USUALLY HAVE TO DRAG MYSELF OUT OF BED, BUT TODAY I FEEL RESTED AND ANXIOUS TO START THE DAY!
KNOCK! KNOCK!
6:15
GET DRESSED, JEREMY, SUPPER'S READY.
I HAVE TO GET A CLOCK WITH A.M. AND P.M. ON IT.
WHAT ARE YOU DOING IN YOUR UNDERWEAR, ANYWAY?

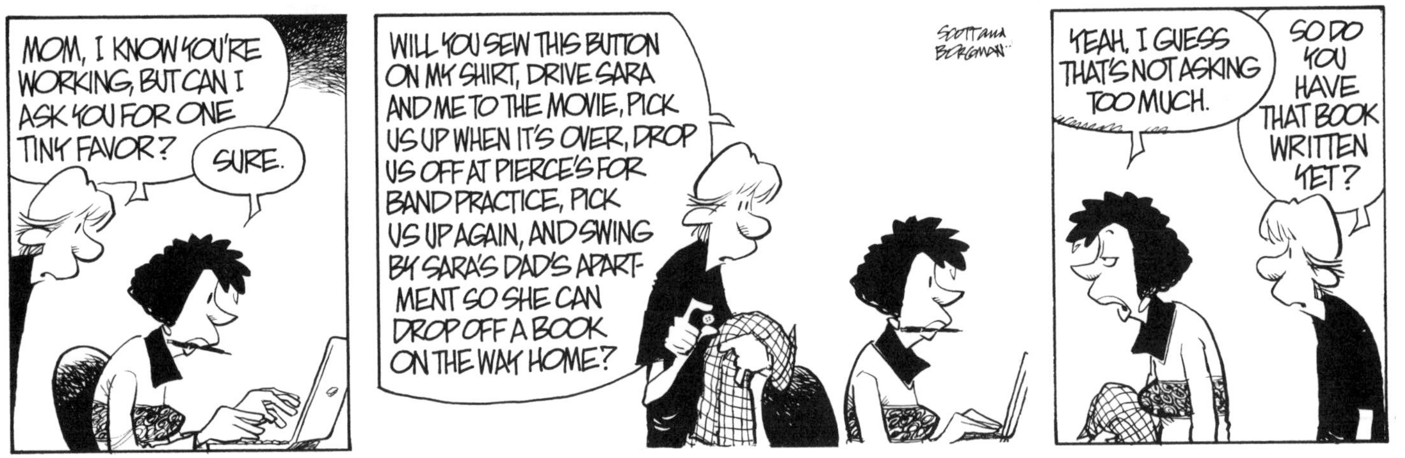
MOM, I KNOW YOU'RE WORKING, BUT CAN I ASK YOU FOR ONE TINY FAVOR?
SURE.
WILL YOU SEW THIS BUTTON ON MY SHIRT, DRIVE SARA AND ME TO THE MOVIE, PICK US UP WHEN IT'S OVER, DROP US OFF AT PIERCE'S FOR BAND PRACTICE, PICK US UP AGAIN, AND SWING BY SARA'S DAD'S APART-MENT SO SHE CAN DROP OFF A BOOK ON THE WAY HOME?
YEAH, I GUESS THAT'S NOT ASKING TOO MUCH.
SO DO YOU HAVE THAT BOOK WRITTEN YET?

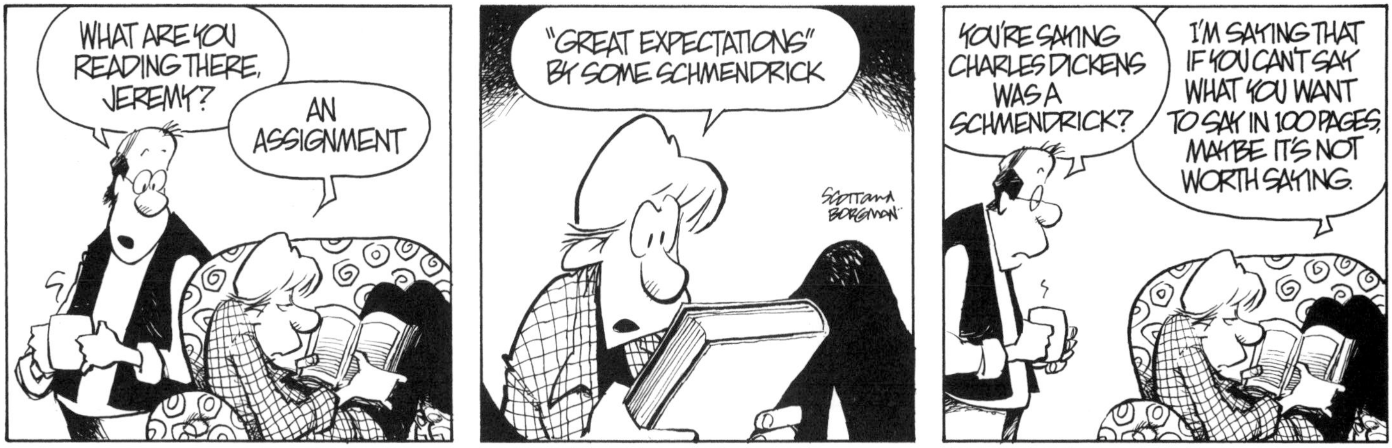
WHAT ARE YOU READING THERE, JEREMY?
AN ASSIGNMENT
"GREAT EXPECTATIONS" BY SOME SCHMENDRICK
SCOTT and BORGMAN
YOU'RE SAYING CHARLES DICKENS WAS A SCHMENDRICK?
I'M SAYING THAT IF YOU CAN'T SAY WHAT YOU WANT TO SAY IN 100 PAGES, MAYBE IT'S NOT WORTH SAYING.

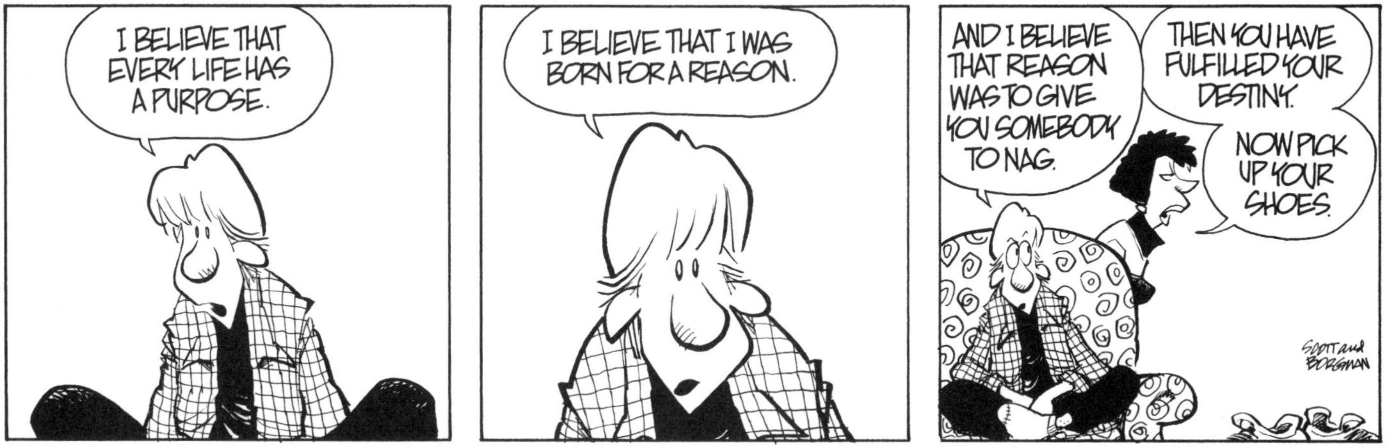
I BELIEVE THAT EVERY LIFE HAS A PURPOSE.
I BELIEVE THAT I WAS BORN FOR A REASON.
AND I BELIEVE THAT REASON WAS TO GIVE YOU SOMEBODY TO NAG.
THEN YOU HAVE FULFILLED YOUR DESTINY.
NOW PICK UP YOUR SHOES.
SCOTT and BORGMAN

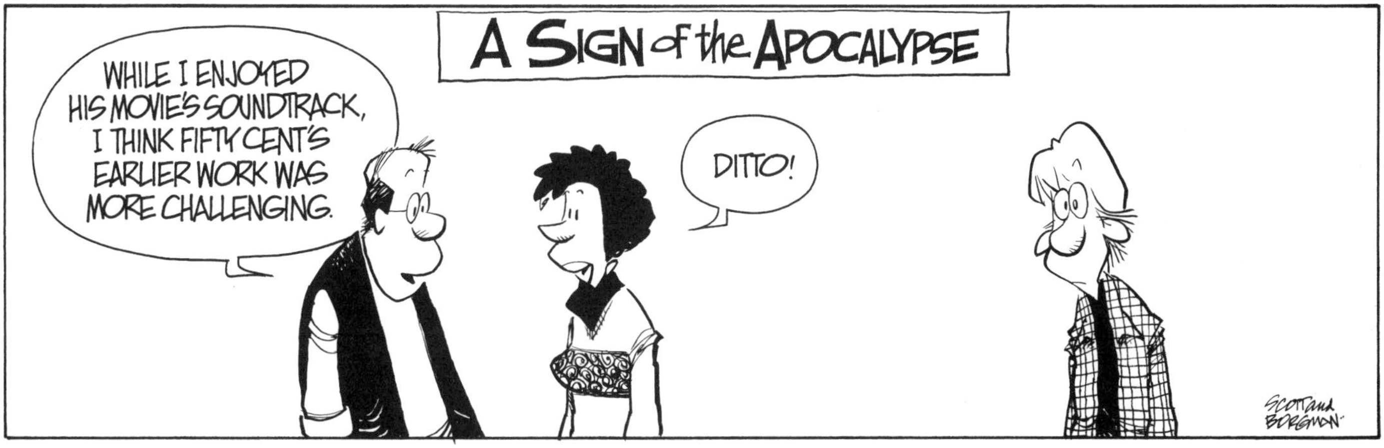
A SIGN of the APOCALYPSE
WHILE I ENJOYED HIS MOVIE'S SOUNDTRACK, I THINK FIFTY CENT'S EARLIER WORK WAS MORE CHALLENGING.
DITTO!
SCOTT and BORGMAN

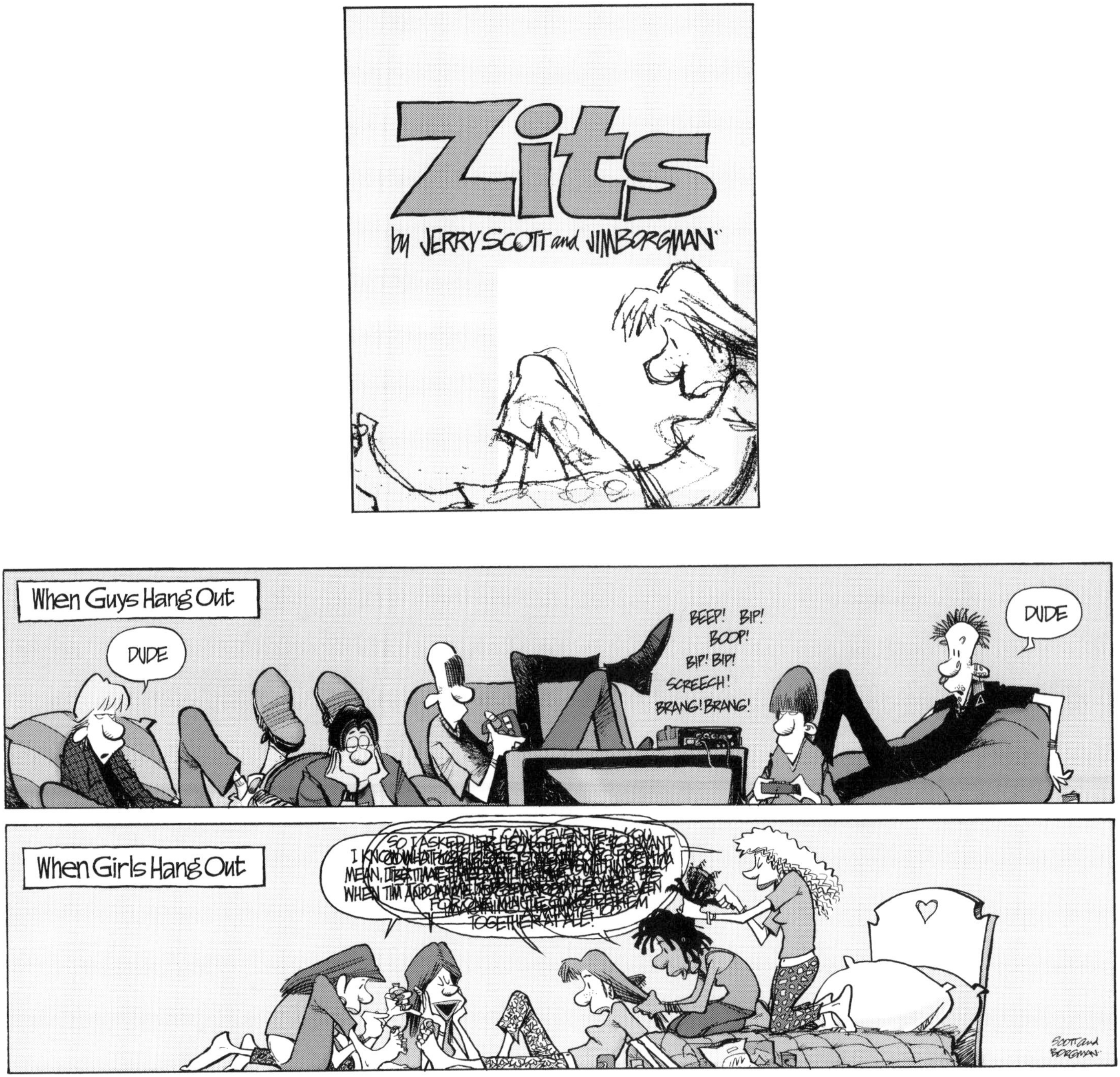

Zits
by JERRY SCOTT and JIM BORGMAN
When Guys Hang Out
DUDE
BEEP! BIP!
BOOP!
BIP! BIP!
SCREECH!
BRANG! BRANG!
DUDE
When Girls Hang Out
SCOTT and BORGMAN

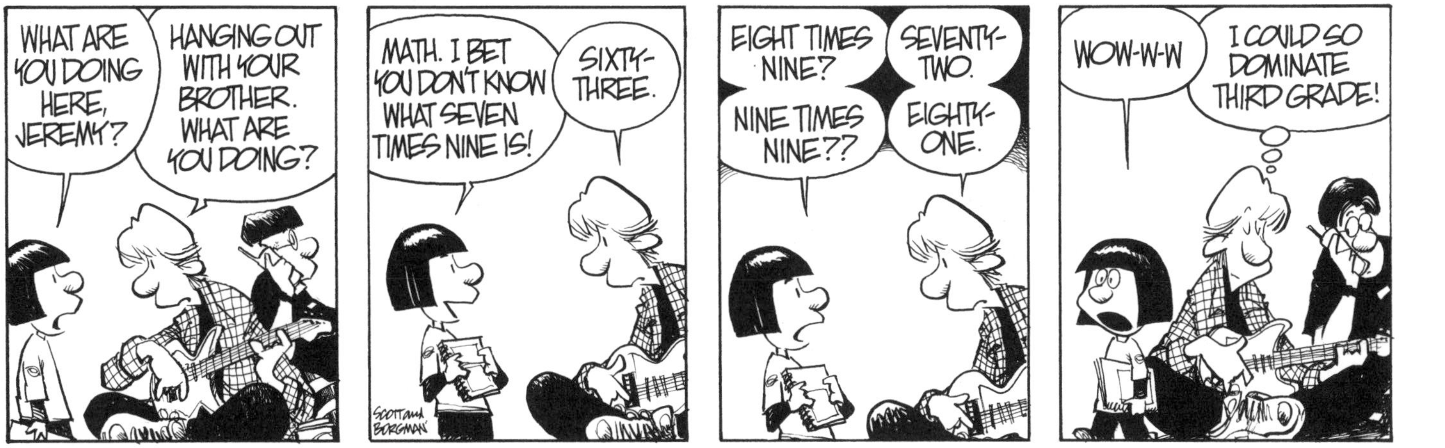
WHAT ARE YOU DOING HERE, JEREMY?
HANGING OUT WITH YOUR BROTHER. WHAT ARE YOU DOING?
MATH. I BET YOU DON'T KNOW WHAT SEVEN TIMES NINE IS!
SIXTY-THREE.
EIGHT TIMES NINE?
SEVENTY-TWO.
NINE TIMES NINE??
EIGHTY-ONE.
WOW-W-W
I COULD SO DOMINATE THIRD GRADE!

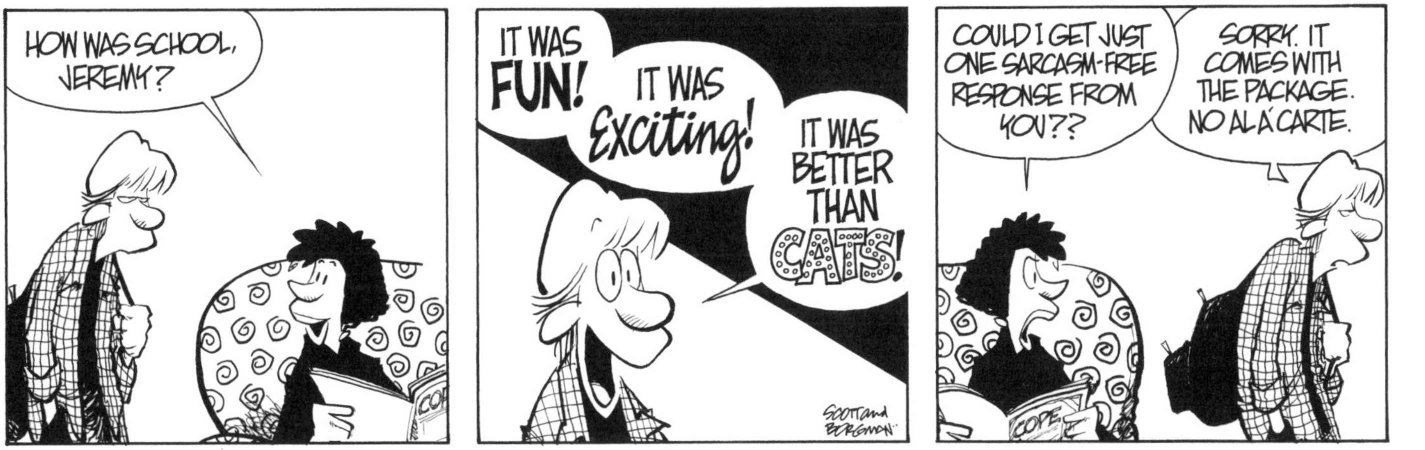
HOW WAS SCHOOL, JEREMY?
IT WAS FUN!
IT WAS Exciting!
IT WAS BETTER THAN CATS!
COULD I GET JUST ONE SARCASM-FREE RESPONSE FROM YOU??
SORRY. IT COMES WITH THE PACKAGE. NO AL A CARTE.

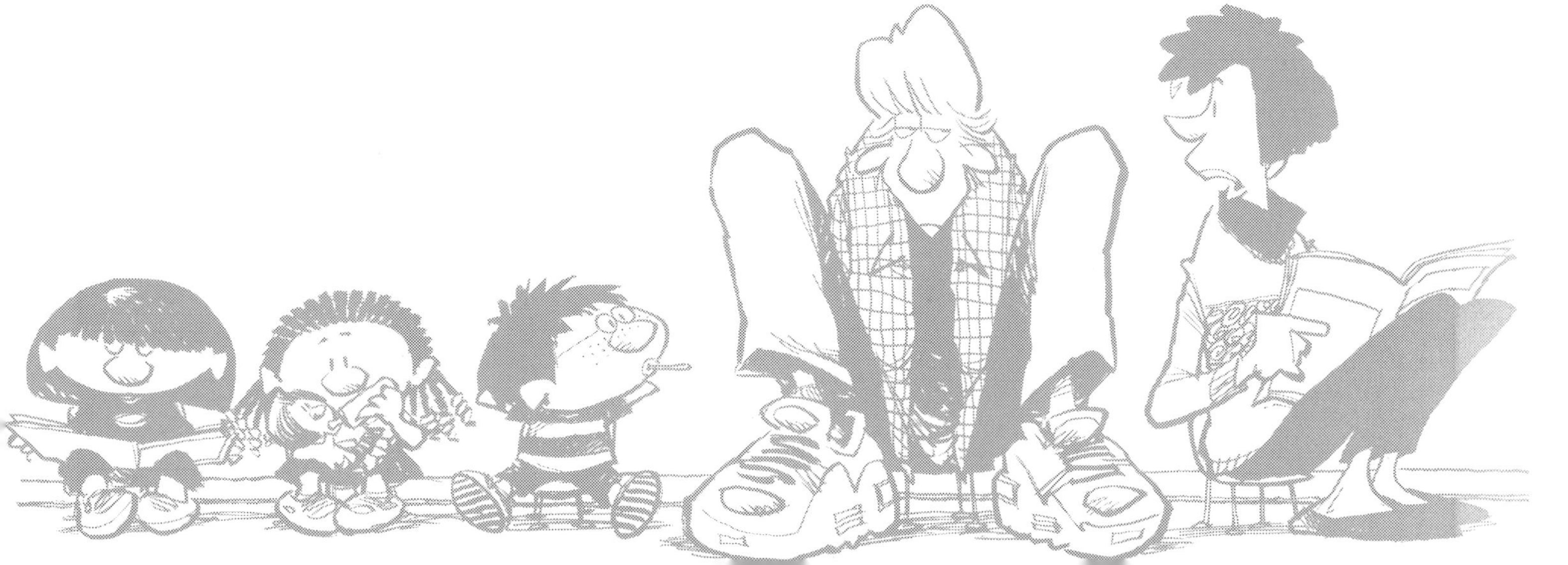

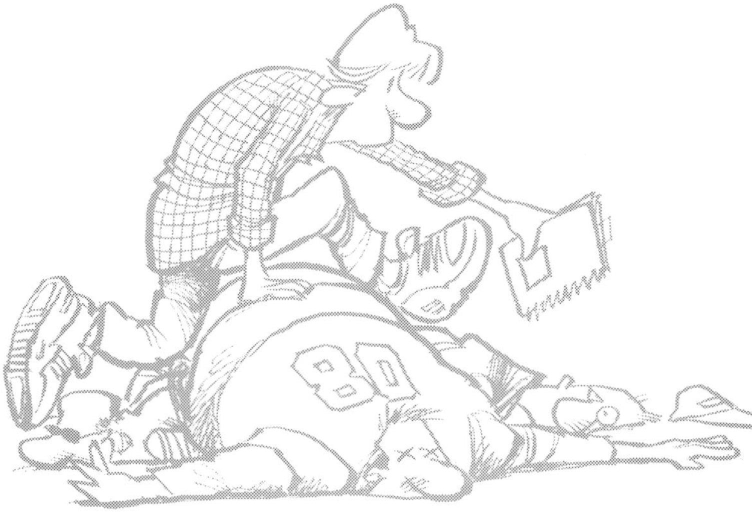

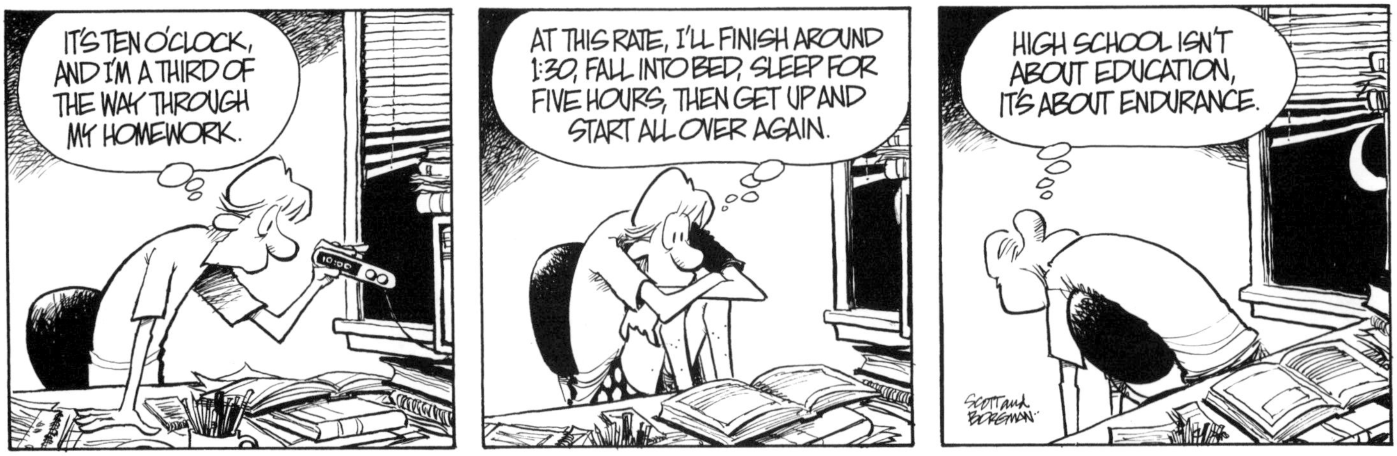
IT'S TEN O'CLOCK, AND I'M A THIRD OF THE WAY THROUGH MY HOMEWORK.
AT THIS RATE, I'LL FINISH AROUND 1:30, FALL INTO BED, SLEEP FOR FIVE HOURS, THEN GET UP AND START ALL OVER AGAIN.
HIGH SCHOOL ISN'T ABOUT EDUCATION, IT'S ABOUT ENDURANCE.

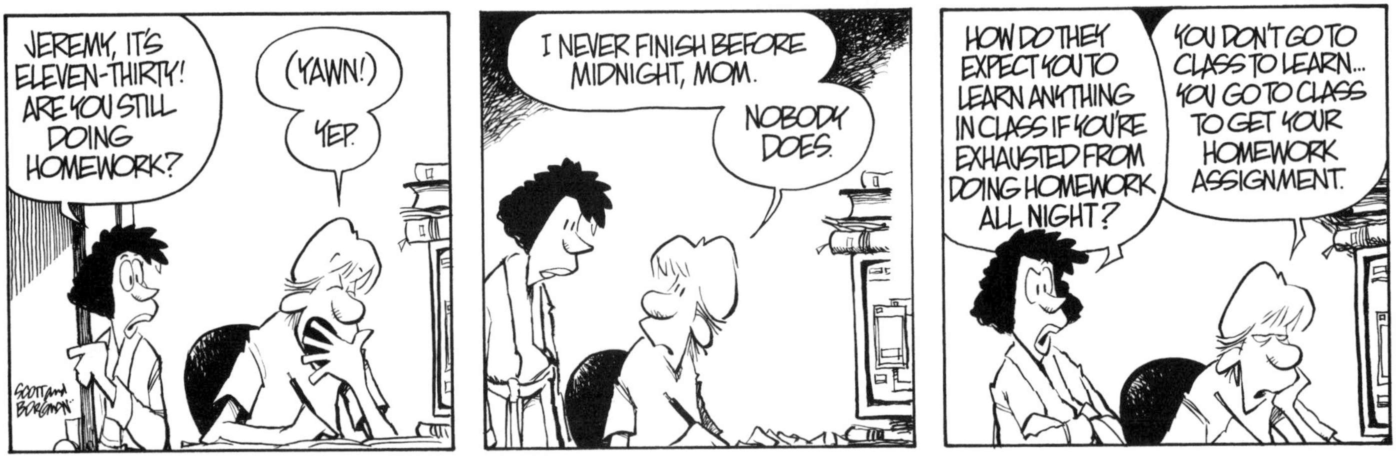
JEREMY, IT'S ELEVEN-THIRTY! ARE YOU STILL DOING HOMEWORK?
(YAWN!)
YEP.
I NEVER FINISH BEFORE MIDNIGHT, MOM.
NOBODY DOES.
HOW DO THEY EXPECT YOU TO LEARN ANYTHING IN CLASS IF YOU'RE EXHAUSTED FROM DOING HOMEWORK ALL NIGHT?
YOU DON'T GO TO CLASS TO LEARN... YOU GO TO CLASS TO GET YOUR HOMEWORK ASSIGNMENT.

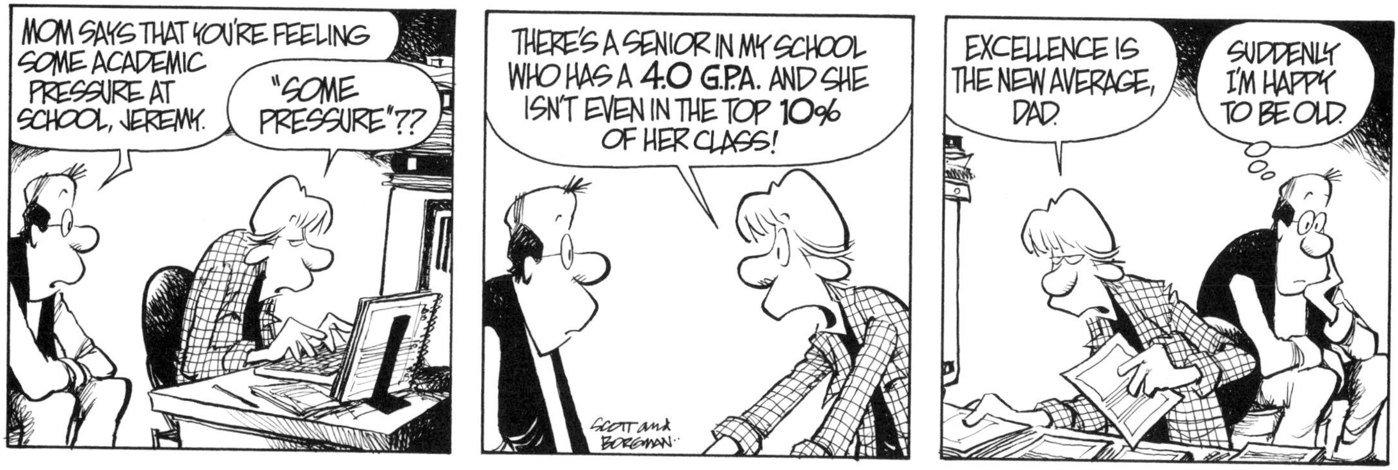
MOM SAYS THAT YOU'RE FEELING SOME ACADEMIC PRESSURE AT SCHOOL, JEREMY.
"SOME PRESSURE"??
THERE'S A SENIOR IN MY SCHOOL WHO HAS A 4.0 G.P.A. AND SHE ISN'T EVEN IN THE TOP 10% OF HER CLASS!
SCOTT and BORGMAN
EXCELLENCE IS THE NEW AVERAGE, DAD.
SUDDENLY I'M HAPPY TO BE OLD.

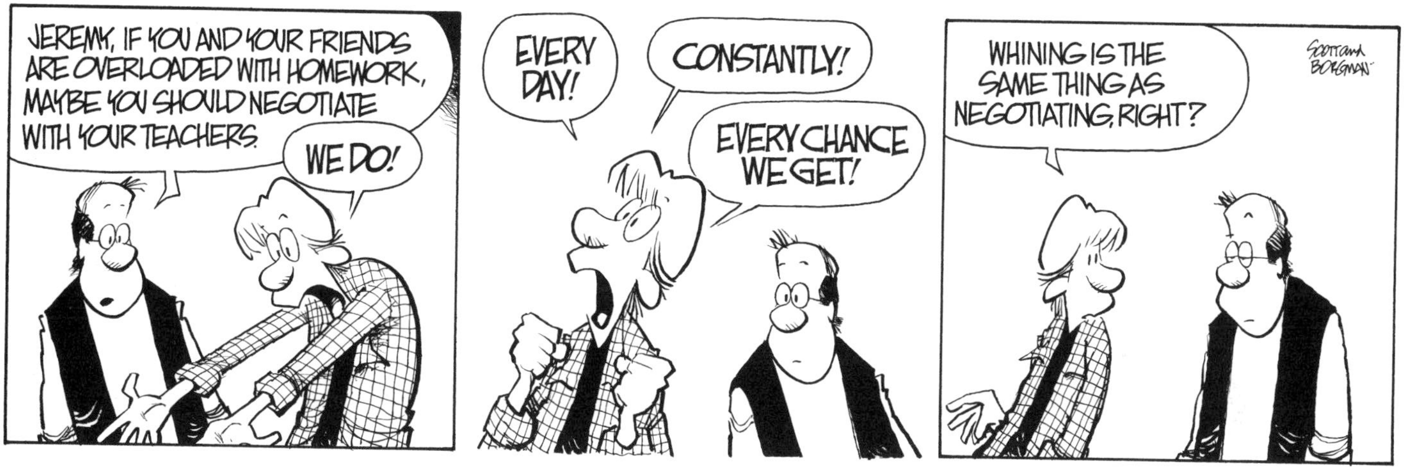
JEREMY, IF YOU AND YOUR FRIENDS ARE OVERLOADED WITH HOMEWORK, MAYBE YOU SHOULD NEGOTIATE WITH YOUR TEACHERS.
WE DO!
EVERY DAY!
CONSTANTLY!
EVERY CHANCE WE GET!
WHINING IS THE SAME THING AS NEGOTIATING, RIGHT?
SCOTT and BORGMAN

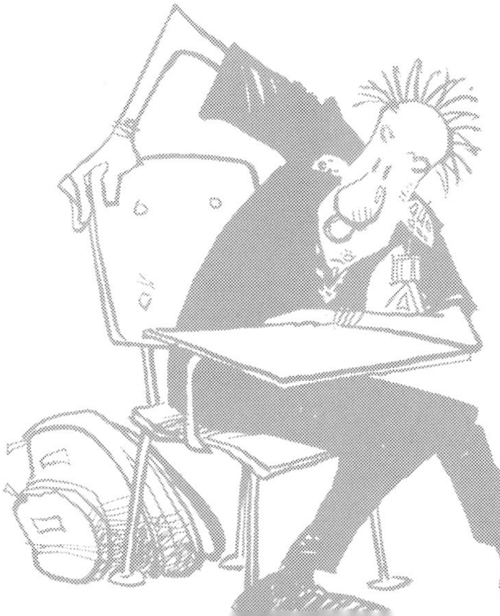

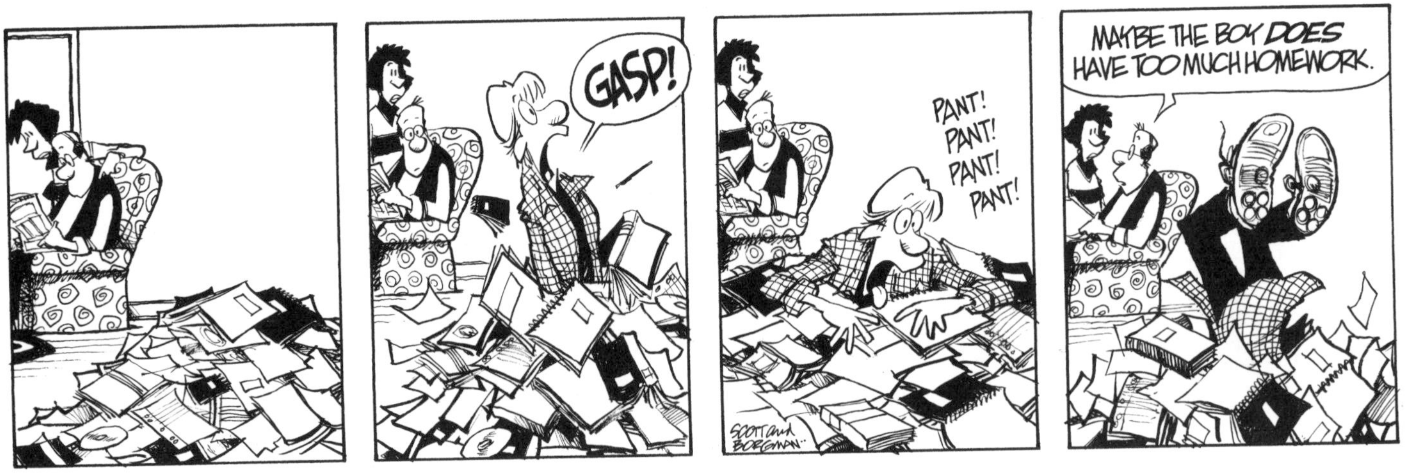
GASP!
PANT! PANT! PANT! PANT!
SCOTT and BORGMAN
MAYBE THE BOY DOES HAVE TOO MUCH HOMEWORK.

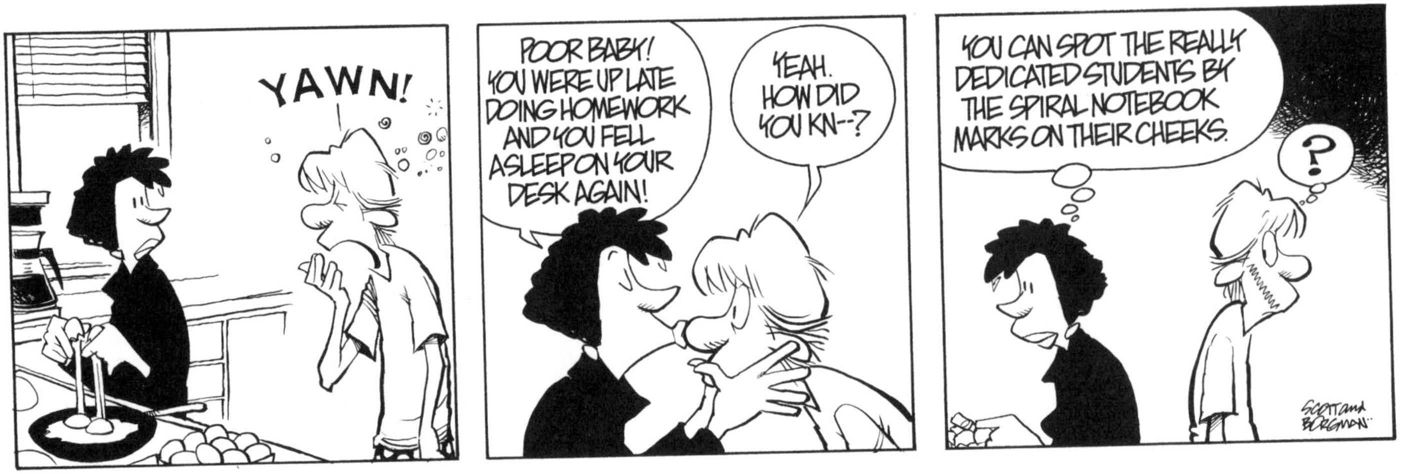
YAWN!
POOR BABY! YOU WERE UP LATE DOING HOMEWORK AND YOU FELL ASLEEP ON YOUR DESK AGAIN!
YEAH. HOW DID YOU KN--?
YOU CAN SPOT THE REALLY DEDICATED STUDENTS BY THE SPIRAL NOTEBOOK MARKS ON THEIR CHEEKS.
?
SCOTT and BORGMAN

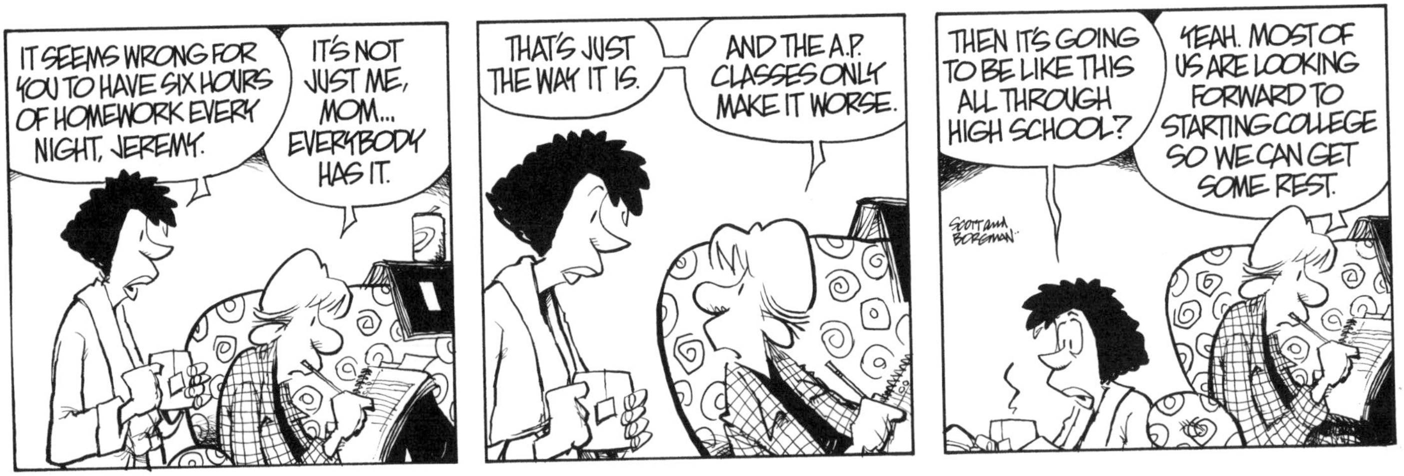
IT SEEMS WRONG FOR YOU TO HAVE SIX HOURS OF HOMEWORK EVERY NIGHT, JEREMY.
IT'S NOT JUST ME, MOM... EVERYBODY HAS IT.
THAT'S JUST THE WAY IT IS.
AND THE A.P. CLASSES ONLY MAKE IT WORSE.
THEN IT'S GOING TO BE LIKE THIS ALL THROUGH HIGH SCHOOL?
YEAH. MOST OF US ARE LOOKING FORWARD TO STARTING COLLEGE SO WE CAN GET SOME REST.
SCOTT and BORGMAN

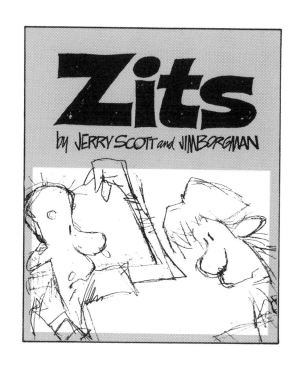

Zits

by JERRY SCOTT and JIM BORGMAN

SARA? IT'S CONNIE, JEREMY'S MOM

OH, HI!

JEREMY MUST HAVE TURNED HIS CELL PHONE OFF.

CAN YOU GIVE HIM A MESSAGE FOR ME?

SURE!

D'JON? SARA.

TELL JEREMY THAT HIS MOM LOCKED HER KEYS IN THE CAR, SO HE SHOULD GET A RIDE HOME WITH HECTOR.

GOT IT.

ZUMA? D'JON. GIVE JEREMY THIS MESSAGE...

'K.

THANKS BRITTANY.

NO PROBLEM. I'LL PASS IT ON.

PIERCE, I HAVE A MESSAGE FOR JEREMY.

GO.

SCOTT and BORGMAN

GIVE HECTOR A RIDE HOME. YOUR MOM LOCKED HER CHEESE IN A JAR.

...OR SOMETHING LIKE THAT.

AND SHE WONDERS WHY I SCREEN HER CALLS...

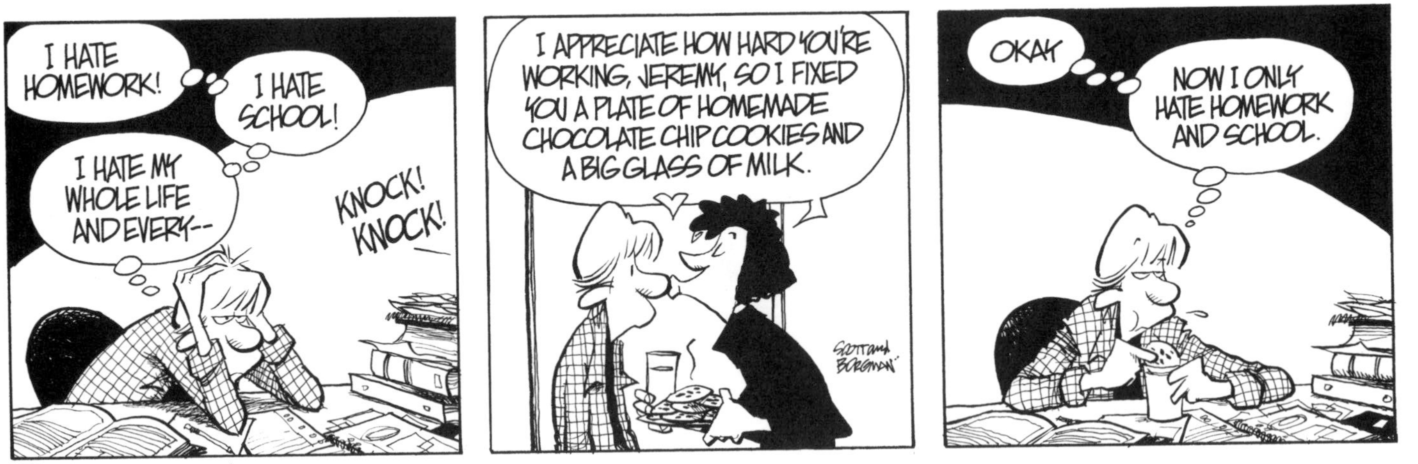
I HATE HOMEWORK!
I HATE SCHOOL!
I HATE MY WHOLE LIFE AND EVERY--
KNOCK! KNOCK!
I APPRECIATE HOW HARD YOU'RE WORKING, JEREMY, SO I FIXED YOU A PLATE OF HOMEMADE CHOCOLATE CHIP COOKIES AND A BIG GLASS OF MILK.
OKAY
NOW I ONLY HATE HOMEWORK AND SCHOOL.

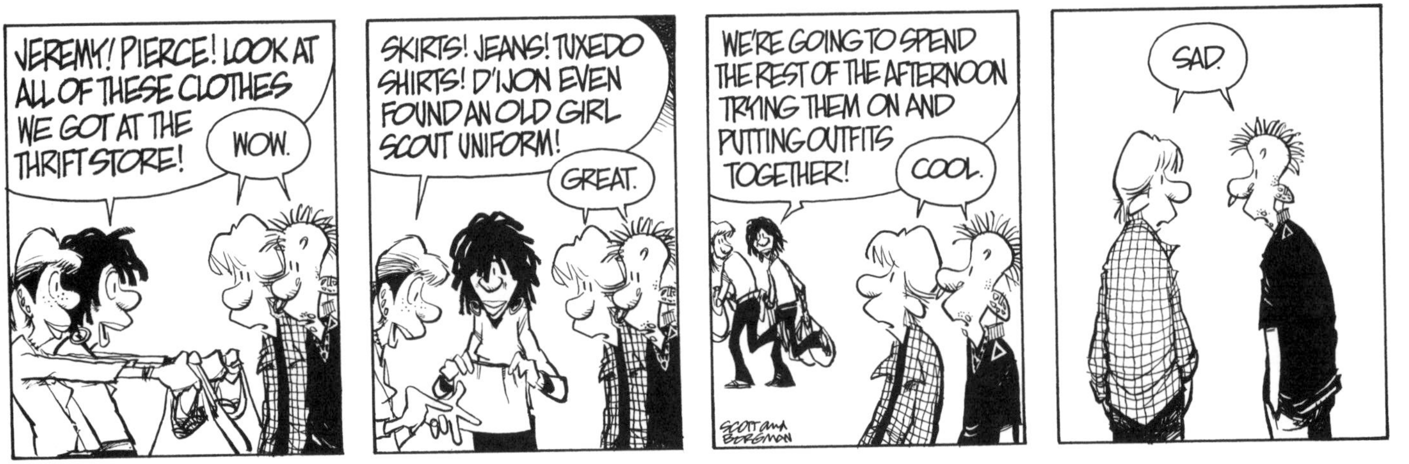
JEREMY! PIERCE! LOOK AT ALL OF THESE CLOTHES WE GOT AT THE THRIFT STORE!
WOW.
SKIRTS! JEANS! TUXEDO SHIRTS! D'JON EVEN FOUND AN OLD GIRL SCOUT UNIFORM!
GREAT.
WE'RE GOING TO SPEND THE REST OF THE AFTERNOON TRYING THEM ON AND PUTTING OUTFITS TOGETHER!
COOL.
SAD.

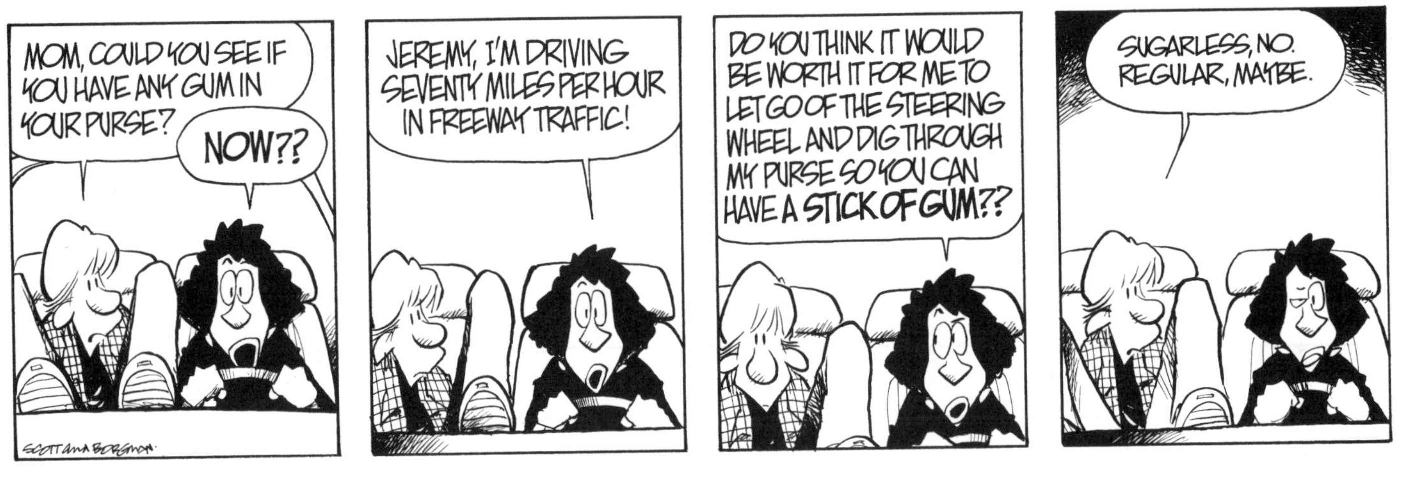
MOM, COULD YOU SEE IF YOU HAVE ANY GUM IN YOUR PURSE?
NOW??
JEREMY, I'M DRIVING SEVENTY MILES PER HOUR IN FREEWAY TRAFFIC!
DO YOU THINK IT WOULD BE WORTH IT FOR ME TO LET GO OF THE STEERING WHEEL AND DIG THROUGH MY PURSE SO YOU CAN HAVE A STICK OF GUM??
SUGARLESS, NO. REGULAR, MAYBE.

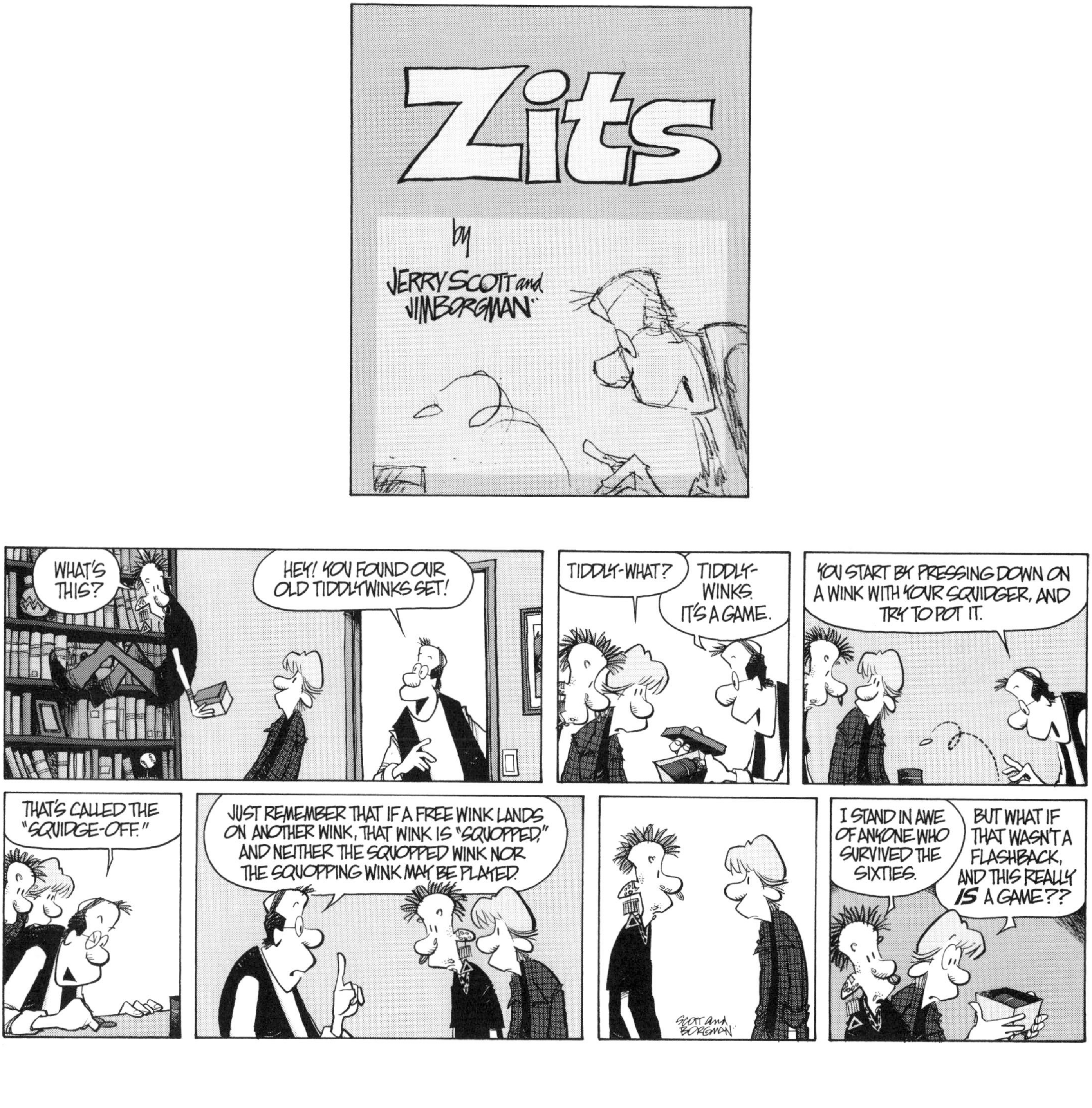
Zits
by
JERRY SCOTT and JIM BORGMAN
WHAT'S THIS?
HEY! YOU FOUND OUR OLD TIDDLYWINKS SET!
TIDDLY-WHAT?
TIDDLY-WINKS. IT'S A GAME.
YOU START BY PRESSING DOWN ON A WINK WITH YOUR SQUIDGER, AND TRY TO POT IT.
THAT'S CALLED THE "SQUIDGE-OFF."
JUST REMEMBER THAT IF A FREE WINK LANDS ON ANOTHER WINK, THAT WINK IS "SQUOPPED," AND NEITHER THE SQUOPPED WINK NOR THE SQUOPPING WINK MAY BE PLAYED.
SCOTT and BORGMAN
I STAND IN AWE OF ANYONE WHO SURVIVED THE SIXTIES.
BUT WHAT IF THAT WASN'T A FLASHBACK, AND THIS REALLY IS A GAME??

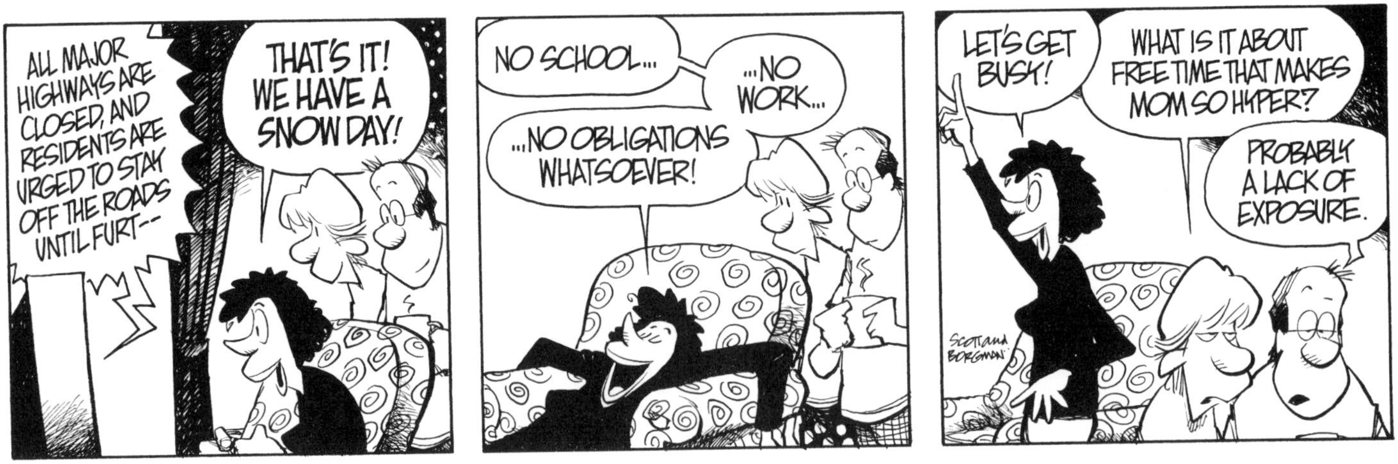
ALL MAJOR HIGHWAYS ARE CLOSED, AND RESIDENTS ARE URGED TO STAY OFF THE ROADS UNTIL FURT--
THAT'S IT! WE HAVE A SNOW DAY!
NO SCHOOL...
...NO WORK...
...NO OBLIGATIONS WHATSOEVER!
LET'S GET BUSY!
WHAT IS IT ABOUT FREE TIME THAT MAKES MOM SO HYPER?
PROBABLY A LACK OF EXPOSURE.
SCOTT and BORGMAN

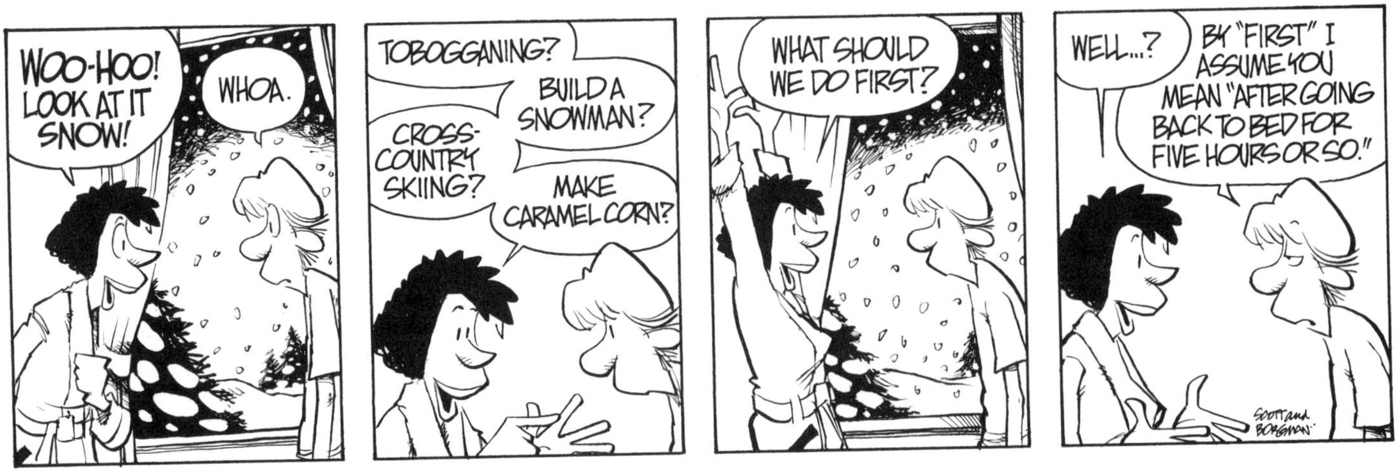
WOO-HOO! LOOK AT IT SNOW!
WHOA.
TOBOGGANING?
BUILD A SNOWMAN?
CROSS-COUNTRY SKIING?
MAKE CARAMEL CORN?
WHAT SHOULD WE DO FIRST?
WELL...?
BY "FIRST" I ASSUME YOU MEAN "AFTER GOING BACK TO BED FOR FIVE HOURS OR SO."
SCOTT and BORGMAN

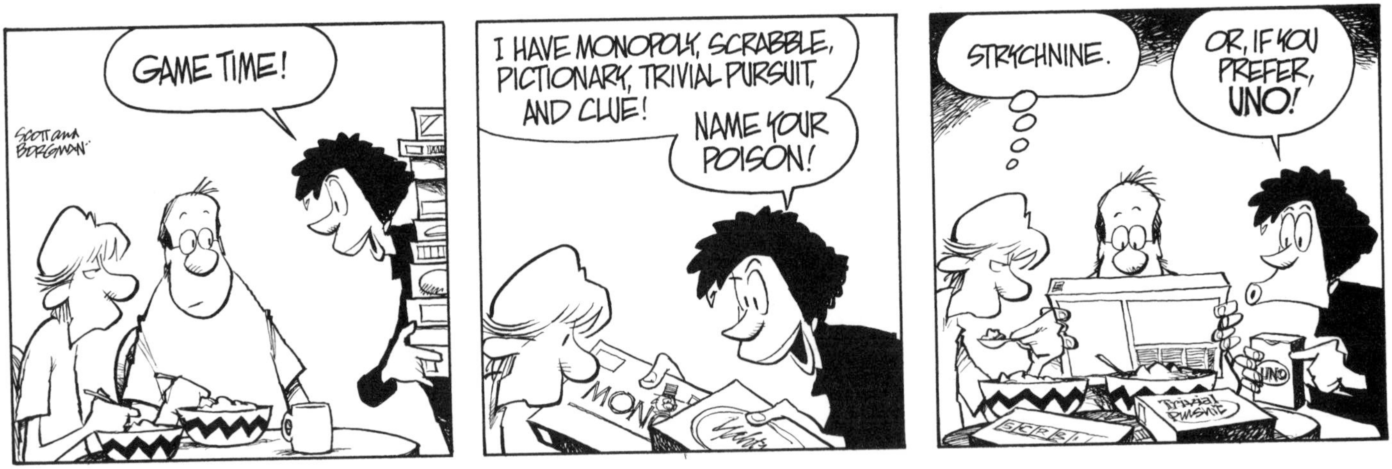
GAME TIME!
SCOTT and BORGMAN
I HAVE MONOPOLY, SCRABBLE, PICTIONARY, TRIVIAL PURSUIT, AND CLUE!
NAME YOUR POISON!
STRYCHNINE.
OR, IF YOU PREFER, UNO!

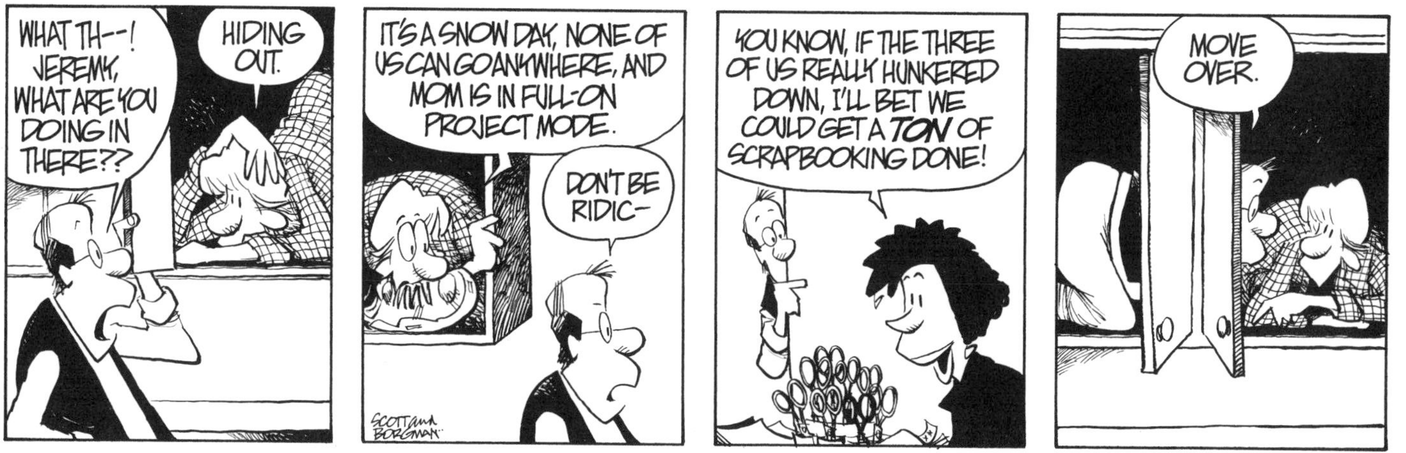
WHAT TH--! JEREMY, WHAT ARE YOU DOING IN THERE??
HIDING OUT.
IT'S A SNOW DAY, NONE OF US CAN GO ANYWHERE, AND MOM IS IN FULL-ON PROJECT MODE.
DON'T BE RIDIC-
YOU KNOW, IF THE THREE OF US REALLY HUNKERED DOWN, I'LL BET WE COULD GET A TON OF SCRAPBOOKING DONE!
MOVE OVER.

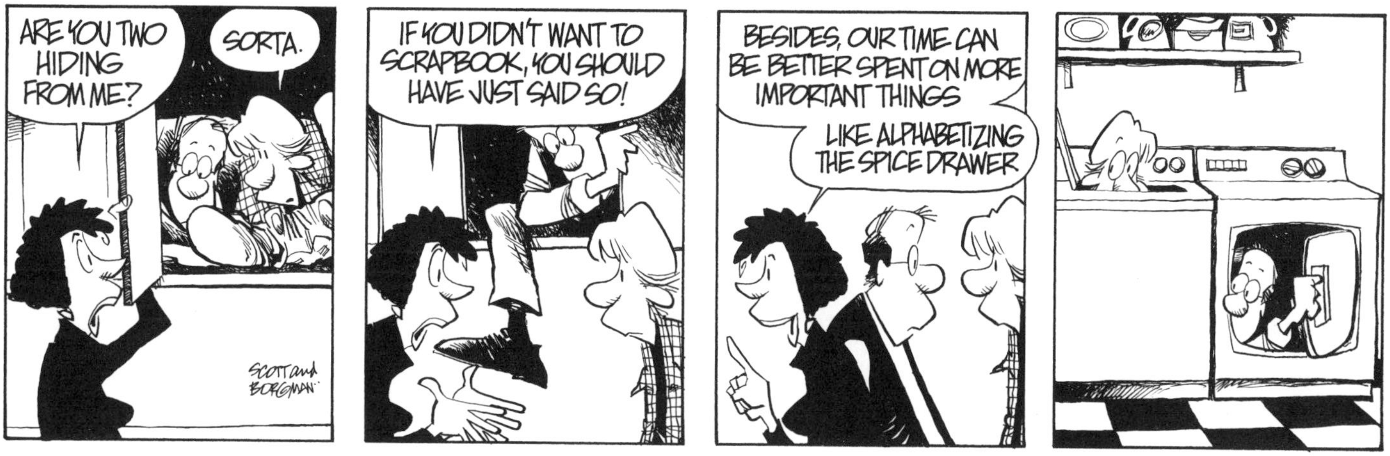
ARE YOU TWO HIDING FROM ME?
SORTA.
IF YOU DIDN'T WANT TO SCRAPBOOK, YOU SHOULD HAVE JUST SAID SO!
BESIDES, OUR TIME CAN BE BETTER SPENT ON MORE IMPORTANT THINGS
LIKE ALPHABETIZING THE SPICE DRAWER

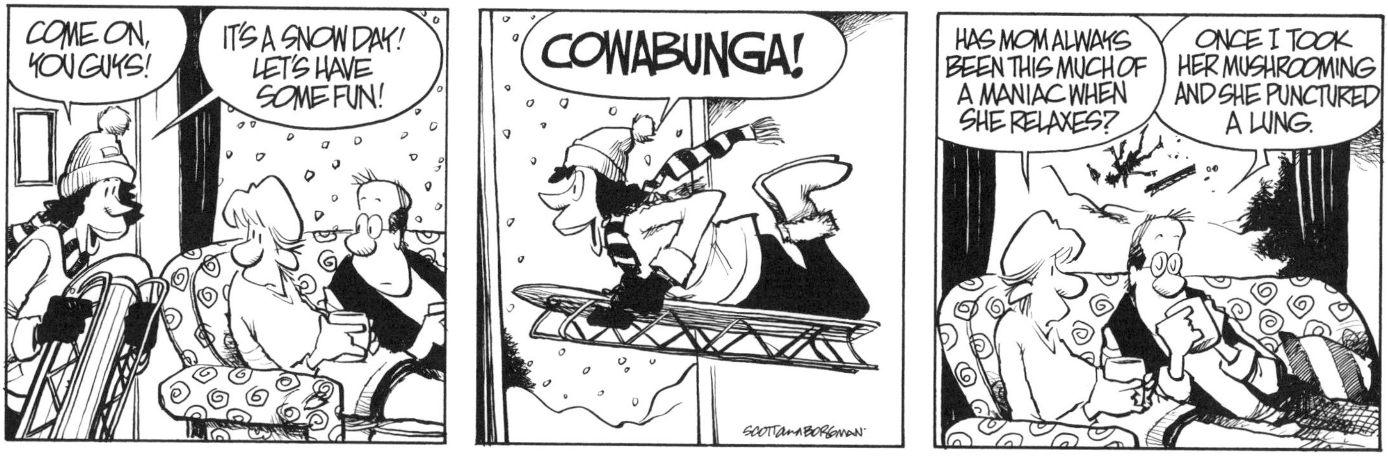
COME ON, YOU GUYS!
IT'S A SNOW DAY! LET'S HAVE SOME FUN!
COWABUNGA!
HAS MOM ALWAYS BEEN THIS MUCH OF A MANIAC WHEN SHE RELAXES?
ONCE I TOOK HER MUSHROOMING AND SHE PUNCTURED A LUNG.

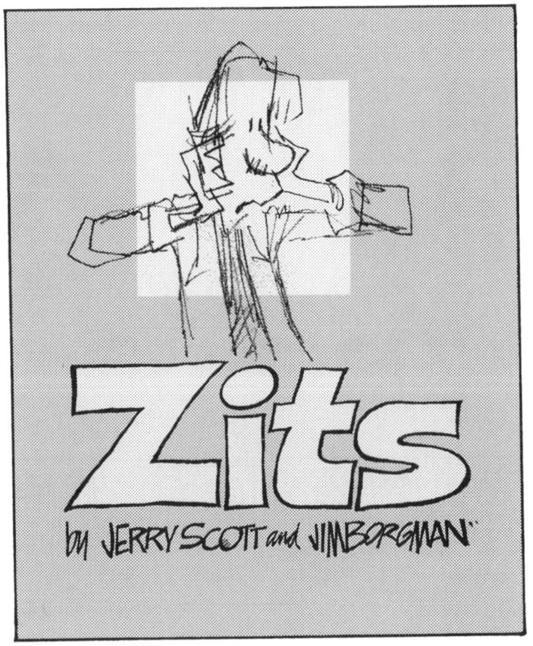
Zits
by JERRY SCOTT and JIM BORGMAN

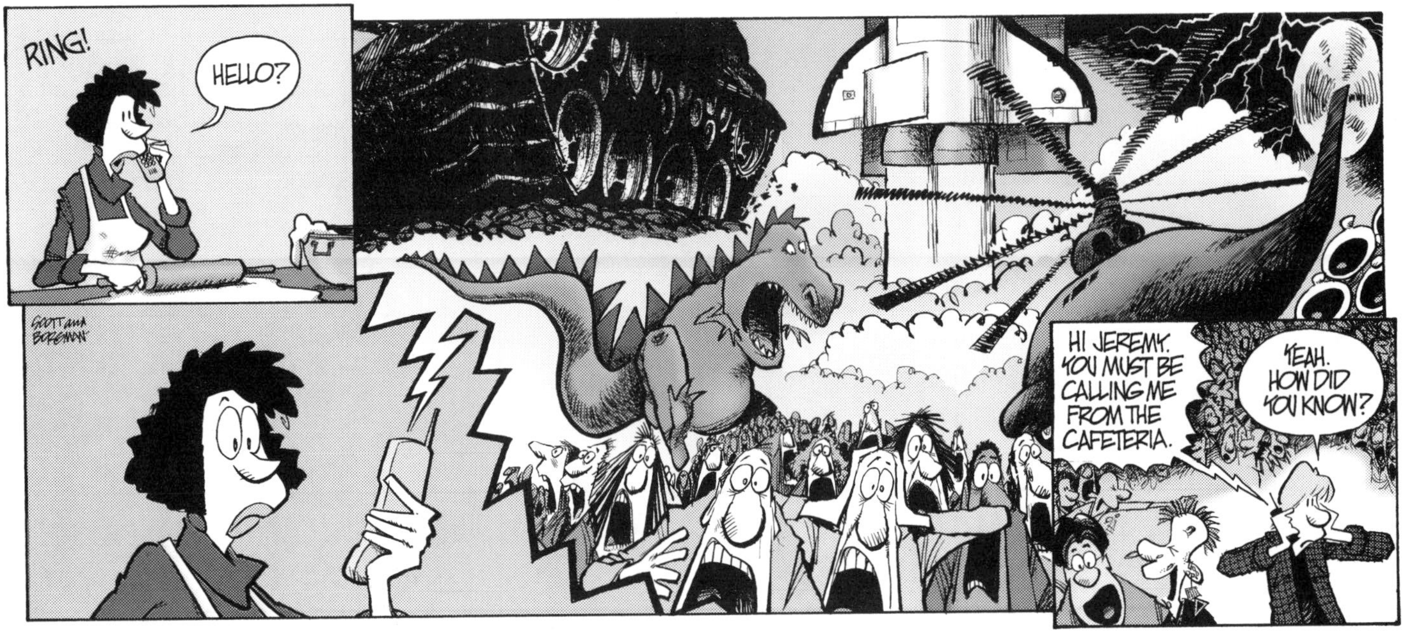
RING!
HELLO?
SCOTT and BORGMAN
HI JEREMY. YOU MUST BE CALLING ME FROM THE CAFETERIA.
YEAH. HOW DID YOU KNOW?

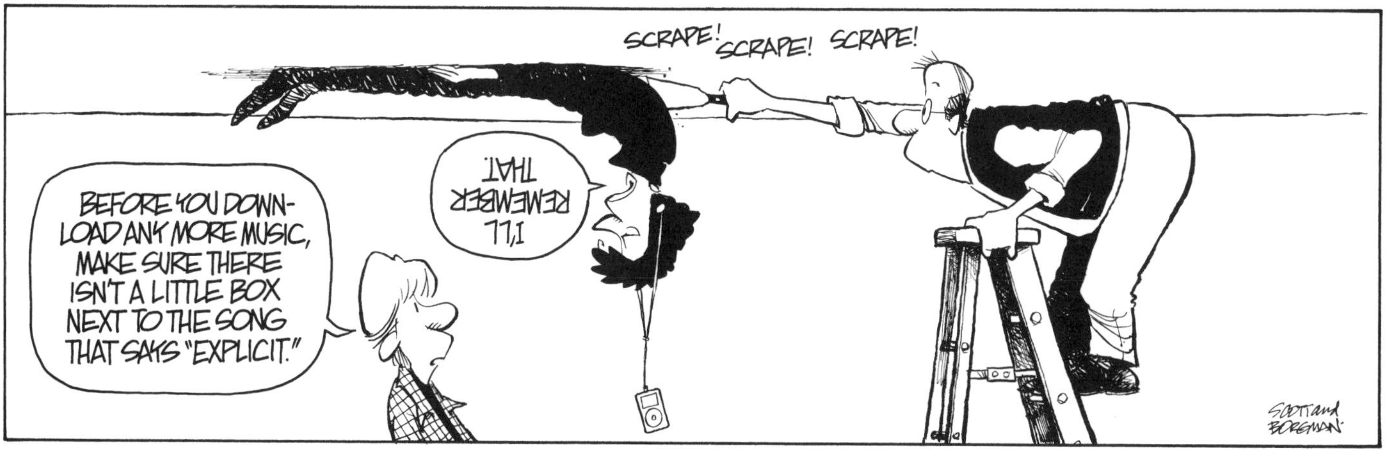
SCRAPE! SCRAPE! SCRAPE!
BEFORE YOU DOWNLOAD ANY MORE MUSIC, MAKE SURE THERE ISN'T A LITTLE BOX NEXT TO THE SONG THAT SAYS "EXPLICIT."
I'LL REMEMBER THAT.
SCOTT and BORGMAN

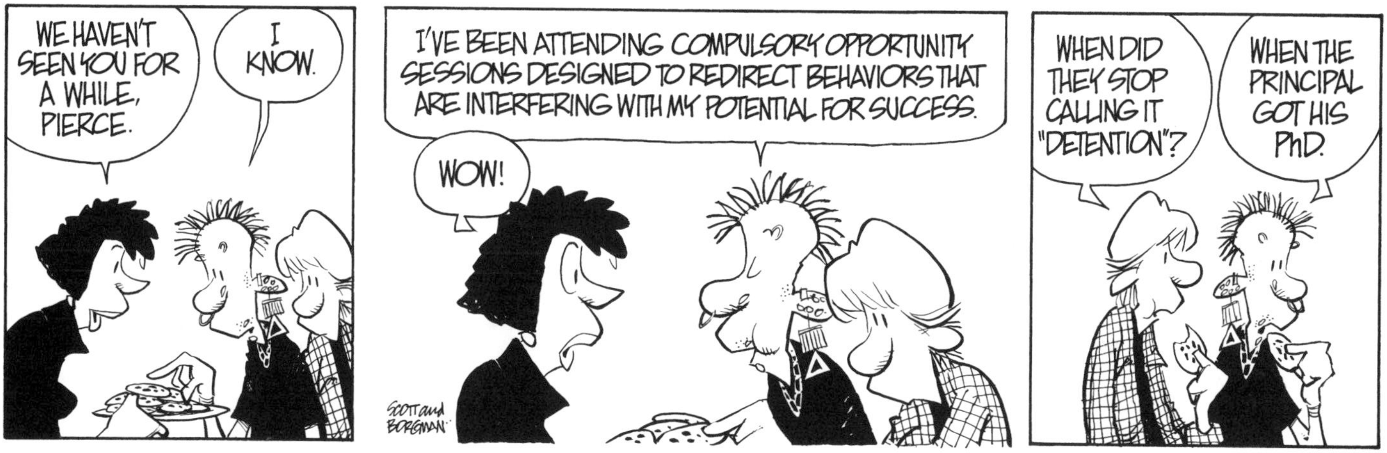
WE HAVEN'T SEEN YOU FOR A WHILE, PIERCE.
I KNOW.
SCOTT and BORGMAN
I'VE BEEN ATTENDING COMPULSORY OPPORTUNITY SESSIONS DESIGNED TO REDIRECT BEHAVIORS THAT ARE INTERFERING WITH MY POTENTIAL FOR SUCCESS.
WOW!
WHEN DID THEY STOP CALLING IT "DETENTION"?
WHEN THE PRINCIPAL GOT HIS PhD.

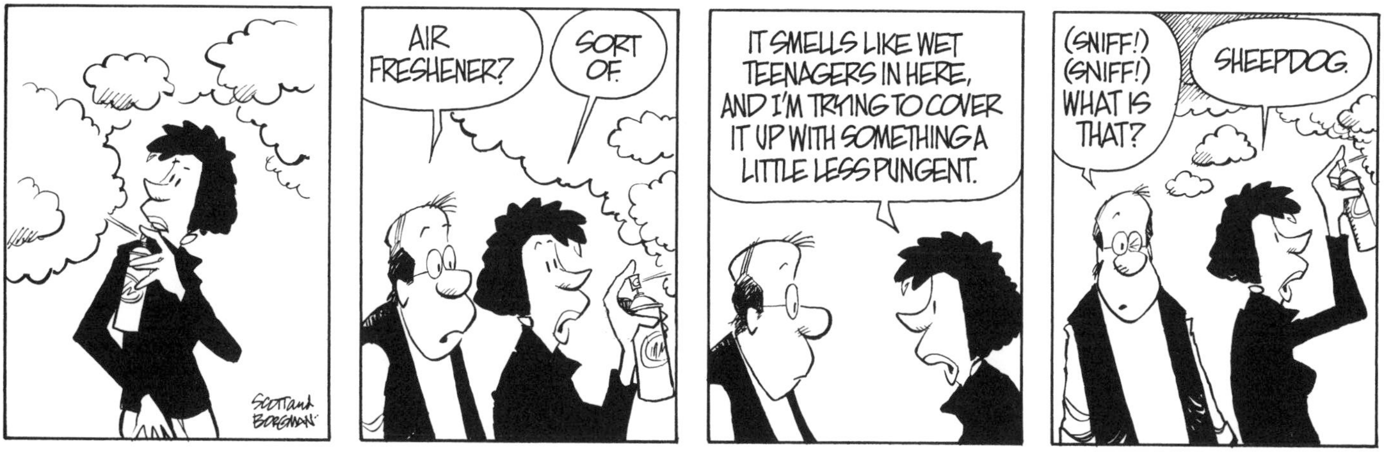
SCOTT and BORGMAN
AIR FRESHENER?
SORT OF.
IT SMELLS LIKE WET TEENAGERS IN HERE, AND I'M TRYING TO COVER IT UP WITH SOMETHING A LITTLE LESS PUNGENT.
(SNIFF!) (SNIFF!) WHAT IS THAT?
SHEEPDOG.

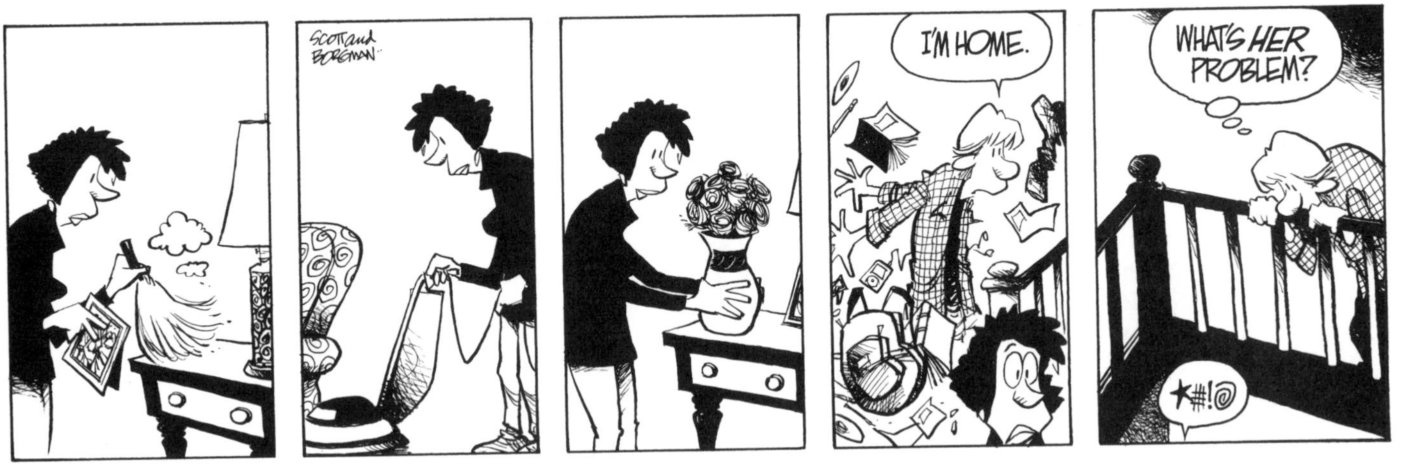
SCOTT and BORGMAN
I'M HOME.
WHAT'S HER PROBLEM?

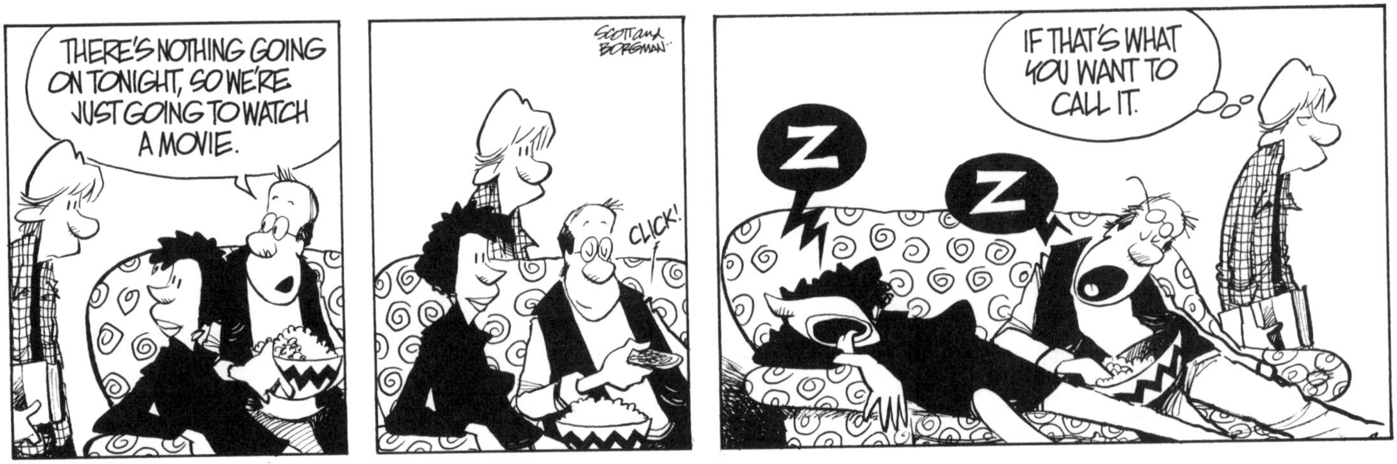
THERE'S NOTHING GOING ON TONIGHT, SO WE'RE JUST GOING TO WATCH A MOVIE.
SCOTT and BORGMAN
CLICK!
Z
Z
IF THAT'S WHAT YOU WANT TO CALL IT.

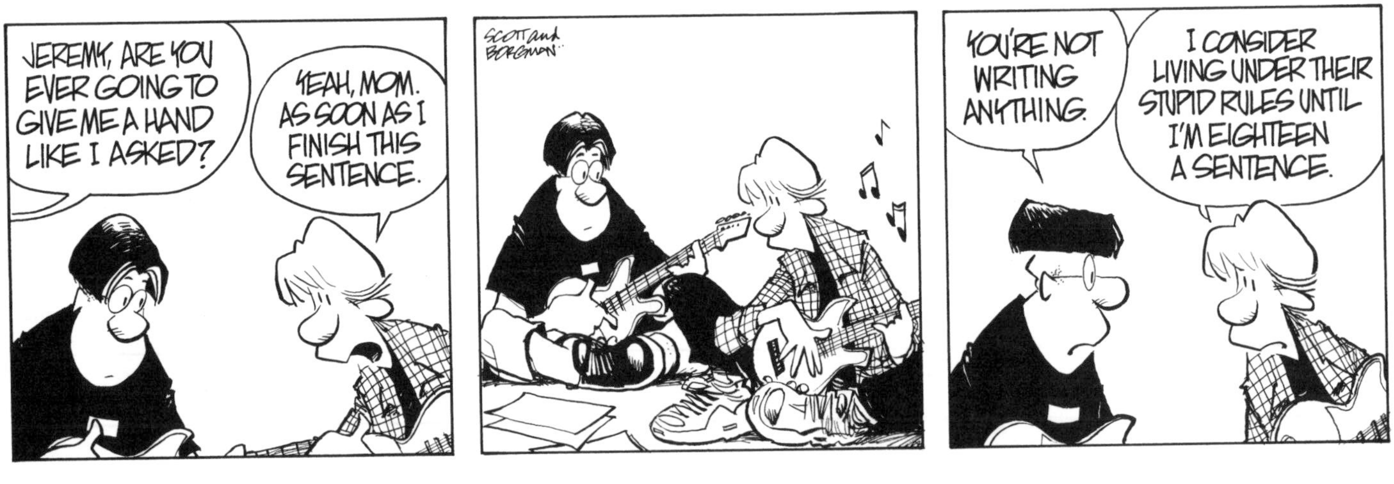
JEREMY, ARE YOU EVER GOING TO GIVE ME A HAND LIKE I ASKED?
YEAH, MOM. AS SOON AS I FINISH THIS SENTENCE.
SCOTT and BORGMAN
YOU'RE NOT WRITING ANYTHING.
I CONSIDER LIVING UNDER THEIR STUPID RULES UNTIL I'M EIGHTEEN A SENTENCE.

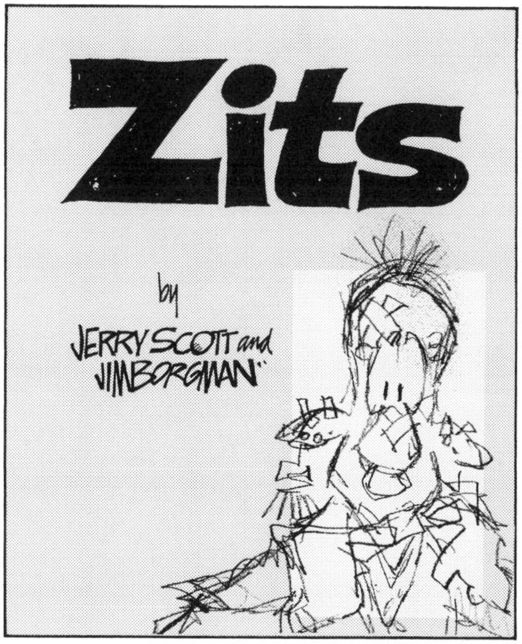
Zits
by
JERRY SCOTT and
JIM BORGMAN

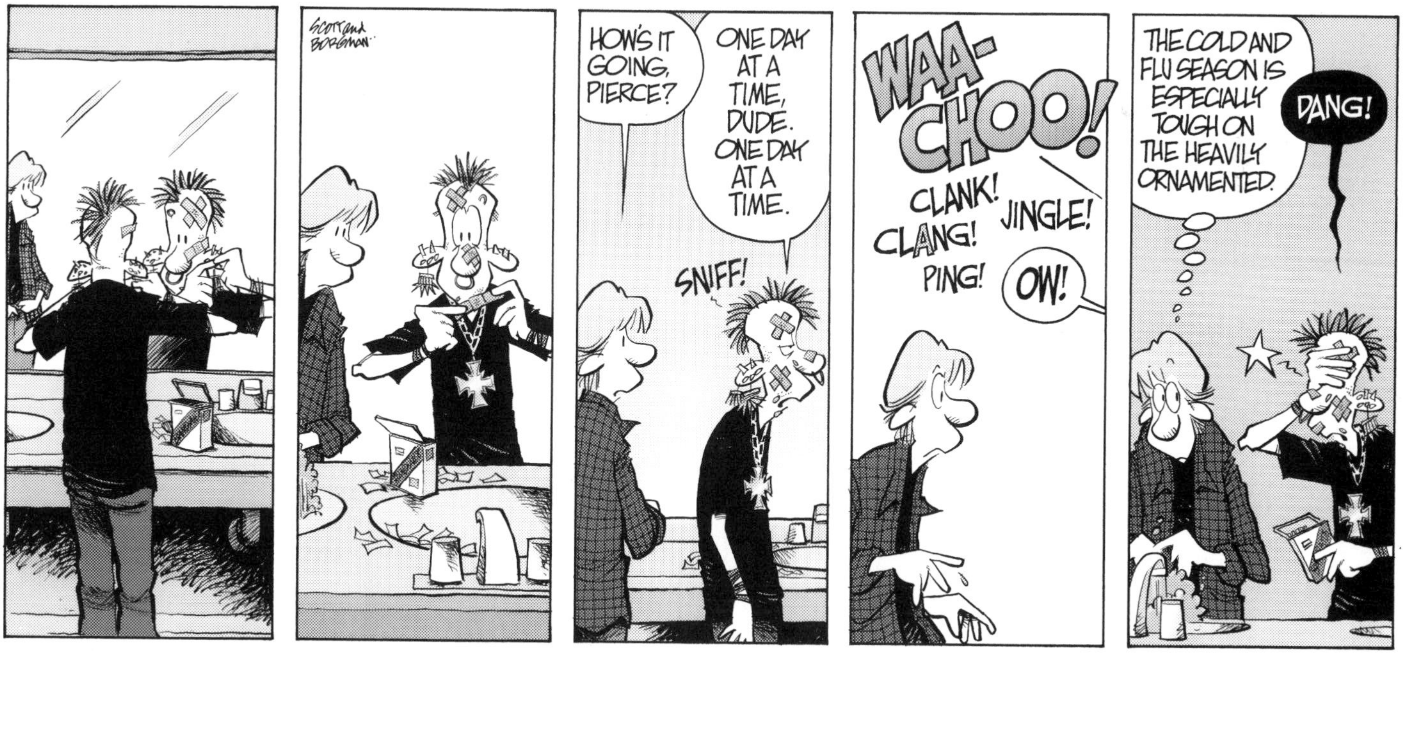
SCOTT and BORGMAN
HOW'S IT GOING, PIERCE?
ONE DAY AT A TIME, DUDE. ONE DAY AT A TIME.
SNIFF!
WAA-CHOO!
CLANK!
CLANG!
JINGLE!
PING!
OW!
THE COLD AND FLU SEASON IS ESPECIALLY TOUGH ON THE HEAVILY ORNAMENTED.
DANG!

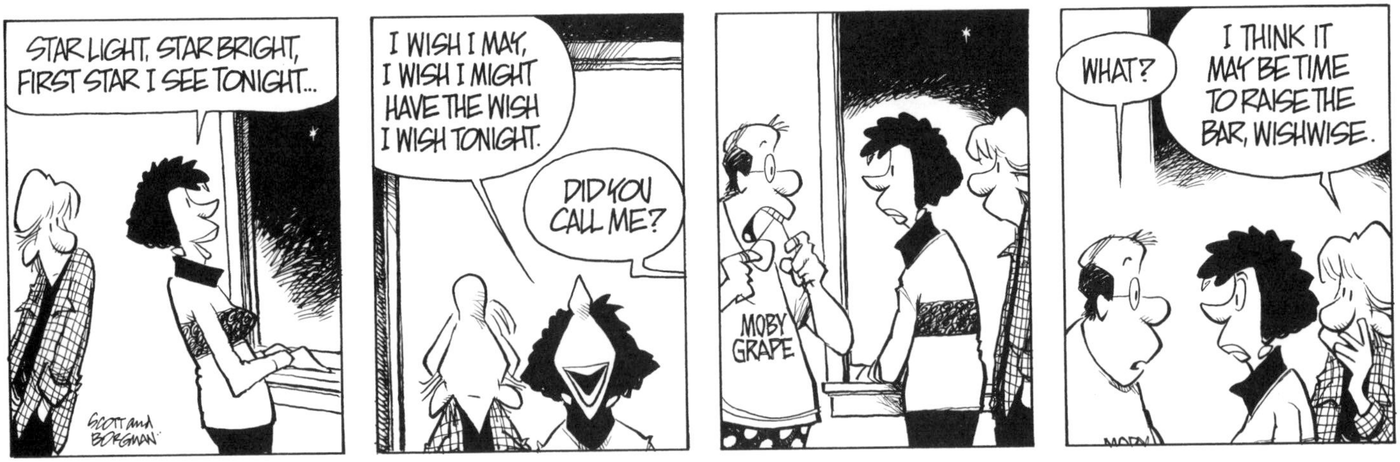
STAR LIGHT, STAR BRIGHT, FIRST STAR I SEE TONIGHT...
SCOTT and BORGMAN
I WISH I MAY, I WISH I MIGHT HAVE THE WISH I WISH TONIGHT.
DID YOU CALL ME?
MOBY GRAPE
WHAT?
I THINK IT MAY BE TIME TO RAISE THE BAR, WISHWISE.

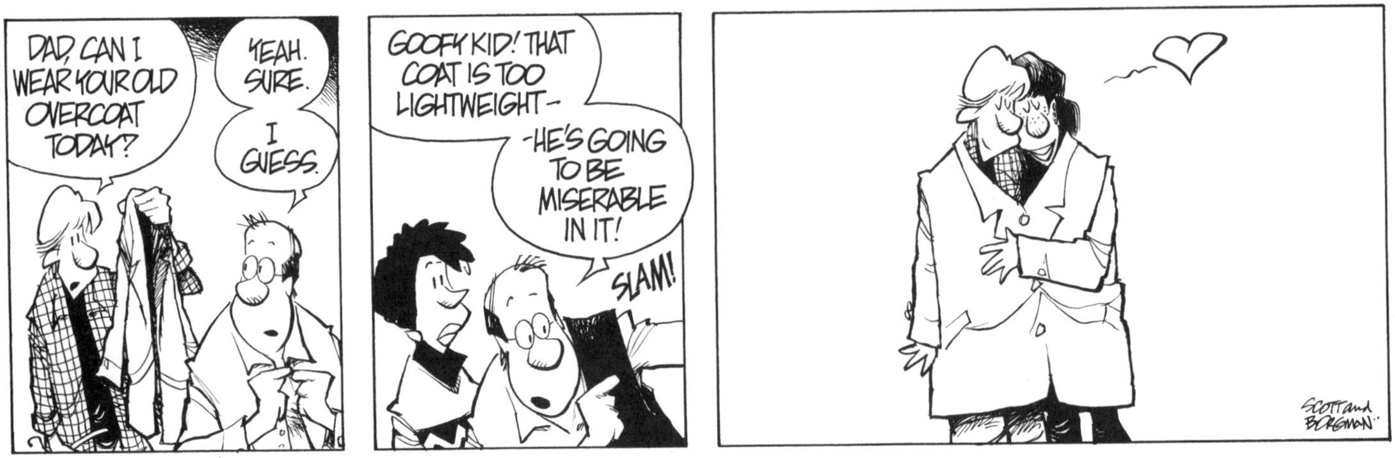
DAD, CAN I WEAR YOUR OLD OVERCOAT TODAY?
YEAH. SURE.
I GUESS.
GOOFY KID! THAT COAT IS TOO LIGHTWEIGHT-
-HE'S GOING TO BE MISERABLE IN IT!
SLAM!
SCOTT and BORGMAN

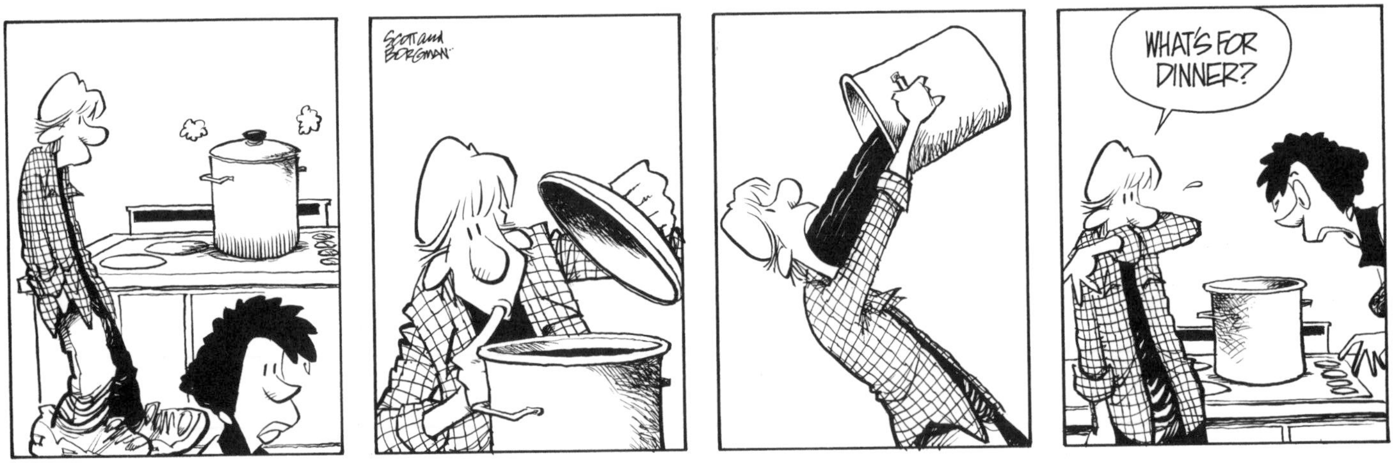
SCOTT and BORGMAN
WHAT'S FOR DINNER?

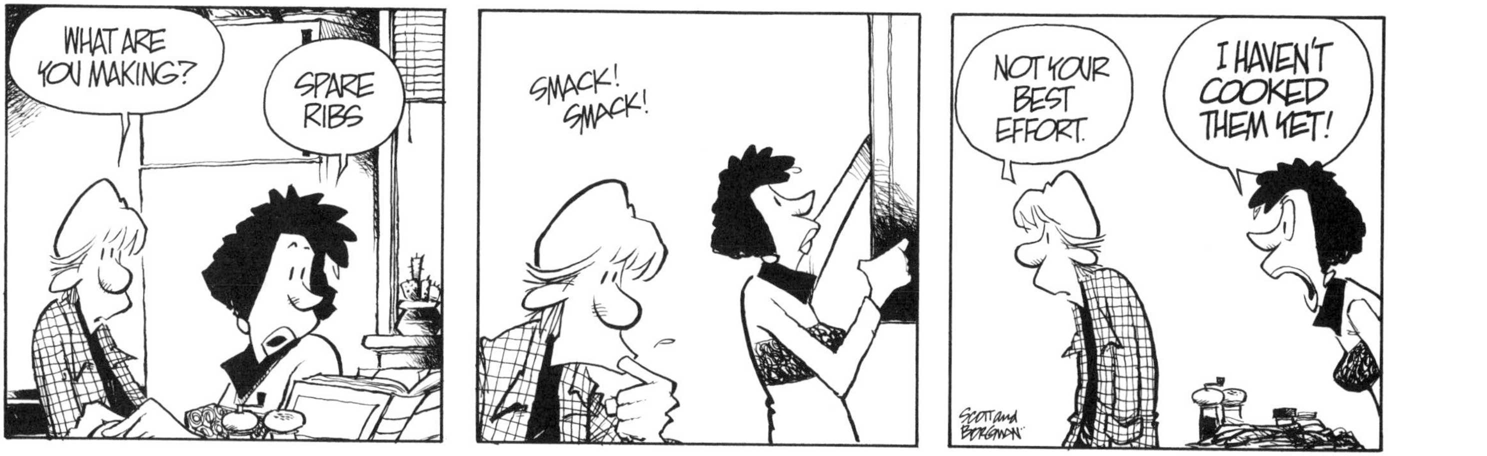
WHAT ARE YOU MAKING?
SPARE RIBS
SMACK! SMACK!
NOT YOUR BEST EFFORT.
I HAVEN'T COOKED THEM YET!
SCOTT and BORGMAN

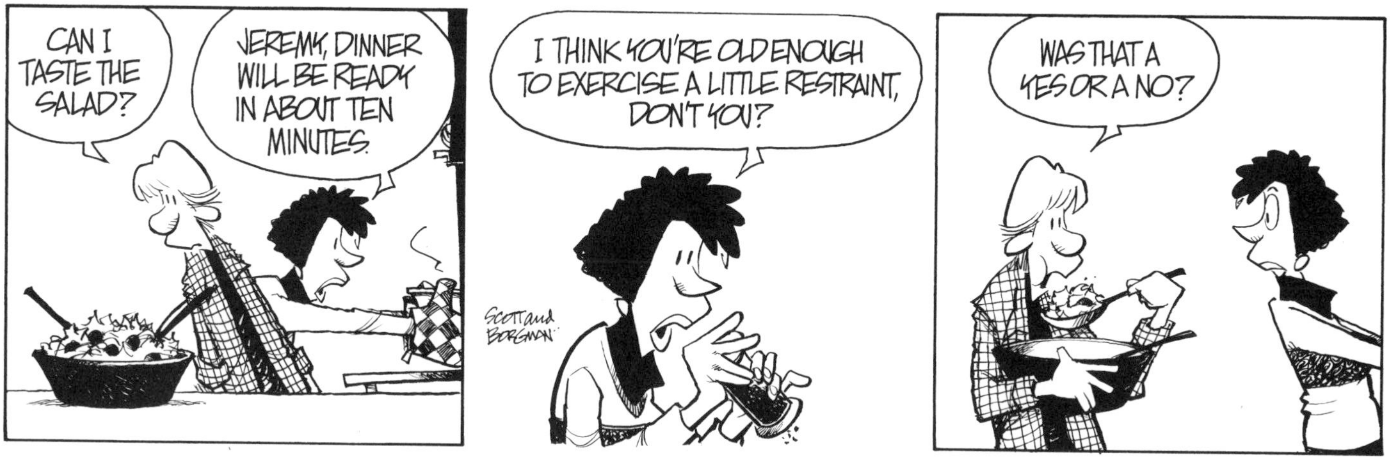
CAN I TASTE THE SALAD?
JEREMY, DINNER WILL BE READY IN ABOUT TEN MINUTES.
I THINK YOU'RE OLD ENOUGH TO EXERCISE A LITTLE RESTRAINT, DON'T YOU?
SCOTT and BORGMAN
WAS THAT A YES OR A NO?

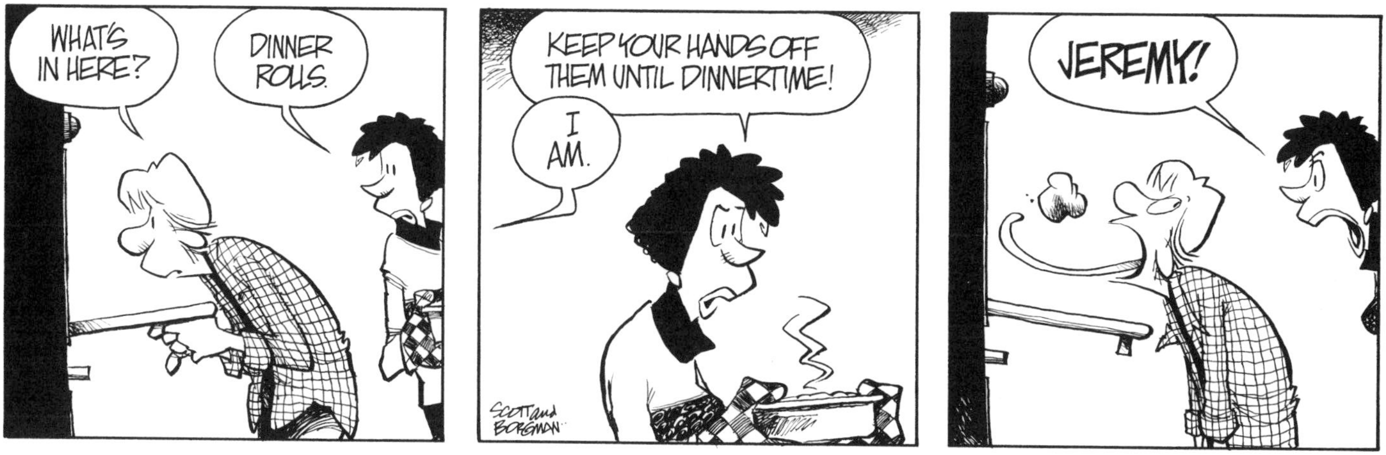
WHAT'S IN HERE?
DINNER ROLLS.
KEEP YOUR HANDS OFF THEM UNTIL DINNERTIME!
I AM.
SCOTT and BORGMAN
JEREMY!

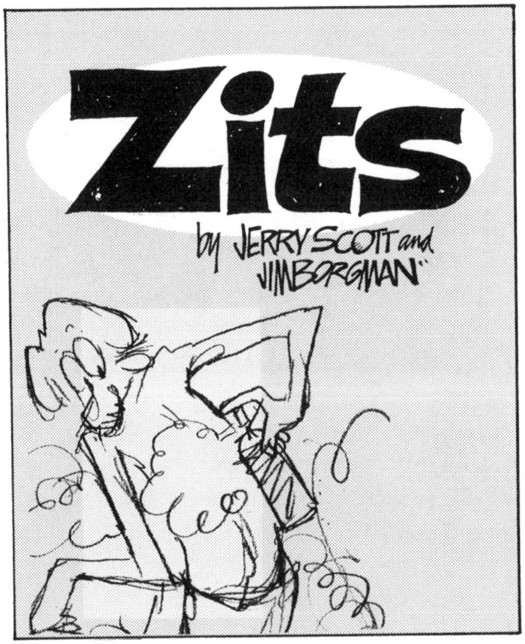
Zits
by JERRY SCOTT and JIM BORGMAN

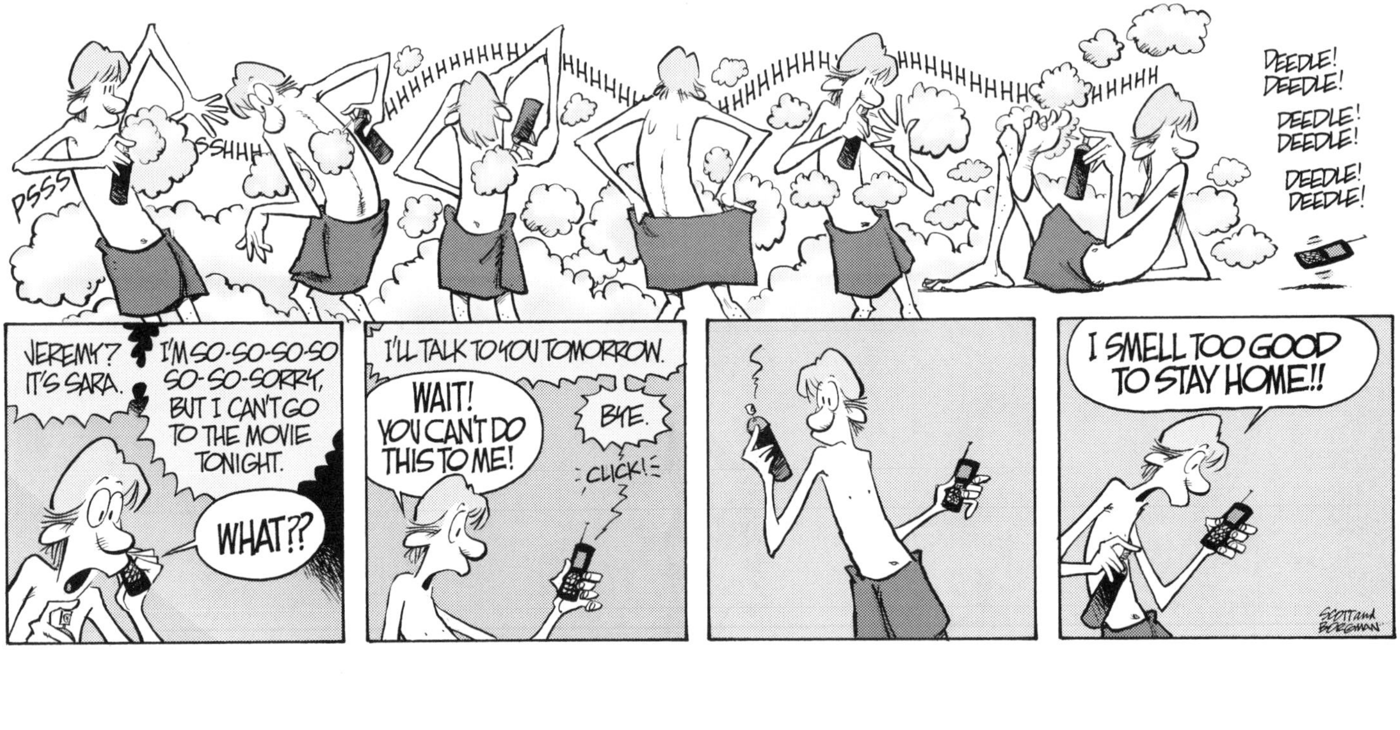
PSSSS
SSHHH
HHHHHHHHHHHHHHHHHHHHHHHHHHHHHHHHHHHHHHHHHHHHHHHH
DEEDLE! DEEDLE!
DEEDLE! DEEDLE!
DEEDLE! DEEDLE!
JEREMY? IT'S SARA.
I'M SO-SO-SO-SO SO-SO-SORRY, BUT I CAN'T GO TO THE MOVIE TONIGHT.
WHAT??
I'LL TALK TO YOU TOMORROW.
WAIT! YOU CAN'T DO THIS TO ME!
BYE.
CLICK!
I SMELL TOO GOOD TO STAY HOME!!
SCOTT and BORGMAN

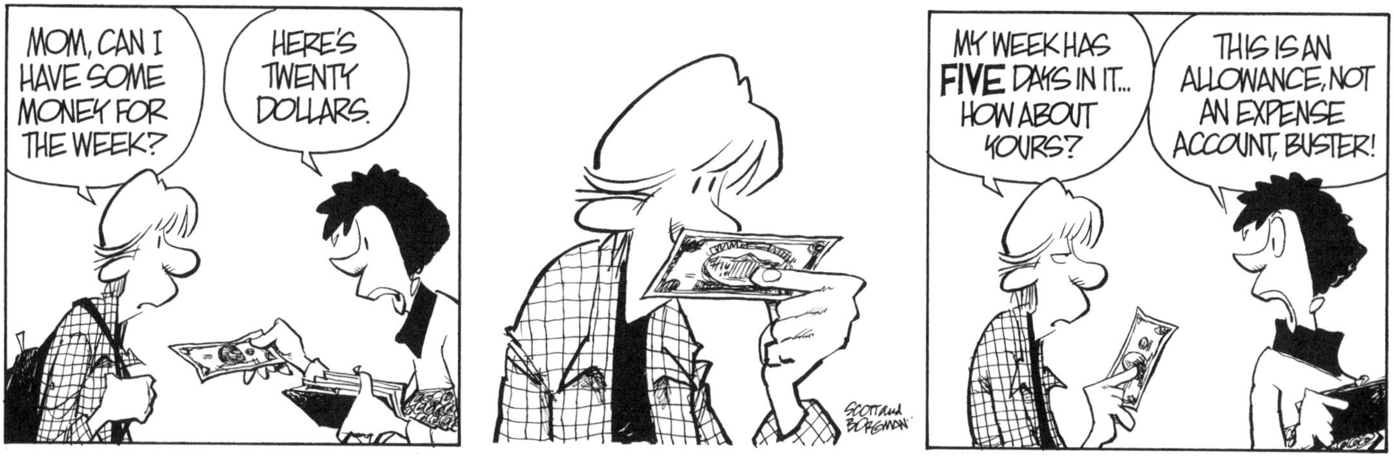
MOM, CAN I HAVE SOME MONEY FOR THE WEEK?
HERE'S TWENTY DOLLARS.
MY WEEK HAS **FIVE** DAYS IN IT... HOW ABOUT YOURS?
THIS IS AN ALLOWANCE, NOT AN EXPENSE ACCOUNT, BUSTER!

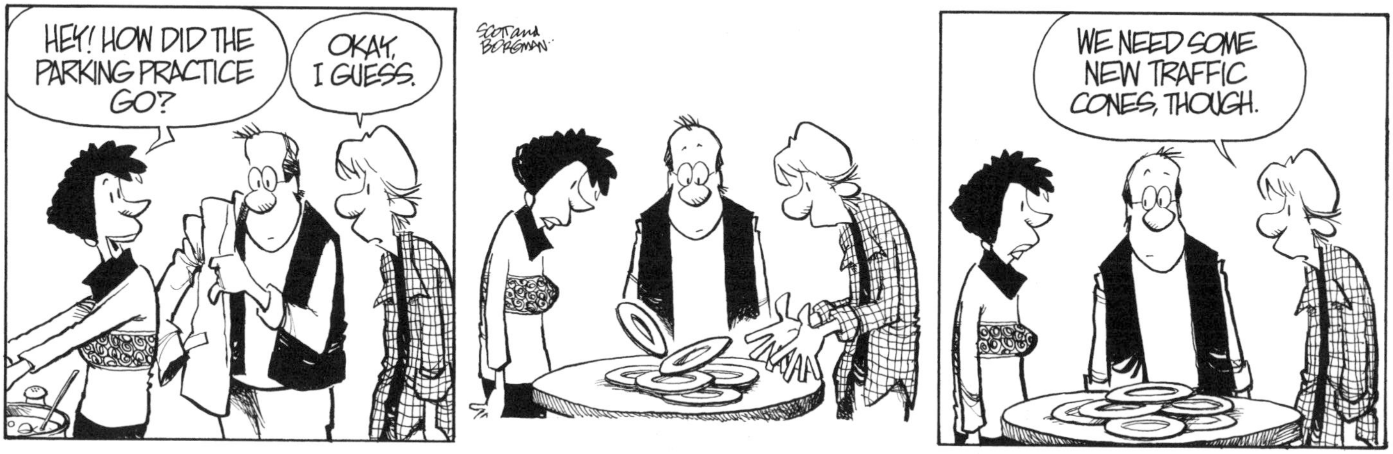
HEY! HOW DID THE PARKING PRACTICE GO?
OKAY, I GUESS.
WE NEED SOME NEW TRAFFIC CONES, THOUGH.

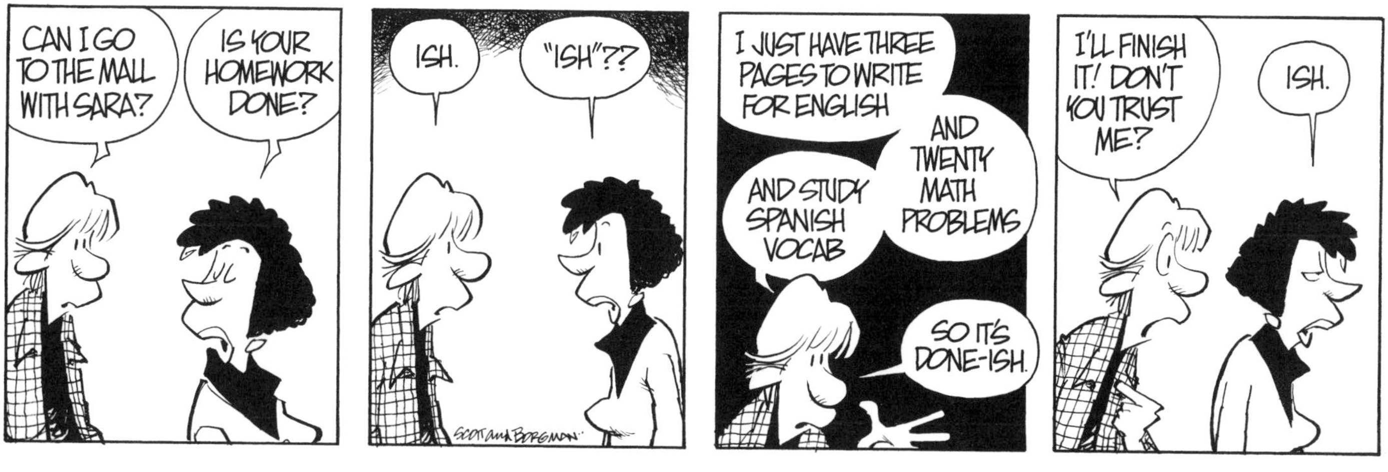
CAN I GO TO THE MALL WITH SARA?
IS YOUR HOMEWORK DONE?
ISH.
"ISH"??
I JUST HAVE THREE PAGES TO WRITE FOR ENGLISH
AND TWENTY MATH PROBLEMS
AND STUDY SPANISH VOCAB
SO IT'S DONE-ISH.
I'LL FINISH IT! DON'T YOU TRUST ME?
ISH.

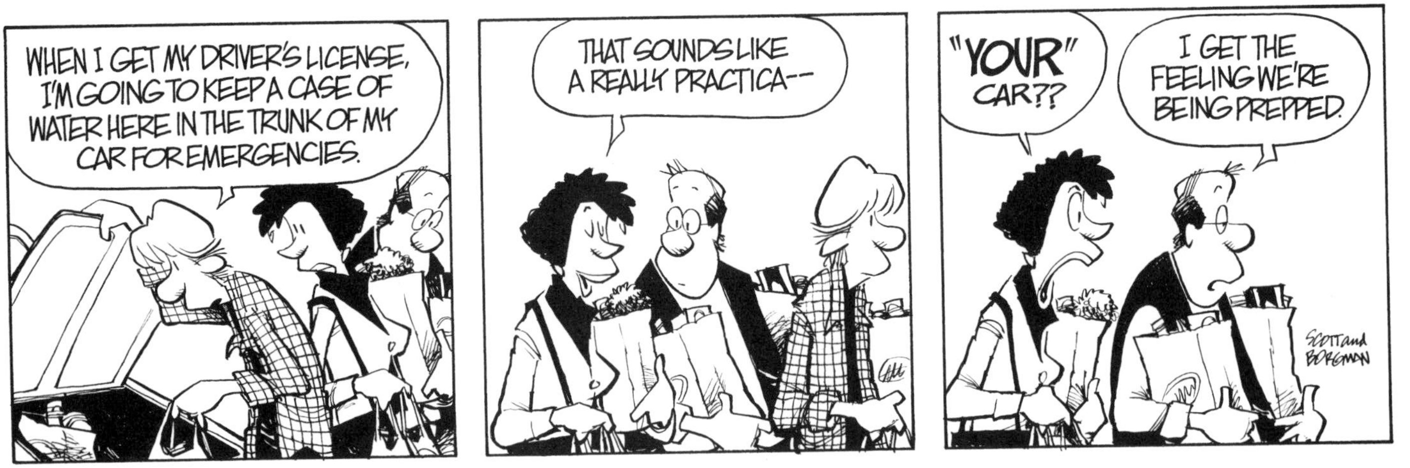
WHEN I GET MY DRIVER'S LICENSE, I'M GOING TO KEEP A CASE OF WATER HERE IN THE TRUNK OF MY CAR FOR EMERGENCIES.
THAT SOUNDS LIKE A REALLY PRACTICA--
"YOUR" CAR??
I GET THE FEELING WE'RE BEING PREPPED.
SCOTT and BORGMAN

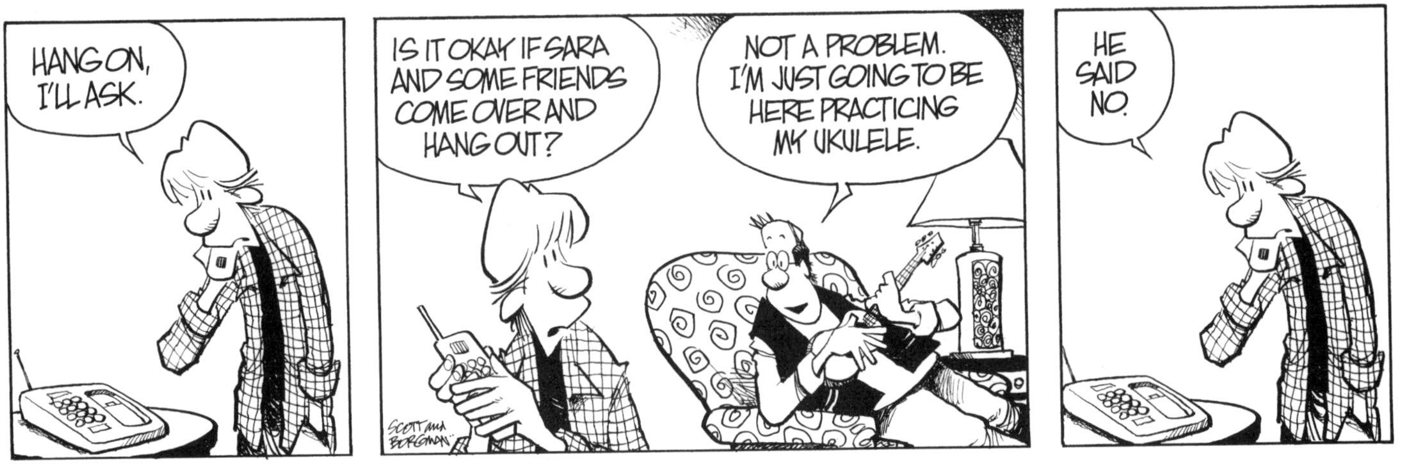
HANG ON, I'LL ASK.
IS IT OKAY IF SARA AND SOME FRIENDS COME OVER AND HANG OUT?
NOT A PROBLEM. I'M JUST GOING TO BE HERE PRACTICING MY UKULELE.
HE SAID NO.
SCOTT and BORGMAN

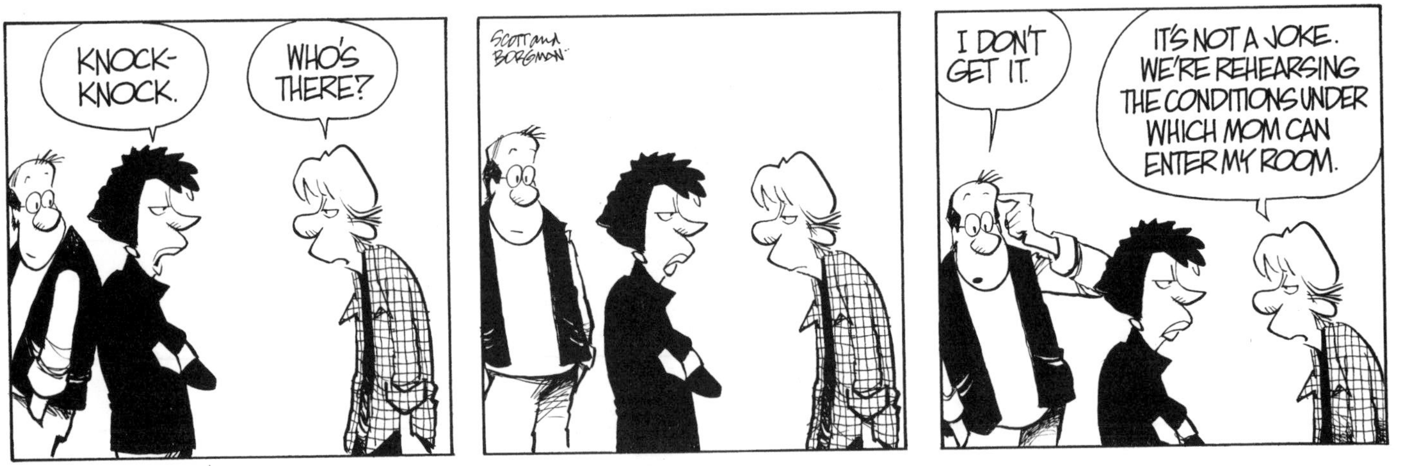
KNOCK-KNOCK.
WHO'S THERE?
SCOTT and BORGMAN
I DON'T GET IT.
IT'S NOT A JOKE. WE'RE REHEARSING THE CONDITIONS UNDER WHICH MOM CAN ENTER MY ROOM.